The Military History of the Russian Empire from Peter the Great until Nicholas II

The Bloomsbury History of Modern Russia Series

Series Editors: Jonathan D. Smele (Queen Mary, University of London, UK) and Michael Melancon (Auburn University, USA)

This ambitious and unique series offers readers the latest views on aspects of the modern history of what has been and remains one of the most powerful and important countries in the world. In a series of books aimed at students, leading academics and experts from across the world portray, in a thematic manner, a broad variety of aspects of the Russian experience, over extended periods of time, from the reign of Peter the Great in the early eighteenth century to the Putin era at the beginning of the twenty-first.

Published:

Peasants in Russia from Serfdom to Stalin: Accommodation, Survival, Resistance, Boris B. Gorshkov (2018)

Crime and Punishment in Russia: A Comparative History from Peter the Great to Vladimir Putin, Jonathan Daly (2018)

Marx and Russia: The Fate of a Doctrine, James D. White (2018)

A Modern History of Russian Childhood, Elizabeth White (2020)

Marriage, Household and Home in Modern Russia: From Peter the Great to Vladimir Putin, Barbara Alpern Engel (2021)

A History of Education in Modern Russia, Wayne Dowler (2021)

Russian Populism: A History, Christopher Ely (2022)

The Russian Intelligentsia: From the Monastery to the Mir Space Station, Christopher Read (2024)

Forthcoming:

The History of the Russian Worker: Life and Change from Peter the Great to Vladimir Putin, Alice Pate

Gender in Modern Russia, Aaron B. Retish

The Military History of the Russian Empire from Peter the Great until Nicholas II

John W. Steinberg

BLOOMSBURY ACADEMIC
LONDON • NEW YORK • OXFORD • NEW DELHI • SYDNEY

BLOOMSBURY ACADEMIC

Bloomsbury Publishing Plc, 50 Bedford Square, London, WC1B 3DP, UK
Bloomsbury Publishing Inc, 1385 Broadway, New York, NY 10018, USA
Bloomsbury Publishing Ireland, 29 Earlsfort Terrace, Dublin 2, D02 AY28, Ireland

BLOOMSBURY, BLOOMSBURY ACADEMIC and the Diana logo are trademarks of
Bloomsbury Publishing Plc

First published in Great Britain 2024

Paperback edition published 2025

Copyright © John W. Steinberg 2024

John W. Steinberg has asserted his right under the Copyright, Designs and Patents Act, 1988, to be identified as author of this work.

For legal purposes the Acknowledgments on p. ix constitute an extension of this copyright page.

Series design by Sandra Friesen
Cover image: National Geographic Magazine, Volume 31 (1917), page 369, panel A. Photographer - George H. Mewes

All rights reserved. No part of this publication may be: i) reproduced or transmitted in any form, electronic or mechanical, including photocopying, recording or by means of any information storage or retrieval system without prior permission in writing from the publishers; or ii) used or reproduced in any way for the training, development or operation of artificial intelligence (AI) technologies, including generative AI technologies. The rights holders expressly reserve this publication from the text and data mining exception as per Article 4(3) of the Digital Single Market Directive (EU) 2019/790.

Bloomsbury Publishing Plc does not have any control over, or responsibility for, any third-party websites referred to or in this book. All internet addresses given in this book were correct at the time of going to press. The author and publisher regret any inconvenience caused if addresses have changed or sites have ceased to exist, but can accept no responsibility for any such changes.

Every effort has been made to trace the copyright holders and obtain permission to reproduce the copyright material. Please do get in touch with any enquiries or any information relating to such material or the rights holder. We would be pleased to rectify any omissions in subsequent editions of this publication should they be drawn to our attention.

A catalogue record for this book is available from the British Library.

A catalog record for this book is available from the Library of Congress.

ISBN: HB: 978-1-3500-3718-2
PB: 978-1-3504-5147-6
ePDF: 978-1-3500-3719-9
eBook: 978-1-3500-3720-5

Series: The Bloomsbury History of Modern Russia

Typeset by Newgen KnowledgeWorks Pvt. Ltd., Chennai, India

For product safety related questions contact productsafety@bloomsbury.com.

To find out more about our authors and books visit www.bloomsbury.com and sign up for our newsletters.

For Victoria
If not for you!

Contents

List of Maps	viii
Acknowledgments	ix
Introduction	1
1 Peter the Great and the Foundation of the Empire	9
2 Russia's Global Empire	53
3 From the Wars of the French Revolution to the Crimean Disaster	99
4 Expanding the Empire in the Wake of Defeat	157
5 The Far Eastern Disaster	195
6 The First World War and the End of Tsarism, 1905–17	241
Epilogue	287
Notes	291
Bibliography	313
Index	319

Maps

1.1	Peter the Great's Azov Campaign	22
1.2	The Narva Campaign	24
1.3	The Great Northern War	34
1.4	The Pruth Campaign	37
2.1	Ottoman Forts around the Black Sea	62
2.2	The Seven Years' War	70
2.3	The First Partition of Poland	78
2.4	The Partition of Poland	83
2.5	The Treaty of Kuchuk-Kainardji	87
2.6	The Second Partition of Poland	92
2.7	The Third Partition of Poland	93
3.1	Suvorov's Swiss Campaign	111
3.2	Expansion into the Caucasus	121
3.3	The Campaign of Napoleon in Russia	124
3.4	The Caucasus after 1828	139
3.5	Treaties of Tukmenchay and Andrianople	141
3.6	Operations in the Crimean War (Ottoman Empire)	149
3.7	The 1856 Settlement Map of the Crimean War	153
4.1	Miliutin's Military Districts	162
4.2	Campaign Map of Russo-Turkish War, 1877–8	171
4.3	Russo-Turkish War in Caucasus, 1877	177
4.4	The Balkans before and after 1878	178
4.5	Conquest of Central Asia up to 1881	193
5.1	Russo-Japanese War Theater of Operations	206
5.2	Port Arthur	225
6.1	The East Prussia Campaign, August 1914	255
6.2	The Galician Campaign, August 1914	257
6.3	The Great Retreat, 1915	266
6.4	The Ottoman-Russian Caucasus Campaign in the First World War	273
6.5	The Brusilov Offensive	277
6.6	The June Offensive and the Defense of Riga, 1917	283

Acknowledgments

This book is the product of thirty-five years of my reading, thinking, writing, and teaching Russian military history. Acknowledgments should start with the people who trained me. They are Norman E. Saul and John T. Alexander of the University of Kansas and Allan K. Wildman and Michael W. Curran of The Ohio State University. Their guidance introduced me to the pageantry of Russian history and instilled an enthusiasm for the topic that remains to this day. After completing my education, I have had the pleasure of discussing Russian imperial and military history with a number of people, all of whom have had an impact on my thinking and whose encouragement has resulted in the pages that follow. This group of people includes Bruce W. Menning, William C. Fuller, Dominic C. B. Lieven, Mark von Hagan, David M. McDonald, Tony Heywood, Chris Read, Alex Marshall, David Wolff, Steven G. Marks, David Schimmelpenninck van der Oye, Jake Kipp, James Robert "Jay" Thompson, and Matthew Schwonek. The faculty research committee of Austin Peay State University generously granted me an academic leave, which provided the time needed to write this book. John G. Tuthill has been a valued copy editor of my work since we were both junior professors at Georgia Southern University. There are a number of scholars in Moscow and St. Petersburg who contributed to my development in the field whose names I will not mention because of the times in which we live. As is always the case, I alone am responsible for the information presented and conclusions reached in this book.

Since this book studies pre-October Russian Revolution history, I have adhered to the dates of the Julian calendar that lagged eleven days behind the European Gregorian calendar in the eighteenth century, twelve in the nineteenth, and thirteen in the twentieth century. In general I have followed the Library of Congress transliteration system without diacritical marks and ligatures. Exception were made for names commonly known in English such as Nicholas instead of Nikolai.

Introduction

At the beginning of the twentieth century, the Russian Empire spanned from the Baltic Sea to the Pacific Ocean and from the northern latitudes of the Arctic to the Black Sea. From its western frontier on the eastern edge of Central Europe to the Far East, military and civilian tsarist bureaucrats administered the empire across the eleven time zones that composed the bulk of the Eurasian landmass. While lacking significant mountain ranges, the topography and vegetation of Russia consisted of every type—from the frozen taiga of the Siberian East to the deserts of Central Asia. Major watersheds existed along the Volga, Don, and Dnieper Rivers to mention only a few. Accompanying this diverse landscape were a multitude of peoples, ranging from the great Slavic peoples of Russia proper to the Central Asian nomads to the forest peoples of Siberia. Simply put, Russia was (and remains) a huge, diverse, and dynamic territory whose history is marked by brilliant episodes of victorious expansion and dark periods of devastating defeats. Such a vast land undoubtedly had the resources to create an empire, but a series of conditions, largely political and military, had to be met before the empire could in fact come into being.

The construction of this empire did not spontaneously happen.[1] It took centuries for the Muscovite rulers of medieval Russia to oust the Mongols first from the heart of their homeland. Once the Mongols had been pushed out of Muscovy proper, the process of empire building commenced, and this process arguably continues until this day. Historians have studied this phenomenal development from every approach and interpretation possible. Many theories have been developed to explain how and why the Russian Empire came into being: Did the Russians aspire to build an empire solely to enrich themselves by obtaining control over territory and the natural resources that existed within? Was the construction of the empire all a gambit to control people and generate wealth that could then be used for Russia and Russians to overcome its backwardness that has long been associated with their history? Or was the motivator of all of the expenditure of effort a logical response to perceived threats to Russia from competitors who sought to control the same resources and territory. The common thread through all of these ideas is that without strong military forces, the Russians could not have built their empire. This book, therefore, examines the role of military history in the creation and development of the Russian Empire between 1689 and 1917.

I aim to explain how the Romanov dynasty's military forces in the eighteenth, nineteenth, into the twentieth century first conquered and then occupied the territory of the largest contiguous land empire in the world. To accomplish the task of fulfilling the state's territorial ambitions, the imperial army became all-pervasive in every aspect of Russian life. This book examines the role and impact of the Russian Empire on world history, first by focusing on what it took to arm, man, and maintain the enormous tsarist's armed force and then by examining the wars and campaigns that they fought as they endlessly expanded the size of their realm. The roots of a Russian plan to construct an empire can be dated to the efforts of the fourteenth-century Rurickian princes of Muscovy to escape from and then replace the power vacuum that emerged with the collapse of the Mongol Empire. Ivan IV, 1530–1584 (the awe-inspiring, also known as the terrible), undertook the conquest of Kazan in 1552 putting the Muscovites on a course to expand into the Eurasian heartland.[2] Despite a host of stunning victories and some dramatic, indeed devastating defeats, Russian expansionist aims and policies came to dominate Eurasia especially after the 1613 ascension of Romanovs to the throne.[3]

Little question exists as to Russian development being different from that of the West. Immense and intense poverty caused by poor soil and a short growing season left the agricultural sector unable to feed the populations of Eurasia. Despite this crushing hardship, the Russians managed to prevail against overwhelmingly strong foes and construct an all-powerful empire by the beginning of the nineteenth century. Building their empire, therefore, results in the overall question of did the Romanovs have a grand strategy that provided them with a master plan that successfully culminated with the emergence and persistence of the Russian Empire? Seemingly, a huge country ruled by an all-powerful autocrat could possess the control needed to organize society and its economy so that all of its resources and assets could be directed at all times toward achieving expansionist goals with little problem. At least one commentator strongly posits that there can be little question that the Romanovs did have a master and systematic plan that governed their imperial activities from the middle of the seventeenth century until the beginning of the nineteenth century.[4] While no further evidence is needed to conclude that since the sixteenth century, when Ivan IV casted off the final vestiges of Russia's dark ages (the Mongol period), the Russians have persistently sought to expand to the furthest edge(s) of the Eurasian landmass, no matter the cost or the challenge. After all, Russia was forever in search of warm water ports to expand trade and to cultivate global connections. And, while always casted as backwards or lagging in development, Russia's leadership understood that to support a plan that pursued expansion while maintaining a stout defense for the realm, the "Empire" would require a sound economic basis that at the very least would provide its military forces with the weapons and all of the other ancillary materials needed to pursue their mission.

This book starts with the reign of Peter the Great (1689–1725) and his efforts to remake his military establishment into an institution embedded in Russian society that could defeat all of its enemies. At the time that Peter came to power, Russia faced two diverse military theaters of operation; he understood that Russia needed a military establishment that had the flexibility to confront enemies who fought with different types of armies. To the north and west stood the Swedes, the Polish-Lithuanian Commonwealth, the Austrians, and the Prussians who by this time had completely invested in what historians describe as the military revolution.[5] As a result, when the Russians fought Western armies at the beginning of the eighteenth century, they encountered well-disciplined troops who were armed with gunpowder weapons to pursue the aims of the state. To the south and east, the Ottomans had become a perennial threat to Ukraine and Crimea where assorted Cossack hosts and the Tatars struggled to maintain their independence as they were slowly losing control over the Danubian-Pontic steppe.[6] These foes fought with cavalry armies using non-gunpowder weapons as they marauded as armed hordes seeking to destroy anything or anyone they perceived as an enemy while looting and pillaging everything of value to them.

The book starts here because Peter created the military system that provided the means for Russia to defeat the Swedes and become the dominant Baltic power, as well as all but compromise Polish-Lithuanian power, and contain the Prussians and Austrians to Central Europe. His adoption of Western European educational customs, technology, and organizational practices sparked new energy into all aspects of Russian life—from the transformation of Russian society to the state's economic development to diplomatic engagement with the world. Above all else it, continued the process of introducing Western military practices and technology into Russia's armed forces. Although Peter's military campaigns to the south and to the east were not as successful, he had built a military establishment that over the course of the eighteenth century would defeat all of Russia's international foes. At the same time he succeeded in forging an irrevocable link that resulted in every Russian serving the state for the purposes of building an empire. Regardless of if you believe Peter the Great was a "reformer," "a revolutionary," "a master of coercion," "a Westernizer," "a Europeanizer," the deliverer of Russia's military revolution, or a bully, a drunkard, or something worse, little debate exists that Peter the Great as the tsar transformed Russia. While he did not forge a grand strategy in which a plan emerged that dedicated all the resources of the state to his military establishment, he did firmly entrench the idea in the minds of Russians that their goal should be to create and maintain a military establishment that would allow them to endlessly expand across the Eurasian landmass.

The book's narrative next exhibits how in the century after Peter the Great's death his successors, especially Elizabeth Petrovna (1741–62) and Catherine the Great (1762–96), combined the use of skilled diplomacy along with the military power they inherited to nurture the Romanov Imperial project. Largely through a combination of diplomacy and military might, the Prussians were contained after the Seven Years' War and the Polish-Lithuanian Commonwealth was erased from the map with three partitions. Catherine the Great gained much of her reputation and legacy, however, after soldiers under her command pushed the Ottomans out of Ukraine and Crimea and forced the assorted Tatar and Cossack hosts off of the Pontic steppe. By the time of her death, the Russian Empire had reached its zenith. With soldier luminaries such as Gregory A. Potemkin and Alexander V. Suvorov at its command, the Russian army enjoyed its age of great captains who left Russia prepared for the challenges of the Napoleonic era.

Keeping to its chronological scope, this book then examines how Russian armed forces under the command of Paul I and Alexander I were severely tested during the Napoleonic epoch. Their ultimate success became a lasting tribute to the recasting of Russian life that Peter the Great started during his reign. Russia emerged in the post-Napoleonic period as the most powerful continental empire for Nicholas I to cultivate. He used his power as tsar to further Russia's ambition against the Turks as he too successfully fought them in 1828-9. Then, Nicholas devoted much energy for the rest of his reign to the conquest of the Caucasus. The Caucasus in fact became the operational training ground for the Russian army in the 1830s and 1840s and were largely pacified in the 1850s.

Russia's reign as the successor to Pax Mongolia, however, was short lived. Her stunning, indeed catastrophic, defeat in the Crimean War (1853–6) at once transformed Russia into one of the weaker Great Powers in the European community. To remedy this shocking military defeat, a debacle so complete that every aspect of Russian life was called into question both domestically and internationally, Russia's young tsar Alexander II ushered in an age of Great Reform. What followed was the complete reorganization of Russian society beginning with the emancipation of the serfs and culminating with the universal conscription reform of 1874. This section of the book that follows the Crimean defeat examines the impact of the military reforms that occurred in the 1860s and 1870s. These reforms, conceptualized and implemented by War Minister D. A. Miliutin, cannot be underestimated! They were and remain just as significant as the reforms of Peter the Great. Miliutin's overhaul of the tsarist military establishment started the process of transforming the army from a dynastic institution where aristocrats commanded peasants into a modern nation in arms where peasants were supposed to become citizens of the empire; the impact of these reforms cannot be overestimated to the fate of the Romanov Empire.

The next section of the book explains how for the rest of their reign the Romanovs mightily struggled with the consequences of their imperial ambitions. The army Miliutin built was used to fight another major war with the Turks in 1877–8. It demonstrated that it had modernized its planning and training capabilities through higher military education, which reinvigorated its training establishment. Tsar Alexander II and especially the tsarevich, the soon to be crowned Alexander III, however, found the violence of the war to be overwhelming—they had little taste for the lethality of the industrialized battlefield. The lessons they learned from this experience was to push back on efforts to modernize the army. Nonetheless, Russian armed forces had marched to the gates of Constantinople in 1878 and created the perception the tsar's army was ready to rejoin the ranks of Europe's Great Powers. The activities of the Russian army in Central Asia throughout Alexander II's reign strengthened this belief as soldiers of the tsar conquered one khanate after another. Yet, in this case, perceptions were deceptive. As the army victoriously marched through the Balkans in 1877–8, command and control weaknesses limited its effectiveness and the requirements of modern warfare—from heavier weapons to more rapid expenditure of ammunition—encumbered its ability to mobilize, supply, march, and maneuver regardless of better levels of military education, staff planning, and training of soldiers.

The final two chapters of the book reveal how systemic weaknesses throughout the social, political, and economic structure of the empire caused the defeats of Nicholas II's armies in the Russo-Japanese War and the First World War. The defeat by the Japanese in every land battle and every major naval engagement sent an undeniable warning to the regime. Reform efforts consumed the military establishment after 1905 but not enough could be done as time was too short before the 1914 start of the First World War. Without question in the post-Japanese War period, the Russian military had a hard-core group of progressively minded officers who embodied the spirit of Miliutin and strove to create a modern nation in arms. Their efforts faced determined and strong resistance, unfortunately beginning with the tsar Nicholas II who fiercely defended his autocratic prerogative. With the exception of Peter the Great and Alexander II, Romanov rulers had little tolerance for reform that might limit their power in any way. In the end Nicholas II's failure to win any war destroyed his army and his navy. No Romanov tsar could survive without the support of his or her officers, soldiers, and sailors. The mutiny of the Russian soldiers in 1917 combined with the inability of the officer corps to seize control of the rapidly spreading rebellion therefore caused the collapse of the Romanov dynasty but not the disintegration of the empire.

Throughout its imperial history, when the future of the regime was at stake, Russia's rulers became and remained wholly dependent on their armed forces to defeat the myriad of enemies they faced on the battlefield. As a result of their expansionist policies, the Russians' military conquered, consolidated, and occupied the territory that formed into a multinational Eurasian Empire. With the period of expansion largely completed by the beginning of the twentieth century, military officers and civilian tsarist bureaucrats struggled to maintain order throughout their empire. As a result of military conquest, the world of the Romanovs (1613–1917) was based on the practice of an all-powerful political center intolerant of the hopes and desires of the vast domains and peoples that they ruled to maintain the huge military force necessary to sustain internal order, defend against all enemies, and expand into new territories whenever possible. As he built his military establishment, Peter the Great connected his country to the political and economic world of Early Modern Europe through victory on the battlefield. His successors then used the military forces they inherited to maintain their firm hold over the governance of their empire while they expanded Russian power in every possible direction. The best of his successors therefore used astute diplomacy, the combination of the strength of their armed forces and what turned into a solid administrative and socioeconomic infrastructure to expand their empire while maintaining domestic order. This book posits that all of these factors together allowed the tsar's armed forces to not only maintain the security of the empire, but also consistently pursue its mission—its plan of expanding the territory that the tsar or tsarina controlled until the 1917 collapse of the Romanov dynasty.

1

Peter the Great and the Foundation of the Empire

The Inheritance

Backwardness and exceptionalism represent ideas that are often ascribed to Russia and its empire. The idea of such backwardness harks back to the origins of any political entity associated with Russia or its earlier incantation Rus. After all, the Slavic peoples who populated Rus were still gathering berries and harvesting honey when or if the Varangians appeared and it was already the ninth century—more than 500 years after the fall of Rome and the rise of Christianity in the West! The staunchly determined part of Peter the Great's personality, his frenetic activity, and his aim to experience as many human activities as possible made him at once inspiring and fearful. He aimed to govern in absolute terms while forging a military establishment worthy of empire. This goal combined with his insistence that all members of society become state servitors regardless of their social standing while in return offering upward mobility to any subject of merit recast the fundamental relationships of all people in Russia with the state and society at the end of the seventeenth, beginning of the eighteenth centuries. Indeed, the Russia Peter the Great inherited was not as advanced as the West, but it was also not too terribly behind the West as a result of the efforts of his predecessors. One of the central points of departure for this study, therefore, is that Peter the Great built on what he inherited on multiple levels. True, he encountered strong and at times savage opposition from some of Russia's most influential families that may well have made him the tyrant that is a part of his legacy.[1] Regardless, he remained undeterred because of his stubborn, hard-boiled determination to enhance Russia's standing in the world. Moreover, central to understanding the scope and extent of his accomplishments, this chapter will start with an assessment of his inheritance in terms of the Russian state, its place in the world, and the type and strength of the armed forces that existed in Russia at the end of the seventeenth century.

Whether or not Peter the Great brought a military revolution to Russia three-quarters of a century after the death of Gustav Adolf depends on its definition. If the emergence of the state's administrative apparatus that could orchestrate its economic infrastructure to provide the means to raise, to equip, and to sustain large-scale professionally trained and commanded armies defines the Early Modern Military Revolution, then the Russians had been engaged in such activities since at least the last half of the fifteenth century. Of course, these developments were not smooth nor did they consistently progress to a clearly understood and accepted end point, but many of the pieces were in place when Peter the Great emerged as absolute tsar in 1696 after the death of his half-brother Ivan V. Something related to Western Europe's military revolution did occur in Russia in the seventeenth century; learning to fight like Western European armies with troops lined up to maximize firepower would only satisfy a part, albeit a critical part, of Russia's military needs. In addition to mastering the Western style of warfare, the Russians still had to contend with a powerful group of enemies who roamed the Pontic steppe. Be they Ottoman, Crimean, or Cossacks, warfare on the steppe still would require hard-hitting cavalry armies throughout the eighteenth century.[2]

Ivan III (1462–1505)—the gatherer of land—started building the Muscovite military establishment that would ultimately throw off the Mongol yoke during and after his conquest of Novgorod. Culminating in 1470–1, Ivan III had gone on the offensive with the aim of reconquering the lands once controlled by the grand prince of Kiev before the Mongol conquest. In addition to the political rationale, Ivan III was also addressing Russia's place in the world by marrying the niece of the last Byzantine emperor. In doing this, he further asserted that, in addition to defending his patrimony, Moscow was the Third Rome and that the center of Orthodoxy should no longer be in Constantinople in the fallout of the Ottomans' victory over Byzantine in 1453. Moreover, he managed to gather limited support for his desire to be known and recognized as tsar among his people and the rest of the world. Regional and global issues aside, how Ivan III solved the challenge of populating the huge expanses of Novgorod with people who would support the absolutism of Muscovy not only exhibits the Muscovite approach toward occupying conquered territory, but would also provide the backbone of the future Russian military establishment. Ivan III oversaw the redistribution of the Novgorodian lands to his loyal servitors, thereby at once demonstrating that Muscovy had little tolerance for conquered peoples while providing a source of new wealth and mobility for his Muscovites supporters.

Thus Ivan III oversaw the rise of a new middle/military service class who ultimately would replace princely retainers (the Boyars). For the exchange of land or being granted a pomestia, the holder of this new land agreed to provide service to the state. In this fashion, these servitors became the leaders of a new cavalry army that would first contain and ultimately push back the numerous steppe armies that threatened Russia from the south and the east.[3]

In creating the pomestia, Ivan III was also centralizing his own authority and the authority of the state particularly over the old service elite, the Boyars. While the Boyars would remain on their own land, the otdel, they would owe service to no one. They believed themselves to be power brokers in Muscovy until Peter the Great made them anachronistic throughout Russia. What ensued was a struggle between the Boyars and the pomeshniki in which the old elite lost their place in Muscovy's social, political, and military hierarchy to a group of younger adventurers. To put their situation into context, in 1550 the Boyars still sat at the very top of Muscovy's state service establishment. Between the oprichnina, the time of troubles, and the rise of the Romanovs, the Boyars would survive Peter the Great's reforms with little more than nostalgic thoughts of past glory. What emerged in their place was a loyal class of servitors, known as the dvorianstvo, who had deeply indebted to Romanov power. They would come to view themselves as Muscovy's first line of defense against all enemies of the state. Thus, the culture of service to the state owes its existence not to Peter the Great or to any other specific tsar. It was, in fact, the product of a process that started when Ivan III first asserted the power of Muscovy beyond its fifteenth-century borders. Slowly, over the course of the sixteenth and seventeenth centuries, the culture of service to the state became embedded in Russian life. Peter the Great may have always had to cope with the shortcomings of individuals and opposition from families and clans, but no one questioned the principle of, or actual service to, the state like the nobility of the Polish-Lithuanian Commonwealth would as it disintegrated and disappeared from the pages of history.[4] Nevertheless, the pomeshniki, or the men who served as leaders and providers of troops, formed a late medieval or renaissance cavalry armed with blades and arrows; they composed Muscovy's middle service class who owed service in return for their estates. The relationship bred loyalty between the middle or military service class and the crown and provided the Muscovites with an army that could compete with the assorted steppe armies who were loyal to various khanates and roamed the territory to the south and to the east of its borders.

The next vital asset that Peter the Great inherited was the expertise of foreigners in Moscow's military affairs who first appeared in Muscovy during the reign of Ivan IV. Ivan IV's August 1552 conquest of Kazan, followed up by the defeat of the Astrakhan Khanate in 1556, marked the beginning of eastward expansion. These two conquests eliminated the remaining vestiges of Mongol power, giving Muscovy control over vast new territories, markets, and subsequent trade. The irony of Ivan IV's conduct is that as he enforces and ascribes legal status to a landholding system (the pomestia), he also begins the process of rendering the pomeshniki obsolete as a military force. He did this by importing the use of gunpowder weapons into the ranks of his forces by creating the Strel'tsy, often translated as musketeers, but more accurately arquebusiers (referring to the weapons they first used), who were the first standing units in the Russian army. The exact date of their formation is open to debate, though it is commonly held that it was between 1545 and 1550 as Ivan geared up to defeat Kazan. Originally recruited largely from free tradesmen who understood the mechanics of gunpowder weapons, the Strel'tsy, unlike musketeers in Western Europe, engaged in a variety of auxiliary duties such as guards, firemen, and policemen when they were not actually fighting on battlefields and in this way emerged as their own social stratum by the time the Romanovs came to power in 1613. Their role on Muscovy's battlefields was not to engage in hand-to-hand combat but to deliver massive firepower from fixed positions, often wooden platforms that they built or from permanent fortifications. When organized and in enough control of the battlefield to assert their will, they used volley fire where the first rank of troops fired at the enemy and then stepped to the rear to reload while a second rank stepped forward and fired. And, in addition to their handguns and muskets, they always carried sabers and depending on the situation they were trained in the use of lances, as well as with large battle-axes that were more commonly used as stands for their handguns. A fundamental difference, however, existed between the strel'tsy and the pomeshniki. Strel'tsy officers were sometimes given land in addition to their wages, while most rank-and-file strel'tsy fought for payment in gold and in grain ration, and unlike their officers, they could act as free agents when not engaged in combat to earn whatever they could on their own.[5]

The Romanovs therefore inherited essentially a cavalry army that had the support of soldiers armed with firearms, a technology largely imported from the West. The importation of European technology, indeed Europeans themselves, sharply increased during the reign of Alexis Mikhailovich (1645–1676) which forms the second significant inheritance that Peter the Great enjoyed when he came to power. After the defeat of Kazan and Astrakhan, and in an effort to forge a link to the Baltic Sea, Ivan IV shifted his attention to present-day Estonia and Latvia where he became bogged down in his long-term Livonian War (1558–83). While his challenges encompassed political, social, and economic, in addition to military issues, the principal reason Ivan IV did not prevail in Livonian was Muscovy's armies had prevailed on the steppe. A different type of army would be needed to fight wars against Western powers. If the Russian state's strategy was shifting from fighting Asian and Turkic to European powers, then its army would need to study and adopt Western ways of warfare before it would achieve success in this new theater of operation. By the beginning of the seventeenth century, the European powers, led by Sweden, were converting their military establishments to standing armies that featured powerful infantry regiments that remained undeterred when assaulted by cavalry forces armed with bladed or pointed weapons because they had gunpowder on their side. Even more of a challenge, just as Alexis promulgated the Ulozhennia of 1649, which enserfed most every Russian peasant to satisfy the long-standing demand of the pomeshniki, not only had their style of warfare lost its dominance on the battlefield, but Alexis learned, as his father Mikhail also knew, the state could not afford to support both the pomeshniki and the strel'tsy. Simply put, during the period between the 1630s and the 1650s, Moscow's military leaders learned that the armed force composed of pomeshniki, strel'tsy, foreign mercenaries, and Cossack and Tatar recruits could prevail against the nomadic armies of the steppe but had neither the know-how nor the equipment to face the power of the Polish-Lithuanian Commonwealth and Sweden.

The decisive event for Tsar Alexis that shifted Moscow's military establishment from an army composed of an aristocratic cavalry and gunpowder specialists was the Thirteen Years' War (sometimes called the Russo-Polish War) against the Commonwealth (1654–67). To meet his crushing manpower needs Alexis introduced conscription in 1658, which, of course, meant that the peasants became victims of a military draft that in November 1658 was defined as the local villages being responsible for one infantry soldier for every twenty-five households. From these recruits Muscovy's armed forces received over 100,000 men by the end of the war. Even more significantly, Alexis found the funds needed to hire foreign military experts to not only command Russian troops but also train future Russian military leaders and soldiers in Western style warfare. In the mid-seventeenth century, therefore, the Russians started to compose large infantry regiments capable of dominating the western battlefield. Much of Alexis's military success can be attributed to the use of his new formation regiments. By 1663, 79 percent of the army was composed of new formation units not counting the Strel'tsy. Their success can be measured by the terms obtained in the Treaty of Andrusovo in January 1667, which gave Muscovy control of Smolensk and the rest of what is now Belorus and the left bank of the Dnieper River (or the eastern part of modern-day Ukraine) including Kiev. The Commonwealth got to keep the territory on the right bank of the Dnieper River. Golitsyn's 1689 invasion of Ukraine failed, yet the transformation of the Russian army continued as his forces consisted of 110,000 armed combatants of which only 17,206 were Dvorianstvo cavalry and Strel'tsy compared to 30,000 new style cavalry and 50,000 new style infantry.[6]

The operational capabilities of the old style cavalry plainly exposed them as amateurs in a world where the role of military servitors were being professionalized. In the middle of the seventeenth century, the pomestia system had obtained an unassailable legal status that propelled the pomeshniki to the height of their political power and social standing. Because of the heightened defense needs of the state, however, it had become economically unfeasible for the middle service class to satisfy the defense needs of the state. Simply put, they did not have the resources to acquire weapons and the rest of the equipment the soldiers of Moscow needed to prevail on the battlefield. Moreover, this gap between Muscovy's military capabilities and that of the West came at a time when all of the European nations were not only adopting mass armies but also providing the economic infrastructure and governmental organization to support the professionalization of their respective military establishments. The Russians could not keep up with these developments, hence the transformation from a medieval-based feudal army to an Early Modern professional army started for them on the mid-seventeenth-century battlefields where they fought a series of wars against the Polish-Lithuanian Commonwealth.

According to Robert Frost, the adoption in the 1630s of new style regiments also reintroduced the practice of advancement for soldiers based on merit, first attempted during the reign of Ivan IV. From this point forward, the idea of reward based on merit became a firm principle within Russia and an essential part of the foundation on which the empire was constructed. Peter the Great understood this and ultimately institutionalized a system designed to reward Russians for state service with his 1722 Table of Ranks.[7] Moreover, what signaled the end of the pomestia system was the 1682 elimination of the Mestnichestvo system. From this point forward all young boyars were expected to serve in the military and as junior officers they were to receive a rudimentary military education complete with practical training that would make them more "professional" in their outlook and, as a result, better able to confront Russia's Western enemies.[8] To infuse this know-how into Russia's military establishment, Alexis hired foreign officers to command new formation regiments while teaching Russians how to command, and at the same time adopting the principle of merit as the sole means of advancement through the ranks. Alexis therefore understood the concept of meritocracy and sought to create a training and operational environment where the best soldiers in the empire rose to the top of the army's command structure if for no other reason than the hiring of foreigners was not sustainable due to the expense.

Opposition to the use of foreigners, however, was evident on levels such as the reluctance of Russians to serve under the command of outsiders. Persistent questions about their loyalty also prevailed throughout Russia. Perhaps more to the point, Russians of the early to mid-seventeenth century were still mired deeply in the idea that the tradition of advancement based on precedent and connections should prevail over any idea of success being linked to the capabilities or the merit of any individual officer in the Russian army. Such attitudes meant that no matter what, the transition to a military establishment where the basis of advancement was merit was going to be a slow process. As a result of Alexis's understanding of the significance of foreigners to Russia's military successes, and despite their cost to the crown, Robert Frost notes that in 1696, at the time that Peter the Great takes sole possession of the crown, the Russian infantry and cavalry was populated by 559 foreigners who served across the ranks from lieutenant to colonel. Thus the argument is made that Alexis laid a firm foundation that his son Peter inherited upon becoming the tsar of Russia. Indeed foreigners had been a part of Russia's military landscape for over fifty years before Peter came to power. Alexis's use of foreigners, therefore, explains why they were in Russia to influence a young Peter not only about the military but also about the world in general.[9] Russians would rise through the ranks of their own army but foreigners would remain in the ranks of the tsar/tsarina's armies until at least the reign of Catherine the Great who was a foreigner herself. And, while the trend was to remove foreigners from positions of power in Russia particularly after the reign of Catherine the Great, both Alexander I and Nicholas I were not opposed to hiring foreigners for their expertise if the situation called for it.

According to Michael C. Paul, the Russian army that Peter the Great inherited when he came to power in many ways represented the tail end of a medieval world where Russia's military power remained linked to an agreement between the middle service class and the Romanovs that dated back to the Ulozhenia of 1649.[10] Simply put, the Russian cavalry at the end of the seventeenth century, the backbone of the Russian military establishment faithfully served their tsar in return for control over their estates and their serfs. The Russian cavalry forces were supported by the Strel'tsy or musketeers who, for the most part, served for wages and for rations although there were exceptions in which for meritorious service they received control of their own estates. Especially during the period leading up to his coming to power, his father Tsar Alexis brought in foreign mercenaries not only to instruct Russians in western arms and tactical practices, but also to command troops on the battlefield. As Alexis fought wars against the Polish-Lithuanian Commonwealth, Muscovy struggled over the question of whether or not the state or the nobleman was responsible for arming, equipping, and compensating troops. For that matter, the state also struggled with the basic question of how to fill its ranks as it had no consistent means to recruit troops nor did their call for volunteers ever end with much success. Perhaps the single facet that separated the Muscovy's medieval military from the Early Modern military establishments of Western Europe was the Russian State could barely afford to pay for its military so in times of peace it did not. As a result, the Russians had to rebuild their army every time they shifted from a peacetime to a wartime footing. Nonetheless, the seventeenth-century Muscovite army enjoyed much military success. Richard Hellie would claim that Tsar Alexis annexed far more important territory to Muscovy's west than Peter the Great did when he defeated Sweden.[11] Peter I did indeed inherit much from his father in terms of military assets and he would take this inheritance and create an empire that persists to this day largely because of the reforms he implement both to his military and to the rest of the state.

Peter the Great

In the century or so leading up to the reign of Peter the Great military reform in Russia had been ongoing and slowly the military of Muscovy was casting off its medieval cavalry-centric armed force and adopting a new military style that focused on the large infantry regiments that were a signpost of the Western European military revolution. Yet the early Romanovs did not have the revenues or the resources to sustain their transforming military forces in times of peace. Peter the Great would take his "military" inheritance and step up the pace of reform within his armed forces while simultaneously institutionalizing a political, social, and economic infrastructure that was based on the enlighten principle of good government. In this age good government was defined as one in which the state's bureaucracy was organized on rational principles, and perhaps more important, all subjects of the tsar were in some fashion bound to serve the state and that their advancement would forever be based on performance and merit regardless of their standing in Muscovite or any other society. While the reforms of his predecessors were instrumental in Russia having the capability to allow Peter to wage war in all but thirteen months of his thirty-five-year reign, his constant reforming provided him with the assets he needed to pursue an empire building strategy based on military conquest and adept diplomacy.[12] In this way, and over the sometimes strenuous objections of the people who had the most to lose, many aspects of Peter the Great's reforms became institutionalized until the 1917 collapse of Romanov power and in some ways would prevail into the twenty-first century.[13]

The stories of Peter's childhood are manifold and need not be recounted in their entirety for this text beyond noting that all biographers agree that in addition to his possessing limitless energy, from a young age he had an interest, indeed a fascination in all things military. From a very young age he was caught in the middle of a vicious power struggle between the families of his father's two wives. No doubt his acute interest in the military finds its roots in the events he witnessed in the 1682 revolt of the Strel'tsy. In the course of the revolt young Peter was traumatized when he witnessed the brutal assassination of his relatives. With his personal safety at stake, Peter and his mother Natalia Narshinkina fled Moscow and took up residence in the village of Preobrazhenskoe. The move in effect exiled Peter from the Muscovite court into the arms of foreigners who were in Russia as "retired" servitors to the crown as these men came to Russia to fight for Peter's father, Tsar Alexis. While Peter did not receive a formal education, the education he did receive came from the information that the foreigners in Preobrazhenskoe shared with him. Some of these prominent foreigners included most importantly the Scotsman Patrick Gordon who in his calm and reflective manner taught the young and future tsar about military affairs in general. Complementing Gordon was the Dutchman Franz Timmermann who taught him the basic principles of fortification and ballistics. If nothing else Timmerman impresses upon Peter about the significance of mathematics in waging a war with gunpowder weapons. The other notable foreigner who helped Peter during this period was the Swiss general Franz Lefort who also taught young Peter about military affairs.[14] While no one in Moscow was paying close attention to Peter he wasted little time and by 1687 he had put together the Preobrazhenskii and Semenovskii Guard's regiments, a new praetorian guard that had started out as instruments of child's play. Using these regiments Peter was able to withdraw to the Troitse-Sergiev monastery in 1689 and gain the support of elements of the Muscovite boyars, foreign officers, and a critical mass of the Strel'tsy to compromise his half sister Sophia's power in 1690. Moreover, in 1691-4, Lefort, Gordon, and Peter I organized annual war games that reached the size of 15,000 men. While the power of the regiments became plain to people in the foreign quarter, Peter's real aim in ordering these exercises was to learn how to command regiments in an operational environment.[15]

The failure of Golitsyn's 1689 Crimean operation opened the door for Peter to assume control over Russia. While he would not become tsar in his own right until the 1696 death of his half-brother Ivan V, the failure of the 1689 Crimean campaign compromised Sophia's support at court and opened the door for young Peter to make a move that would secure his position on the throne of Russia. Oddly, because of his geographic location, Peter had a fascination for ships and everything related to them. From a young age he understood that one vital asset to Russia being able to expand on a global level would be its ability to build and maintain ships of every size and type. His recognition of the impact of sea power on the strength of a state may have played a role in his decision to first challenge the Ottomans at Azov, but that campaign was in fact the another act of a war that had been ongoing with the Ottomans since 1686 when Russia joined the Holy League. The Holy League was originally organized by Pope Innocent XI who convinced Leopold I, the Habsburg emperor who also ruled over the Papal States and the Holy Roman Empire and Jan III Sobieski, king of the Polish-Lithuanian Commonwealth, to contain the Ottoman Empire's efforts to occupy all of Central Europe. The Venetian Republic joined soon afterward, and Muscovy became a member in 1686 once the Poles and the Russians determined that the Turks were a much greater threat to their sovereignty than to each other. At its inception, therefore, Peter's campaign was grounded in an attempt to placate the expectations of his Holy League allies by containing Ottoman power as much as possible. The point of the campaign was not much different from the goals of all of Peter's military adventures—by gaining access to the Sea of Azov, his plan was to deliver goods from the Don River basin hopefully via the Black Sea. Likewise, opening up to international trade while expanding his kingdom's reach and hold over more territory exhibited for the rest of the world to see that the Romanovs sought nothing less than to make Russia a world power on an equal footing with the rest of Europe. In addition to impressing the Ottomans and making a statement to the Europeans, Peter chose to wage war in Russia's south to reveal to the assorted Cossack hosts, the Tartars, and anyone else paying attention that he intended to impose Russian power wherever he could. In 1695, however, he sought to reduce the fortress at Azov with a large force of Muscovite troops—some 120,000 men of which the bulk were old style cavalry and Strel'tsy. In fact, only around 30,000 of these troops served in the newly composed guard's regiments, thereby demonstrating that it would take time for Peter to integrate his style of warfare into Russia's armed forces. Thus, in 1695 Peter's massive July assault on Ottoman positions in and around the fortress at Azov failed because the Turks kept resupplying themselves from the sea. The young tsar learned the hard lesson that no matter how large the army might be, it was not going to be enough to reduce any fortress that is able to maintain a supply line with its main base of operations.

In response to his failed 1695 campaign Peter spent the winter of 1695-6 in Voronezh where under his direction the first Russian naval assets were built for use in his next campaign against the Turks. Peter left Voronezh in May 1696 with his new navy under the command of Lafort and began the process of laying siege to the fortress at Azov. Meanwhile another largely cavalry army supported by Ukrainian Cossacks under the command of Boris Sheremetov assaulted the fortress from land and cut it off from its base of supply. The fortress surrendered on July 19, 1696, suffering little damage, which meant that Peter I combined armed forces had taken control of a largely intact position that had once been owned by the Ottomans. But, much to his chagrin, in the aftermath of the campaign, Peter had to admit that the main reason his campaign succeeded was that over the winter of 1695-6 he made an appeal to the Western Christian powers for aid in defeating the Ottomans. The appeal for aid resulted in German engineers and Austrian gunners traveling to the theater of operations where together they taught Russians about the proper deployment of artillery and then how to use it effectively in a siege. Meanwhile, the use of Ukrainian and Don Cossacks to reduce the fortress' ramparts would cast in the mind of Peter the idea that the horsemen of the steppe were an important military asset and therefore useful addition to his armed forces if he could command their loyalty. Indeed the defeat of the Ottomans at Azov so impressed the Muscovites that they would provide funds for the continued construction of ships for a Russian navy that would be instrumental in Peter's next military adventure against Sweden. Yet, it should also be noted that while the Turks were defeated at Azov, Russia did not have access to the Black Sea because the Ottomans continued to control the vital straits of Kerch. Moreover, the Russians still remained in a state of war with the Ottoman Empire—a problem that would remain until the final collapse of the Turks in 1918—and holding on to the gains of 1696 would not be automatic or guaranteed. For the time being, however, Peter remained vexed over how he, in the end, was dependent on western experts for his success in the 1696 campaign and as a result he decided that he needed to go to the West to learn as much about everything that he could possible absorb, hence the cause for the Great Embassy of 1697–8.[16]

While tales of the incognito tsar Peter touring and working in the shipyards in Amsterdam or the many other stops on his Great Embassy make for great reading and reinforce the image of Peter the Great as an energetic if somewhat out of control royal, the affairs of state simply did not stop because he sought to live and learn as an ordinary person. In addition to learning as much by rote as he possibly could, Peter also sought to build alliances specifically to refocus his attention from his southern frontier to the Baltic Sea basin. To pave the way for this shift Russia's diplomats sought negotiations with the Ottomans first to resolve the remaining questions of the Azov campaign and then to adopt an armistice. The aim of this shift was to redirect Peter's attention to his northern advisory, the Swedish Empire. The last stage of the cycle of the northern war conflict(s) started in the summer of 1700 when Peter the Great joined a military alliance with Frederick IV, king of Denmark-Norway, and Augustus II, king of the Polish-Lithuanian Commonwealth and elector of Saxony. Their aim was to confront and defeat Charles XII, king of Sweden, who sought to gain control of the entire southern coast of the Baltic Sea along with its immediate hinterland. This alliance cleared the way for the Russians to sign on to the two significant treaties of Karlowitz on January 26, 1699, and the treaty of Constantinople in 1700. The document signed at Karlowitz was the product of a two-month summit that occurred between the Ottoman Empire on one side and the Holy League that formed in 1684 specifically to confront what proved to be the last major Turkish threat to Western Europe. This coalition consisted of the Holy Roman Empire, the Polish-Lithuanian Commonwealth, the Republic of Venice, and Muscovy. The Ottomans were forced to accept this treaty because they had repeatedly lost battles in the final stages of a conflict they had been fighting with the Holy League since 1683. While Peter I only gained a two-year truce with the Turks as a result of this treaty, the big winner was the Habsburg Empire that won control over much of Hungary, Slovenia, and Croatia. The Ottomans never threatened Central Europe again and the Habsburgs emerged as the regional power in southeastern Europe that they remained until their demise in 1918.

The Treaty of Constantinople was signed on July 13, 1700, between Peter the Great and the Ottoman Empire and it ended the cycle of conflict that had been going on between themselves since the mid-1680s. Peter dispatched Yemelyan Ignatievich Ukraintsev to the Porte in Constantinople in search of the sultan Mustafa II's recognition of Russia's success at Azov in 1696. Not only did he gain such recognition but he also secured control over an inlet southwest of Azov where Peter immediately commenced in the construction of what became the Port of Taganrog. As the new home of the Azov flotilla, Taganrog became the major base of operations for the Black Sea's fleet until Catherine the Great conquered Crimea. In return Peter the Great dropped his claims to territory in the lower Dnieper River region, thereby turning it into a demilitarized zone as both parties agreed not to build more fortifications for the time being. Russia also dropped its claim to the Kerch straits, which meant that Russian ships would not have free access to the Black Sea. There was much more to this treaty as the sultan and Peter the Great sought to impose order over the chaos of their mutual frontiers through various agreements such as Muscovy no longer would pay tribute to the Crimean Khanate breaking a cycle of payments that had been ongoing since Mongol occupation. Or, the sultan promised his loyal Crimean Tatars would not attack Russia in return for the tsar's promise that the Don and Zaporoshian Cossacks, both groups that had pledged loyalty oath to him, would not attack the Ottoman Empire. As a nod toward future harmonious relations each side agreed to exchange prisoners of war, Russian pilgrims were promised free passage to holy sites, and most important, the sultan finally agreed to permit the stationing of a permanent Russian diplomatic representative in Constantinople. Finally, Peter the Great and Mustafa II agreed that this agreement would last thirty years, thereby creating the impression that the Treaty of Constantinople signified an eternal peace between Russia and the Ottoman Empire.[17]

The high-level diplomacy that brought peace between the Ottomans and Europe and Russia resolved long-standing hostilities but no one was genuinely in the mood for peace. Instead, they all had other conflicts to fight. Parts of Western and Southern Europe were about to be consumed by a dynastic crisis that would result in the War of Spanish Succession, 1701–14. The succession of the childless Charles II of Spain would completely distract Louis XIV of France to the situation in Northern Europe and the Baltic where the Great Northern War, or the last war in the cycle of Northern War that largely Sweden, Denmark-Norway, Poland-Lithuania, and Muscovy had been fighting throughout the sixteenth and seventeenth centuries.[18] Thus, in the aftermath of the Treaty of Constantinople, Peter the Great directed the formation of a Baltic anti-Swedish coalition composed initially of himself, Augustus II "The Strong" of Saxony-Poland-Lithuania, and Frederick IV of Denmark-Norway who together sought to compromise the power of Charles XII's (king of Sweden) hold over the Baltic Sea basin. Like most wars, at its outbreak in 1700 no one expected this war to last

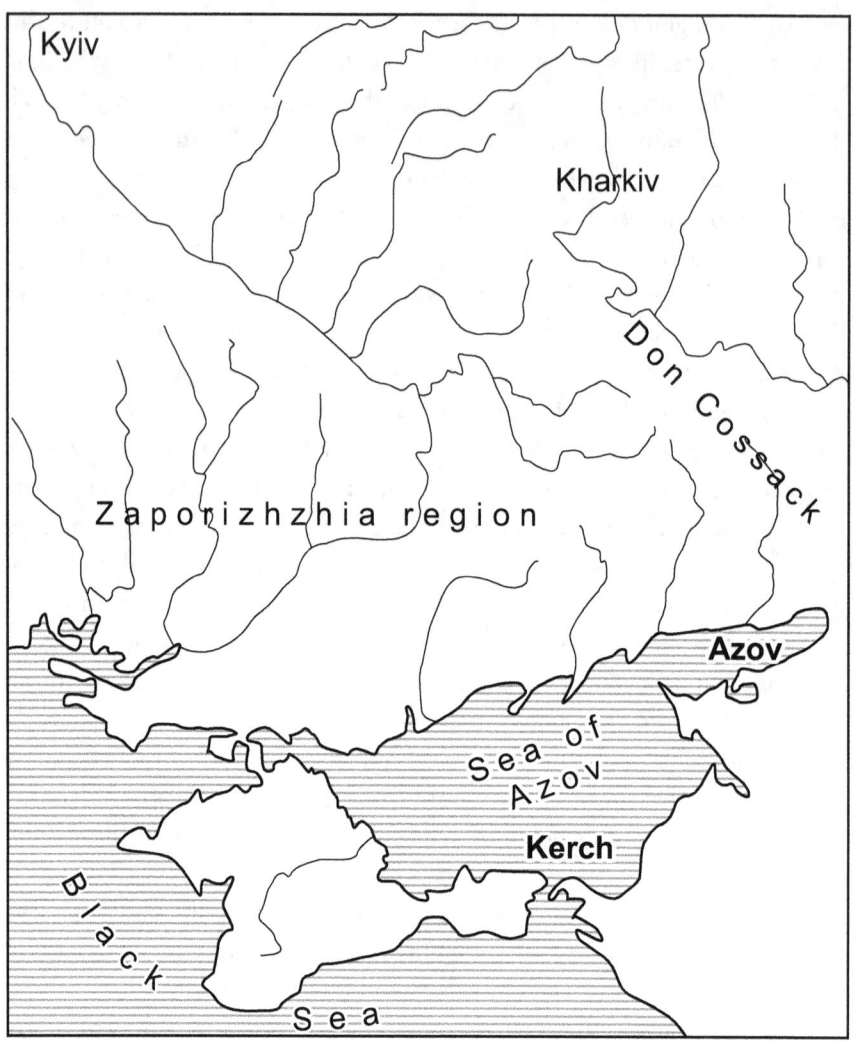

Map 1.1 Peter the Great's Azov Campaign.

twenty-one years. Yet in 1700 there was nothing extraordinary about the start of this war. After all, Peter was at once addressing a serious threat to his power across the Northern reaches of his empire while asserting the emergence of Russia as a factor in Great Power politics. He could not hesitate to make a move against Sweden because while the Ottomans had agreed to peace, there were still threats, mainly from Cossacks and Tatars, that persisted across the Muscovite's southern frontier. To add to the challenge, Sweden represented a very different type of foe for the young tsar. Charles XII was the heir to Gustav Adolf and the military revolution that had transformed warfare in the early seventeenth century. Arguably, the Swedish army of this time was the most proficient across Europe, or at the very least in the Baltic region. But, the stakes were too high and waiting did not seem like an option as the potential always existed for Sweden to build its own coalition and become so strong that the window of opportunity to compromise Charles XII's power might close.

As Peter I struggled to gain a foothold in the Sea of Azov, he simultaneously addressed the Baltic and its environs to continue the persistent practice, since Ivan III, of expanding his power through conquest and then occupation of the conquered territories to gain control over resources. The competition to gain control over and exploit the Baltic's lucrative trade became fierce as the sixteenth century progressed as a result of the availability of ever increasing quantities of grain, timber, pitch, potash, hemp, flax, wax, hides, and furs. Not surprisingly, all belligerents in the Great Northern War understood by the beginning of the eighteenth century that the real key to power in the region was controlling ports and riverheads where all trade coming in or out of the interior had to pass. For example, the status of the city of Riga highlights why conflict between Charles XII and Peter the Great became inevitable. While Sweden controlled the port, it did not control the month of the Dvina or the river itself. This situation was rapidly becoming unsustainable because Charles XII needed to expand his revenue stream while Peter the Great wanted control of Riga to monopolize the trade and to strengthen Russia's presence on the Baltic.[19] Moreover, the appearance of a Russian flotilla on the Sea of Azov was not lost on Charles XII and while there were no Russian ships to threaten Sweden's control of the Baltic Sea, it now had become a possibility that the king could not afford to ignore.[20]

As the eighteenth century dawned, Sweden was in a difficult position. She had reached the zenith of her power by the mid-seventeenth century as a result of the work and campaigns of Gustav Adolph during the Swedish phase of the Thirty Years' War. During that war he demonstrated that Sweden's new model army, one populated by trained recruits who were commanded by professional officers all supplied and funded by the state, could defeat any irregular or mercenary army. But in the second half of the seventeenth century, it became clear that Sweden could only support its professional army if it could pay for itself. The country did not possess the internal resources and the extent of their empire was not providing enough revenue to finance the army. As Charles XII was rising to power, the Swedes had concluded that the only way they could maintain their place in the world was to continue to expand the size of their empire specifically to finance their army in the field.[21] When Charles XII came to the throne at the age of fifteen in 1697, he had two assets that

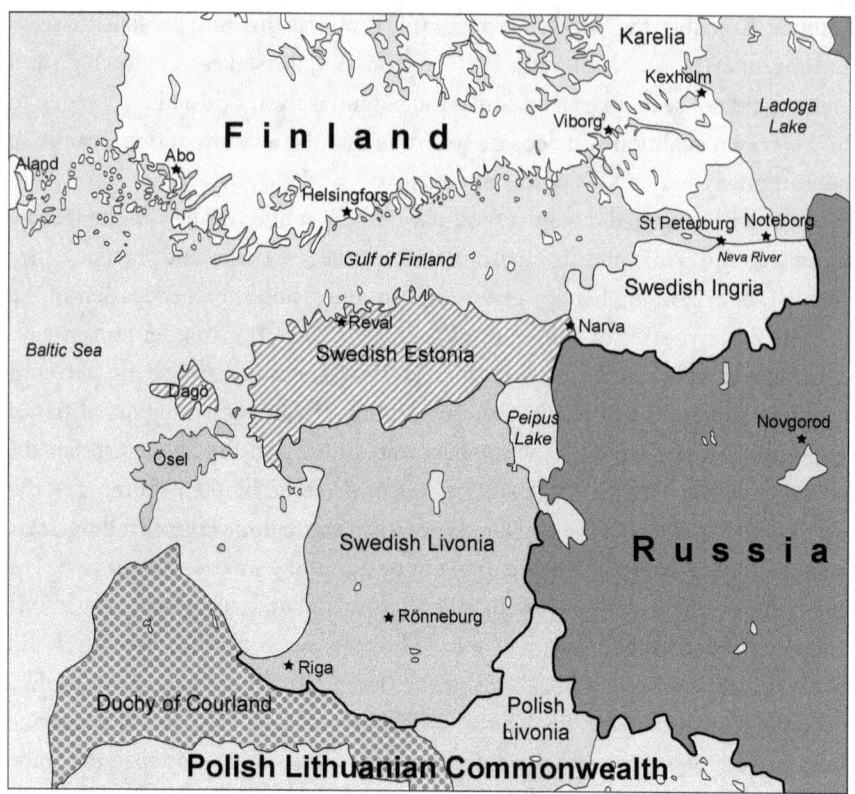

Map 1.2 The Narva Campaign.

supported Swedish strategy. The first was his fervent desire to be a successful and victorious warrior who would build a powerful and unassailable Swedish Empire. The other was that his father Charles XI had built up a professional military organization that consisted of twenty-three infantry regiments composed of 30,000 soldiers and eleven cavalry regiments composed of 11,000 horses.[22] In addition to the standing force structure, Charles XI had also created a regional recruitment system where the burden of supplying troops fell on the regions from where these troops were inducted. This system had tremendous support across Sweden. Nonetheless, once Charles XII came to power he and his supporters suffered from one intractable problem. His goal was nothing short of imperial expansion of Sweden into territories on the southern shores of the Baltic and as far into the hinterland of both Russia and the Commonwealth no matter the cost. Sweden's concentration of strength especially on the southern shores of the Baltic inspired all of the people who lived there to support the growing power of Muscovy.[23] Another problem facing Charles XII was that his main ally—France—was getting deeply embroiled in the War of Spanish Succession as conflict commenced in the Baltic region.

The first major clash of this conflict occurred in what is now Estonia when Peter the Great laid siege to a Swedish fortress, the fortress of Ivangorod originally built by Ivan III, at the headwaters of the Narva River. Peter's assault on Navra was actually the final campaign of a coordinated plan that had started when Augustus II, king of Poland/Lithuania and elector of Saxony, attacked Swedish Livonia in February 1700 and Frederick IV, king of Denmark and Norway, occupied Schleswig and Holstein in March of the same year. The young tsar went into the Narva campaign with much confidence not only because of the successful operations of his allies but also because his reorganized army was now composed of the guard's regiments he created as his elite servitors and new model infantry regiments. Peter I started building a system of siege works at the end of September 1700 with the aim of launching an artillery bombardment on the Swedish position. The Russian shelling of Narva started at the end of October after Peter I had concentrated some 35,000 troops in the region. The Russians, however, proved to be no match for the Swedish military. While Charles XII would contain the operations of both the Poles and the Danes under his direct command, a Swedish relief force approximately one-third the size of the besieging Russian forces arrived at Narva on November 19, 1700, and in short order smashed the forces of Peter in the midst of a blinding snowstorm and sent them packing. The Russians were to lose over 8,000 men and approximately 145 guns or all of the artillery that they brought to the field of battle. Peter, himself, was caught away from any point of command as the battle unfolded and was left with having to endure a humiliating defeat.[24]

In the aftermath of this battle Charles XII enjoyed continuous success in his campaigns on the southern shores of the Baltic while Peter the Great set upon the task of rebuilding Russia's military establishment. Initially, Charles seemed unstoppable—he first forced his way across the Dvina River and invaded Courland in July 1701 and then Lithuania proper in January 1702. Later in the year, in July, he defeated a combined Saxon-Polish Army in Kliszow, which resulted in a period of continuous campaigning that reached its apex in July 1704 when Swedish forces fully occupied the cities of Warsaw, Krakow, Poznan, Thorn, and Elbing. Moreover, as a result of his many successes Charles XII was empowered to become influential in Polish politics, which resulted in his ousting of Augustus II as king of the Polish-Lithuanian Commonwealth. He abdicated once the Swedish army occupied the bulk of his domain. Ultimately, August II, Peter I's ally, renounced the throne at the Treaty of Altranstadt on

September 24, 1706, and was then replaced with Sweden's candidate Stanislaw Leszczynski who was elected king of the Commonwealth under duress by the Polish land magnets at the same time. After General Karl Gustaf Rehnskiold crushed a combined army of Saxons and Russians at Fraustadt in February 1706, the path lay open for a general invasion of Saxony proper, which Charles XII ordered in his continuing effort to gain control over as much territory as possible on the southern side of the Baltic Sea. By this point in the conflict the Polish-Lithuanian Commonwealth was in serious distress and Charles XII still was not taking Russia as a serious adversary.

Charles XII, however, made a huge mistake when he underestimated the will and determination of Peter I. Although the defeat at Narva was bruising both in its military impact and on the reputation of the young tsar, Peter I remained boldly determined to lift Russia out of its medieval past and recast his land as a great European power. In all but ignoring Peter I, Charles XII did not pay sufficient attention to the defensive needs of the southern Baltic coast and this was a shortcoming the tsar deduced and exploited. He started campaigning in this territory as he simultaneously rebuilt his army with the aim of eliminating all dependency on the old middle service class, the pomeshniki/Dvoiranstvo cavalry, and any surviving elements of the Strel'tsy. Not surprisingly, Peter I therefore addressed his weaknesses by appointing Prince Boris Alexeievich Golitsyn to rebuild the cavalry arm of his armed forces. His efforts can best be measured by noting that in 1707 he had organized approximately 27,000 men into twelve cavalry regiments. Instead of the pomeshniki exclusively populating the ranks of this force, the main qualifying attribute for being allowed to serve in the new Russian cavalry was horsemanship. Men from all social classes were accepted based on how well they handled horses. And, while little question exists that upper-class men had better opportunities to learn horsemanship, what should not be lost in Golitsyn's work was that the cavalry was now a service where qualifications and merit played a role in acceptance and advancement. Opposition from the old Boyars of Muscovy, the use of qualification, and merit as a means to professionalize Russia's cavalry cropped up almost from the moment Peter first commanded it. That opposition would persist throughout the eighteenth century in various ways and means, but the concepts nonetheless became embedded in the Russian army and would persist—sometimes to greater and lesser degrees—until its collapse at the beginning of the twentieth century.[25]

In the wake of the defeat at Narva, one of Russia's glaring weaknesses, that of the lack of much of an industrial base to support eighteenth-century warfare, became clear. So desperate was the situation that one of Peter's old confidants, Andrei Andreevich Vinius, scoured the Baltic region for church bells to confiscate and melt them down so that their metals could be recast into cannons. The historian Christopher Duffy makes a claim to 25 percent of Russian's church bells being remade into over 200 cannons in the aftermath of the battle of Narva. Indeed, this act made Peter's determination to win at all costs clear to every Russian![26] He further charged the Scottish major general James Bruce who had the technical know-how to build an effective artillery force for the Russian army. For the most part, he alone designed the weapons and most importantly the carriages that gave the new force mobility and from which the weapons could be fired. True to the spirit of Peter's goal of learning from western expertise, after creating artillery regiments along western lines, Bruce also introduced a training regime designed to provide the army with future generations of Russians trained as artillery specialists.

In addition to providing the army with an organizational plan for its development in 1705, Peter I ordered it to adopt a document written by ex-Austrian Lieutenant General G. B. Ogilvy entitled: *Plan and Arrangement for the Army according to Foreign Practices*.[27] Composed in thirteen dictums, the document provided an organizational structure of the imperial army that would, for the most part, persist until the Napoleonic interlude changed everything. According to Ogilvy's guidance, the standard infantry regiment in the Russian army would now consist of 1,400 men and would be split into two battalions. Seven years after the disaster at Narva, in 1707 the army consisted of two guard's regiments, forty-seven line infantry regiments, five elite grenadier regiments, thirty-three dragoon regiments, and one artillery regiment.[28] Once Peter I had established the semblance of branch services in the military, he was faced with the daunting challenge of coordinating their efforts especially not only during times of war but also during peacetime when planning, training, and supplying a standing army continued to challenge the economic infrastructure of the Russian Empire. Toward achieving a modicum of command and control within his army after the disaster at Narva and for when it engaged enemy forces, Peter I created the Supreme War Council to oversee all military activities in his realm.[29] The council would endure periods when it was politicized to the point of making itself irrelevant but it would persist as a vital planning and coordinating unit especially in times of war until the reign of Paul I. Moreover, it demonstrated that while Peter I wanted to maintain authoritative control over all aspects of his realm, he also understood that he also needed bureaucratic support for those moments when he could not be present to make decisions from command to planning decisions. To this end he created a system in which his confidants advised and sometimes made decisions that affected the course of a war.[30]

Although Peter drew on foreigners to reorganize his armed forces, he was also keenly aware that the army needed an infusion of new blood in his leadership cadre, which ushered in the rise of Boris Petrovich Sheremetov (of Azov campaign fame) and of Alexander Danilovich Menshikov, his childhood friend. Together they defeated Swedish forces first at Ersestfer on December 30, 1701, and at Hummelshof on July 17, 1702. These successes not only demonstrated that Peter remained undeterred as a result of the catastrophic disaster at Narva but also paved the way for a general invasion of Livonia or the territory that formed the bulk of the borderland of Russia and the Polish-Lithuanian Commonwealth. Notably, during the summer of 1702 while campaigning in Livonia, Peter would meet Marta Helena Skowronska, a woman of a lower-class background and he would soon marry her after she converted to Orthodoxy and changed her name to Catherine.[31] More to the point, also in the summer of 1702 Sheremetov with 30,000 soldiers laid siege to the fortress at Notebourg, which was situated on an island where the river Neva flowed out of Lake Ladoga and into the Gulf of Finland. The Russians stormed the fortress on the night of October 10–11 and upon reducing it Peter occupied it and renamed it Schlusslburg. These actions in the spring, summer, and fall of 1702 effectively cut Charles XII off from the eastern side of the Gulf of Finland.

By the spring of 1703 Peter expressed his belief that Russia's hold on the Gulf of Finland was secure and permanent when he started the construction of the new capital of his empire, St. Petersburg. Shortly after he had a three-room cabin built from where he would direct and participate in the construction of St. Petersburg while living in domestic bliss with Marta Skowronska soon to be Catherine I. While Peter designed and laid out his imperial capital, his armies continued to pursue Russia's relentless strategy against Charles XII and his forces and recaptured Narva in August 1704. This victory opened the door for Russia to invade the Polish-Lithuanian territory in and around the southern shores of the Gulf of Finland. This campaign culminated at the end of January 1706 when the Russians were defeated in front of Riga. This defeat forces Peter's line of operations away from the sea and as he seeks to destroy the Swedish army in the Commonwealth's interior. Fortunately, the Russians found support from the local populations who actually preferred to be occupied by Russians than the Swedes! The campaign of 1706 then resulted in a Russian invasion of Saxony on September 6th that forced Charles XII to rethink his next move as the tide of the conflict shifted to Peter the Great's favor.[32]

During the period between Narva and the 1709 Battle of Poltava, Peter also strove to eliminate the need for foreigners in the Russian army. He sought to replace them with Russians trained and educated to serve their tsar. This task succeeded to the point where by the 1721 end of the Great Northern War only 12.6 percent of the officers consisted of non-native Russians.[33] This transformation of Russian military leadership started to assert itself in mid-April 1707 when a Russian War Council met at Zholkiv and developed a strategy for engaging in operations for the next and what proved to be the decisive stage of the war. While Peter was campaigning and winning local engagements along the southern shores of the Gulf of Finland, Charles XII had systematically defeated the Danes (who until this period effectively controlled the entrance of ships into the Baltic Sea by charging a toll), the Saxons, and most importantly the Poles. These events culminated with the realization that nothing stood in the way of Charles XII from invading Russia proper. To this end, the Russians adopted the strategy of first giving up once and for all on Augustus II and then Peter issuing the command to withdraw his army into his kingdom's interior. Moreover, in preparation of a general invasion, Peter develops and implements a scorched earth policy that aimed to destroy anything of use or value to the Swedish army. This policy effectively deprived the Swedes of anything of practical use, as it made them vulnerable to defeat as their supply lines stretched further and further into Russia from their operational base in Stockholm.[34] Thus as the 1707 campaigning season ramped up, Charles XII concluded that Russia's withdrawal into their interior revealed weakness so he left a small force of approximately 9,000 troops in the Polish-Lithuanian Commonwealth while using the rest of his army to invade Russia.[35]

Still in 1707 Charles did not appreciate the potential power of the Russian army or the determination of Peter I to prevail in his efforts to gain control of the Gulf of Finland. What followed was a two-year odyssey for the Swedish king that culminated with his crushing defeat at the battle of Poltava in June 1709. Charles XII grievously miscalculated when he arrogantly decided not to secure his supply lines. Rather, he believed that his supplies would catch up to his movements, hence he left the environs of Livonia and marched toward Moscow. Russian forces, however, kept pressuring him to move south into Ukraine, which he did believing he would find supplies as he marched. The September 28, 1708, Battle of Lesnaia became the prime example of the character of this part of the war as a Russian army numbering around 28,000 men under the command of Menshikov and Mikhail Mikhailovich Golitsyn fought a Swedish force of some 12,000 men commanded by General Adam Ludwig Lewenhaupt and Berndt Otto Stackelberg to a standstill. While stalemated on the battlefield, the reinforcements that Charles XII was counting on never made it to his main army as they looted their supply wagons and disappeared into the night of September 28/29. More catastrophic for Charles was the complete abandonment of the approximately 4,500 wagons of irreplaceable supplies. Not only did this result in Charles searching desperately for another source of supply, it meant that the Swedish army was destined to spend the winter of 1708–9 trapped deep in the Ukraine without adequate food and shelter let alone a robust supply of arms and ammunition.[36]

Simultaneous with his efforts to resupply his forces from Sweden, Charles first sought supplies from his newly installed ally, the king of Poland, Stanislow Leszczynski. But as a Swedish puppet he had little local support and was therefore unable to provide Charles XII with supplies. In fact, as a result of continuous conflict, the Polish-Lithuanian Commonwealth was bereft of any supplies useful for an operational army. Once it was clear that the Commonwealth would not provide anything to his military effort, Charles attempted to get the Zaporizhian Cossacks to switch to his side in an effort to find a source of supply for his forces now effectively cut off from Sweden. The status of Cossacks throughout Ukraine had been transforming throughout the seventeenth century as tsars, sultans, and kings of the Commonwealth sought their loyalty.[37] The Cossacks since the 1648 revolt of Bogdan Khmelnitsky had sought to create their own homeland out of the Ukraine. By the beginning of the eighteenth century and especially because of the persistent spread of Russia's power, the window of opportunity for Cossack autonomy was closing. Charles XII and his Swedish armies, therefore, offered another and what proved to be the last chance for the Zaparochian host to gain control over what they perceived to be their home territory. Thus, the Swedish king informed Hetman Ivan Stepanovich Mazepa when they met at Smorgon that Peter I was scheming to replace him (Mazepa) as leader of the Zaporozhian host with Alexander Menshikov. Mazepa believed this accusation and considered it to be tantamount to a betrayal by Peter the Great to the promises made by his father Tsar Alexis Mikhailovich in the 1654 Treaty of Pereyaslav. In that treaty the Cossacks promised to provide the Romanovs with military support if in turn the Tsardom of Muscovy provided the Cossacks with support to defend against the persistent raids of the Crimean Tatars. Relations between the Cossacks and Peter the Great had been souring as the tsar kept drafting the Cossacks to fight the Swedes in Poland and to be laborers for the construction of St. Petersburg. By 1708, Mazepa was concerned and faced public questioning about securing of their territory when so many men were elsewhere serving the tsar. When Charles offered him a princedom composed of all Cossack lands in return for his switching sides and fight for the king of Sweden, Mazepa made the fateful decision to join him in his conflict with Peter I. Much to Mazepa's chagrin, he soon learned that he, like Charles, had miscalculated the power of and the support that Peter I had across the land as only 3,000 Cossacks joined him in the Swedish ranks. Upon learning of Mazepa's decision to switch sides in October 1708, Peter branded him a traitor, informed Cossackdom that they would be hunted to their deaths if they followed Mazepa into the Swedish army but that they could also receive amnesty if they supported the election of a new hetman by their own rada or council.[38] Peter's action resulted in the election of Ivan Skoropadski as the new hetman of the Zaporzhian host. Then Menshikov promptly led a force into Baturyn, Mazapa's capital, on November 13, 1708, and razed the city while slaughtering most of its inhabitants.[39] As a harbinger of his fate, Baturyn's rich store of provisions and supplies were lost, thus foiling Charles XII's best chance to properly resupply and shelter for winter.[40] Despite the Swedish invasion of Russia and Ukraine, the challenges and threats of the southern frontier remained ever present if not because the Ottomans and the Crimean Khanate maintained powerful military forces, then in the numerous insurrections that occurred across the Don region in 1708 as various Cossack hosts sought to seize control of Azov, Peter's recently won foothold in the south.[41]

While never forgetting the instability of his steppe frontier, in the winter and spring of 1708–9, Peter I had to focus on the main theater of operations as the war with Sweden was reaching its major turning point, the Battle of Poltava. The route to Poltava was a meandering affair especially since it occurred deep in Ukraine when Charles XII's objective was Moscow and St. Petersburg. Clearly the Russians were learning how to fight on the Early Modern battlefield using the same technique as her adversaries. As opposed to their capabilities at Narva, in the Poltava campaign the Russian army now engaged the Swedes with every intention of aggressively seizing the initiative and controlling the battlefield throughout the engagement. In addition to concentrating his forces, Peter has also developed logistical capabilities that had his army well supplied when they confronted the Swedes in the spring and summer of 1709. Even more significant, by the time of Poltava the Russians under Peter's insistence developed a strategy that included trading space for time, destroying everything of military value in front of the campaigning Swedish army and any of her allies, and concentrating his (Peter's) forces for a climactic battle after Charles XII's poorly supplied forces had endured a winter in the field. The results of Peter's military efforts were a strong and confident Russian army confronting and poorly supplied, morale sagging Swedish army outstand a hamlet in Ukraine.

Peter, now taking an active role in the command of his army, chased Charles's army of some 30,000 Swedish troops and 8,000 Cossacks around Ukraine in the spring of 1709. Charles, seeking to create a base from which he could concentrate his forces and launch his advance northward toward Moscow, chose Poltava and laid siege to its fortress at the end of April.[42] Once Peter realized that Charles had chosen Poltava as the place where he sought to build a strong point, he immediately set off to get there and take command of his army. He did not arrive until June 9th and after assessing the situation called for a War Council to meet on June 16th. With all of his exuberance and boundless energy, Peter insisted on the commencement of operations the following morning, which he did when he commanded his approximately 45,000-men army to cross the river Vorskla six miles north of Poltava and begin the process of enveloping the Swedish army. In the midst of this high drama, and adding to the excitement of the moment, Charles was hit by some flying ordinance on June 16 and was forced to command the battle from a stretcher. Swiftly realizing what Peter sought to do, and short on everything from men to powder, Charles ordered a retreat toward Poltava while he magnificently concentrated his forces to prepare for a strike against Peter the Great. The strike ensued early on the morning of June 27, 1709, when the Swedes attacked the Russian forces at 3:30 a.m. in a gambit to catch them asleep. The Russia's pickets, however, raised the alarm and they seamlessly formed up, deployed their infantry with great effect because of their organization and response to commands, and promptly seized the initiative. By the middle of the day Russian artillery was blasting the Swedes from the battlefield. By the end of the day the Swedes were fleeing in disarray leaving 10,000 dead, wounded, and prisoners. Charles XII and a small group of supporters fled to Turkish territory and would be heard from again inside of two years.[43] The final act of the Battle of Poltava occurred on June 30th when Menshikov caught the rest of the Swedish forces operating in Ukraine now under the command of General Lewenhaupt and forced him to surrender the balance of his army of approximately 16,000 men. In the end, the campaign cost Sweden her entire army that had been conducting operations in Ukraine. Some 9,000 men had been killed and over 18,000 had been captured; the rest had been wounded or fled into the landscape. In addition, the entire baggage train of the Swedish army in Ukraine had been lost. While Charles XII's defeat in 1709 was complete, he still had a few options left, thus the war was far from over.[44]

Veterans of the Battle of Poltava may not have realized that they had participated in a battle that would change the course of world history. They most probably did, however, understand that Russia's armed forces had undergone a transformation in its operational capabilities that had ushered in a new age in its history, one in which they would be a dominating, and hence victorious, force in most battles against not only adversaries riding off of the steppe but now European opponents with their Early Modern "revolutionary" armies. At the very least the victory at Poltava symbolized the coming of age of the Russian defense establishment. From this time forward the Russian military would consider its primary mission to be to expand their power and authority as opposed to defending from enemy invasions of the homeland. While the Russians would never be immune from hostile threats, invasions of Russia proper would be few and far between after the decisive defeat of the Swedes at Poltava. Moreover, in domestic terms, victory at Poltava also became the event that legitimized the Petrine reforms, persistent opposition notwithstanding. When the Russian kingdom came together behind Peter I to support his army so it could defeat the Swedes at Poltava, it also revealed a new and higher level of support for the Russian monarchy. Brian Davies, taking from Richard Hellie, notes that while the military victory alone exhibited the professionalization of the Russian army, what followed was a "second state service revolution" where the duties and responsibilities of everyone but especially the dvorianstvo were dramatically enhanced, that is, the Russian nobility finally accepted that Peter the Great now demanded of them a lifetime of service. More significant to Russia's future as a Romanov kingdom, in accepting Peter's demands, they agreed to strengthen the power of the tsar and the firmness of his autocracy. Perhaps in a final nod to the memory of the Times of Troubles, Russia's aristocrats of all levels—from the scions of Boyars to the emerging landed gentry (former pomeshniki)—were now willing to submit to the power of a royal autocrat in exchange for their security and prosperity, which became the foundation of the new Russian Empire.[45]

Did the Poltava campaign represent the emergence of a new style of warfare as Christopher Duffy claims?[46] There is no question that Peter the Great soundly defeated the Swedes at Poltava. On a certain level Duffy is correct but Russia winning so big at Poltava had more to do with Peter I adopting a European style of warfare as opposed to something new. Russia's military, like all Early Modern armies, was transitioning from feudal cavalry to mass infantry armed forces. The challenge for all of these countries was developing the infrastructure to support such forces. The Russians may have taken longer than the rest of Europe, but Peter the Great made sure that once his nation did develop an Early Modern army, that it was going to be an important factor in first European, and later global affairs. Poltava was a turning point in history; it started the process that would culminate in the 1721 Treaty of Nystadt and this document made Russia

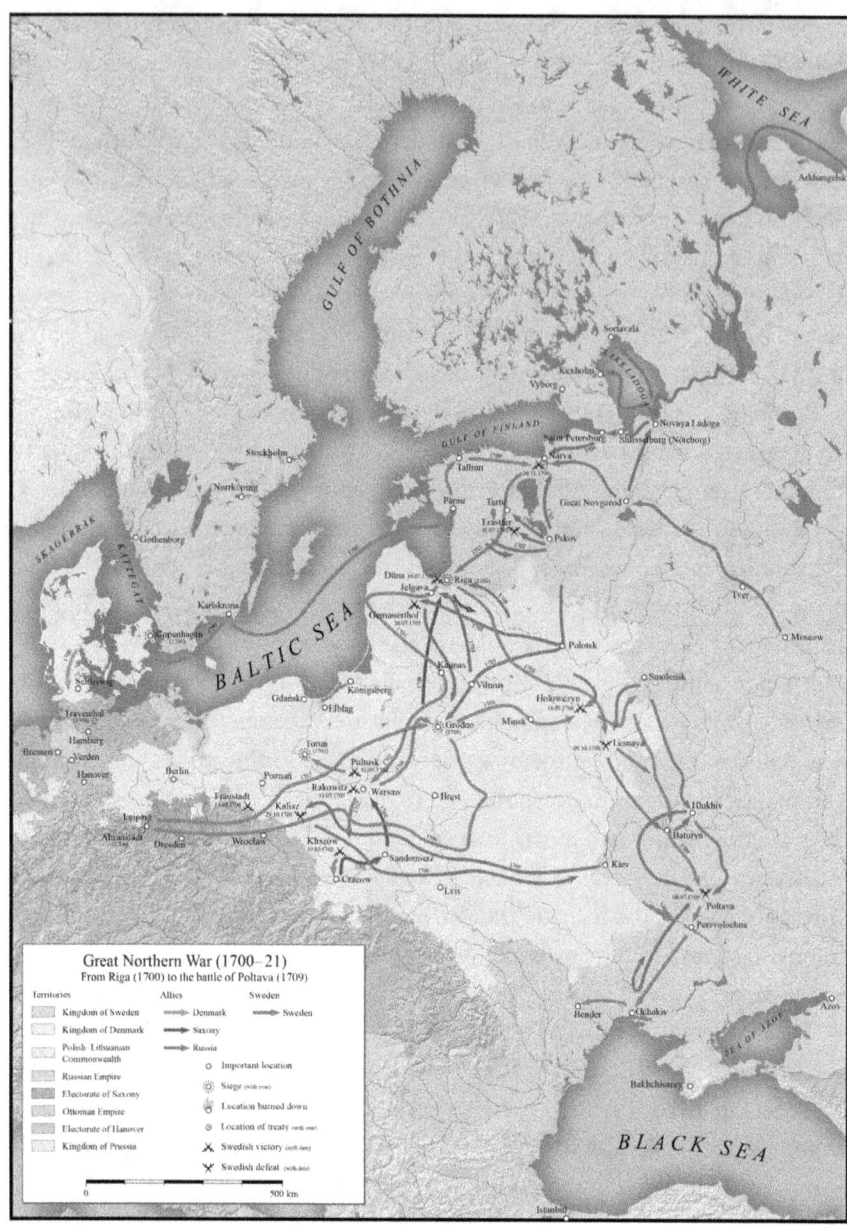

Map 1.3 The Great Northern War.

a Baltic power, something first sought by Ivan IV. While there were still a dozen years left in Peter's Great Northern War, Sweden's defeat at Poltava turned into a harbinger of the war's outcome. After being defeated in the Great Northern War, neither Sweden nor any other power would challenge Russia as the dominant power in the region of the Baltic Sea and its environs.[47]

Although the die was cast, no one clearly knew this in 1709, and Peter I's immediate task was to consolidate his victory both in military and in diplomatic terms. First, Russia's victory at Poltava undermined Charles XII's position in the Polish-Lithuanian Commonwealth. In specific terms this meant that Stanislaw Leszczynski had lost the power behind his throne. On October 9, 1709, this reality sunk in when Peter I signed a new treaty with August II that promised him Russian troops to defend the Commonwealth. The next day he signed a pact with Prussia aimed at preventing Swedish forces from having sanctuary in their territory as they fled Poland in the coming onslaught of Russian forces. The day after that, Peter I signed a pact with Denmark designed to cut off Sweden from the west.[48] All of this diplomatic activity set the stage for the armies of Peter to launch a campaign in the summer of 1710 to oust Sweden from the Gulf of Finland. He reduced and defeated the powerful Swedish fortress at Vyborg in June, most notably building a power siege train to complete the destruction of Charles XII power at the eastern edge of the Gulf. Contributing to the seeming invincibility of Russian armed forces was the decisive defeat and reduction of the fortress at Riga by Count Sheremetov in July 1710. Gaining control of Riga paved the way for Russian forces to occupy all of Livonia and this in turn opened the door for the emerging Tsarist Empire to become a regular trading partner within the old Hanseatic League, thereby allowing Peter to achieve one of his basic strategic goals.[49] These series of actions culminated with the capitulation of Estonia and Livonia when first the Livonian nobility surrendered to Russian forces at Riga on July 5th and then the Estonian followed suit at Tallinn on September 29th. Here Peter confirmed the traditional status of each group of nobles and they in turn agreed to be the tsars' subjects. While Sweden did not accept this new status quo until the 1721 Treaty of Nystadt, the decisions of the Baltic nobility to join forces with Russia effectively ended Swedish power on the southern side of the Gulf of Finland.[50]

As Peter consolidated his hold over the southern and eastern sides of the Gulf of Finland, he also incessantly demanded that the Ottomans make Charles XII surrender, and barring that to be forced out of his sanctuary in the Ottoman Empire. Charles, of course, agitated for the Ottomans to join him in a coalition against the Russians. In 1710 Charles succeeded in getting Sultan Ahmed III to coalesce around like-minded Ottoman bureaucrats, and he violated the 1700 Treaty of Constantinople to declare war on Peter the Great. The tsar in turn now found himself engaged in a two-front war in which he fought Early Modern Swedish forces in the north and a combined Ottoman/Crimean steppe army to the south. Nevertheless, in the summer of 1711 an Ottoman/Crimean-Tatar force that numbered some 200,000 men invaded Moldavia and ultimately surrounded a combined force of some 42,000 Russians, Moldavians, and Cossacks on the river Prut in July. Here Peter I learned that while he had a new army with "modern" firepower capabilities, he still was not the master of his universe. Simply put, he was so heavily outnumbered that the tsar had no choice but to surrender. The surrender, known to history as the Treaty of Prut(h), signed on July 21, 1711, at first appeared as a document that confirmed the Ottomans' overwhelming and decisive victory on the river Prut. It required the Russians to evacuate Azov and to destroy all Russian fortifications, especially at Tangorod that Peter the Great had been building to consolidate his hold over the Sea of Azov since his victory there in 1696. Yet, after a short while, rumors started to circulate inside the sultan's court that Grand Vizier Baltaci Mehmet Pasha, commander of the forces in the field in Moldavia, had accepted the bribe of tsarina's jewels in return for allowing Peter the Great to exit the battlefield, thus forever putting a stain on the Ottoman accomplishments at Prut.[51]

The disaster at Prut cannot be understated. The loss of Azov was a major blow in prestige and to Peter's overall southern strategy. He was just as far from gaining access to the world via the southern frontier of his empire as he had been when he set off on his original Azov campaign in 1695. Moreover, a clause in the Treaty of Prut allowed for Charles XII the right to return to Sweden via the Polish-Lithuanian Commonwealth. In addition, the campaign (sometimes called the Russo-Ottoman War of 1710–11) started with the Ottomans blatantly violating a prior treaty, which forever made them a treacherous, untrustworthy foe on their southern border. While every tsar/tsarina would negotiate their share of armistices and peace treaties with the Ottomans, the Russians never put much faith in any of them and would subsequently remain in a perpetual state of conflict with the sultan(s) until their mutual collapse in 1917/1918. The story of Catherine I jewels may be apocryphal, but the idea that a Turkish pasha in the seventeenth century accepting a bribe for personal gain is entirely within keeping of our understanding and image of the bureaucrats of the Ottoman Empire. Perpetual conflict as opposed to eternal peace along Russia's southern frontier would result in this long border from the Bosporus straits, through Anatolia, to Armenia and the Caucasus becoming a training ground where

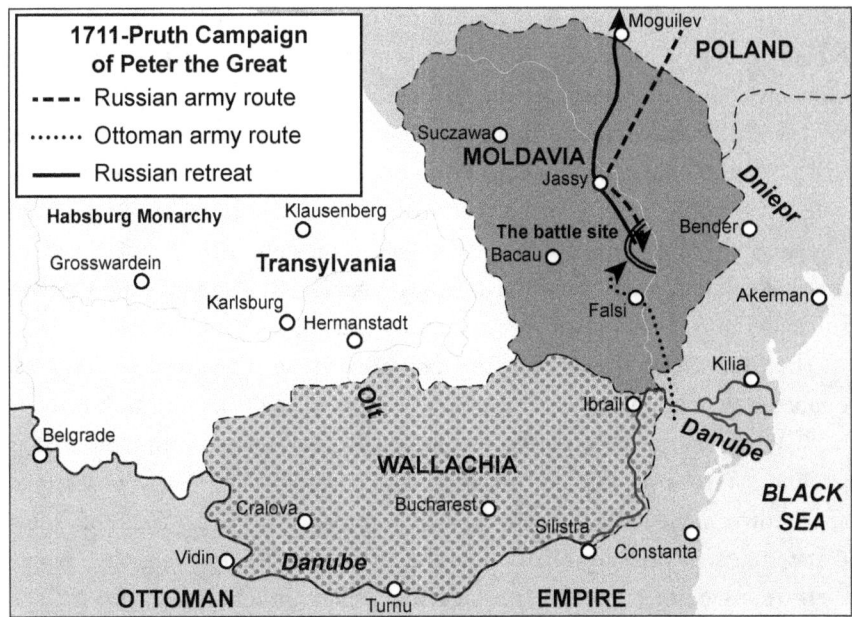

Map 1.4 The Pruth Campaign.

officers of its army would learn not only about the many intractable differences that existed between them across their extensive frontiers, but also in the art of command for officer and soldiering for soldiers.[52] Peter the Great laid out the strategy regarding the Ottoman Empire throughout his reign. In the end, he did not enjoy much success in the south, but he did set the process in motion that would let his successors, especially, Catherine the Great push the Ottomans off the northern side of the Black sea and continue to maintain pressure on the Turks throughout the high age of imperialism.

After the debacle at Prut, Charles headed to Sweden, and Peter returned to the Baltic theater of operations. There, the tsar discovered that despite having a common enemy and the mutual goal of defeating and removing all aspects of Swedish power from the European continent, much tension existed between his allies the Poles, Danes, Prussians, and Saxons over territorial claims. After the defeat of the Swedish fortress at Stettin in September 1713, the course of the war directed Peter's attention to events occurring on the northern side of the Gulf of Finland where Russian forces had also been conducting operations. The invasion of Finland had become a strategic necessity because of the construction of St. Petersburg. Russia's new imperial capital would not be secure until her defense establishment controlled the Karelian Isthmus and the territory adjacent to its north, east, and west. This defense requirement resulted in the invasion of Finland proper in the summer of 1713, and at the same time Russian forces were reducing Stettin and they also occupied Helsinki/Helsingfors. By February of the next year all Swedish troops had been pushed to the west coast of Finland and at that point the Battle of Storkyro/Isokyro occurred where the Russians soundly defeated the Swedes and forced them out of Finland proper. The invasion of Finland in 1712–14 was the last major land campaign of the Great Northern War but still the conflict continued because Charles XII was not yet prepared to surrender himself or any aspect of his sovereignty or his nation to the Russians.

The Great Northern War now took on a maritime aspect as Peter I saw an opportunity to establish if not command control of the Baltic Sea with his new navy. What transpired was a series of events that culminated with the Russians gaining control over the Gulf of Bothnia as a result of the Battle of Gangut, also known as the Battle of Hango, in the summer of 1714. The chain of events that resulted in this naval battle was the attempt by the Russians to resupply their troops engaged in operations in southern and western Finland by sea. The Swedes had stationed a blockade fleet off the southern coast that had successfully prevented Russian supply ships from landing war materials beginning in May 1714. A cat-and-mouse game ensued throughout the summer that resulted in heightened tensions over control of what had become a vital supply line. The battle took place north of the Hanko Peninsula on July 27, but the real prize turned out to be the Aland Islands in the middle of the Gulf of Bothnia, which the Russians were able to occupy after the fighting ceased. Under the command of Admiral Fyodor Matveyevich Apriksan some ninety-eight Russian galleys overwhelmed a Swedish force under the command of Admiral Gustav Wattrang who was caught with only eight galleys in front of his enemy. Indeed, the Russian fleet was so large for the space in which it was fighting, only twenty-three ships actually engaged in battle! This battle proved to be the last major engagement in which galleys, ships powered by men rowing with oars—a classification of ships that had been used since ancient times—fought to control the sea. Moreover, it also bears the legacy of being the first major Russian naval victory—operations at Azov notwithstanding. While Peter the Great was still working on building his own battle fleet with ships of the line that could compete with Swedish naval power, in the summer of 1714 this aspect of his navy was not prepared for battle. His solution to the challenge was to grossly outnumber the Swedes with his galleys. The galleys, being smaller and lighter, handily outmaneuvered the much heavier Swedish ships, especially on a calm day as the Russians were not dependent on the wind. Once the Russians occupied the Aland Islands, they used them as a staging base to raid Sweden repeatedly. The city of Umea, for example, was burnt to the ground on September 18, 1714, and after it was rebuilt it was razed again in 1719, 1720, and once more before the treaty of Nystadt in 1721.[53]

One of the products of the conflict with Sweden, and no doubt a result of Peter's efforts to modernize Russia's armed forces, was the development of a body of regulations that would govern the training, organization, and operations of the tsar's army at the beginning of the eighteenth century. This systemization of the thinking that governed the future development of the armed forces would lead not only to the establishment of Russian military organization for the balance of the eighteenth century but also to the growth and evolution of military doctrine throughout the Imperial period. While the operational impact of the seventeenth/eighteenth-century military revolution on the European battlefield manifested itself in the form of large, well-trained, mass infantry units, the Russians still could not afford to give up maintaining large cavalry formations because of its steppe frontier. Peter I understood the significance of "modern" infantry units, and he moreover struggled to eliminate the political power of the old pomestia-based cavalry, but he could not eliminate the use of large cavalry formations. Such formations did run counter to the teachings and lessons of the military revolution, but Russia remained a very large landmass. In addition to fighting European armies in the Great Northern War, Peter I had to remain mindful of the threats that persisted on his southern frontier, be it from the Ottoman armies, or from unruly Cossacks, or from the host of Tatars that roamed the southern steppe. As a result, Peter developed a large standing army using his guard's regiments as his model for the emergence of mass infantry units while maintaining the same amount of cavalry as the old Muscovite state to defend Russia's wide open spaces. In this fashion Carol Stevens notes that in 1705–6 the Russian field army consisted of thirty-three dragoon regiments, forty-seven foot units, two guard's regiments, and an artillery train.[54] Overall, Peter's army valued mobility, which is why he avoided set field battles unless he knew that he could command the battlefield as he did at Poltava. Yet, what did change was the role of the cavalry transitioning from being a striking arm of the military to one that operated in more of a support role, taking on tasks such as reconnaissance/intelligence gathering and guarding the flanks of mass infantry units.

Not surprisingly, in the period between the battles of Narva and Poltava the drive toward a set of regulations that would define both the organizational structure and the operational conduct of the Army was heavily influenced by the work of the foreigners who Peter the Great, in some cases, personally recruited while on his Grand Embassy.[55] The process started with the adoption of the 1698 Regulations that was drafted by the Austrian general Adam Weyde, which was designed to provide the army with a routine for holding draft levies among tax-paying commoners in order to provide soldiers for the ranks. Weyde's scheme envisioned a standing army that was trained and supplied by the state and could vary in size between 60,000 and 80,000 men depending on the tsar's needs.[56] These regulations meant the adoption of an organizational structure that did not include the Strel'tsy who still persisted in the ranks. Eventually the Strel'tsy were relegated to garrison service, but their ultimate fate was to become too impoverished to support themselves in their profession of arms. The survivors totaling some 24,000 men transformed into tax-bearing state peasants who no longer had to serve if they paid the state a pittance of one ruble per year as their tax burden.[57] But the pressing issue after the defeat at Narva was to develop a recruitment process that would provide the manpower necessary to fill the ranks and prepare for the next round of battle with the Swedes. The lack of accurate census data from any source—church or state—hampered efforts to develop a consistent policy, and thus recruitment practices were in a perpetual state of transformation throughout Peter's reign. At the height of the crisis in the post Narva period, the state would resort to calls for volunteers and in this fashion according to Brian Davies in the period 1701–9 the Russian army inducted 138,000 men, which proved sufficient by the Battle of Poltava.[58] Despite the assorted schemes and undertakings to raise troops, the army still remained dependent on foreign customs and practices for ideas about engaging in combat as well as for the more mundane challenges such as its overall organization. In the aftermath of Narva and as a result of efforts to reconstruct his shattered forces, by 1707 the army consisted of two guard's regiments, forty-seven line infantry regiments, five elite grenadier regiments, thirty-three dragoon regiments, and one artillery regiment.[59]

Then, asserting his own ideas, Peter I drafted "Rules of Combat" in 1708, which became the basis for the tactical instructions found in his "Military Statute" of 1716. Both of these documents focus on unifying the role of the infantry as the primary fighting arm of Peter the Great's army. Little doubt exists that in keeping with his methods of acquiring knowledge the 1716 Statute combined the best ideas from the works of German, French, Swedish, Dutch, and English military thinkers and political leaders. Much of the statue defines the organization of the army in war and peace by explaining the duties of officers and soldiers. Training routines are codified to exhibit the requirements for field service.

Confirming his desire to comprehensively overhaul every aspect of this military establishment, the tsar also included a section that identified crimes and their assorted punishments those convicted would suffer for their transgressions. The most lasting effect of this statue however was the creation of the oath that every officer and soldier would take to swear their allegiance to the tsar and his empire upon induction into his armed forces.[60] In the course of the long Northern War, therefore, Peter I institutionalized his reforms all while developing a style of warfare for his empire that sought to always combine his forces in a fashion that allowed him the flexibility to shift from the offensive to the defensive. He further introduced the creation of a navy largely not only to support his army's operations but also to have the capability to further develop trade with the rest of the world. He accomplished this all while maintaining a system of fortifications to defend against incursions on Russia's southern frontier.[61]

While no significant military campaigns were mounted by any of the belligerents in the waning days of the Great Northern War, the death of Charles XII by a flying projectile during the siege of the Danish fortress of Fredriksten (located on the southern part of the long Norwegian/Swedish border) on November 29, 1718, marked the beginning of the end of the Swedish Empire. Having no children at the time of his death, the crown moved to his sister Ulrika whose husband, known as Frederick I, negotiated a series of treaties that at first aimed to allow him to marshal the forces needed to stop the periodic raids where Russian forces pillaged sites on Sweden's eastern seaboard. As the diplomatic process unfolded this series of treaties culminated with the end of the Great Northern War. Untangling the assorted claims of all the Baltic nations started with the treaties of Stockholm that were signed respectively on November 9, 1719, and January 21, 1720. These two treaties were followed by the Treaty of Frederikborg that was signed on July 3, 1720. Together these three treaties resolved territorial claims between Sweden and Poland/Lithuanian and Saxony, Prussia, Denmark/Norway, and even the province of Hanover. While the *status quo ante bellum* was restored between Sweden and Poland/Lithuanian and Saxony, Prussia gained control over towns of Stettin, Damm, and Gollnow, and part of Swedish Pomerania while Hanover gained control over Breman. Moreover, at Frederiksborg, Denmark gained complete control over Schleswig and Sweden forfeited her duty-free rights to transit across the Oresund Sound, the stretch of water that separated Denmark and Sweden at Zealand. In addition, the Swedes paid Denmark a substantial sum of money to regain control over any other Swedish territories that the Danes occupied in 1720. Despite all of these diplomatic efforts, the war and, more to the point, the Russian threat to

Sweden remained until a treaty could finally be negotiated between the two main belligerents. Finally on September 10, 1721, the two sides signed the Treaty of Nystad, which formally ended the second Great Northern War. According to its terms, after Russia evacuated its troops from the Aland Islands and from most of southern Finland, Sweden, ceded to Peter I Estonia, Livonia, and Ingria, the piece of land where he was building St. Petersburg. The tsar also insisted on controlling the strip of Finnish Karelian immediately to the north of his new capital to defend its flank. The tsar's stunning success can best be appreciated when recognizing that Russia now had control of the Gulf of Finland from Vybourg to Riga. In addition, the Swedes agreed to pay the Russians the enormous sum of two million silver thalers as reparations for the cost of the war. Moreover, both the Swedes and the Russians recognized that the Baltic nobles would be allowed to keep their Lutheran faith and their independent system of self-governance and taxation. With the end of the war, not only was the Swedish Empire removed from the pages of history, so was Swedish absolutism. Without the support of its landed elite, the Swedish monarchy accepted the demise of its standing and the emergence of their own "Age of Liberty," which witnessed the shift in power from the monarch to a parliament with limited suffrage.[62]

As disastrous as the outcome of the Second Great Northern war was on Sweden, the war represented a major turning point for the Russians in their now centuries-long endeavor to construct their own empire. As V. O. Kliuchevskii famously noted, from the time Peter the Great ousted his half-sister Sophia in 1689 until his death in 1725, he was at war with someone in all but thirteen months of his reign.[63] Judging from his conduct, he considered himself to be at war on two fronts. After defeating Sweden and gaining the marvelous terms of the Treaty of Nystadt, the tsar's attention shifted immediately to his southern front where, through the folly of the Prut campaign, he had lost his foothold on the Sea of Azov and potential access to the Black Sea. To regain a foothold in the south, Peter I started constructing a defensive line between Pavlovsk on the Don and Tsaritsyn on the Volga designed to contain the Crimean Tatars. Then, sensing a weakness with the Persian Empire's hold on the western and southern shores of the Caspian Sea, Peter sent an expedition by both land and river down the Volga that by September 1723 had resulted in the conquest of Reshut and Baku. The Persians recognized their loss of influence and withdrew from the Caspian Sea, which strengthened Russia's connections to the Far East. Meanwhile, Peter ordered the eastward expansion of the Empire by pushing through the unruly Ustyak Tatars and building forts across southern Siberia. In this fashion the Russians constructed their first outpost on the Kamchatka Peninsula, and it was from there that Peter the Great ordered the famous Danish cartography/navigator/explorer captain Vitus Bering on his voyage to determine if any type of land bridge existed between Russia/Asia and the American continent. Indeed, the only reason he stopped his persistent military and diplomatic campaigns was due to his untimely death on January 28, 1725.[64]

Sustaining the Army

The image and memory of Peter the Great remains strong in Russian history for many more reasons than the success of his military operations and diplomatic coalition building. His activities resulted in not only the complete overhaul of the army, but also the generation of the economic infrastructure that provided both the arms and munitions needed to wage continuous warfare as well as contributed to the vital issue of generating revenues that ultimately enhanced tax collection throughout the empire. Moreover, his incessant reforming efforts may well have been rooted in his never-ending desire to strengthen his military establishment, but they also resulted in the restructuring of Russian society. The extent and impact of his reforms were summed up by Evgenii V. Anisimov as: "The soul tax system of assessment introduced in 1724 was not abolished until 163 years later, in 1887. The last recruiting levy took place in 1874—almost 170 years after the first. ... the Governing Senate, created by Peter in 1711 was liquidated only in December 1917, some 206 years after its formation."[65] Although this study does not aspire to provide a complete account of all of Peter's reforming activities, it cannot lose sight of how the motivation for most all of Peter's reforms are linked to his efforts to build an army that could respond to the burgeoning empire's various and differing military challenges on an assortment of frontiers and boundaries. Peter I understood that he needed to at once enhance the military capabilities of the state while at the same time build the infrastructure to supply a new mass standing army with everything from guns and bullets to uniforms, rations, and shelter. The unquenchable needs of his armed forces therefore required a never-ending restructuring of every aspect of state life and would therefore leave an indelible mark on Russia that exists arguably until this day.

The most basic need of any army, of course, is soldiers. Because of the 1649 enserfment of Russia's peasants, Peter I had ready access to large numbers of men whom he could draft to serve in his armed forces. A central challenge to any recruitment process for soldiers, however, was that the state did not have accurate demographic data since no census had been taken since 1678. In addition to this vexing problem, the state's administrative apparatus did not have the organizational structure or the bureaucrats needed to enforce a troop levy at the beginning of the eighteenth century. Thus a recruitment levy was created that was irregular and largely dependent on what Peter the Great thought was needed in terms of manpower at any given time. After the battle of Narva, the manpower shortage within the ranks became so dire that at first Peter I demanded one man per ten households be inducted into the army. He would back off to a certain degree and shifted the requirement to one man per twenty households after absorbing and providing sufficient replacements for those lost at Narva.[66] According to John L. H. Keep, by 1709, such assorted levies had recruited some 138,000 soldiers into the army in time to be available for the Battle of Poltava. After Poltava and after the panic of 1711 (Purt), Peter the Great scoured the land searching for and ultimately inducting 50,000 new recruits into the army. A system of regular levies started in 1713 based on rates that ranged from 1 man per 40 households to 1 man per 250 households depending on the needs of the state, which, of course, was highly dependent on the course of any of Peter's wars. Ten such levies were held between 1713 and 1724 with the overall result of the drafting of some 153,000 recruits in the period when the cycle and intensity of conflict was slowing down, not that Peter ever stopped planning for and fighting wars. The recruitment levies became the bane of the taxpaying population (i.e., the serfs) existence as it was not originally clear how long they would be forced to serve. But once in the army, it usually meant service in the ranks for life, hence the emergence of the not uncommon practice of holding mock funerals for beloved family members who had ended up becoming recruits. Or perhaps worse yet a powerful indication of how clearly service in the ranks was dreaded; it was also not uncommon for a peasant to maim himself—cut off a finger, shoot himself in the foot—to avoid service in the ranks of the Imperial Russian army. Although the mantra of Peter the Great's modus operandi was to standardize all state activities along rational, indeed professional lines, he was not above singling out groups of people for special recruitment practices, something, for example, necessary to keep as many Cossacks in the Russian service as possible. At the time of Peter's death, he had called for and then orchestrated some fifty-three levies of which twenty-one were general and thirty-two were partial, meaning they had been called at irregular times and because of manpower shortages caused by the swinging tide(s) of his many wars. In the end it is estimated that a total of some 300,000 men were recruited into the Russian army during the reign of Peter the Great.[67]

Although creating, developing, and implementing a recruitment system for soldiers was daunting, transforming or recreating the officer corps challenged the basic political structure of Russia. After all, one of the inheritances of the Romanovs had been the military service class, the pomeshchniki, who supplied off of their pomestia's a retinue of men who together formed the bulk of the cadre of Muscovy's officer corps. Moreover, this system based on the exchange of land tenure for service to the state had another, higher layer of aristocrats whose power within the state structure could not be ignored. This group, the boyars, had ancestral roots that traced their lineage to the grand princely families that had populated the Russian landscape since the time of Kiev but more likely from the time when Muscovy consolidated its power before casting off the Mongol yoke. While much ink has been spilt over the rebellious strel'tsy, Peter also had to contend with unruly Boyars who usually sought greater personal power within the state even at the expense of the Tsar.[68] From this mass of people Peter struggled mightily to construct a professional officer corps. Not surprisingly, his ideas about military professionalism were the product of his engagement with Europeans from the time of his childhood. Thus, the tales of his early military campaigns usually note that foreign luminaries advised and in some cases commanded the tsar's troops in battle. Not only because the Russians resented taking orders from foreigners who had command over their fate, Peter the Great sought to develop the means for Russians to educate and train themselves to lead their troops into the battle. The challenge to this was that by the seventeenth and eighteenth centuries, the essential tool, the key to the professionalization of almost anyone, was their gaining access to education that would teach technical and general literacy. While much could and was learned through the experience of military operations and through command experiences, much more knowledge was needed to prevail on the battlefield.

Besides providing practically endless conflict for experimentation, Peter the Great sought to transform his officer corps through social reform that included the creation of formal educational institutions in Russian. Russians had served the state at least since the reign of Ivan III (1462–1505). Codifying this service to the state was the rigid set of precedence that were embodied in Russia's notorious system of social control known as *mestnishstvo* that Peter's half-brother Feodor eliminated in a 1682 decree that he issued as tsar shortly before he died. The elimination of an arcane system that rewarded service tenure as the best path to gain more power and authority was a gift of enormous magnitude for Peter.

While he sought to compel both aristocrats and nobles to serve throughout the Great Northern War, Peter was never satisfied with their response, so in 1722, after the war's conclusion, he created the Table of Ranks. The table divided state service into three paths (civil, military, and naval) that consisted of fourteen ranks. It sought to make every member of Russia's upper classes responsible to serve the state and to reward them for being successful in their endeavors. The reward was advancement up the table that would lead to more status and presumably more wealth and power. Men who started at the bottom of the table (rank 14) and progressed to the sixth rank gained the status of nobility. In this fashion Peter sought to create a meritocracy that rewarded competency as opposed to lineage.[69] Nothing, however, came to symbolize the meaning of the table nor caused more aggravated feelings between the crown and his elite than the clause that prevented the inheritance of rank and status from one generation to the next. Moreover, Peter's regulation that everyone was responsible to serve the state for life resulted in aristocrats seeking to reform such practices well into the reign of Catherine II the Great.[70] Demonstrating a degree of favoritism toward his navy, Peter launched the modernization of education in Russia beginning in 1701 when he opened the school of mathematics and navigation. Staffed largely by foreigners, this school opened the door to a technical education in Russia where until this point in history the only type of education offered was either religious or done via private tutors for the very wealthy. Starting with a technical school Peter led the way for the introduction of a secular educational system in which the arts and science were emphasized, thus paving the way for the growth (although very slowly) of secular education in Russia.[71]

Through military service, therefore, Peter sought to instill in the conduct of his subjects the dual practice of state service and advancement based solely on the question of merit as opposed to lineage. Regardless of the theory of meritocracy governing the advancement of soldiers, Peter I's efforts to unify command found him increasingly dependent on soldiers who gained experience during his father's reign, gaining control over the army's high command in the period after the disaster at Narva. True, Alexander Menshikov was of low-birth origins but Boris Petrovich Sheremetev (1652–1719), Feodor Mattveievich Apraksin (1661–1728), Ivan Ivanovich Buturlin (1661–1738), and Anikita Ivanovich Repnin (1668–1726) all emerged as commanders during Peter's reign and were all scions of the traditional service elite.[72] The continued service of such elites revealed that the Table of Ranks was a reformed continuation of the old practice of the old *mestnishstvo* system. In addition, although young Peter created guard's regiments for childhood play, by the time he reached his majority, these units had become the vanguard of his concept of Russia's future military elite.[73] While his efforts to impose the custom of meritocracy as the source of professional advancement were rooted in his burning desire to create a system that would put the best possible people in command of the army, opposition to the practice almost undermined the reforms of Peter I after his death. The idea of meritocracy was never lost on the empire's subjects, but as the eighteenth century progressed, constant refinement of the system ultimately resulted in an officer corps, especially the men in the Imperial Guard's regiments, gaining extensive influence over the empire's ruler and ruling elite. Thus, as the eighteenth century progressed, one of the unintended consequences of the reforms of Peter the Great was the politicization of the Army's office corps, which reached its apex in December 1825 when officers of the guard attempted to overthrow the Romanovs.[74]

Regardless of political consequences and with the understanding that the backbone of any military establishment was its officers, soldiers, and weapons, Peter the Great also realized that his large standing army would need state-provided provisions if it were to remain an effective fighting force able to defend against all foes while maintaining offensive capabilities. Building the logistical base to maintain his military in peace and war therefore challenged both the administrative organization and industrial capacity of the state. On the administrative side, Peter the Great gutted the many different bureaucracies called chancelleries (prikazy) that control limited aspects, such as one that controlled cloth and another that controlled thread, often with overlapping jurisdictions creating an endless source of petty conflict, and transformed them all into one central, uniform system of administration. The emergence of the Administrative College after the defeat at Narva started the process of centralizing and streamlining the state's operation, but their creation came unsystematically and tentatively. The reorganization of the state's administration was enormous as the number of prikazy would decline from fifty-five in 1699 to thirty-five in 1701.[75] The transition from medieval to Early Modern administrative institutions gained further momentum from Peter I's decision to build and move his capital to St. Petersburg. With the founding of St. Petersburg in 1703, many of the prikazy moved from Moscow where they were renamed kantseliarii, which alone revealed a transformation in administrative organization as it meant these medieval institutions entitled (Prikaz) were being remade into European style governmental agencies. Thus F. M. Apraksin's Admiralty Chancellery, James David Bruces's Artillery Chancellery, and Gavrila Ivanovich Golovkin's Ambassador's Chancellery all moved to St. Petersburg in the period after the victory at Poltava.[76] More to the army's immediate needs, the tsar created a Provisions Chancery under the command of Iakov Fedorovich Dolgorukii on February 18, 1700, that oversaw the supply of everything from food to uniforms to weapons. In addition, he created a War Ministry (Voennyi Prikaz) that was responsible for the administration and organization of new regiments and larger military formations, the training of officers, the recruitment of soldiers, and the maintenance of discipline throughout the ranks.[77] Both of these administrative structures along with the command structure of the army would be unified into the military college that was created in 1718 as a part of Peter the Great's overall effort to rationalize all aspects of Russia's government including its armed forces.[78]

Peter's constant state of being engaged in warfare was the engine that drove the development of industry during his reign. The industrial enterprises that did emerge in the first quarter of the eighteenth century were fashioned almost entirely to meet the needs of Peter's ever demanding military establishment. Yet an accurate assessment of Russia's economic growth in the first half of the eighteenth century is elusive at best because even Arcadius Kahan could not produce compelling output statistics for the period of Peter I's rule.[79] Indeed, defining what made for and did not qualify as a factory alone is controversial for this period of Russian history. Nonetheless it is clear that Peter I did insist on the development of a production base that could supply his military with the weapons, munitions, uniforms, boots, and everything else that an army needed to become or remain operational depending on the circumstances of the moment. To this end Peter the Great established state iron, copper, and silver mines and perhaps, more importantly, initiated geological surveys to determine how much mineral resources he could exploit for state purposes.[80] With the iron ore that he mined from the earth Peter had the resource he needed to feed his own iron foundries and armament works. By 1725, therefore four iron foundries existed in the Urals with the city of Tula becoming the principal armory center of the empire. Recognizing a constant and ever growing need for weapons of all types—from cannons, to small arms and bayonets, he built additional armories in St. Petersburg and Moscow as well.

As he built out his ever increasing capacity to provide his troops with weapons, he also encouraged the development of a woolen textile industry specifically to provide uniforms for his soldiers. At first Moscow became the center for textiles but regional centers started to develop during Peter's reign in Vladimir, Khar'kov, Astrakhan', Yaroslavl', Estonia, and Livonia. Once Peter established the woolen industry, other textile manufacturing plants expanded the type of material being processed as linen, silk, and cotton followed over the course of the eighteenth century. While he encouraged Russians to develop the skills to become autonomous entrepreneurs, he also understood better than most that while the state could provide a captive workforce—usually serfs assigned to factories—it needed educated and skilled people to design, build, and manage a factory. To this end, and especially after his Grand Embassy, and like his father Tsar Alexis, he never hesitated to invite skilled foreigners to come to Russia and share their expertise. The need for the expertise of foreigners never ceased, which was made clear when he opened the Admiralty dockyard in St. Petersburg in 1696 to build naval and merchant ships. By the end of the eighteenth century, it was the largest industrial complex in the empire that was supported by ancillary industries that ranged from the harvesting of trees for lumber to the manufacture of sailcloth, rope, and other nautical accouterments needed to provide equipment for the Imperial navy. The best estimates claim that because of Peter I's insistence and boundless energy, the number of factories, that is, enterprises that built items through a production process grew from 80 to 200 over the course of his reign.[81]

The emergence of industry and manufacturing, especially the ore extracted from silver mines, generated much needed capital to finance a new army that was dependent on the state for all of its supplies. Revenue collection, therefore, and collecting enough to finance a burgeoning military establishment became another central concern for Peter the Great. Simply put, all of Muscovy's forms of revenue collection were inadequate to finance the military that Peter built. While he introduced a number of different types of taxation, with the 1705 beard tax being the most notorious, none of these taxes addressed the perennial fiscal shortcomings of the Russian state until he introduced the 1718 poll tax. The poll tax was designed to simplify tax collection because it moved from the old Muscovite system that tried to differentiate tax rates according to variables based on the ability of a family to pay taxes to a tax that every male serf and state peasant had to pay. At the same time as he imposed a poll tax on Russia's peasantry, Peter also ordered the first census of the Russian population to be taken in the eighteenth century because it was not clear in the waning days of the Great Northern War how many people populated the Russian Empire. After some initial vacillation in 1725, the poll tax settled in at a rate of 80 kopecks per peasant. In addition to the poll tax, peasants were also obliged to provide their lords with either obrok or barshchina labor service as a means for Russia's landed aristocrats to tend to their fields. While the people who lived in towns were also required to pay a poll tax at a higher rate (in 1725 it was 1 ruble, 25 kopecks), Russia's nobles and aristocrats did not pay the poll tax as their service to the state was considered to be the means by which they met their fiscal obligations to the tsar and the empire.[82] To complete the overhaul of the revenue collection system, Peter I created what could be considered his most important administrative organization in the state's bureaucracy—the Office of Tax collection (*Ratusha*), which actually represented a consolidation of tax collection agencies from the Muscovite period. Together, all of these bureaucratic entities aimed at imposing and collecting tax revenues did greatly enhance the ability of the state to accumulate capital. Yet the Russian Empire suffered from persistent financial shortfalls because the share of the military's expenses consisted of 62 percent of the state's budget in 1680 and 78 percent in 1701 in the midst of the post Narva scramble to rebuild the army. As the Early Modern State orchestrated their rise to global power through the construction of empires, they were all in similar financial shape that can best be described as strained and overextended.[83] Persistent state deficits were not an uncommon problem for all the belligerents of the Great Northern War

As all of his biographers agree, Peter I's energy was endless. His aim to create and then build a state administration based on rational principles not only sought to capture the spirit of the times in which he ruled but, more importantly, to provide Russia with the organizational structure not only to conquer the territory needed to create a global empire, but also to govern it once it existed. In addition to creating new parts of a governing structure, he also demanded that his nobility serve the state on a level perhaps not obtained by any other European monarch of the period. Of course, nowhere was this demand for service better met than when Russians of all social classes served in the military establishment. Yet it should not be overlooked that state service was fulfilled on many different levels and by nonmilitary servitors. After all, the Table of Ranks did include the civil side. Peter the Great, therefore, created a governing Senate on February 22, 1711, to accomplish two tasks. The first and most pressing was to have a bureaucratic device that was empowered to govern the country in his absence or when he was off campaigning against the Swedes, the Turks, and the host of Russia's other enemies who marauded on her southern frontiers. The other cause for the creation of the Senate was to replace the Old Boyar Duma with an Early Modern governing entity. Peter I, of course, appointed the original ten members to the Senate with a blend of his supporters and in 1714 moved it from Moscow to St. Petersburg. Once in St. Petersburg, the tsar rapidly expanded the powers of the Senate so that it oversaw the consistent and equal implementation of laws and application of justice while controlling all trade, finances, and military affairs. By the time of his death, the Senate was the empire's supreme governing body that had the power to control the day to day affairs of the empire. In keeping with this center of power the Senate proclaimed on September 22, 1721, that Peter I was Father of the Fatherland, that he was Peter the Great, and that from this time forward he should be recognized as Emperor Peter, Tsar of the Russian Empire. Thus, the Senate in 1721 formally proclaimed the birth of the Russian Empire by decree and by the middle of the eighteenth century, the rest of Europe recognized Russia as a global empire, indeed one of Europe's Great Powers.

Peter's boundless energy therefore resulted in the establishment of an armed force that was responsive to Russia's people and their culture. He borrowed from the groundwork laid by his father and did his very best to discard everything else regardless of what his opponents propagated. He did his best to address the duplicitous administrative structure of the old Muscovite state with reforms based on the idea of constructing a government and a bureaucracy based on rational thought. As a young tsar and throughout his reign, he struggled with the challenging questions of recruitment and the vexing problem of raising enough funds through taxes to finance his military. In addition, Peter the Great strove to cast aside the custom of rewarding servitors based solely on loyalty and lineage. To this end, the tsar sought to build his meritocracy based on providing educational opportunities to his nobles. After addressing his government and his peoples' needs, Peter rewrote the regulations of his army that touched on every aspect of military life from the training of soldiers to expectations for discipline and codes of justice. Then, he developed a style of warfare that provided his forces with the ability to confront and win against the standing armies of Europe and the nomadic armies of the steppe. Most significantly for the future of the Russian Empire, he founded a navy that started with operations in the Sea of Azov but also had over fifty ships in the Baltic stationed at the Admiralty quay in St. Petersburg or at the new fortress on the island of Kronstadt. Upon his death, he left his heirs with a military system that, through continuous reforms, would conquer the Eurasian landmass and replace the power vacuum that occurred when the Mongol Empire collapsed over the course of the fifteenth century. For these achievements he was and remains Russia's truly great leader!

2

Russia's Global Empire

The death of Peter the Great marked the beginning of a century-long process that culminated in what some historians refer to as the golden age of Imperial Russia history. As a consequence of Peter I's reforms Russia's eighteenth century featured both the expansion of his Imperial vision along with a reordering of society. Together what occurred after fits and starts was the ascendency of a defined group of Petrine era aristocrats who provided the foundation of the Romanov's political and financial support. The enormity of change foisted on Russia's elites by Peter the Great naturally produced a reaction that intensified when Peter I's suddenly died in 1725 at the age of fifty-three. In the immediate aftermath of his death, a power struggle ensued between his ardent supporters and those members of Russia's elite who resented his reordering of society along western lines. Complicating this already tense situation was Peter I's decision to eliminate his son Alexis, the natural heir to the throne out of concern that the tsarevich would not continue his reforms. Alexis's death combined with Peter I's edict that the sitting tsar would be responsible for appointing his successor offers another sordid tale from Russian history. Regardless of the ensuing drama, the lack of a proper heir in 1725 led to an era of palace revolutions from Peter's death until Catherine II's seizure of power in 1762. In this period, despite or because of the strong machinations of a small clique of noblemen, there were eight *coups d'état* that defined the Russian process of political succession during that era. With the passing of each tsar and tsarina, the officer corps played an increasingly larger role in selecting a successor, and the loser and his/her supporters endured arrest, exile, and the loss of property and privilege. Each one of these events added another chapter in the manifold struggles between the supporters and opponents of Peter I's reforms. As the century progressed, each coup represented not only the coming to power of another leader of Russia but also another episode in the developing relationship between the military and the crown. Indeed, without the ardent support of the guard's officers, there would not have been the coups in 1762 that brought Catherine to power. By the time of her 1796 death, the Imperial Guard reigned supreme in not only the military, but also the political establishment.[1] The experiences of the eighteenth century therefore reveal that without gaining the support of the nobility, the Russian imperial autocracy could not have survived the struggles for power that routinely emerged during each transition of power that occurred from the death of Peter I to the rise of Catherine II.

The struggle culminated with the ascendency of guard's officers as military leaders and political activists. The rise of the imperial guard also signified the transformation of Russia to the service state Peter I envisioned. Yet in the course of Peter I's reforms being enacted, his idea evolved from a purely service state into a garrison state whereby the guard's officers determined who reigned and who did not. The irony of this reordering of the state is that it occurred largely because the Petrine elite gained their emancipation from state service as the empire, hence its military requirement, grew in the latter half of the century. With each regime change every aspect of the relationship between political and military power could be challenged—from tax levies, to the recruitment of soldiers, to the state's military expenditures both in war and in peace. Estimating how much Peter's new army cost the Russian State at the time of his death is, at best, an educated guess because of the substandard (by today's standards) recordkeeping of the Russian State. After all, no accurate records exist that reveal the size of the tax-paying population. One of Peter's aims in implementing a poll tax was to standardize the tax burden of everyone. Such standardization required accurate census data, which the early Romanovs sought to compile but never quite achieved. After determining that there are no sources that will provide definitive numbers, John L. H. Keep's estimates that in 1725 the Russian State expenditures were 9,141,000 rubles of which 73.2 percent was spent on the armed forces.[2] Peter the Great, therefore, made his army and navy the center of his reforming, indeed modernizing, efforts to strengthen the Russian Empire while continuing the pursuit of his idea of empire. His successors considered the military's expense to be unsustainable and thus began the struggle between the staunch modernizers who sought to maintain the nature and pace of Peter's reforms versus the last gasps of the scions of old Muscovy. The debate over the cost of maintaining a military force capable of perpetually expanding the size of the empire would not be resolved until the reign of Catherine the Great (1764–1796). Perhaps Catherine II's greatest accomplishment was that despite the never-ending challenge of recruiting, training, and maintaining a large and expensive standing army, by the beginning of the nineteenth century all

Russians envisioned living in a world that included themselves ruling a large and ever-expanding Eurasian Empire.

This chapter will examine how Peter the Great's successors struggled to achieve the goal of expanding the size and the holdings of the Russian Empire through diplomacy and military conquest. A strong Germanic influence repeatedly appeared at court throughout the eighteenth century that offered an alternative to the military establishment that Peter created and envisioned. Regardless of who won or lost the succession struggles, whether supporters of Peter's reforms or not, by the end of the eighteenth century the Russian military had pushed its enemies further to the west, the south, and the east. This chapter will therefore focus on the European and Ottoman theaters of operations because while each ruler from Peter the Great to Catherine the Great encouraged Russian settlers to set out for eastern or south-eastern lands (Siberia, the Caucasus, and Central Asia), this was the period when Russia defeated and eliminated the Polish-Lithuanian Commonwealth from the map of Europe and contained both Swedish and Turkish power. Moreover, the Russians developed diplomatic relations with the Germanic powers of Austria, Prussia, and the Holy Roman Empire that maintained a relative amount of peace throughout Central Europe until Napoleon conquered the continent with his armies of the French Revolution. Throughout it all, regardless of how alliances came together and fell apart, the Russians continued to develop and enlarge commercial relations with Great Britain that prompted lucrative Baltic trade that withstood the test of time and, even more importantly, contributed to the vital economic development of the country. The combination of military power, astute diplomacy, and economic development resulted in the emergence of the all-powerful Russian Empire that existed at the end of the eighteenth century.[3]

During her reign Catherine II emerged as Catherine the Great because of her military success. Under her tutelage the size of the empire's population more than doubled and a Russian "way of war" emerged that would be used by the Romanovs until the end of their regime. Peter the Great's sweeping reforms made Russia a major power in the European community of nations. By the time Catherine II was done, Russia would be a global power. To understand this development, this chapter will also examine how Russia's armed forces were organized, reformed, trained, and supplied while the empress struggled to defeat her internal opposition of which the most notable was the Cossack renegade Emil Pugachev. This chapter, therefore, examines how over the course of the eighteenth century the Russian Empire came into being because Romanov leadership developed a military system that had the capability to defeat all of its international foes while at the same time providing the state with an instrument that embodied its ideas and practices.

In the Aftermath of Peter's Death

In the period immediately following the death of Peter the Great, his handpicked successor, his empress Catherine I, immediately sought out ways to reduce the poll tax burden of the peasants. Her efforts did not result in much success largely because she died of tuberculosis on May 6, 1727. Her handpicked successor was Peter the Great's grandson, the son of Peter I's disobedient son Alexis, Peter II. His reign would also be very short as he succumbed to smallpox in 1730. Peter II was only twelve years old when he came to power, and his youth combined with his early demise limited what he could do in military affairs. In fact, he showed little interest in Russia's armed forces. He let the navy fall into disrepair and limited the size of the army when he banned the right of serfs to volunteer, which had the effect of tightening serfdom as the individual serfs lost one of the few means they could employ to escape their bondage. If Peter II had lived, he would have represented a huge victory for the opposition in Russian for two reasons. The first was his treatment of Peter the Great's close friend and one of his principle advisors Aleksandr Danilovich Menshikov. Menshikov had been so instrumental to Catherine I that she agreed to a marriage between his daughter Maria to the young Peter II. When Peter II rose to the throne, Menshikov in his role as power broker took the young tsar into his own home and sought nothing less than to have full control over his actions. Peter grew tired of Menshikov's heavy hand and with the support of the Dolgoruki family managed to have the former favorite of Peter the Great stripped of all of his rank and privileges in September 1727 and shortly thereafter exiled to Siberia where he died in 1729. The other symbol of the opposition's victory was Peter II effectively moving the capital of Russia back to Moscow. At least one historian however speculates that Peter was not so much interested in moving to Moscow for political reasons as he could engage in his passions of fishing and hunting, which was far better in Moscow and its environs than St. Petersburg. Regardless, the five-year period between the death of Peter the Great and the ascension of Empress Anna were a time of relative peace, a time when the drive for empire did not determine the course of state policy and neither tsarina nor tsar expressed much interest in the state's military forces.[4]

Anna Ivanovna

Anna Ivanovna (1693–1740) was the daughter of Ivan V, the developmentally disabled tsar who co-ruled with Peter the Great from 1682 until his death in 1696.[5] Her mother, Praskovia Saltykova, raised Anna in a disciplined and austere household. At the age of seventeen, Peter the Great arranged for her marriage to Frederick William, Duke of Courland, who died within a year of the nuptials and left her to rule Courland for some twenty years. In 1730 her life was transformed when she was contacted by Russia's Supreme Privy Council with an invitation for her to succeed to the throne of the Russian Empire as one of the sole living heirs of Peter the Great. Indeed, the Dolgoruki tried to get Peter II to leave their clan the throne by royal decree, but the severity of his smallpox overwhelmed him before he could sign any such document. Prince Dmitri Mikhailovich Golitsyn, as the senior member of the council, engineered Anna's rise in part not only because of her experience in governance but also because she had never remarried and therefore did not have a legitimate successor to the crown, thus leaving the question of succession in the future an open book. This was an important part of the Privy Council's rationale when they decided to offer Anna the throne because their ultimate aim was to redirect the main nexus of power from the tsar to the council itself. The instrument by which the council attempted its bureaucratic *coup d'état* was a document simply called the "Conditions," which sought to limit the empress's power by making her follow the Swedish model whereby a monarch was responsible to the state. In the Russian case, the Council's Conditions attempted to make the tsarina responsible to them (The Supreme Privy Council) on significant matters of state, including the right to declare war or to call for peace, or to impose taxes or to spend state revenues. Moreover, she could not promote or appoint people to the top four rungs of the civil service, nor could she grant estates or villages at her discretion, nor could she punish an unruly nobleman without a trial from his peers. To gain the throne, Anna signed the Conditions in January 1730, but before she could arrive in Moscow to assume the throne, a dispute emerged within the Russian nobility about the future of the empire.[6] Sometimes portrayed as a rebellion of the old aristocrats and the young nobility because the Golitsyns and Dolgorukis dominated the Supreme Privy Council, what in fact happened in Russia in the winter of 1730 was Anna's own *coup d'état*. While sources mention that a cohort of nobles petitioned Anna to create some form of representative institution for Russia, with the backing of her Saltykov family and, most importantly, the officers of the imperial guard, on February 25, 1730, Anna disbanded the Supreme Privy Council and reasserted her power as the autocrat of Russia.[7]

As Bruce Menning has pointed out, in the eighteenth century the only institution more powerful than the army was the autocracy and perhaps the church. The eighteenth century was unquestionably the golden age for the Imperial Army as it defeated Charles XII, Frederick II, and ultimately Napoleon. Just as important, the eighteenth century is also the period when the army enjoyed its age of great captains in the person(s) of Piotr Alexandrivuch Rumiantsev, Grigory Aleksandrovich Potemkin, and Alexander Vasilievich Suvorov.[8] While the military, indeed all of Russia, wandered through the possibilities of its future in the wake of Peter the Great's death, both the armed forces and the continued expansion of the empire clearly found their way starting with the rise of Anna. Her personal seizure of power launched the process that culminated by the end of the eighteenth century with a firm bond being formed between the crown and the imperial guard's officers corps. She took further action to cement this bond with the formation of the first Cadet Corps Academy by her Ukaz (the Empress' decree) on July 29, 1731. On the one hand, the establishment of this school was following in the Petrine tradition of introducing higher educational opportunities for subjects of the empire. On the other hand, the first Cadet Corps established the tradition of the state providing an education to Russia's elite subjects free of charge but only for the sons of the aristocracy and the nobility. The establishment of this school sparked the creation and the addition of numerous Cadet Corps Academies across the empire so that by mid-nineteenth century twenty-three such institutions existed. The aim of these schools was to provide young noblemen with a foundational education that would make them literate in language, literature, mathematics, religion, and history. In addition, the students would receive rudimentary instruction in all aspects of soldiering to prepare them for the day when they would join the ranks of the army as a junior officer. While education was clearly one goal of the Cadet Corps Academies, so was indoctrination into the armed forces and its service culture. While not always the case, it was not uncommon for boys as young as seven years old to be sent to the Cadet Corps to begin their training to serve the crown. The young age of these children upon their enrollment in the Cadet Corps created another challenge for the state. Enrollment in the Cadet Corp marked the formal start of their service to the state. Thus, young men who enrolled in these schools at the age of seven would complete their mandatory state service of twenty-five years at the age of thirty-three. If they survived their service as relatively young men, they would muster out of the ranks with little to do beyond managing a family estate.[9]

Creating the Cadet Corps Academies, however, was only the beginning of Anna's mark on the Russian armed forces. In addition to an educational institution, Anna also created a third guard's regiment to compliment the two from Peter the Great's era and to further reward the people who brought her to power. Baltic Germans who became subjects of the empire in the aftermath of the Great Northern War filled the ranks of this regiment, the Izmailovskii Regiment. The creation of a guard's regiment for the Baltic Germans also highlights that she stood accused of letting the Baltic Germans dominate, if not totally control, Russia during her period of rule. While the Golitsyn and Dologuki cabal sought to limit the power of the throne, Anna, who was not well known in Muscovite circles, took the support she had in 1731 to empower the troika of Baltic Germans beginning with her lover Ernst Johann Biron, Ostermann, and, most important for the purposes of this study, Baron B. Kh Minnikh. Under Anna, Minnikh became chief of Ordinance, governor general of St. Petersburg, and president of the Military College. In fact, he would dominate military policy throughout Anna's reign, arguably making him the first great captain of Russia's eighteenth century.[10] He would be the first, but not the last leader of the eighteenth century who sought to circumvent the spirit of the Petrine military reforms through the adoption of as much of the Prussian military system as possible. Using the authority of his offices and with the approval of the tsarina, he formed a Commission in 1731 to reorganize the army. Originally Minnikh intended to maintain the same number of regular infantry regiments (thirty-eight) as had been operational at the end of Peter the Great's reign. In 1731 besides creating the Izmailovskii Regiment, he also expanded the size of the army by adding three new infantry regiments and one Life Guard Cuirassier Cavalry Regiment for a total of 10,000 additional soldiers to defend the realm against its enemies to the west and to the south. His aim throughout the decade was to maintain the army's strength at 90,000 regulars in the core or European Russia during peacetime that could readily be expanded to 100,000 men in wartime. In addition, he organized what became known as the lower Persian Corps to defend the southeastern frontier of the empire. It consisted of 33,500 troops divided into seventeen infantry and seven dragoon regiments. The last component of the army during Anna's reign was a mixture of garrison regiments, militia, and Cossack irregulars that readily added up to another 100,000 men. While combining all of these forces in a time of crisis would have been all but impossible because of the vast distances of the empire, in total Minnikh had the potential of mobilizing over 230,000 troops if a moment of dire emergency should occur.[11]

Minnikh's reforms, however, were not limited to the size of the army or its disposition. He recognized and understood the need for Russia to have an army capable of fighting both a European force and assorted Ottoman, Tatar, and other tribal hosts to the south, but he opposed the core thinking behind the Petrine school of military operations. The emergence of Minnikh, therefore, set off a struggle between advocates of the Petrine school and those who believed in the Prussian school that taught very different customs and practices on the battlefield.[12] The romance with the Prussian style of warfare was very much a product of the Early Modern/Enlightenment period of rational thinking that culminated in the training of a well-disciplined force schooled and drilled in the use of concentrated firepower by tactical units when engaged in operations. In theory and practice, such troops prevailed on the battlefield because of their overwhelming firepower. Peter the Great, however, understood that such infantry units had a place on his battlefield, particularly when confronted with a European power such as the Swedes. Nevertheless, on the open steppe where Russia confronted an assortment of enemies, flexibility, mobility, and the shock imposed by the cold steel of an assault with bayonets were far more appropriate. Thus, the Petrine style of warfare sought to accommodate the complete military needs of the empire while the Prussian school believed that "modern" firepower would ultimately prevail against any enemy. Unfortunately, the question of appropriate styles of warfare became enmeshed in the political struggle that persisted between the supporters of Peter the Great's reforms and the advocates who sought to return to the period of Muscovite rule. Indeed, style of warfare defined which side of the struggle a particular reign supported throughout the balance of the eighteenth century. Yet, as is often the case, the lines between each side may not have been as well defined as historians seek to make them. Minnikh, for example, continued building fortresses and creating fortified lines across the southern frontier, a practice that had deep roots in Russian strategic planning and was endorsed by the Romanovs from the time of the reign of Mikhail (1613–45).[13] Moreover, for allegedly being a staunch supporter of medieval Muscovy and its mores, Anna moved the capital back to St. Petersburg in 1732.

Be that all as it may, in the course of her reign Anna would fight two wars that contributed to Russia's drive for an empire while also establishing a precedent that eighteenth-century wars with the Ottoman Empire started over the Polish question. Although not understood during Anna's reign, her conflict with Poland represented one of the opening events in the long saga that culminated with the final partition of the nation in 1795. The vexing issue for the Poles, centered on the question of executive authority or who would be king. The death of King Augustus II in 1732 sparked the war of Polish succession that occurred in 1733–1735. The king's death set off a power struggle between the Russian/Austrian backed Augustus III of Saxony and Stanislas Leszczynski, a former ally of Charles XII who had the backing of France. The 1715 death of Louis XIV had distracted the French in the final phase of the Great Northern War, resulting in their failure to back a resurgent Poland that could then act as a bulwark against the emerging Russian Empire. In August 1733, despite Russian and Austrian warnings, the Sejm backed Leszczynski making him Stanislaw I, believing that the French would provide military support if their action resulted in a conflict with Russia. Depending on the skill of the Irish General Peter Graf von Lacy, a veteran of service under Peter the Great who got to know Anna when he appointed governor of Riga in 1729, the empress ordered him in July 1733 to start concentrating troops in Courland in case the Sejm did not back the Russian/Austrian candidate for the throne. Lacy subsequently launched Russia's invasion of the Polish-Lithuanian Commonwealth at the end of the summer and marched to Warsaw where he faced token resistance. After quartering in Warsaw for part of the winter, Lacy marched on Danzig where Marshall Minnikh took over command of Russia's forces to command the siege of the city that was defended by a combination of Polish, French, and Swedish forces. In June 1734 the French tried to land 2,200 reinforcements to relieve Danzig, and the failure of this effort resulted in the city capitulating on July 8th and Stanislaw I taking flight to Prussia, thus ending this brief conflict.[14]

Tsarina Anna's 1735–9 Russo-Turkish War turned out to be an outgrowth of the war of Polish succession that had just been resolved.[15] Throughout the war, the French had been agitating for the Turks to invade Russia. Clearly, the French viewed the growth of Russian power in Eastern Europe as a threat to their imperial designs of the time. While the Russian sought to avoid a two-front war, the flight of Stanislaw I allowed them to respond to Ottoman pressure in a warlike fashion. For the Russians, the warmongering of the sublime Porte offered them the opportunity to redress Peter the Great's defeat at Prut. Beginning in 1735 both Minnikh and Lacy started gathering forces in Ukraine for future operations against the Sultan's army. These plans turned into open conflict in 1736 when they launched a two pronged offensive designed to at once occupy Ukraine and then to restore Russian power at Azov. At first they achieved their objectives as Minnikh overcame the Perekop fortress line and was able to launch an attack on the Tatar capital of Bakhchaserai. This attack forced the Tatars to flee into the hills of Crimea, but Minnikh could not pursue and obliterate his enemy because his troops first had to halt due to exhaustion and, in the midst of their stoppage, disease broke out within his forces that ultimately compromised their integrity. Left with no other option, Minnikh retreated into Ukraine to rebuild his army over the winter of 1736–7. Lacy, who had marched to Azov, now found his army without forces to defend his flank also retreated into Ukraine. The war would continue through another season of campaigns, but what became clear as this war progressed was the Russians could not project their power to the theater of operations in sufficient force to prevail because of its remoteness.[16] Moreover, maintaining the integrity of the army was further complicated by the outbreak of assorted diseases that the eighteenth-century world could not contain. Perhaps the outcome might have been different if the Russians had received support from their allies, the Austrians, but the Habsburg's emperor Charles VI was directing his attention to convincing the rest of Europe to recognize his pragmatic sanction of 1713 that was designed to ensure the smooth transition of power to his daughter the future empress Maria Theresa. Thus, the Turkish War of 1739 taught the Russians that projecting power to their south was going to require more than the training and maintenance of a cavalry army capable of broad and vast maneuvers on the steppe. An important and often overlooked

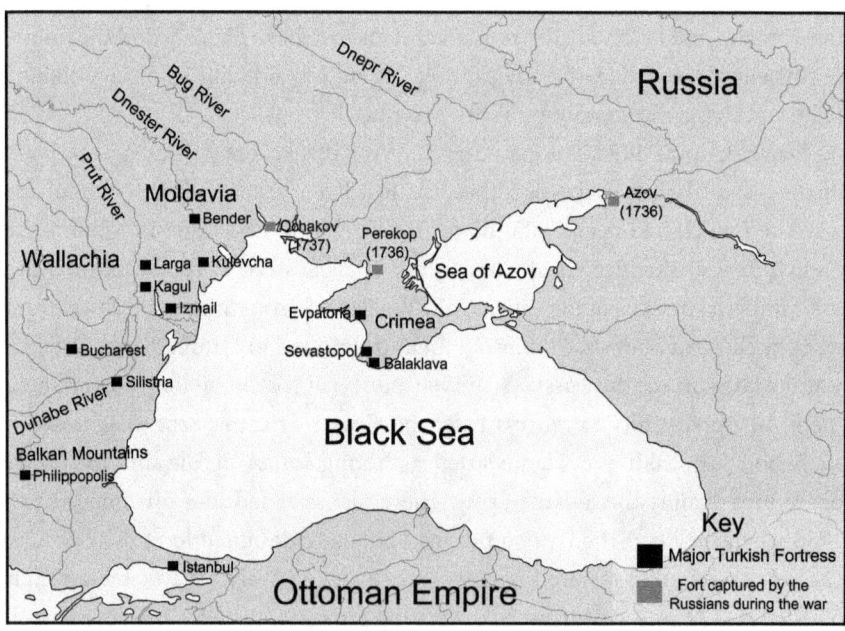

Map 2.1 Ottoman Forts around the Black Sea.

outcome of this war was the lesson the Turks took from their experience in this conflict. While the Russians could not sustain their operations, the Turks also could not stop them, nor could their allies the Crimean Tatars. As a result, the Turks decided the time had come to regroup and strengthen their armed forces for a later date, which they knew would be coming as Russia continued to grow stronger.[17]

Elizabeth Petrovna

After a brief interregnum following Anna Ivanavna death in 1740, Elizabeth Petrovna, one of Peter the Great's surviving daughters, the product of his marriage to Catherine I, came to power as a result of a *coup d'état* supported by the officers of the imperial guard in 1741.[18] She immediately banished the supporters of the Prussian model from court, thereby compromising the power of, most importantly, Minnikh. Overall, this turn of events was a huge blow for the Baltic Germans at court. She then named the Irishman general P. P Lacy commander in chief of the army and told him to restore the army to the principles Peter the Great had established in his 1716 military statue. One of the first tasks that Elizabeth Petrovna sought to address therefore was military reform and, in the end, Lacy would be instrumental in returning the army's administration and organization back to its status as defined by Peter the Great. She would be so grateful for his endeavors that Lacy would be promoted to the rank of Field Marshal. Lacy succeeded because he never underestimated the desire of Elizabeth Petrvona to restore the image of Peter the Great to the army's rank and file. He, moreover, had learned that reforms cannot be rushed nor can they be successful if political support for some type of consensus cannot be formed around the impending change. The aim of restoring Peter the Great's legacy resulted in the young empress and General Lacy to agree on a common goal that they hoped to achieve through reform, but international events unfolded that required attention as well.

Before Lacy or anyone else could invoke any reforms, however, Russia had to resolve a minor challenge from Sweden. In terms of relations among nations, the Russo-Swedish War in 1741–3 was in fact a distant continuation of Anna Ioannavna's 1736–9 Russo-Turkish War. As was the case on the Pontic steppe in the 1730s, the French convinced the Swedes that the time was right for them to challenge some of the terms of the 1721 Treaty of Nystand. Specifically, the aim was for Sweden to reassert its supremacy over Finland, hence they declared war on Russia in 1741. Elizabeth viewed this as a direct threat to the Karelian Isthmus, and especially the town of Vybourg. Losing Vybourg opened the road to Peter the Great's city of St. Petersburg, which had become the undisputed capital of the empire. As a result, Elizabeth, after failing to resolve the impasse through diplomacy, ordered Marshal Lacy to mobilize a force to march on Sweden. He did this in the spring of 1743 by gathering 36,000 troops who then marched around the southern shore of Finland. By late spring/early summer, Russian forces had marched as far west as Helsingfors (Helsinki) and Abo. True to form, promised French support never materialized for the Swedes. The Swedes, now fearing for the invasion of their homeland, decided that prudence was the better part of valor and agreed to the 1743 Peace of Abo, which formalized Russia's claim dating back to Peter's I time over southern Finland. While there would still be a minor Swedish presence in northern Finnish territories, Finland was now well on its way to becoming a grand Duchy of the Russian Empire which it would remain until the 1917 revolution.[19] As a reward for his victory, Lacy was given command of the Russian forces stationed in and around Riga from where he would administratively control the occupied territories of what was now Northern Latvia and Southern Estonia.

The early period of Elizabeth's reign also witnessed the rise of Aleksei Petrovich Bestuzhev-Riumin, first as vice-chancellor from 1741 to 1744 and then as chancellor from 1744 to 1759. Benefiting entirely from the purge of the Prussians at court, Bestuzhev-Riumin effectively became Elizabeth's foreign minister and from this position he cemented the strategic alliance with Austria during the War of Austrian Succession (1740–8). His aim was to use this alliance to contain Prussia's involvement in Baltic and Polish affairs. Moreover, Bestuzhev-Riumin used his time as chancellor to promote the strengthening of relations with Great Britain largely to make them a significant factor in Baltic trade. At the same time when Elizabeth was imposing Russian power in Central Europe, the empire's southern frontier remained largely quiet because the Ottomans had decided after 1739 to disengage in European affairs, thus ushering in a period of reform and reflection for the Sublime Porte as it contemplated its place in the future. The relative period of calm, therefore, gave the Russian army under Elizabeth Petrovna the time it needed to reorient its place in Russia back to what her father Peter the Great had originally envisioned for his armed forces.[20]

After the Swedish War, Elizabeth remained suspicious of Prussian elements in the army, which prevented the promulgation of any substantive reforms. As events in Europe were heating up into what would become the Seven Years' War, Elizabeth finally agreed to a recommendation from her Military College to convoke a new commission in 1754 ostensibly to update Peter the Great's 1716 military statue. Under the leadership of General Major Zakhar Chernyshev and with the assistance of Peter Panin in 1755, they (Chernyshev and Panin) drafted a new set of regulations entitled *Description of the Infantry Regiment's Structure*. In it they maintained the Petrine notion that the central strength of the Russian army should remain in its infantry (both guard and non-guard) regiments. As such they organized the core of the army to consist of 162,000 men of which approximately 130,000 were in the infantry and the rest were in the cavalry. During this period elements within the army vigorously debated questions about the nature of and the roles and missions of the cavalry. Early Modern European infantry formations needed heavily armed cavalry troops guarding the flanks of their squares and depended on cavalry to do this first and foremost.[21] This was not to be the case on the Pontic steppe. Instead confronting the Ottomans, the Tatars, numerous Cossack hosts, and many indigenous peoples across the steppe required light, highly maneuverable, and versatile troops trained to fight in a wide variety of roles. Not surprisingly, and keeping in the Petrine tradition, Chernyshev's commission mandated that the cavalry should maintain a mix of hussars and dragoons who could satisfy the mixture of missions that confronted the Russian cavalry across its empire. The artillery also benefited from the work of the Chernyshev commission, which discovered an unorganized mess upon evaluating the status of this service branch. To clean up the mess the artillery corps was enlarged and equipped with approximately 140 new heavy weapons and then organized into two regiments that could be attached to infantry units as needed. Adding to the modernization of the artillery corps, the Commission wrote a new set of regulations in 1756 entitled the *Generalitet* that represented the first comprehensive set of orders for the heavy guns. These regulations defined how to organize and to train Russian artillery troops to concentrate their firepower for greater effect.[22] During this period the artillery started to take the lead in technological progress as the Russians, in the midst of the Seven Years' War, introduced a special Corps of Bombardiers that had greater maneuverability on the battlefield because they were equipped with a new and secret howitzer, which with its high trajectories and steep angle of descent brought a new dimension to the battlefield.

As these reforms responsible for the reorganization of the Russian army were running their course, Prince Wenzel Anton Kaunitz Rietberg, Austrian state chancellor and minister of foreign affairs, orchestrated the 1756 Treaty of Versailles, which is better known to eighteenth-century history as the Diplomatic Revolution. This act of diplomacy was responsible for realigning relationships such that Austria and France joined forces against Prussia and Great Britain. This treaty included the dynastic deal that promised the infant Austrian princess Maria Antoinette to the French *Dauphin*, the future Louis XVI. Such a diplomatic realignment could well have alienated Russia from her longtime ally, the Austrians. In the true Shakespearian tradition of "politics makes strange bedfellows," however, Elizabeth and her advisors were unfazed by this transformation in political affairs. Russia and Austria still had the common interests of containing Frederick the Great's Prussia, they both remained committed to containing the Ottoman Turks, and eventually both Elizabeth and Austrian Empress Maria Theresa set their empires on the course that concluded with the complete partition of Poland. Indeed, the Diplomatic Revolution of 1756 was not at all directed toward Russia. Instead, Kaunitz sought to prevent France from becoming involved in what was brewing into the chain of events that would culminate with the outbreak of the Seven Years' War. The French, having failed in their efforts to expand their power into Central Europe and the Baltic, elected to disengage in such affairs and direct their energy toward the Western Hemisphere, which cleared the way for them to confront the British in what became known as the French and Indian War. At the same time the Austrians and Russians enlisted the additional support of Saxony and surprisingly Sweden, thus forming the coalition that became embroiled in the Seven Years' War in an effort to contain the power of Prussia and their young king Frederick II whose military prowess would earn him the reputation of being Frederick the Great.[23]

Setting the stage for what became the Seven Years' War (1756–63) was actually the last act in the struggle that started when Frederick the Great seized control of Silesia in the aftermath of the 1740 death of the Habsburg Charles VI and the rise to power of his daughter Maria Theresa. This bold act by Frederick II precipitated the Austria Wars of Succession (1740-8) and set Central Europe into turmoil and on the path that would culminate with the outbreak of the Seven Years' War. With the outbreak of the Seven Years' War, Russia's primary theater of operation was in East Prussia so Elizabeth sent an army of 80,000 men into the territory in 1757. The campaign was administered through a bureaucratic body known as "The Conference of St. Petersburg," the leader of which was Elizabeth's longtime chancellor Alexei Petrovich Bestuzhev-Riumin. He then promoted his friend General Stepan Fyodorovich Apraksin to the rank of field marshal and gave him command of seven army corps composed of the aforementioned 80,000 men who became the vanguard of the invasion of East Prussia in the spring of 1757. The Russian army enjoyed initial success with the defeat of the Prussians at the battle of Gross-Jagersdorf on August 30, 1757. Frederick II's army, overwhelmed by the invasion, retreated to Konigsberg, the old Teutonic fortress city. Lacking logistical support, Apraksin did not press on with his attack and instead ordered his troops to withdraw east of the Vistula River where he set up a camp and prepared his army to retire into winter quarters. Once ostensibly in its winter quarters the army allegedly waited as word had reached it from St. Petersburg that Elizabeth Petrovna was about to fall victim to her abusive lifestyle and die. Instead Apraksin died, some sources noting, under a cloud of accusations, that he had been bribed by Prussian agents to not pursue their king in the campaigns of 1757. Others noted that as the empire waited for Elizabeth's demise, he had a stroke while awaiting the judgment of a military tribunal about his conduct on the battlefield.[24]

Regardless of Apraksin's status at the time of his death, the war continued and Elizabeth chose this moment to appoint General William Fermor to take command of the army even though he was a Minnikh protégé. Greatly aggravated at Apraksin's lackluster performance, the empress wanted a new military leader known for having an aggressive style of command when engaging the enemy. True to his reputation Fermor immediately ordered the army out of its winter quarters with plans to immediately resume operations. Before the Russian army's impact could be made on the battlefield, Frederick the Great went on the offensive and in the ensuing actions defeated French and Austrian armies on the battlefield—first the French at Rossbach in Saxony on November 5, 1757, and a month later he defeated the Austrians at the Battle of Leuthen on December 5, 1757. These two victories, combined with his laying siege to the city of Breslau and reducing it into surrender on December 20, 1757, cemented the reputation of Frederick II as a great military leader in history. More important to the moment, the clear and present threat of Frederick's Prussia as a menace to everyone's security convinced the French to maintain a presence on the European side of the global conflict, and at the same time, resulted in the British declaring war on the Austrians. This declaration was accompanied with British loans to the Prussians that provided them with the financial means to continue fighting the war. But, this string of successes so exhausted the Prussians that they could do little to halt Fermor's thrust into East Prussia, which ended with the occupation of Konigsberg on New Year's eve 1757. After his success at Konigsberg, Fermor received orders from the Conference in St. Petersburg to occupy all of East Prussia, but as he prepared to move westward into Brandenburg and Pomerania, his army ran out of supplies. Thus, in the early part of 1758, a lull of sorts existed throughout the areas of conflict while all sides regrouped and resupplied. By the middle of the summer of 1758, however, it became clear to Frederick that the

Russians and Austrians were trying to combine forces to threaten Berlin, the very heart of his kingdom. His maneuvers to prevent such a meeting of allied armies culminated with the Battle of Zorndorf on August 14, 1758, a battle that occurred not far from Frankfort-on-Oder, with each side suffering some 12,000 killed and a similar number of troops wounded. Zorndorf, therefore, is noted as one of the bloodiest battles of the period. In the course of this engagement, Frederick II tried to outmaneuver the allied forces by means of a flanking motion. When Russian defensive squares blocked his attempt to outflank them, he switched to a frontal assault, which was the cause of the bloodbath. Although shaken, the Russian line held largely because of the support of both the artillery and cavalry in an early example of Elizabeth's army deploying its forces in a combined operation. At the end of the battle, both armies retired from the battlefield to lick their wounds with no decisive winner.

In the battle's aftermath Elizabeth relieved General Fermor of his command for not pressing home the attack so that his army could combine forces with the Austrians and march on Berlin. His replacement, Count Pyotr Semyonovich Saltykov, renewed the offensive in June 1759 and invaded Prussia with 40,000 men. He was supported by an Austrian army of 20,000 men under the command of General Ernst von Loundon. They combined forces just east of Frankfort-on-Oder and fought a Zorndorf-like battle at Kunersdorf on August 12, 1759, with a much worse outcome for the Prussians. For starters, Frederick the Great was almost captured by a roving band of Cossacks just off of the battlefield on the day of battle. The Prussians suffered grievously compared to the allied forces with some 18,000 casualties plus the loss of 178 field artillery pieces. The Russians and Austrians literally swept aside all opposition on their drive to Berlin, but, again, the supply problem bedeviled both sides and the campaign fell apart, especially after the two allies started to argue over the eventual spoils of their victory. Given the supply situation, the Russians again withdrew east of the Vistula to set up winter quarters, a maneuver that Frederick the Great would describe as the miracle of the Brandenburg campaign because there was little he could do to stop the Russians from marching across Prussia.[25]

After being promoted to field marshal in the aftermath of the battle at Kunersdorf, in 1760 Saltykov pressed on with a campaign across northern Germany with the goal of occupying Pomerania and ultimately seizing control of Berlin. Orders from the Conference in St. Petersburg, however, forced him to consider other options. In an effort to resolve the army's perpetual logistical challenges, the Conference directed Saltykov to lay siege to the port of Kolberg, which he did with troops under the command of General Pyotr Aleksandrovich

Rumiantsev. Collectively along with Austrian forces under the command of von Loundon, they fought a series of skirmishes known as the battles of Silesia, which kept the Prussians on the defensive. With the situation seemingly under control, Saltykov marched on Breslau with the intention of meeting Lounden and once again tried to combine forces to march on Berlin. Loundon, however, suffered a devastating defeat at Leignitz on August 4, 1760. Saltykov, ill and disgusted with the Loundon and the defeat of the Austrians, became enraged when he learned of the overall allied indecision about most everything, so he remanded his command to General Fermor who had remained with the operational army after Elizabeth dismissed him from command after Zorndorf. To try to obtain some type of positive result for the 1760 campaign season, Fermor ordered General G. G. Totleben to organize a flying detachment of Cossacks to launch a raid on Berlin at the end of September. They occupied Berlin on September 28, 1760. After charging the Prussians reparations of 1,800,000 thalers and seizing some 5,000 prisoners, the Russians withdrew across the Oder River and spent the winter around Danzig and its environs.[26]

The Conference of St. Petersburg then set Russia's strategy for the next year (1761) when it ordered a two prong offensive into East Prussia. The first thrust was to strengthen the siege of the fortress at Kolberg. The aim of this campaign was to capture the fort and use it as a supply base that would once and for all resolve the army's supply problem. The second part of their strategy was to invade Silesia with 50,000 troops under the command of General Alexander Borisovich Buturlin. Frederick II did not have the troop strength to contain and defeat the Russians, but the Prussian king was too crafty a military leader to get trapped in an open battle with a superior enemy. Much to Buturlin's frustration, he spent August and September chasing Frederick the Great around Silesia without achieving a decisive result. Meanwhile, Rumiantsev in a combined operation of army and naval assets surrounded and cut off the fortress Kolberg in September and forced it to surrender on December 5th as the Prussians inside ran out of supplies. The victory at Kolberg was the last one for the Russians in the Seven Years' War. Although it set Russia up to launch a decisive campaign in the spring of 1762, Elizabeth Petrovna died on January 5, 1762, with her armies poised to conquer Prussia and once and for all defeat Frederick the Great. With her death and the rise of Peter III to the throne, the army was ordered back to a peacetime footing as the new tsar, who worshiped Frederick the Great, wanted nothing to do with further conflict with Prussia.[27]

Without question the operations of the imperial army in the Seven Years' War plainly revealed that Russia's armed forces were on par with the other armies

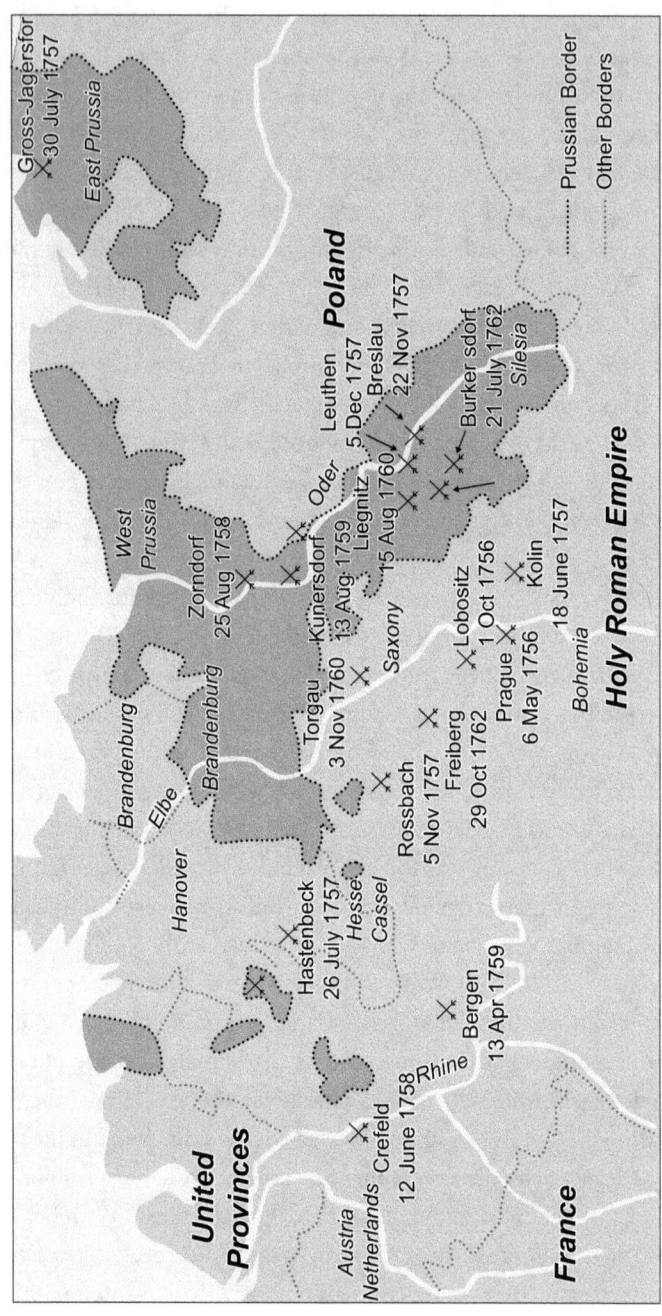

Map 2.2 The Seven Years' War.

of the great European powers.²⁸ Elizabeth Petrovna may not have expanded the size of the empire, but her reforms designed to strengthen the military establishment met with great success; her efforts permanently institutionalized the administrative, organizational, and operational ideas of her father Peter the Great, at least in military affairs, and at the end of 1760 the army stood in Central Europe strong and victorious. Evidence of a fighting style based on the principle of combining operations among all of the service branches—infantry, cavalry, artillery, and navy—had taken shape especially during the latter stages of the Seven Years' War. Moreover, a brain trust emerged during this period largely through the activities of P. A. Rumiantsev and Alexander Vasilovich Suvorov that paved the way for the age of the great captains who would command Russia's armies for the rest of the century. This military establishment would emerge as the most powerful in Europe first by the time of Catherine II's death and then after it played a significant role in defeating Napoleon after 1812. Moreover, the teachings and conduct of Russia's late eighteenth-century military leadership remained influential in the strategic thinking and practical training of the armed forces for the rest of the Romanov period of rule and well into Soviet history. While maintaining force structure at both the soldier and officer ranks would always present a challenge to the army, Elizabeth's charisma successfully wedded the military to the crown. The main factor that limited capabilities during her reign was logistics. The army had the know-how and enough of a technological base to fight both their European and steppe foes, but moving men, equipment, and supplies around the vast spaces of the empire remained problematic at least until the middle of the twentieth century. Financing the military establishment for the grand plans of its political leadership also remained a perpetual problem that the Romanovs would never adequately resolve. The drive toward empire based on the principles that Peter the Great first inculcated into the realm, however, remained firm as they evolved through the century.²⁹

This transformation in Russian power became further embedded in the mores of the empire as a result of the series of events that followed the death of Elizabeth Petrovna. As per Peter the Great's law of succession, Elizabeth, who never married nor had children that history has been able to identify, selected her successor. For this honor Elizabeth chose her older sister Anna Petrovna's son (not Anna Ivanova who ruled from 1730 to 1740) Peter, whose father was Duke Karl Friederich of Holstein. Elizabeth wasted no time in naming Peter her successor in part because she wanted to reinforce her dynastic claim to the throne by making Peter the Great's grandson tsarevich. Her sister, having died soon after his 1728 birth and Karl Friedrich death in 1739, made Elizabeth's decision to bring Peter to Russia in 1742, shortly after her rise to the throne, an even better choice because at least in appearance he came to Russia without any strings attached. Peter, however, turned out to be quite the challenge for Elizabeth and her courtiers to mold into the next tsar. Self-conscious due to a heavily smallpox-scarred face, socially inept (as became completely clear after his marriage to the future Catherine the Great), and with an annoying habit of occupying his time playing with lead soldiers, Peter did little to nothing to endear himself to anyone in the twenty or so years he lived in Russia before becoming tsar.

Peter III

Despite his February 18, 1762, manifesto, "On the Granting of Liberty and Freedom to All the Russian Nobility," to emancipate the Russian nobility from compulsory state service being one of his first acts as tsar, Peter III could do nothing to please the servitors who populated his court. And, then trying to shift political power back into the hands of Peter the Great's Senate, thus re-empowering the old aristocracy, Peter III still managed to further alienate himself from the army and nobility in his 186-day reign.[30] He also managed to alienate himself from the church after he made clear his intention to secularize all of its landholdings. Limited by his overall physical and social awkwardness—a stunning contrast to the gregarious Elizabeth Petrovna—Peter, as Peter III, lost the support of the army, beginning with the Preobrazhenskii and Izmailovskii guard's regiments for abruptly ending the Seven Years' War and immediately ordering the adoption of Prussian style uniforms and drill. He then sought to institutionalize the process of Prussification when he disbanded Elizabeth's War Cabinet and appointed a special military commission commanded by Zakhar Chernyshev with orders to rewrite the drill manual to conform to the Prussian way of war.[31] When he realized that his efforts to transform the army were going nowhere via the commissions he created to oversee reform, he pushed matters via decrees. Officers of the Guard interpreted these actions to mean that the tsar had imposed a pro-Prussian military and foreign policy on them, which was aimed at supporting his hero Frederick the Great but was at its core considered either not in the best interests of the realm or at worse treasonous. He did not help his cause when he created his own guard corps—the Holstein Guard—which he proclaimed to be the model for the entire army, which was a direct challenge and insult to the imperial Russian guard. The army's leadership viewed his reforms with contempt and disdain and was not prepared nor did it desire to have Frederick the Great as their ally. Besides making accusations of treason, they feared that what Peter really had in store was an invasion of his home provinces of Schleswig-Holstein to restore them to Denmark, a goal that his father had tried to achieve before dying.[32] The army's leadership, simply put, believed that Peter III had discarded its magnificent victories in the Seven Years' War because he worshiped Frederick the Great, and this perception provided the essential backdrop to the gathering of forces that coalesced into a *coup d'état* that not only ousted him from power in June 1762 but also led to his assassination.

Since Peter III's historical legacy was formed by the people who ousted and assassinated him beginning with his wife, there is still cause to question his reputation in Russian history. Over the course of his time in power he issued 220 decrees all aimed at reforming the society that Peter the Great had organized specifically to support the construction of his empire. His emancipation of the nobility is emblematic of the intent of his reforms, but his actions still need to be reconsidered to view his reign outside of the reputation ascribed to it in the aftermath of his assassination.[33] Whether or not Peter III's attempt to emancipate the nobility was aimed at building a base of support for himself will never be known because of his fate. His death, however, did not eliminate the question of the nobility's relationship to the crown. Their so-called emancipation lacked specific terms other than they were now free to travel abroad. The lingering concern among Russia's aristocrats in the wake of being granted newfound freedoms was about the costs. If the nobility was no longer going to be required to serve the state, then questions about future obligations to the state needed to be answered. Their concerns mainly centered on the state imposing huge tax levies to compensate it for the lost service. While Russia's upper classes did not want to endure a life of mandatory service to the state, they also did not want the perpetually cash-poor regime to burden them with excessive taxes. Peter's decree in itself came as a huge surprise to the nobility and no one understood better the stress and tension his emancipation caused throughout Russia than his wife, the person who orchestrated the coup against him, Catherine II.

Catherine the Great

By the time of her death, Catherine would indeed be labeled as "Great," but on the night of June 28, 1762, when she and her cabal of supporters seized power, she was known as Grand Duchess Ekaterina Alekseevna. As she came to power, she had to manage a host of challenges that began with first placating the Army's High Command and guard's officers. Then, she had to convince all of Russia's nobility from the highest aristocrats to the service gentry as well as the church hierarchy that she would rule in accord with their wishes and desires. The demands of these challenges were extreme especially for Catherine II, because like her husband Peter III, she was not a Russian, rather she grew up as Princess Sophia Augusta Frederika from the minor German principality of Anhalt Zerbst. Elizabeth Petrovna had brought her to Russia in 1745 at the age of sixteen specifically to be Peter III's bride. In her seventeen years in Russia, she embraced the orthodox faith and the mores of Russian society and its court on a much higher level than Peter. She expected and prepared for the moment when Peter III's support would wither by endearing herself to the officers of the Preobrazhenski and Izmailovskii guard's regiments. Her connections ran deep; one of the commanders of the Preobrazhenski regiment was her lover Grigorii Orlov but perhaps more significantly, she had the support of Kyrill Razummovskii who was hetman of Ukraine and also an officer of the Izmailovskii guard's regiment. How widespread the support was for her is difficult to estimate because of the conspiratorial activities of the participants of the coup. More important to understanding this moment in Russian history is how she first pandered to the guard's officers by appearing at their barracks and then wearing their uniform when she rode at the head of their regiment as they went to arrest Peter III. Then, after the tsar's arrest, Catherine quickly consolidated power by gaining the support of significant political leaders such as Nikita Panin, Peter Sheremet'ev, and Chancellor A. P. Bestuzhev-Riumin. In addition, she also emerged unscathed from the assassination of Peter III who was murdered allegedly trying to escape from his captors on July 6, 1762, a mere eight days after the coup that ousted him.

Upon consolidating her support, she set out to reform Russia according to the teachings of the enlightenment that was sweeping through Western Europe in the eighteenth century. Like Peter the Great, Catherine saw the way forward through the lens of Western European ideas, technology, and society. Purported to have read Voltaire and Montesquieu at the very least, Catherine tried to portray herself as the enlightened despot who through the imitation of Western, especially French culture, would modernize Russia by establishing a rule of law that meted out justice based on the ideas and expectations of people for their society. Moreover, Catherine also envisioned herself as the person who would spread educational opportunities throughout her realm, thereby continuing a major enterprise started by Peter the Great. The ideas behind these reforms were first articulated in her famous Nakaz (instruction) of 1767 that called for the gathering of information upon which a future commission would redraft the laws of Russia. This idea would mature with the convocation later in the year of the Legislative Commission of 1767 in which 564 delegates from all the provinces and representatives of all social classes congregated to rewrite the laws of the land. While the Commission ultimately produced little in the way of reform because, like all "enlightened despots," Catherine did not like the idea of sharing power with anyone, she nonetheless infused higher ideas and levels of thinking into the body politic of Russia. And, while she also worked to build schools throughout Russia and at the same time struggled to introduce assorted levels of local administrations and governments to strengthen the long reach of the central government in St. Petersburg, Catherine's legacy that makes her "Great" is wrapped up in two accomplishments that would define Russian society for the next century and the Russian Empire until today. First, she maintained harmonious relations with the nobility, which ushered in their golden age in Russian history. More important and significant, she never lost touch with the base of her political support, the officers of the guard's regiments. With their support she would do more to build the Russian Empire than Peter the Great.[34]

All of her domestic accomplishments aside, Catherine II would fight two major wars against Turkey, dismantle the Polish-Lithuanian Commonwealth, and push Russian power further into the Caucasus, and in so doing not only continued the pursuit of Empire, but also expanded the size of Russia more than any other Russian leader at any time in all of history. To first organize and then oversee the entire enterprise, she set up the Military Commission of 1762, which became the driving force behind her policymaking and the operations of the army until her death. This Commission, working in unison with the Military College during the course of Catherine II's reign, doubled the size of the army to approximately 400,000 men while restoring the Petrine ratio of twice as much infantry as cavalry. The Military Commission ultimately defined the role of the infantry as to deliver decisive firepower on command. The roles of the cavalry included shock attack, screening, reconnaissance, securing the flanks of deployed infantry units, and pursuing the enemy when it fled from the battlefield. Their recent experiences had taught Russia's military leadership that to defend their empire against all of their enemies, the army needed heavy cavalry to fight in Northern and Central Europe and light cavalry to fight across their southern frontier. While coming to terms with their various needs in cavalry, it was also during Catherine's reign that the artillery corps was reorganized into three branches—regimental, field, and siege—to define its assorted roles on the battlefield. Still it was not a unified service branch since most guns were assigned to regiments that developed their own regulations. Most importantly, the Commission focused the army's work on maintaining discipline, enhancing training, and always providing adequate logistics and reliability in both peace and war. Moreover, largely through her educational reforms, the army's officers were indoctrinated to teach the entire army what they stood for and would always defend the faith, tradition, and heritage of mother Russian.[35]

As her armies were sorting themselves into becoming the largest and most powerful forces in all of Europe, Catherine set out to manage the politics of empire building first through diplomacy. While she had the reputation of using her amorous side to impose her will on friend and foe alike, she also had strong men advocating and negotiating on behalf of Russia. Especially since the reign of Anna Ivanova, Russia had maintained a strong alliance with the Austrians, mainly to stand in unison against the Turks. Austria's 1756 Diplomatic Revolution, however, reoriented the Russians largely because after their meddling in the Baltic and with Sweden in the 1730s; St. Petersburg did not trust the French. When she came to power, therefore, Catherine intended to remake Russian foreign policy, which she did starting with the removal of Elizabeth's chancellor A. P. Bestuzhev-Riumin, who had become a devoted Austrophile and replacing him with Nikita Ivanovich Panin (1718–1783). Panin was a diplomat who had served as Ambassador to Sweden in 1747–60 and then as tutor to Paul, the son of Catherine and Peter III. His reward for being instrumental in delivering the support of the Guard to Catherine at the time of the coup was his appointment as president of the College of Foreign Affairs. With his control over foreign policy unchallenged, Panin would emerge as one of the most powerful men in Russia outside of the army. He worked well with Catherine to maintain the Petrine idea of rewarding meritorious service with promotion through the table of ranks, but he also represented his class by convincing Catherine II that there should also be a path open to the highest levels of her government to people who served the state for long periods. To accomplish this, Panin favored restoring as much power as possible to the Petrine era Senate so that Russia's natural leaders—the old Muscovite era aristocratic families would have a stake in the empire's governance. Thus, Panin became instrumental in assisting Catherine II in building political consensus among Russia's aristocrats.[36] More importantly, however, shortly after her coming to power, Panin suggested to his tsarina that the empire, in the wake of the Seven Years' War, needed a prolonged peace so it could gather its strength, which put an end to the threat of a war with Denmark and started Russia down the path of a rapprochement with Prussia. Panin, despite the adverse circumstances that cropped up at the end of the Seven Years' War, recognized that the impact of the conflict had resulted in Europe dividing into two (bipolar) blocs that consisted on one side of France and Austria and on the other Prussia and Great Britain. In 1763 Panin's rise to prominence continued when he got Catherine to endorse his idea of constructing a Northern Accord that by design would be composed of Denmark, Prussia, and Britain. Catherine the Great's decision to support this diplomatic avenue marked the end of the Austro-Russian alliance, at least for the time being. What Panin saw in such an alignment was gaining the support of Great Britain. As the British Empire gained strength in global affairs, Panin was forward thinking enough to recognize that Russia stood to gain both commercially and diplomatically through the development of harmonious relations with the UK. Throughout Catherine's reign, therefore Britain and Russian became great maritime commercial trading partners with their efforts focusing on Baltic/Russian goods such as bar iron, sailcloth, hemp, and timber. Moreover, Panin recognized that Great Britain and her royal navy had emerged as a counterforce more valuable than the Austrians in Russia's struggles against the Ottomans. The precursor to the emergence of the Northern Accord was the Treaty of St. Hubertusberg, February 15, 1763, which formally ended the Seven Years' War in the East and paved the way for the development of a new strategic relationship between the northern European powers. In the summer of 1763 Catherine II enlisted her empire's old adversary Frederick II the Great to join Russia in its Northern Accord, thereby prompting a strategic realignment that placed the tsarina in the position to address her first strategic challenge, the status of the Polish-Lithuanian Commonwealth.[37]

The Polish question had been a serious foreign policy issue from the moment the Romanovs came to power in 1613. Under Catherine the Great's leadership, the question of the status of the Polish-Lithuanian Commonwealth would finally be resolved with the partition of the nation and its disappearance from the map of Europe until 1918. While in hindsight the partition of Poland is portrayed as a logical culmination of eighteenth-century diplomacy and warfare, there was nothing logical or predictable about the course of events that culminated in the disappearance from the map of a state that had been the most powerful nation in seventeenth-century Central Europe. Catherine II's initial plan for Poland was to create the image that it was a strong and useful ally that could act as a bulkhead against any military adventurism coming out of Western Europe. Yet, at the same time, she did not want the Commonwealth to become a threat to Russian security as had happened during the Times of Trouble at the beginning of the seventeenth century. Panin, therefore, attempted to orchestrate a policy in which Russia cultivated the idea that Poland and Catherine II were partners while Russia increased its hegemony over the Commonwealth. Thus, he pursued a policy of outwardly claiming to support a strong Commonwealth while in fact he sought to tame and reel in any attempts by the Poles to strengthen their autonomy and their nation. Polish magnates and lesser nobles rebelled because they correctly understood that the Russians would always be a threat to their autonomy and their "Golden" Liberty. This along with the Polish magnates and clergy zealously guarding and protecting the hegemony of their Roman Catholic Church were the perpetual sources of conflict between Poland and Russia. The situation intensified in 1763 because Poland needed a new king as August III was on his deathbed when Catherine came to power. The immediate challenge for the future of Poland became finding a king who could placate the magnates while doing Catherine's bidding. Reform-minded magnates would seek to strengthen the power of their monarch to the point of making their choice unacceptable to Catherine and the Russians.[38] Further complicating the scenario was that the stronger Russians became within the Commonwealth, the

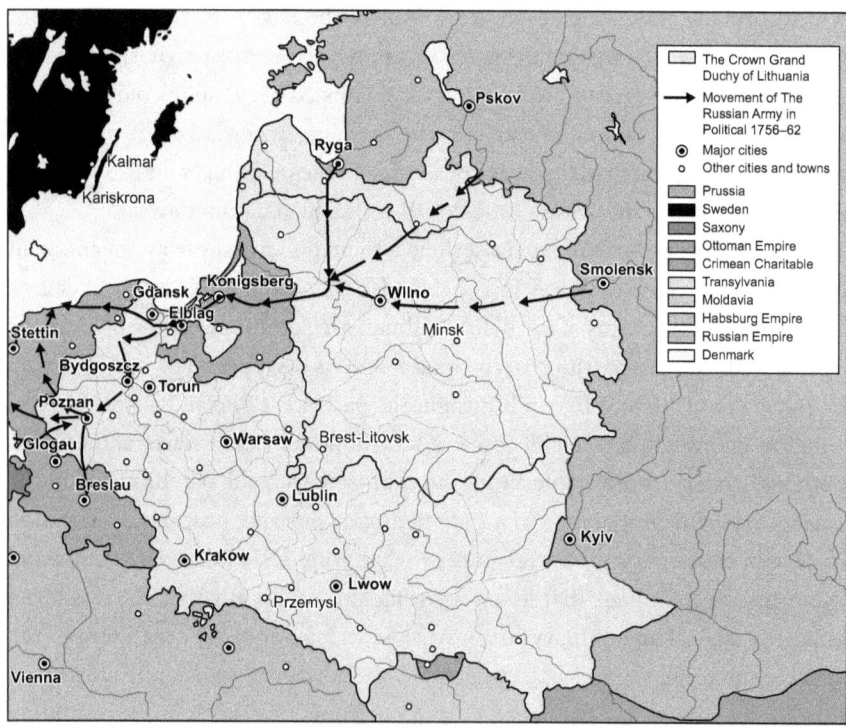

Map 2.3 The First Partition of Poland.

more alarmed the Ottomans became because they considered the Poles to be the buffer between themselves, the Russians, and Ukraine. Regardless of the Ottoman threat, Catherine II's goal was to reduce Polish and Saxon influence in the eastern Baltic while she strengthened her relationship with Frederick the Great if for no other reason than to remove him as a threat to Russia. Frederick II's machinations fit those with Catherine II because he wanted to maintain the semblance of a balance of power between himself, Russia, and Austria.

Augustus III died on September 24, 1763, and Catherine appointed Stanislaw Antoni Poniatowski (1732–1798), one of her former lovers as the new Polish king. She immediately sent N. V. Repnin, Panin's nephew by marriage to Warsaw as her ambassador and stationed Russian forces on the Commonwealth's frontier. Frederick II then deeply implicated himself in Russia's Polish policy when he signed a mutual defense alliance pact with Catherine II in St. Petersburg on March 31, 1764. Through this treaty he agreed to act in concert with Russia's Polish policy as long as the Russians respected religious toleration in Poland. Despite opposition from within the army, Panin as the recognized leader of Russian foreign policy now acted on his belief that Poland could play an important role in their struggle with the Tatars and the Ottomans. In 1764, therefore, he encouraged Poniatowski to build his army to 50,000 men and to allow the Russians to base troops between the Dnepr and Dnestr Rivers. With the military question seemingly under control, Catherine II beginning in March 1764 sought to orchestrate the next vital step in her Polish policy, which was to get the Polish nobility to acknowledge the accession of their new king. Using Repnin as her agent, she started to pour money into Poland to bribe the magnates to support an election of Poniatowski as king, which the Diet did on September 7, 1764.[39]

In a classic carrot and stick exercise, resistance to Poniatowski started to grow immediately after his election when both the Prussians and the Russians made it clear that they now expected the Poles to sign a formal alliance before the Polish Crown Army could expand in size. Both Catherine II and Frederick II had become concerned that the Polish magnates were going to rebel because of the heavy-handed interference of the Russians and the Prussians in their internal affairs. In an attempt to reign in the Poles who sought independence from Russia, Catherine reversed course and after agitating for the Poles to eliminate the crippling constitution device, the *Liberum veto*, she insisted on its inclusion in the Polish legislative process.[40] Even more vexing for the Poles was the now understood Russian and Prussian demand for religious tolerance, which appeared to be a nod toward liberal enlightened ideas, but was actually designed to protect the Orthodox Christians and Protestants in the Commonwealth. Understanding the intent of this policy alienated the Catholic magnates who dominated the Polish body politic from the machinations of both the Russians and the Prussians. Because of this Polish resistance, Catherine II threatened military intervention and had 40,000 troops under the command of General Ivan Petrovich Saltykov poised to invade the Commonwealth if the Diet did not accept the abovementioned demands in the form of what became known as the Toleration Bill.[41] The Polish diet polarized into Poniatowski's supporters and radicals who opposed Russia's heavy hand in Polish politics as they debated the Toleration Bill. Their inability to reach a compromise resulted in the radicals breaking away and forming their own association known as the Bar Confederation (as it was formed at the fortress of Bar in Podolia) under the leadership of the famous patriot and soldier Casimir Pulaski. With the support of France, the radicals at Bar signed articles of Confederation on February 29, 1768, and promptly declared war on Russia. Throughout this period the Russian response to the collapse of political unity in Poland's Sejm that resulted in the emergence of a group of breakaway radicals was to send more troops into Poland. As a result, by early 1769 over 66,000 Russian troops in the Commonwealth were inflaming the situation throughout the countryside. Meanwhile, a loose group of Cossack irregulars menacingly operated throughout the territory striking fear into the hearts and minds of their victims.

The Russian buildup captured the attention of Ottoman Sultan Mustafa III especially since the presence of Russian troops inflamed his border with the Commonwealth. After all, the presence of Russian troops in Poland had been the *casus belli* for the Russo-Turkish Wars of 1711–13 and 1735–9. Meanwhile, a loose group of Cossack irregulars agitated among Ukrainian peasants for them to oppose the Polish magnates who supported Russia's challenge to the Commonwealth not because they supported Russia but because they saw an opportunity to carve out their own nation from all the turmoil. This group coalesced into a viable force that represented itself as a political entity that existed to defend the rights of Catholics against Orthodox invaders. By May 1768, their agitation had matured into the Haidamak revolt, which is considered the last great revolt of Ukrainian peasants against their Polish overlords. While the revolt would last until the summer 1769, two events occurred in June 1768 that would define its significance to the growing tensions of the region. The first was the brutal massacre of some 2000 Jews, Ukrainian Uniates, and assorted Polish collaborators at the town of Uman in the middle of the month. Further inflaming the situation, the conflict(s) associated with the revolt spilled over into Ottoman territory near the city of Balta, also in mid-June. Balta, on the Moldavian side of the Ottoman/Commonwealth border, was an important market town, which meant the sultan had rapid and relatively accurate reports that informed him that over 1,000 of his subjects had been massacred by a Zaporozhian host. These Cossacks were not irregulars as they were considered to be Russian subjects. After June 1768, therefore, the sultan prepared to declare war on Russia if they did not withdraw their forces from sensitive border regions. Catherine the Great, however, was not prepared to withdraw her forces until the Polish question was resolved. In the end, Panin's Northern Accord was supposed to bring peace to buy Russia time to recover from the Seven Years' War and for Catherine II to consolidate power. But the key to the Accord was taming Poland and efforts to do that led to the projection of the Russian army into the Commonwealth and this occupation ended up threatening the Ottomans, which led to the Russo-Turkish War of 1768–74.[42]

Mustafa III declared War in 1768 for a host of reasons that started with the Russian army being solidly entrenched in Ukraine because of Catherine II's efforts to control the politics of the Polish-Lithuanian Commonwealth. These troops were poised to attack Crimea and were menacing to Wallachia and especially Moldavia, which made both the Orthodox and Muslim populations of these regions restless for good cause. This situation combined with a shift in attitudes of assorted Cossack hordes, especially the Nogai, culminated in these irregular forces, critical to the status and control of the Pontic steppe, shifting their allegiance from the porte to the tsar, which made the sultan edgy. Indeed, Mustafa III, convinced that the Russians were not leaving Ukraine anytime soon, believed the security of his entire northern frontier was in doubt.[43] The sultan did not take his decision to go to war lightly since by the second half of the eighteenth century the Ottoman Empire was well on its way to becoming the sick man of Europe. Outsiders viewed his armies as an undisciplined mob; his government, because of its corruption and incompetence, was incapable of organizing or administrating its military resources. Overall, the Porte was becoming decentralized as power progressively shifted from Constantinople to the provinces. International encounters beginning with the 1683 failed siege of Vienna had not gone well for the Ottomans. While they were able to stem the tide at Prut in 1711, every other encounter with the rest of the world had ended in defeat. Defeat at Azov in 1696, a failure to gain strategic objectives as at the treaties of Karlowitz and Constantinople in 1700, and the conclusion of the 1735–9 War where the Treaty of Nis gave Azov back to the Russians and further acknowledged Russian control over the Zaporoshian region or what is today the southeastern Ukraine together had severely weakened Ottoman standing as a great power. In fact, when Mustafa III declared war on October 6, 1768, he ended a twenty-nine-year period of peace where the official thinking out of Constantinople had been to deliberately avoid war and to use the interregnum to reorganize and reform both politically and militarily—two goals never accomplished for the remainder of the history of the Ottoman Empire.[44]

The Russian presence in Poland simply did not end because of the Turkish declaration of war. Rather, Russia now found itself engaged in a two-front war—one over the fate of Poland and the other against the Ottomans and their assorted allies on the Pontic steppe. After the Haidamak revolt, Catherine II sent additional troops to Warsaw under the command of General P. I. Olits who controlled a brigade commanded by A. V. Suvorov. Suvorov, to tame the Polish rebels, marched his brigade south from Warsaw to Krakow, thereby chasing his adversaries into the foothills of the Carpathian Mountains. As 1769 turned into 1770, the French were able to revitalize the Polish cause by sending troops under the command of General Francois Charles Dumouriez who not only reenergized Polish troops but also convinced them to draw up an alliance with Grzegorz Antoni Oginski, the grand hetman of Lithuania. By 1771 this alliance of Polish magnates, Lithuanian troops, and French supplies kept Suvorov and the Russian army occupied as each force chased the other around what is today the core of Poland. Suvorov managed to bottle up the majority of these forces at Lublin, but about 1,000 or so escaped to the citadel at Krakow where a siege ensued beginning in January 1772. Meanwhile, in the next month Catherine II, Frederick II, and Maria Theresa agreed to the first partition of Poland, which became a fact after the citadel at Krakow surrendered in late July. Once occupied in August, the three powers orchestrating the demise of Poland formally ratified the first partition on September 22, 1772. While Suvorov was miffed that as he lifted the siege Austrian troops arrived to occupy what became their share of the partition, the Poles and Lithuanians had to digest the loss of 30 percent of their sovereign territory to the Great Powers in this series of events known to history as the First Polish Insurrectionary War. The Russians believed that more of Poland should have gone into their sphere of control, but because of the war they were also fighting against the Turks, by the fall 1772 Catherine was willing to take less of Poland to better use her resources to continue her campaign against the Ottoman Empire.[45]

While Ottoman forces suffered from multiple defects, they still numbered over 600,000 in 1768, which made them formidable and a danger to the security of the Russian Empire. Nevertheless, a war against the Porte also meant another

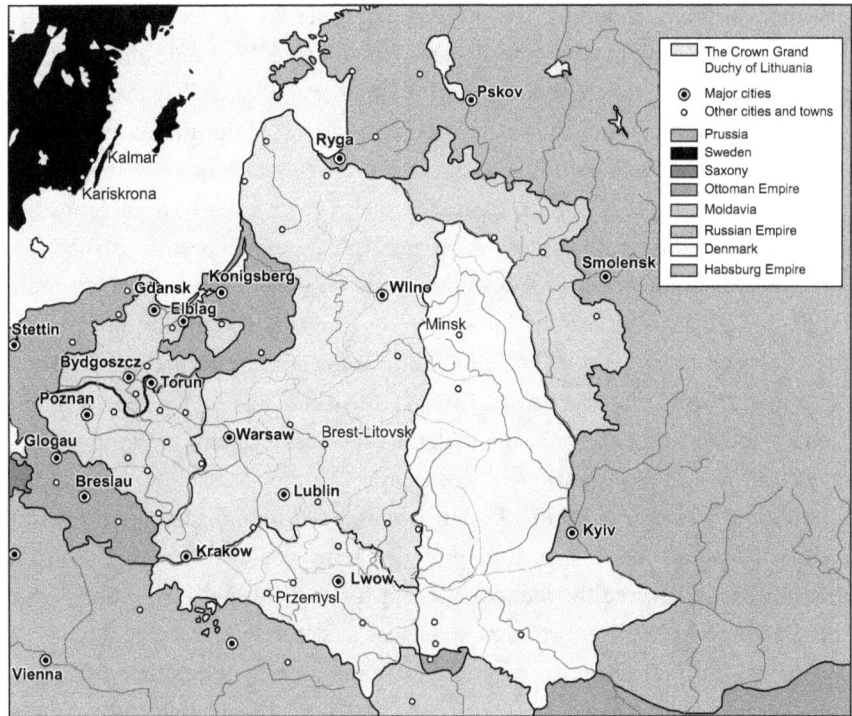

Map 2.4 The Partition of Poland.

confrontation with the pesky mounted troops of the Crimean Khanate. The Khanate had been a major source of opposition both to the rise of Muscovy and to the emergence of the empire in the seventeenth century. At its height, it could mount 80,000 horse troops and was notorious for launching vicious raids into southern Russia. In the first half of the seventeenth century, it has been estimated that they captured and enslaved 150,000–200,000 Russians. Their power, however, had been vastly weakened by the middle of the seventeenth century because of the rise of the Romanovs, yet they nonetheless represented another threat to Russian armed forces. The Cossack hordes represented a threat to everyone as they remained unruly and usually available to the highest bidder. By the time of the 1768–4 Russo-Turkish War, however, their chaotic existence had been organized by the Russians into three major groupings—the little Russian Cossacks of Ukraine, the Zaporopzhian Cossack who resided in the lower reaches of the Dnieper, and the formidable Don Cossacks although various and assorted Cossack hosts would continue to exist well into the nineteenth century. From the time they first came to power, the Romanovs had a policy of recruiting the Cossacks either by agreement or by coercion to swear allegiance to the tsar in return for them remaining free and agreeing to serve as irregular troops in the Russian armed forces. Always an ill-disciplined horde, both the sultan and the tsar/tsarina usually sought their support in times of conflict, but by the latter half of the eighteenth century they were more likely to side with the Russians than not. The Romanovs offered the Cossacks more freedom to govern themselves while also promising them a respectable role in their armed forces. Since the seventeenth century both the Ottomans and Romanovs had been constructing a horizontal chain of strong fortresses that could on the one hand serve as supply outposts and secure locations for settlers on the steppe. On the other hand, these fortresses also served as staging grounds for military formations in times of conflict. By the outbreak of war in 1768, the Turks had built a line from the Danube to the Crimean Peninsula to denote the borders defined by the treaties of Karlowitz and Constantinople, while by 1740 the Russians were working on building what turned into 18 fortresses and 140 redoubts across their vast southern frontier. These fortresses provided both sides with staging grounds that ultimately became the launching point for their military operations once they had built up sufficient strength to engage in battle.[46]

Against the huge Ottoman army, the Russians, already committed in Poland, could muster only around 150,000 troops that had been organized into three armies. The First Army, the largest of the three, consisted of 80,000 men under the command of Prince Alexander Mikhailovich Golitsyn and formed up near Kiev. Its mission was to invade the Ottoman provinces of Wallachia and Moldavia. The Second Army of some 40,000 troops was under the command of General Piotr Aleksandrovich Rumiantsev and had the mission of defending the huge wide arc that stretched from the Bug River to the foothills of the northern Caucasus. The fortresses and redoubts throughout this region would be critical to him fulfilling his mission. The Third Army was a small force of some 15,000 men under the command of General P. I. Olits whose task was to guard the Russian rear and prevent any Polish patriots from complicating the situation in the south. The Turks, taking advantage of proximity and location of forces, struck first in the late fall of 1768 when they launched a two-prong assault on southern Ukraine from the fortress covering the Dnepr estuary. Using a force of Tatars, the Ottomans struck out into the Donets Basin while the Crimean Khan led an attack on Elizavetgrad. Rumiantsev contained the strike into the Donets Basin, but lacking sufficient force there was nothing he could do to prevent the occupation of Elizavetgrad. The khan, fearing that Rumiantsev might organize a counterattack that would push the Tatars into the open steppe, instead optioned to loot Elizavetgrad for all it was worth and then withdraw to the Crimea.[47]

This set the stage for A. M. Golitysn's 1769 invasion of Wallachia and Moldavia, but he got bogged down trying to surround and cut off the fortress at Khotin, which covered the middle flow of the Dniester River. The failure of his troops to reduce the fortress via a siege demonstrated his weakness as a commander. In the end, the Turks gave up on the siege of Khotin largely because Rumiantsev had launched operations in the region of Bendery and Ochakov, which perplexed the Ottoman military establishment, and in this confusion, Golitsyn finally reduced the fortress, thereby giving the Russians a victory although they did not obtain their strategic goal of occupying the two provinces. In the aftermath of this campaign, Catherine II recalled Golitsyn to St. Petersburg and gave him a Field Marshal's baton and remanded Rumiantsev to the First Army while giving command of the Second Army to Peter Panin, the brother of her foreign minister Nikita Panin. In the field, the first part of 1770 was spent reorganizing the army while enhancing its training routine. From St. Petersburg the Military Council ordered that Panin's Second Army should launch a thrust toward the Danube and that Rumiantsev should guard the flanks of this troop movement. Rumiantsev was first busy with his reorganization that aimed to eliminate the Third Army, using its troops to reinforce the two remaining armies in the field. He was also busy constructing the new magazines and depots needed to resolve perpetual and vexing supply problems. Once he had resolved the administrative and organizational challenges of the moment, Rumiantsev, using his experience of the previous year, in addition to intelligence gathered in the theater of operations, had concluded that the Ottoman forces were much weaker than what was understood in St. Petersburg. As a result, in mid-May, Russian armies started a maneuver across the theater of operations that culminated in three decisive victories that decided after the better part of a century of struggle the question of who would control the Pontic steppe. Here Rumiantsev's emphasis on training as he reorganized his forces would pay huge dividends as his armies exhibited the deft capability of moving from marching columns into compact squares that could both provide offensive thrust and defensive rigidity in quick order and on command. First, he overran the Turks at Bendery on the middle flow of the Prut on June 17, 1770. Then, on July 7, he repeated his success some 30 kilometers further south on the river Larga. The Russian army's moment of glory came on July 21 when Rumiantsev's battle squares bottled up the Ottomans at Kagul. Here some 35,000 disciplined Russians formed into squares and annihilated some 150,000 Turks.[48]

In addition to seizing the initiative on land, 1770 was also a good year for the Russian navy. With a force of four capital ships and four fire ships, Admiral

Samuel Greig sailed from the Baltic to the Mediterranean and confronted a Turkish fleet at the Bay of Chesme off the coast of Asia minor. Using superior sailing skills and better command and control, Greig was able to defeat a fleet four times his size and then by the end of June bottle up the Turkish fleet in the Dardanelles effectively cutting them off from Turkish possessions in the Aegean Sea. This may have been the first occasion when Russian maritime prowess impressed friend and foe alike in Western Europe![49] The year of unprecedented Russian successes was capped off when Panin's Second Army forced the fortress at Bendery to capitulate in the middle of September. All of Russia's victories sent the sultan and his advisors into a tailspin that drove the Porte to the peace table. But neither side was ready to agree to terms, so 1771 was the year that the Russians would invade Crimea. The Second Army, now under the command of Prince V. M. Dolgorukov, marched into Crimea in May and with improved logistics thanks to Rumiantsev's efforts, his Second Army occupied the entire peninsula by the middle of the summer. But, still, the sultan would not sue to end hostilities so the war dragged on for two more years with campaigning on both sides of the Danube before the Ottomans finally agreed to peace terms. For his astute administrative conduct and aggressive military leadership against the Turkish enemy Catherine II's first Turkish War became known as Rumiantsev's War, and he therefore became one of the empress's Great Captains.[50]

The Treaty of Kuchuk-Kainardji, signed by the Porte on July 21, 1774, was a landmark in diplomatic history that remade the world of the Pontic steppe. Its terms started with the status of the Crimean Tatars and Nogai host who were formally declared to be independent. In fact, the Khanate now became dependent on Russia and in 1782 would be annexed outright after clashes between Christian and Muslim inhabitants of the territory. The Ottomans formally ceded the seaports at Azov, Kerch, and Kinburn, thereby resulting in the return to Russia of the territory lost at Prut in 1711. More significantly, the Russian navy and its merchant ships were given direct access to the Black Sea. From this point on the Russians would maintain a permanent fleet on the Black Sea that exists to this day. In addition, the Russians gained control over territories between the Dnieper and Bug Rivers. The Ottomans also renounced their claims to territories in the northern Caucasus, thereby ending any further aspirations to expand in that direction. In keeping with the tradition of Great Power diplomacy, the Russians submitted a bill to the sultan for war reparations in the amount of 4.5 million rubles to cover the cost of the war. In a nod to the Austrians, both sides agreed that the Habsburgs gain control over the northwestern part of Moldavia, soon to be renamed Bukovina. The clause in the Treaty, however, that opened the

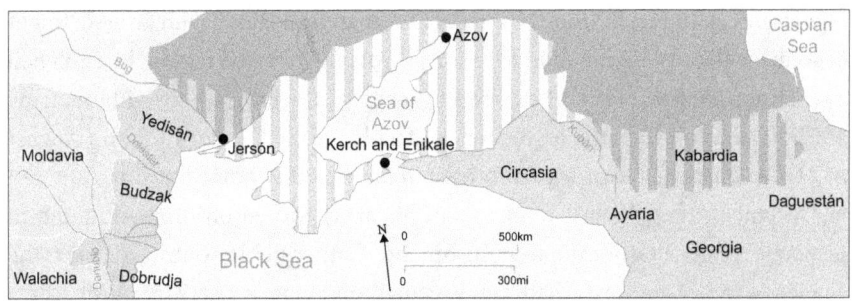

The stripped areas are territories gained by the Russian Empire by the end of Catherine the Great's reign

Map 2.5 The Treaty of Kuchuk-Kainardji.

door to future conflict was that in return for regaining control in Wallachia and Moldavia, the Sublime Porte had to recognize that Russia now gained the official right to act as the protector of all orthodox Christians who lived in her realm.[51]

In the midst of what should have been the greatest moment in the history of her regime, Catherine the Great had to contend with a widespread peasant rebellion that, in the end, required units from the regular army to be transferred from Poland and from the Ottoman campaign to suppress the unruly renegades. This rebellion, known to history as the Pugachev revolt, was a reaction to the ever-increasing power within the state and authority over the land of the gentry that the Romanovs encouraged, indeed legislated, in return for their support to the empire. While such a power arrangement ushered in the golden age of the nobility, the peasantry paid the price as the state slowly stripped away whatever freedoms they had remaining after their enserfment in 1649. Emelian Pugachev was a renegade Cossack from the Iaik host of the Don Cossacks who, after service in the imperial army, became disaffected toward the regime and before he was done had managed to create a movement composed of 30,000 followers whose host marauded the wide expanses that existed between the Volga River and the Urals in 1773–4. Political suppression and harsh economic conditions combined with initial support from peasants, Cossacks, and Old Believers fueled the movement. Moreover, Pugachev's claim that he was actually Peter III, Catherine's II assassinated husband, further contributed to the explosion that swept across the land. As their estates were being destroyed by the rioting masses, the gentry were terrorized and at the mercy of the brigands because the state had few institutions or troops in the region that could impose order in the midst of chaos.[52] Colonel I. I. Mikhek'son, a veteran of the recent Seven Years' War, the conflicts in Poland, and the recent Turkish War, was transferred to the area of the rebellion at the end of 1773 to take command of the situation. Using both regular forces and fresh troops from the Ottoman front along with an assortment of soldiers already stationed in garrisons across the affected region, he launched a strike across the Volga and chased Pugachev to Tsaritsyn where with his army of 5,000 men forced battle on the rebels at a place called Chyorny Yar on August 25, 1774. Pugachev escaped from his pursuers at this point but was captured in December after the last remnants of his army turned on him. Although in principle opposed to capital punishment, Catherine II, outraged over the challenge to her authority, had him executed on January 21, 1775, in Moscow's Red Square.[53] His death, however, did not end the memory of his movement nor end the state's reaction to the breakdown of authority that occurred across a vast section of the Russian Empire. After a brutal campaign of suppression against the inhabitants of the rebellious region, Catherine the Great would spend the rest of her reign seeking to establish local provinces that had garrisons and political leadership that could respond to any future such emergency. In addition, the rebellion served as a turning point in the relationship between the crown and the Cossacks. The policy of the Russian Empire heretofore toward the Cossacks would be to slowly but methodically reduce their privileges and turn them into another branch of the imperial army.[54]

Not surprisingly, Catherine the Great had not heard the last from the Ottoman Empire. Her decision to tour her newly won and annexed territory in Ukraine and Crimea in May and June 1787 combined with her many meetings with Austrian Emperor Joseph II sparked much consternation and discussion in Constantinople that centered on efforts to redress some of the more outrageous conditions of the Treaty of Kuchuk-Kainardji. Turkish advocates for rekindling conflict were further encouraged when the British and French lent their unconditional support to Abdul Hamid I, the reigning sultan. Such support convinced the sultan to demand that Russia return the Crimea, which Catherine II and her government interpreted as a *casus belli* and subsequently declared war on the Porte on August 19, 1787. Regardless of the ill timing of the sultan's conduct as he would also soon find himself at war with the Austrians, the Turks mobilized more rapidly and opened this conflict with an attack on the small Russian fortresses at Kinburn, which stood across from the Dnepr River estuary and was key to the Russian position in Crimea. Luckily for the tsarina, Alexander Suvorov was in command of this fortress and through his leadership the fort and its troops withstood assaults from the sea and from land that occurred throughout September 1787. The battle reached a climax on October 1 when the Ottoman's navy landed 5,000 marines and then supported their advance with seaborne gunfire through fifteen fortified defensive lines that approached Suvorov's central position. This advance took most of the day and in the late afternoon when the leading elements of this invasion had reached the effective range of the fortress's heavy guns, Suvorov gave the order to counterattack, thereby unleashing his artillery batteries. After the initial barrage, the general then ordered his troops to attack the Turks with fixed bayonets and the application of the cold steel in battle so shocked the Turks that they fell back in retreat. Meanwhile, Russian galleys had maneuvered themselves between the shoreline and the Ottoman ships, and while they took a beating, they obscured the Turkish view of the battlefield, which in turn compromised the naval support for the invading troops. As a result, the fortress at Kinburn held, the Russian strategic approach into Crimea was secure for the balance of the war, and Russian armed forces emerged victorious and confident.[55]

With Crimea secure much of 1788 was spent laying siege to the Ottoman Fortress at Ochakov on the mouth on the Dnieper River by two Russian armies, one composed of 37,00 troops under the command of the aging Rumiantsev and the other composed of 50,000 troops under the command of one of Catherine II's most loyal servitors, Gregory Aleksandrovich Potemkin. By this point in Catherine's reign Potemkin's power had eclipsed all other contenders at court as his connections to the tsarina were so close that he had been promoted to the rank of field marshal after the 1783 annexation of Crimea. At the same time, he was also made the president of the War College and shortly after that, Catherine II started referring to him as the commander in chief of the army. Further extending his power, Catherine appointed him governor-general over the territory won from the Turks, which the Russians referred to as New Russia. His power by the time of the outbreak of this second conflict with the Turks was unassailable; clearly G. A. Potemkin was one of Catherine II's most favorite generals and another of her Great Captains.[56] While he did his best to avoid a frontal assault on the Turkish positions at Ochakov, as winter rapidly approached he orchestrated an attack that combined elements of his nascent Black Sea's fleet with his army, which together inflicted heavy casualties on the Turks. On December 6, his forces finally conquered the fort and its garrison. Yet, at the same time in the winter of 1788 the Russians found themselves fighting alongside their Austrian allies in Moldavia. Fortunately for the Austrians, the Russian commander on-site was none other than A. V. Suvorov who came to the rescue of Russia's Habsburg allies after he marched his troops some 85 kilometers to reach the field of battle on September 11. What ensued was a decisive victory at the battle of Rymnik where Suvorov deployed his heavily outnumbered troops into battle squares that ultimately prevailed with the support of Austrian cavalry.

In the meantime, Potemkin conducted his own siege at the fortress of Bendery, which forced its capitulation on November 3, 1789, and further strengthened Russian power in Moldavia.[57]

Although the Russians had prevailed throughout the war, the Turks mustered one last effort to turn the conflict in their direction by first attempting to gain control of the Danube theater of operations and then launching simultaneous offensives in Crimea and Kuban. Their efforts were thwarted starting with their failure to contain the emerging Russian Black Sea fleet that supported the reduction of the last Turkish stronghold on the northeast shore at Anapa. Their efforts to assault the Kuban also failed so that by the late summer of 1790 all attention had shifted back to the Danubian theater where Field Marshal Potemkin had maneuvered troops through Bessarabia to surround and cut off the reportedly impenetrable Ottoman fortress at Izmail. When the assault started to waiver in late autumn, Potemkin had the good sense to call in Suvorov who stormed the fortress with 30,000 troops on December 11. The capture was especially brutal as over 26,000 Turkish defenders lost their lives by the time the survivors of Izmail capitulated. Still, the Turks would not surrender and continued the war into 1791, but after losing again in open battle at Machin on June 28, 1791, the cost of the conflict finally caught up with the Porte. Indeed, the scope of the French Revolution, the realization that the French monarchy was endangered, had transformed the international situation. Before getting any deeper into a conflict with the Ottomans all of Europe's powers shifted their attention and resources to defending against the growing French threat. Given the gravity of the French situation, the time had come for concluding the war in South Russia. What followed was the Treaty of Jassy that Potemkin largely negotiated. Signed on January 9, 1792, the treaty forced the Ottomans to formally recognize the annexation of Crimea, the ceding of Odessa and Ochakov to Russia, and that the Dniester River would be the new internationally recognized frontier between Russia and Europe. While the status of the Ottoman frontier in the eastern part of their empire did not change, the conclusion of this conflict also made clear that the Turks had lost the ability to spread their power any further into the Caucasus and Central Asia.[58]

In the midst of her second Turkish War, Catherine II also had to contend with what proved to be the final attempt by Sweden to win back some of the territory it had lost dating back to the reign of Peter the Great. In the summer of 1788, while the bulk of Russia's army was in the south fighting the Ottomans, Sweden's king Gustav III planned an invasion of the Gulf of Finland to land troops some 25 miles west of St. Petersburg at Oranienbaum, which would then serve as a launching point for an invasion on the Russian capital. Catherine the Great and her political cohort had deduced that Gustav was not only seeking the restoration of what is today Finland to his empire, but that he also wanted to win a war against Russia to consolidate his political power. His grandiose plan however was dependent on his navy commanding the Baltic Sea, which was soundly denied to him by Admiral Samuel Greig at the Battle of Hogland on July 6, 1788. This defeat prevented the Swedes from landing troops at Oranienbaum. Moreover, as the Russian navy gained control of the sea, the tsarina's army under the command of General Valintin Musin-Puskin beat back a Swedish invasion of Finland with 14,000 troops that had been hastily drafted into service. While Gustav III did not win a single battle during this war, he would continue to wage war against Russia in 1789 and in 1790. For Catherine II, this war was a nuisance tying down troops and more significantly preventing the Russians from transferring ships from the Baltic to the Black Sea where the Russian navy was always significantly weaker than their Ottoman adversaries. In addition to the major conflict with Turkey, the situation in the Polish-Lithuanian Commonwealth was headed toward the Second Partition, and the French Revolution had evolved into the chaos that would culminate with the Reign of Terror. Simply put, although Russian forces had landed in Swedish territory and had largely destroyed the Swedish fleet when Gustav III attempted an invasion at Vyborg in June 1790, Catherine the Great decided the war was not worth her time and effort. Meanwhile, Gustav III was running out of financial and material resources to continue the war and with the conflict never being popular in Sweden, he sued for peace on August 3, 1790. On Catherine II's orders, the offer was immediately accepted the warring sides agreed to a *status quo ante bellum* and they signed the Treaty of Varala on August 14, 1790.[59] Even with the Russian Empire engaged in a major conflict on its southern frontier, the Swedes could not prevail and they had fought their last war against the Romanovs.[60]

Despite defeating both Sweden and the Ottomans, there was no rest for the Russian army in the aftermath of these respective conflicts because of the situation in Poland/Lithuania. Reformist elements in Poland had had their fill of King Stanislaw Poniatowski's and his supporters' collaboration with the Russians. Largely inspired by the events in France, the reformers who were coalescing around Thaddeus Kosciusko drafted what became known as the May 3, 1791 constitution in an effort to enfranchise a larger part of the Polish body politic to represent the interests of the nation. Fearing an outbreak of radical Jacobinism, the Russians occupied Warsaw in the summer of 1792 forcing Kosciusko to flee his country's capital. This prompted the second partition of Poland, which formally occurred on January 23, 1793, when Russia and Prussian signed a treaty that revoked the Polish constitution of May 3, 1791, and provided for Russia and Prussia to each annex more territory. The Russians now moved their frontier 250 kilometers west and gained access to a direct route to the Balkans. These events paved the way for the third partition of Poland. Polish patriots, outraged by the high-handed way they were being treated by the Russians and the Prussians, rioted and rebelled against foreign occupation in the spring of 1794. Kosciusko took command of Polish forces and by the summer would claim to have 70,000 troops who were mostly armed peasants under his command. Both Catherine II and Prussian King Frederick William II were quick to mobilize troops to crush the rebellion, which they did largely under the command of General Suvorov. After a summer of campaigning, Suvorov would first defeat Polish patriots at Maciejowice on October 10, where Kosciusko allegedly fell off his horse and proclaimed *Finis Poloniae*. Nevertheless, the rebels who held the bridgehead into Warsaw at Praga failed to get the message and they held out while Suvorov united his army with Prussian forces under the command of General Johann

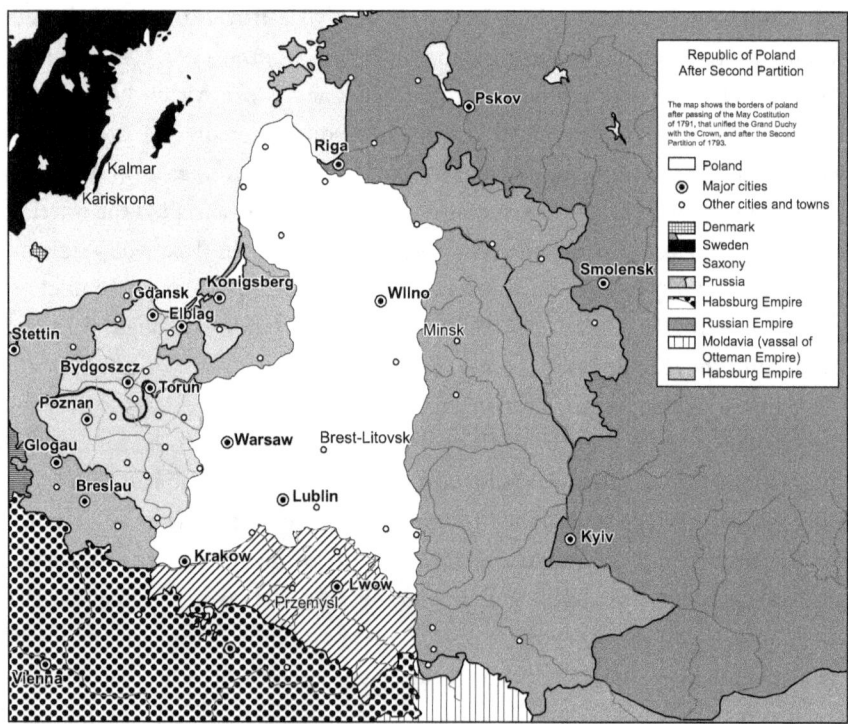

Map 2.6 The Second Partition of Poland.

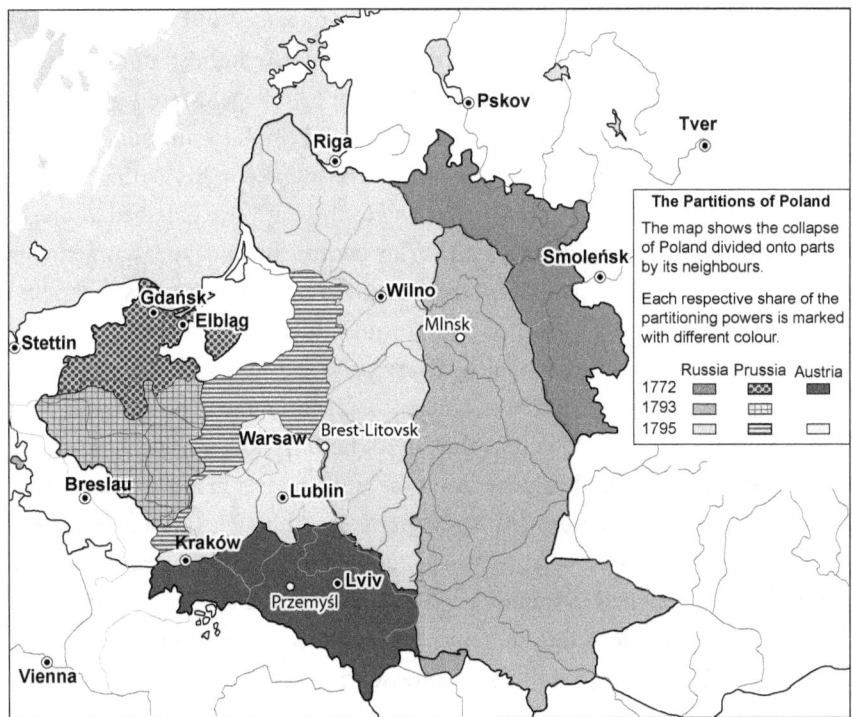

Map 2.7 The Third Partition of Poland.

Fersen before Warsaw and launched a brutal and bloody assault against the Polish position. After enduring repeated cavalry strikes on October 24, 1795, the Poles capitulated after losing thousands of their men. While the insurrection ended at this time, the third partition did not occur until January 15, 1797, when Austria, Prussia, and Russia signed an agreement that formally removed Poland from the map of Europe for the following 123 years.[61]

The Russian Way of War

By the end of her reign, Catherine the Great had built a military that had delivered victory after victory in almost every conflict that she fought. From these experiences a Russian way of war emerged that would be refined and reformed throughout the rest of imperial history and beyond. She profited from the organizational, administrative, and operational genius of her military leaders and their success resulted in them being identified as Great Captains. Their experiences stretched from the Seven Years' War until the early stages of the Napoleonic epoch. The legacy of P. A. Rumiantsev and G. A. Potemkin as commanders of the operational army and then as administrators of newly conquered territory inscribed them in the army's heritage. More significantly, the work and teachings of A. V. Suvorov provided the Russian military forces with ideas about doctrine and training that were adopted in his lifetime and are arguably a part of Russian military thinking to this day.[62] He emerged as one of the leading commanders in the Russian army because he came from comparably humble noble origins, which meant that he moved through the ranks slowly and only after distinguishing himself as a successful battlefield commander.[63] In 1795 after a half a century of distinguished service to the Romanovs, a career that started before the Seven Years' War, Suvorov was considered to be both eccentric and innovative because of his thoughts on soldiering and his risk-taking on the battlefield. He expressed his ideas about the military arts in a manuscript now known as *The Art of Victory* (*Nauka Pobezhda*). Although he came of age at the height of the period of eighteenth century when linear tactics and intensive troop training designed to impose rigid discipline prevailed, The *Art of Victory* inculcated mobility, flexibility, initiative, and agility into the operational conduct of the Imperial Army.[64] He further expressed his now famous triad of speed, assessment, and forceful hitting power, encouraging his troops to move fast, size up situations quickly and accurately, and then push headlong into an attack. He did not fear helter-skelter formations if they meant that his soldiers seized the initiative and chased the enemy in relentless pursuit. The *Art of Victory*, therefore, provided the Russian army with the operational guidance that resulted in it defeating its host of widely different enemy armies.[65]

Perhaps more importantly, early in his career, Suvorov witnessed the difficulties Frederick the Great had replacing combat losses because of the high level of training he imposed on his troops. Suvorov, allowing for the lower educational level of Russian peasants, decided that training in his army had to be above all else comprehensible for her soldiers. The root of his training method started with the knowledge that he had to transform raw, uneducated recruits into fighting troops when they were still digesting that they would most likely never see their home village again. The genius behind the training that these disgruntled men encountered was Suvorov's insistence on building high morale and good health. The process started with him deemphasizing corporal punishment and prescribing a work routine that encourage soldiers to pay attention to their health and diet while providing adequate living conditions. Breaking from Petrine practices and challenging tradition, he ordered his officers to see to the well-being of their troops before they saw to their own needs. First and at a minimum, he prescribed that soldiers have a secure place to rest, had hot meals including vegetables, learned to boil water before consumption, and that proper field sanitation had to be considered and provided for wherever the army built a camp at the end of a march. The enforcement of these basic health standards reduced mortality rates while increasing the combat readiness of troops. While lax discipline could not be tolerated, officers were expected to build a rapport with their soldiers that would not only strengthen their self-confidence but also teach that everyone from their subaltern to the tsar would take care of their needs. Their training routine must have been physically demanding because under Suvorov's tutelage Russian soldiers developed the reputation of being able to march long distances rapidly and then seamlessly maneuver onto the battlefield. In addition, this well-lubricated machine was trained to engulf the battlefield with well-aimed infantry fire; Russian soldiers were also taught to unleash their fury on the enemy with fixed bayonets as the brutal shock of a confrontation with cold steel usually resulted in the flight of enemy troops.[66]

Placing such emphasis on soldiers and soldiering served the Russian military establishment well throughout its history and therefore represents the core of Russia's style of war-fighting. The military, however, needed endless support from all other aspects of Russian society. Most important for the future was the training of officers. While its eighteenth-century custom was to provide such training only for the children of the nobility, embedded in their preparation as future officers was a military education that became more rigorous as the century progressed. Empress Anna Ivanovna did indeed create Cadet Corps academies to reward and generate noble support for her throne. The schools, once created, took on a life of their own as they expanded their curriculum to encourage the development of soldiers who also had the overall education to become critical thinkers. As a result, by the beginning of the nineteenth century, the Russians had a military educational system in place that could and would be modernized and expanded to continue to train officers who could understand the growing challenges and complexities of the modern battlefield. And, while education of officers and training of soldiers became a vital part of the growing and continued success of the military, all rulers of Russia in the eighteenth century understood the need to support and encourage continued growth of the empire's economic infrastructure. Without factories to make weapons and munitions, there would be no army and no empire. A. V. Suvorov's legacy was as the person who, after Peter the Great, contributed the most succinct and practical ideas for how to train and use Russian troops. Through his experiences as a commander of troops in the field and in battle, he further developed his ideas into a military doctrine about the training and supplying of troops so they had complete confidence in their mission. This philosophy became the key to success in times of war. When the system was working, the power of the state's bureaucracy and economy provided the army with the rest of its needs so that it could wage victorious wars. Because of the success of armed forces at the time of Catherine II's death, there could be little question that the Russians had developed a military system that had fulfilled the expectations of Peter the Great.

Conclusion

When Catherine II died of a stroke on November 6, 1796, the accomplishments of her military had so strengthened the Russian Empire that its permeance as a European power was beyond question. Her successful reign was unquestionably a product of her own strength and authority over all matters domestic and international. Her strategic successes, however, represented a continuation of Romanov policy that had existed, in some cases since the family came to power. After all, the first two Romanov tsars, Mikhail and Alexis, constantly waged wars with the Polish-Lithuanian Commonwealth. This cycle of conflict continued until, using the power of her armies to back her demands, Catherine II, in partnership with the Austrians and the Prussians, partitioned the Commonwealth off the map of Europe. Just as significant, by the end of the eighteenth century and, after waging another cycle of long continuous conflict with the Ottomans, the imperial Russian army had gained complete control of the northern laterals of the Black Sea as well as the Sea of Azov. They had driven the Ottomans out of Ukraine so that the western boundary between the two empires rested in Moldova while also applying pressure on the Sublime Porte's eastern flank, in the Caucasus. In addition, the collapse of the Commonwealth combined with the Ottomans losses resulted in the Cossack hosts finally brokering a deal with the Romanovs that gave them special status as the "special forces" of the Russian Empire. This along with the collapse of Crimean Khanate brought an end to the perennial problem of Russian settlements on this frontier living in fear of the next raid from nomadic steppe warriors. Of course, the Ottoman Empire still existed and almost every other Romanov tsar would fight a war against them. The success of Russian arms in the eighteenth century therefore transformed the strategic picture between the two empires for the rest of their respective histories because the Pontic steppe had finally been tamed.

Catherine the Great's reign is often first thought of in terms of her desire to "enlighten" Russia with the ideas and customs of the West in an effort to create a path for her empire to be recognized as an equal by all of the European powers. She largely accomplished this task not through any attempt to "modernize" Russia as much as she managed to cultivate a military establishment that won great victories on the battlefield. Her greatest military victories were against the Ottomans but her shrewd diplomacy, especially concerning her relationship with Austria and Prussia, resulted in a stabilization of Russia's western frontiers after the final partition of Poland. It was also because of her military that during her reign Sweden became a nonfactor as a Baltic power. Russia did indeed emerge from the eighteenth century with an empire backed by a military establishment that had the size and resources to dominate on the battlefield as well as in the higher politics of the age. While never a dominating economic power, Russia's society had developed to the point where it could muster the economic resources needed to maintain and to continue to expand the size of its empire. Yet challenges still lay in front of the empire. The Ottomans may have been weakened by the rise of the Russian Empire in the eighteenth century but the Sublime Porte still existed and, more importantly, still controlled the vital maritime entrance into the Black Sea. Conflict would exist between the Ottomans and the Romanovs until both empires disappeared from the map of Europe after the First World War. The more immediate concern, however, was the impact the French Revolution was having on European power relationships. Catherine was one of the first to realize that none of Europe's monarchs could embrace any aspect of French liberal politics without compromising their absolute authority. When the course of the French Revolution produced Napoleon Bonaparte, every European military establishment had to rise to the occasion. Some did better than others but, in the end, the Russian army marched all the way to Paris, which proved to be the crowning achievement of Peter the Great's military system that had been refined, reformed, and made supreme by his successors.

3

From the Wars of the French Revolution to the Crimean Disaster

While replete with fits and starts, Russia's eighteenth-century military history in every aspect from education, training, supply, to actual war fighting can best be assessed as being tremendously successful. Peter the Great did lay the foundation for the creation and development of a military system that provided his successors with the capabilities to emerge as the dominant power on the continent after the Russian army defeated Napoleon. Their eighteenth-century victories had been so complete that Sweden would be reduced to the small Scandinavian state that it remains to this day and Poland would be removed from the map of Europe altogether. Moreover, while Austria and Prussia would both at one point or another challenged the empire's security, Russian arms contained both threats to their realm. One of the central accomplishments of both Peter the Great and Catherine the Great resulted in the spread of Russian power not only to the West and North but to the shores of the Black Sea. Developing the capabilities to become the master of the battlefield set the stage for Russia's emergence as Europe's only superpower after the defeat of Napoleon. A huge price however was paid for the state to emerge with the most powerful military establishment in the world in 1815. In the aftermath of Peter the Great's reign much of Russia's economic development, especially after the rise of Catherine the Great, was based on military needs. The question of state authority in relation to Russian society also became a factor in the rise of the military in domestic affairs. Politicians became increasingly dependent on the support of factions within the imperial guard's officer corps to gain and remain in power. Their power within the civil-military establishment could not be questioned even when Paul I sought to compromise their authority during his short reign. Regardless of the strengths and weaknesses of the Romanovs' military system, it decisively rose to the occasion when Napoleon conquered the European continent, not only ousting the French from Russian after the 1812 invasion but liberating Europe and ultimately occupying France itself before order was restored to the continent at the Congress of Vienna in 1815. Without the power of Russia's armed forces, this history of Europe would have occurred in a much different fashion.

At the same time that the Russians defeated every other Western military power in the eighteenth century and conquered the French at the beginning of the nineteenth century, they also confronted and contained a powerful and menacing enemy to their south. Every nineteenth-century Romanov ruler except for Alexander III fought a war against the Turks and, with the exception of the Crimean War, prevailed thereby extending the strength of their state to the shores of the Black Sea. Thanks to these numerous conflicts being framed around a political/diplomatic series of events known as the "Eastern Question," the struggles with the Ottoman Empire became well chronicled for students of history.[1] Equally significant as the defeats of Sweden and Poland for the history of the empire, Russia's military developed specialized means to defeat the hostile forces that existed on her southern and eastern frontiers. During the first half of the nineteenth century this conflict centered on the Caucasus because the Russian, the Ottoman, and the Persian Empires found themselves in competition for control over this strategically vital territory. Developing an adroit mix of irregular forces, largely Cossacks, and building fortresses that together formed defensive barriers, the Romanovs slowly developed the capability first to contain the Turks and then to maintain a security zone against all other opposition to their growing empire. From these zones the Russians learned to implement unconventional means to defeat their foes because conventional forces—large disciplined troop fighting in linear formations—were fat targets for the irregular forces engaged in the nineteenth-century version of asymmetrical warfare. Necessity, therefore, resulted in the Russian military becoming experts in unconventional means of warfare. While it took half a century to develop the different types of forces needed to simultaneously fight Western armies and Ottoman armies, possessing the combination of conventional and unconventional capabilities gave the appearance that nothing could defeat Russian armed forces at the time of Catherine II's death.

At the beginning of the nineteenth century and especially after 1815 Russian policymakers could count on the strength of the Russian military to confront and contain any challenge from the West. Moreover, such military strength factored into Imperial dreams and designs aimed at creating further opportunities for the Romanovs to push the limits of their realm beyond the Caucasus into Central Asia, Siberia, and the Far East. While the eighteenth-century rulers had ordered what turned out to be isolated campaigns in the Caucasus and Central Asia, a systematic policy of conquest was orchestrated for these two regions first by Nicholas I and then by Alexander II. As a wide assortment of hostile elements were always present, the nineteenth century proved to be the period when Romanov power would spread across the rest of the Eurasian landmass. If the overall aim of the Imperial project was to replace the Mongol Empire, then by the end of the nineteenth century the Romanovs could claim success! Without question the tsars built their empire only after they created a military establishment that became well versed in fighting both conventional and unconventional styles of warfare. When the Russian army marched into Paris in 1814 it had reached a height of success and glory that it would not match again until the Red Army marched into Berlin in 1945. The army continued its conquest by first subjugating the Caucasus, then defeating the Turks in a decisive conflict in 1828–9, and ultimately emerging as the gendarme of Europe during the reign of Nicholas I. Yet, for all of its accomplishments and its splendor and glory, the empire let itself become irreparably weak by the 1850s. This chapter examines how the Russian Empire transformed from being the European superpower that defeated Napoleon, one of the greatest military leaders in all of history, to being soundly defeated by a coalition of European powers on their own territory, the Crimean Peninsula in 1855–6. Such a dramatic collapse of Russian military power had not occurred since Peter the Great's reforms and offers students of this history a cautionary tale about how remaining static in a dynamically changing world leads to catastrophe.

The Military Reforms of Paul I

Unlike every political succession that occurred in the eighteenth century, there was no question who would succeed Catherine the Great upon her death. While rumors persisted about her son's pedigree, no one questioned the legitimacy of the long-serving and allegedly long-suffering son Paul who became Paul I upon her death. Regardless of the level of abuse—real or imaginary—Catherine the Great and Paul I were alienated from each other his entire adult life. As a young man Paul I aspired to be a military leader but Catherine saw to it that he had no influence, let alone basic mentoring in military affairs. Her conduct toward her son supports the rumor that he was not her son at all![2] When Paul was old enough, he fled the capital and established his permanent residence at Gatchina, a country estate some 70 kilometers southwest of St. Petersburg.

At Gatchina Paul ruminated over the shortcomings of Catherine's army and, without much education or training, concluded that its major deficiency rested in the realm of organization and discipline.³ Paul considered the Russian army to be an institution that depended on connections and wealth as opposed to skill, knowledge, and capabilities. Catherine II's court, according to Paul, had become too relaxed and therefore imposed little or no discipline over itself, the army, indeed the entire government especially in the last decade of her reign.⁴ Much to the chagrin of the officers who, although aged, had defeated the Prussians in the Seven Years' War, Paul I idolized Frederick the Great and therefore viewed the Prussian army as a model for the Russian army to adopt in matters of order and discipline.⁵ Once Paul came to power, he imposed reforms on his army based on the adoption of the Prussian idea and way of war as he understood it. Paul I therefore followed in the footsteps of his purported father Peter III and Empress Anna Ivanova. All three believed that the Prussian way of war imposed order and discipline on the army that translated into success on the battlefield. For Paul the process started with the standardized uniforms and the adoption of precision drill until the soldiers mastered the manual of arms and the officers learned to conduct slavishly mechanical maneuvers that were always designed to defeat an enemy with overwhelming aimed fire from all weapons available.⁶ Ignoring that the Imperial Russian army of the late eighteenth century was, if not the best, then one of the best fighting forces in Europe, Paul became fixated on questions of appearance and decorum on the parade ground during peacetime drills and maneuvers. In the short run his focusing on non-warfighting tasks compromised morale, thereby reducing the overall military effectiveness of the army. In the long run, Paul's insistence on appearances of the troops especially in ceremonial pass and reviews in front of the tsar became an embedded tradition within the military much to its detriment long after his reign.⁷ The young tsar had chosen to impose foreign ideas and customs on military policy(s), which, in the end, would alienate him from the imperial guard's officers who were the power brokers at court. This did not bode well for his long-term future of his reign.

The great debate in military circles during the reign of Paul was about whether Russia had developed its own native military tradition from the time of Peter the Great or whether it would remain dependent on importing its traditions from others. Trying to resolve questions on everything from the development of tactics to the equipment used on the battlefield caused much friction between the army and Paul I. Paul I, often portray as either erratic, irrational, and sometimes as simply being mad, nonetheless persistently applied his policies if for no other reason than to compromise the privileged status of the guard's officers and their regiments within the army that his mother has used to establish Russia as a dominant military power. Rooted in Paul I's military reforms were also his attempts to impose political reform on Russia. He rejected the power of the guard's officers because by the time he came to power they rarely saw combat. Instead the officers of the guard had become the praetorian guard whose main function was to defend and guard the tsarina and her capital from all internal opposition. By Paul I's reign there could be no worse fate for a guard's officer than to be posted in some remote region, away from the crown where they would be forgotten in the empire's backwaters. He developed this disdain for the leading elements of the imperial army during his long reign as tsarevich. Just like Peter the Great, he prepared for the day he became tsar by first building up a loyal cohort of officers and soldiers outside of the capital. Thus, Gatchina became his base of power where he composed a force that included 19 officers, 2,300 soldiers, and 12 guns. He also had support units of jaegers, artillery, and cavalry. Most if not all of the officers were Baltic Germans or Prussians who defected to the Russian army. The soldiers tended to be deserters from the regular army who found a safe haven in being Gatchina soldiers. Everyone adopted Prussian style uniforms. Paul I also created a new rank and proclaimed himself a "General-Admiral" as he viewed himself, like Peter the Great, to be an expert in naval affairs. Paul I sought to recreate Frederick the Great's idea of Potsdam at Gatchina.[8] Gatchina therefore made the guard's officer understand that it represented the place from where their new tsar would seek to weaken their privileged status within the army and at court.

When Paul came to power the first thing he did was bring his Gatchina corps to St. Petersburg to serve the role of his praetorian guard and displace the imperial guard's officers from their political influence at court.[9] This was his way of taking control and imposing his thoughts and ideas over the entire army. The Guard Corps still remained an exclusive cadre within the army, but Paul I reasserted that the best path to becoming an officer was to earn it via service and meritorious promotion. By 1799 Paul I had expanded the guard's corps to 14,000 officers with its soldiers organized into four infantry regiments, one jaeger battalion, three cavalry regiments, and one artillery battalion. Exacerbating his relations with the guard's officers, he forced them to wear Prussian-style uniforms and to endure the appointment of Gatchina trained disciplinarians as new instructors in drill and especially in the manual of arms. Longtime veterans found these reforms to be an insult to the army's traditions. Continuing his Prussianization of the army, in 1796 Paul I ordered the implementation of

Prussian-style field regulations on the cavalry and infantry. He wrote similar regulations for the artillery in 1797. Achieving excellence through the adoption of Prussian military practices required the type of training and precision that could be obtained through persistent parade ground drill; rigid discipline and precision became the key to success with Paul's military system.

Paul's reforms and new regulations did much to undermine the traditions and the customs of the military that were first defined in Peter the Great's Ustav of 1715 and further refined in the Catherine era Ustav of 1763. The aim of Paul's training regime was to create an army that was trained to form into battle squares to concentrate his forces and have them able to fight offensive and defensive battles. The great Captains—Rumiantsev, Potemkin, and especially Suvorov—trained their armies to have much greater flexibility to maneuver according to the situation that confronted them when in battle. Despite his Prussian proclivities, Paul did believe in one-time honored Russian tradition. As a part of the concentration of maximin force, his troops were trained to shock the enemy by brandishing the cold steel of their bayonets when they charged out of their battle squares. Besides training the cavalry to act as the eyes and ears of the army when it marched, he also ordered his mounted troops to safeguard the security of the army flanks when it was engaged in operations. To his credit, Paul sought to simplify the army's persistent logistical challenges by eliminating baggage trains in favor of loading soldiers up with individual supplies and creating resupply depots along their path of operations. To further control the cost of the military, he reduced its overall size from 250,000 infantry men to 201,000. By the time the size of the cavalry, artillery, and irregular forces (Cossack) were added to the total Paul had an army of 450,000 men making the military half the size it had been at the time of Peter the Great's death. At the same time, he reduced the size of the cavalry at the expense of the light horse units that were indispensable in steppe warfare in favor of the Prussian style heavy cavalry. It boiled down to this ... Paul demanded that his army train to provide disciplined and overwhelming fire at a concentrated point when ordered to do so. In an effort to further strengthen the force of Russian firepower, Paul I took an interest in artillery and concluded that he should remove field pieces from army regiments and created eight separate field artillery regiments. Importantly, and as a direct result of Paul I's decision to redeploy his artillery pieces, Russia's artillery was equivalent to anything Napoleon could muster when he invaded Russia.[10] Despite having enough artillery when Napoleon turned on Russia, Paul I nonetheless remained determined to train his army to fight like the Prussians did in the late eighteenth century. Instead of preparing the army for maximum flexibility given the variety of enemies Paul faced, Paul's military reforms caused his army to return to the era of linear tactics that had died a slow death in the second half of the eighteenth century.

According to Bruce Menning, Paul's reorganization of the operational army turned its administrative clock back fifty years right before the empire was going to face the supreme challenge of the wars of the French Revolution.[11] One of Paul's most basic shortcomings was, however, he never experienced combat so he did not understand that there was no direct link between looking smart and performing military drills well to achieving success in battle. Perhaps worse, Paul would not listen to nor take advice from any of Catherine II's military leaders. Not even the great A. V. Suvorov could persuade Paul to reconsider his ill thought-out plans. When the impact of his new tsar's reforms became clear the old Generalissimo allegedly commented: "We have always beaten the Prussians … Why imitate them now?" Such sentiment got the general exiled to his estate in Smolensk province until Paul I needed him in Russia's initial encounters with the French military after Napoleon came to power.[12] Meanwhile, he became obsessed with minutiae hence he spent two to three hours a day on parade grounds demanding perfection in the presentation of his troops in uniforms. Indeed, his agitation over appearance evolved into the tsar's biggest problem with his officers, which was his making them wear Prussian-style uniforms. They were tight through their mid-section. They did not want to tie their hair into uncomfortable wigs. They especially did not want to learn the minutiae of Prussian-style drill.[13] The tsar also failed to understand that the more simple thinking Russian peasants would have a much harder time mastering Prussian-style drill, especially the manual of arms. The Gatchina spirit that came to symbolize the tsar's insistence on drill, parades, uniforms, maneuvers, awards, and punishment came to symbolize everything that was wrong with Paul in the minds of Catherine's favorites. It did live on, however, until the end of the Romanov dynasty in the form of excessive parade ground drills becoming the norm of the imperial army's training routine. Without question, Paul I saw to it that military parades became synonymous with the concept of tsarist power.[14]

What Paul I missed, indeed all of Europe may have failed to comprehend, was the impact of how the French revolutionary idea and then the revolution itself would transform military forces from dynastic to national armies. As this transformation occurred the Russian army, already considered a powerful force because of its numerous eighteenth-century victories, remained an army first and foremost loyal to its tsar and his dynasty. Its backbone consisted of serfs who had been chosen by lot to serve at the desire of the tsar/tsarina and his/her dynasty and noble officers who saw their service as a means to achieve greater status in Russia. Its cadre was composed of nobles with the largest portion of its leadership cohort emanating from the guard's regiment milieu. This milieu was fostered in elite military schools that had been created in the first part of the century to reward the nobility for their service. Service to the state was their *raison d' etre* especially after 1762 when service became voluntary, their need for additional income not provided by their estates notwithstanding. This was not the case for the bulk of the empire's population as they borne the burden of conscription.[15] While the lower classes had to provide recruits, taxes, or service directly to the state, the nobility chose military service because after the reforms of Peter the Great, serving in the military had become far more prestigious than working in the civil service.[16]

Paul I Napoleonic Challenge

Paul's angst toward his mother over all matters but especially military did not change that his empire still faced the same strategic threats that had confronted Russia since the Romanovs came to power. In addition, the French Revolution's threat to the established order, especially after the 1793 execution of Louis XVI, transformed the strategic environment in Europe forever. At the time of his accession to the throne, his greatest threat was perceived to come from the Ottomans who had not at all given up in their struggle against the Russian tsars. Because the threat from the south remained the same, Paul understood and therefore prepared for war against the Ottomans as well as with the nomadic hordes that still might support the Turks. One advantage that Paul I had over his predecessor in the perpetual struggle with the Sublime Porte was the Cossacks had largely pledged their allegiance to St. Petersburg and they made for the perfect soldier in this type of warfare. At the same time that Paul came to power, the excesses of the French Revolution had reached a low point, which in fact proved to be a calm before the storm, better known as Napoleon, swept across Europe. To this end, all Europeans kept an eye on France out of concern that the liberal radicalism of French politics might infect the rest of the continent and challenge all established authority. For Paul, the potential threat of the French Revolution meant he could not ignore that Russia might find itself engaged in a military struggle on his western frontier. The challenges of Russian foreign relations made it imperative for them to have the flexibility within the military establishment to confront both the Ottomans and the Europeans, perhaps simultaneously.[17]

Paul's efforts to reorganize the army and the state's bureaucracy along with his Prussianization of the military not only alienated the highest ranking members of the officer corps from the throne but also left large numbers of the nobility disaffected from the crown. At the time of Catherine the Great's death, Russia was in the midst of committing 50,000 troops to the anti-French cause. Not much had been done to formalize any aspect of these plans before the empress's death and, as is well known, Paul not only sought to distance himself from all of his mother's policies and practices, he also intended to cut back on all military spending as the Russian state had a bad habit of overspending its revenues. Paul's initial policy toward the French Revolution, therefore, was to distance Russia from Western entanglements while he reformed his military to de-Catherinized Russia. Perhaps in keeping with the irrational character of his foreign involvements, Paul became interested in fighting the forces of the French Revolution when they occupied Malta. Not only did the French seizure of Malta lead to a Russian navy operating in the Mediterranean, it also resulted in Paul I joining the Second Coalition that was struggling to contain the French army in the aftermath of Napoleon's first major military victories in Italy. The threat of the French Revolution subsequently afforded Paul I the support necessary to pursue what can best be described as his erratic foreign policy.[18] This latitude allowed him to withdraw from the anti-French cause in 1800 even though the consequence of this action was to alienate Russia from the Austrians along with most other peoples across Central and Northern Europe. His actions in the Baltic had the empire on the verge of war with the British. The irony of his shift in foreign policy meant that for a moment Paul I became the only Romanov to foster harmonious relations with the Ottoman Empire as both sought to contain the spreading influence of the French.[19]

The October 17, 1797, Treaty of Campo Formio acknowledged French gains in Italy and concluded the wars of the first coalition, with only Great Britain still at war with France. Yet mistrust prevailed especially between the French and the Austrians. Tensions were on the upswing when, on his way to his ill-fated invasion of Egypt in June 1798, Napoleon bombarded and invaded Malta when Grand Master Ferdinand von Hompesch zu Bolheim refused to cooperate with the French. In response to the occupation, many of the Knights dispersed and some ended up in St. Petersburg where later in the year they elected Paul I as Grand Master of the Knights of Malta. While perhaps odd to elect a Russian tsar to such a position, there was a history of relations between Russia and Malta that dated back to the reign of Peter the Great. French policy toward Malta combined with the persistent request of the Austrians for assistance in their effort to contain the revolutionary regime finally persuaded Paul I to join the newly forming second coalition in May 1798.[20]

After joining the coalition, Paul divided his military forces and simultaneously engaged them in three separate theaters of operations. First, he sent an expeditionary corps under the command of General Johann Hermann to operate with the English in Holland. Then he sent a force to Italy to operate with the Austrians under the command of Field Marshal Suvorov. And last, he sent a fleet from the Black Sea into the Mediterranean to operate with the British and Turks under the command of Admiral Fedor Ushakov.[21] While Ushakov sailed to the Ionian Islands, his ships also participated in the blockade and siege of Corfu, which capitulated on March 3, 1799. Then he went up the West Coast of Italy and seized Brindisi and imposed a blockade on Ancona. Russian sea power was at its height in the Mediterranean and, while the Turks did not like it, the operations of the Russian navy at this time largely contributed to the period of good relations enjoyed by the Turks and the Russians during the Second Coalition.[22] Meanwhile, General Hermann found himself in command of a composite force of 17,000 troops who, while ill equipped, landed in Holland in September 1799. They had formed up with 31,000 British troops outside of Plymouth, UK, and then landed with the intention of dislodging French troops stationed in the village of Bergen. But the Russian and British forces failed to support each other and Hermann ended up a prisoner of the French. In November, the Russians and the British left the Netherlands to the French, but the seeds for cooperation between the two powers had been planted.[23]

The final operation in this phase of the war was the epic campaign of Suvorov in the Alps. The story of Suvorov and Paul I begins with the general's self-imposed exile to demonstrate his rejection of the tsar's efforts to reform the army in the period following Catherine the Great's death. Exhibiting his rational side, and perhaps responding to pressure from his new allies, in February 1799 the tsar reinstated Suvorov and gave him command of an army. Not surprisingly, Suvorov, ever loyal to the crown, accepted his rehabilitation and followed his tsar's orders to lead a Russian army into Central Europe. Paul I gave Suvorov carte blanche to operate as he saw fit … so respected was the Field Marshal for his leadership and command of troops in battle. The Austrians, as Russia's major ally at the start of the campaign, proved of little value as Suvorov intended to fight his own style of war, which meant he was going to fight a hard-hitting mobile war. By April 1799 he had at his command a 50,000-troop combined Russian army and he would use it to defeat some of the French republic's top generals, such as General Barthelemy Louis Scherer and General Jacques Entienne Macdonald, and regain for the Austrians what they had lost in 1796–7. Napoleon, however, never matched his skills against the Russian Field Marshall as the Corsican was busy getting chased out of Egypt at the time of Suvorov's Italian campaign.

On April 16, 1799, Suvorov put the French army to flight at Cassano. This victory resulted in the city of Milan opening its gates to the Russians the next day and the defeat and disintegration of the Sicilian Republic. Suvorov now intended to invade France proper by moving his forces through the Po Valley, but Sheer was replaced by General Jean-Victor Moreau who redrew his forces into Piedmont and started to receive reinforcements via Switzerland. When Suvorov advanced on Turin, Moreau withdrew into Genoa effectively meaning that the French had abandoned northern Italy. Meanwhile, Macdonald who had been operating in the south of Italy advanced north so Suvorov decided that he could use his advantage of controlling interior lines of transportation and communication to defeat each army in detail. Now based in Alessandria, Suvorov, in command of 34,000 primarily Russian soldiers, started marching late in the evening of June 4, 1799. Over the next thirty-six hours his troops marched 85 kilometers to engage in what turned into a four-day battle on the river Trebbia. The Russians routed Macdonald and Moreau's effectiveness was largely compromised as it was needed to support the remnants of Macdonald's forces. As both sides suffered heavy casualties, there was a lull in the action that resulted in Suvorov's next victim, General Barthelemy Catherine Joubert, who marched troops into northern Italy in an effort to support the army of the Republic. Joubert met his fate at Trebbia on August 4, 1799, when an allied force bottled up the French. With help from the Austrians under the command of General Michael Friedrich von Melas in reducing the right flank of the French, the Russians poured into the town in the late afternoon.[24]

All forces were exhausted after this engagement, but in the following days Suvorov grew weary of Austrian excuses and shortcomings and proclaimed he was breaking away from the Habsburgs and taking on the French by himself in Switzerland. In Switzerland General A. M. Rimskii-Korsakov waited for the Marshal with 30,000 troops. This meant that Suvorov had to cross the Alps to join forces with Rimskii-Korsakov. Lacking his own cavalry to do reconnaissance work, he followed the Austrian instructions to take the shortest route possible across the Alps. But this left him on the wrong side of Lake Zurich with no good roads to link up with Rimskii-Korsakov. The march across the Alps was fraught with transporting equipment, not to mention men through rugged mountainous terrain, all while being confronted with heavy French resistance. Meanwhile, on the other side of the lake, Rimskii-Korsakov was confronted with an aggressive

French army under the command of General Andre Massena. Suvorov then was faced with a twelve-day march across intersecting valleys and the forbidding Kinzing and Pragel Passes. This all ended badly for the Russians as Rimskii-Korsakov lost 18,000 men and 26 guns in one of Russia's worst defeats of the eighteenth century on September 15 near Zurich.

Suvorov's troops now exhausted and running out of everything from bullets to rations marched through the Moutatal Valley reaching Glarus on September 20, 1799. From Glarus the Russians marched into the Panixer Pass where in blinding snow they fought a bitter rear guard action that resulted in the loss of over 200 men and all of their heavy guns. They would emerge in the valley of the upper Rhine on September 26 at llanz. On October 7 he finally caught up with the remnants of Rimskii-Korsakov forces at Lindau. Twelve days later he established winter quarters in southern Bavaria. Once military operations halted in the fall of 1799, Paul I recalled Suvorov and promoted him to the rank of generalissimo for his service in northern Italy and Switzerland.[25] Suvorov's Italian campaign revealed that the Russian army could more than hold its own against the French showing that Suvorov's determined tactics could prevail against a nationally inspired army. The key to it all was that flexibility and expediency governed Suvorov's conduct—he never feared switching from the offensive to the defensive as the situation required. He exuded confidence unlike any of his peers in all of his endeavors. When he decided to march to the river Trebbia, his army covered some 53 miles in a day and a half and then immediately engaged in a victorious battle. This operation confirmed his teachings about the value of speed and mobility, and most importantly, it proved that Suvorov's training and command practices, that is, his making sure his troops knew him on a personal level, translated into good morale throughout his forces, which in turn meant that Russian troops were ready to follow the commands of their leader. In addition, with his 12,000 men, he was outnumbered by the 19,000 French troops, but his bold plan, combined with the momentum of his movement, demonstrated that a well commanded army could overwhelm superior numbers.[26] Suvorov did not waste his reserves and proved masterful in the timing of unleashing his Cossacks when he needed to intimidate his enemy. Although he would die in May 1800, his legacy as one of Russia's greatest military leaders prevails to this day.

Paul's wars of the French Revolution ended with the collapse of the Second Coalition in 1800. He withdrew into Russia in possession of an army whose strength was in its system of conscription, training, and organization. Russian soldiers were physically strong and capable of responding to a way of war that required them to be flexible in everything that they did. They remained intensely

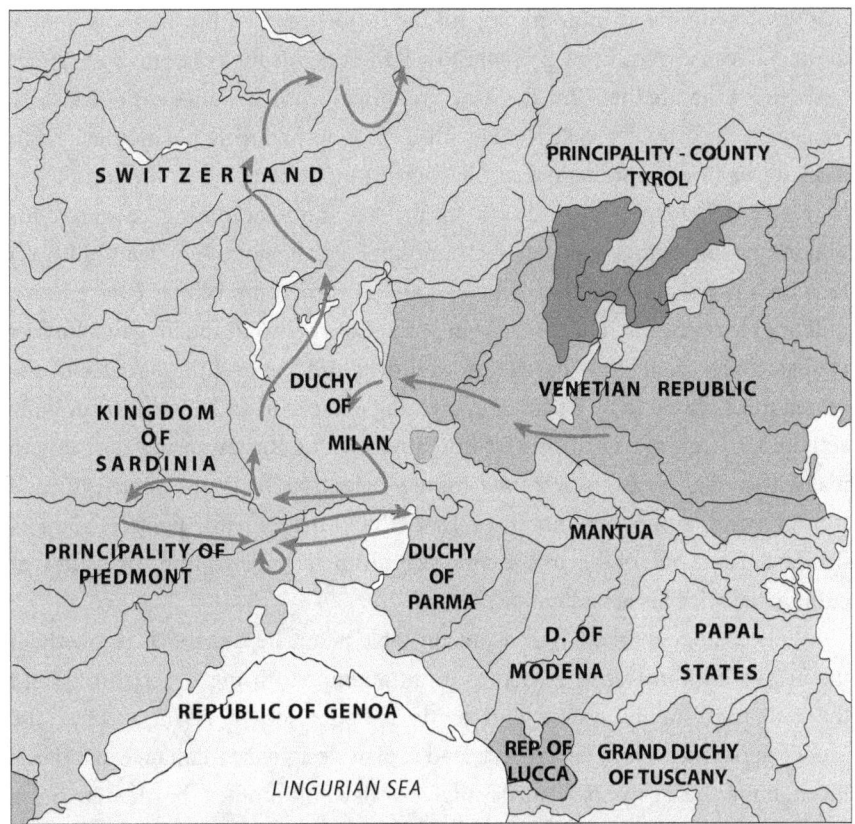

Map 3.1 Suvorov's Swiss Campaign.

loyal to their leaders because with role models like with Suvorov, Russian soldiers believed in their commanders' ability to prevail in battle. Moreover, the army was enjoying the fruits of Peter the Great's efforts to make it independent of foreign goods for its supplies. For example, Russian iron factories in Tula competed with the West in terms of quality and quantity of weapons produced as their capabilities had been expanding since the Great Northern War and that would continue through the Napoleonic period. Remarkably it had developed a surge capacity so that in 1797 they made 24,438 weapons of all calibers, a number that they increased to 43,388 weapons in 1799. In raw numbers the Russians were outproducing the West; in 1803 Russia's entire industry produced 163,000 tons of cast iron compared to England's 156,000 tons and France's 80–85,000 tons.[27] In addition, by 1801 Russia's cloth and wool factories provided all uniforms for the military, and its leather factories supplied all boots and harnesses. The problem for the textile industry was their mills produced goods that would command more money on the export market. But this was denied to them because of military pressure to sell their goods for below market rates.[28] Such heavy-handedness by the tsar combined with his incessant desire to transform the army from its status within the empire during his mother's reign has led to a body of thought that questions if the state had become completely militarized. Evidence in addition to the economy becoming co-opted for military purposes that supports such thinking usually notes how Paul I's Russia took on a marshal appearance when he all but turned the Winter Palace into a military barracks much to the chagrin of the Court. The argument gains further credence because of how parade ground drill and the ensuing parades of the armed forces came to be a part of everything associated with Paul and his daily activities.[29] Regardless of Paul's efforts to reform the Russian army and state to make it leaner, less expensive, and more efficient, he had so alienated himself from the core group—the nobility—that offered the emperor political support that he became vulnerable to the coup that ultimately ousted him, an event that culminated with his assassination.[30]

While history marked Paul as an unstable actor, he did much to overhaul the army's administrative structure in an attempt to bring order throughout the military's supply system and to do a better job of taking care of the army's personnel. First, he orchestrated a plan designed to enhance standards throughout the army. Not surprisingly, unlike his mother, he demonstrates a strong interest in the welfare of his troops as he saw to their quartering by building barracks, thus starting the process that would evolve into military colonies by the end of the Napoleonic period. He also insisted on the use of harsh discipline and military punishment through military courts for both officers and soldiers. Paul's determination to standardize uniforms throughout the army was his effort to put everyone on the same level, which meant even the guard's officers had to compromise their appearance that did little to unify the various segments of the Officer Corps but was part of a larger effort to reduce their role in politics. Perhaps his best action for the long-term betterment of the army was his insistence on the retirement of superannuated and anachronistic officers, especially if he considered them dead weight or political opposition in the guard's regiments. In addition, Paul was determined to reduce spending on the military. Nonetheless, for all of his foibles, Paul did impose better financial control over the army by creating an auditor's office in the military college and by also creating an office of inspector general to supervise the standardization and the execution of regulations. To stop the imposition of troops on civilians for quartering, he furthermore built barracks to house the troops across the empire.[31]

To this end, he tried to streamline the army's administration that started a reform process that would culminate in 1802 with the creation of a War Ministry that shifted power away from the nobles in Peter the Great's War College. More important to the administration of the army, he also created a Military-Field Chancellery that organized and administered the billeting and supply of troops throughout the empire in an effort to economize the military's supply system. Finally, although his reforms and erratic methods of governance ultimately lead to the loss of support, he also created the Imperial Suite to replace Catherine's military council believing that in doing so he was finally undermining the army's leadership cadre who so loyally served the empress. While he envisions the Suite to be the army's early modern idea of a general staff, it evolved into the institution that provided a harbor for Russia's highest aristocratic servitors in the late nineteenth/twentieth century.[32] Paul's military system therefore remained fraught with favoritism and the associated inequalities despite his best efforts to eliminate such practices. Yet, this dynastic army beat the French revolutionary army in Italy in 1799 albeit without Napoleon's presence. It would continue to serve their tsar well until the mid-nineteenth century by steadfastly refusing to adopt European military models best defined through the introduction of mass conscription, the democratization of the officer corps, and the adoption of modern technology. Indeed, a large percentage of Russia's military still had tremendous faith in the use of Paul I's parade ground drills as a fundamental part of their army's military training.

Alexander I and the Russian Empire's Finest Hour

As per his 1797 law of succession, Paul's eldest son Alexander I became tsar as a result of the March 1801 coup that culminated, much to the new tsar's angst, with the assassination of his father.[33] To say the least the 24-year-old's inheritance, as well as his standing within his own family, was complicated because of the fraught nature of the relationship between Catherine the Great and her son Paul. Unlike her treatment of Paul, Catherine imposed her will on the education and training of Alexander I to someday become the emperor of Russia. Alexander I was raised in the best tradition of the enlightenment (through the Russian lens) and upon becoming tsar, he initially indicated proclivities toward reforming his empire to make it be more in line with enlightened principles. But it was not to be because of the times in which he lived! The specter of Napoleon forced Alexander I to become the wartime leader of the empire in one of the most dramatic moments in all of Russian history. After spending over a century competing with the West to gain a foothold among the Great Powers while fighting persistent challengers to their southern and eastern frontiers, the Russian army prevailed during the desperate days of the summer and autumn of 1812 and then destroyed French military power in 1813-14. The Russians had developed a way of fighting best embodied in the recent memory of Suvorov and the experiences of the eighteenth century. Ultimately the Russian military defeated the French on their own territory without much help from allies or a coalition until the enemy had been forced back into Europe. The war plan of 1812 was a calculated effort to defeat Napoleon by preventing him from fighting the type of warfare that he had mastered in defeating all of Europe's Great Powers, especially between 1805 and 1807 and by planning to fight a long war. A dreadful price was paid—the homeland was invaded; the enemy was denied everything of value when they adopted a scorched earth policy that left the theater of operations in tatters. The city of Moscow was occupied and destroyed. Causalities to this conflict required an extraordinary recruitment of men into the armed services. But, once the damage had been absorbed, the military system created by Peter the Great and further developed throughout the eighteenth century overwhelmed the French after they had exhausted their resources and could not maintain a supply train capable of providing their troops with even a fraction of what they needed to wage war in the depths of a Russian winter. Moreover, once the Russians started marching westward after the French abandoned Moscow, they did not stop, albeit with the support of the rest of Europe's Great Powers, until they reached Paris and dispatched Napoleon from his seat of power. Above all else, this magnificent feat of arms was a tribute to the ability of Russia to provide arms, armaments, foodstuffs for soldiers, and, above all else, horses, not only to the cavalry but for the supply train itself, which supported and ultimately provided this massive army with the weapons, munitions, food, and fodder that it needed to march all the way to Paris and destroy French military power. The final result of the Napoleonic interlude resulted in Russia emerging as Europe's sole superpower.[34]

Russia's path to the position of supremacy, however, started with the Peace of Luneville (1801) and the Peace of Amiens (1802) that signaled the end of the Second Coalition. Alexander I designed to use the period brought on by the treaties to strengthen the administrative and organizational side of the army and his government. This is the period when along with his closest collaborators (Adam Czartoryski, Nikolai Novosil'tsev, Count Pavel Aleksandrovich Stroganov, and Viktor Kochubei) the tsar formed his "Unofficial Committee" to consider and to eventually limit the extent to which his government would pursued liberal reforms. While no fundamental change would occur that resulted in the creation of some form of participatory governance or in addressing the increasingly vexing question of serfdom, he nonetheless firmly rooted the idea that reform was in Russia's future.[35] Regardless of his hopes and desires for Russia, none of Alexander's domestic plans would gain much traction because of the impact Napoleon had on Europe between 1801 and 1807. At first Alexander naively sought to engage with Napoleon on a diplomatic level believing that he could work with the French leader to create a universal peace that in turn would allow him to concentrate on internal reform. Napoleon's sour relations with Great Britain and menacing toward the Austrian Empire and the rest of Central Europe, however, undermined all diplomatic efforts in 1804–5.[36] Alexander did not view these developments as a direct threat to Russia, but he did see them as a threat to international norms, the balance of power, and therefore a threat to the peaceful order of Europe. Yet, like his father, Alexander wanted to be a part of a coalition to contain Napoleon but he also wanted the Austrians to shoulder the heavy burden of war fighting so that Russia could disengage from the conflict if her interests were not being served. Whether or not Alexander found himself in a difficult position that necessitated his joining what became the Third Coalition or if he actually sought to enhance Russia's power in the world, he nonetheless agreed to the overtures made to him by British Prime Minister William Pitt in April 1805 and joined the Third Coalition that the European powers organized to contain Napoleon.[37]

Alexander I went to war against Napoleon in 1805 with a 300,000-man army in which his father's reforms had only partially taken effect. While the Russians had learned to combine arms by forming into corps that consisted of infantry, cavalry, and artillery, these corps operated as independent regiments. The order of battle therefore made it awkward for them to combine forces and deliver a decisive blow. According to the terms of the coalition, the Russians believed they marched into Central Europe with the Austrians providing them with supplies, especially rations for the tsar's soldiers and fodder for their horses. When the Austrians failed to deliver promised supplies, the Russians without their own supply train took what they needed from the land to subsist.[38] The forces that marched into Central Europe numbered around 75,000 men under the command of Field Marshal Mikhail Illarionovich Kutuzov and General F. W. Buxhowden. The tsar expected a short victorious war and did not attempt to mobilize any more troops for this operation. The 1805 campaign, however, turned into a disaster because there was no coordination between allies. Austrian Field Marshal-Lieutenant Frederick M. L. von Mack invaded Bavaria before Kutuzov arrived with his army. The Austrians were trapped and surrounded after a series of skirmishes and surrendered at Ulm on October 17, 1805. Mack's defeat left Kutuzov exposed, but he performed a masterful retreat that, after losing Vienna to the French in November, culminated with the devastating defeat at the Battle of Austerlitz on December 2, 1805.

The defeat was a great victory for Napoleon because he was outnumbered 90,000 allied troops to his 70,000. Napoleon prevailed because he outthought and then outmaneuvered the Russians. Confusing the situation further, Alexander I tried to fire Kutuzov right before the battle and take over command of the army that was disastrous because he did not know what he was doing. The Russians fell into a Napoleonic trap by attacking the French right flank in strength, which is exactly what Napoleon wanted as it meant the Russians and Austrians did not unite into one operational front. Napoleon's plan was to conceal troops on the Pratzen Heights to attack the center of the Russian forces after the bulk of the allied army had been committed to the attack on the French right flank. On the day of battle the heights were covered in mists, which aided the French cause. The French also badly needed Marshal Louis-Nicolas Davout (d'Avout) and his III Corp to arrive from Vienna in time to reinforce General Legrand's men on the right flank, which they did within a 48-hour window. While Napoleon struck his decisive blow around 9:00 a.m. the outcome of the battle was not known until the end of the day when the French finally forced the Russians, who had stubbornly resisted throughout the day, from the battlefield. When the battle ended, some 36,000 allied soldiers were dead to the French who lost only around 9,000 soldiers. Austerlitz is considered one of Napoleon's greatest victories. Alexander I departed from this period of the war realizing that Russia had a lot to learn before her army would be ready and prepared to fight the French in any future battles.[39]

Napoleon seized the moment and on December 4, 1805, he imposed the Treaty of Pressburg on the Austrians in which Emperor Francis II recognized French gains dating back to the 1797 Treaty of Campo Formio and in addition lost land to Bavaria, Wurttemberg, and Baden. These three principalities then became Napoleon's allies and were occupied by the French army. Venice was also stripped from Habsburg control and promised to the future, what Napoleon described as, the kingdom of Italy. Forcing the Austrians to pay 40 million francs in war indemnities made the treaty harsh but not disastrous for the fate of the Habsburg throne in the immediate aftermath of the war. In the long run, however, the Treaty of Pressburg spelled out the end of the Holy Roman Empire, which Napoleon formally replaced with the Confederation of the Rhine the next year. The Hohenzollern in Prussia considered the situation and came to the conclusion that Napoleon sought to use this new Confederation of the Rhine to act as a string of buffer states that he intended to use to control Central Europe. As a result, the Prussians walked away from this moment in the conflict insulted and more importantly believing they would be Napoleon's next target. They went to war in 1806 to preempt any of Napoleon's future plans.

The Russian army was allowed to disengage and return to their home territory, which suited Alexander as it gave him time to digest the lessons of his first major engagement with Napoleon. While for the time being Austria had lost its desire to continue the struggle, the Prussians had not as they rightly sensed that a new opportunity for control over Central Europe had now presented itself and, not surprisingly, the heirs of Frederick the Great did not want French troops occupying territory populated by German-speaking people. The flash point in this instance was the province of Hanover, which the French had occupied in 1803. In the course of the War of the Third Coalition Hanover had been occupied by the Swedes in an effort to keep the province neutral. Despite their best efforts the conflict over control of Hanover intensified after the Treaty of Pressburg as the British tried to make dynastic claims, the Prussians made cultural claims, and the French made their revolutionary claims over this territory. In the end, all of these disputes over a German principality resulted in the emergence of a Fourth Coalition composed of Prussia, Russia, Great Britain, Sweden, and Saxony, all of whom had the common goal of stopping the spread of the French Revolution and the growing power of Napoleon. What followed was a complete disaster for the Prussians and the Russians as both ended up losing their autonomy in foreign affairs after signing the Treaty of Tilsit.[40]

The major story of the Wars of the Fourth Coalition was the obliteration of Prussia at the Battle of Jena-Auerstedt in October 1806. Like General Mack at Ulm the year before, Prussian king Friedrich Wilhelm III sought battle with Napoleon before his allies, which effectively meant the Russians, marched their armies into Central Europe. After nineteen days of campaigning the French invasion of Prussia culminated with the occupation of Berlin on October 27, 1806. The Royal family with its most loyal servitors escaped to their ancestral homeland in eastern Prussia where they would link up with the Russian army near Konigsberg. Napoleon then proclaimed the Berlin Decree on November 21, 1806, that announced to the world the birth of the Continental System. Realizing that in addition to his continental enemies Napoleon could not contain the British because of their control of the sea and understanding that the British Empire was a looming threat, the emperor chose this moment to launch an economic war against them by banning all trade between Europe and the UK. By the end of the year he got King Frederick Augustus I of Saxony to switch sides by making his duchy a kingdom and promising his new ally that he would rule over the newly created Duchy of Warsaw. Angered by the ensuing invasion of Poland, Alexander I ordered General A. T. Bennigsen to halt Napoleon's march toward Russian territory. The Russians then fought the French to a draw at the bloody battle of Eylau in early February 1807 with each side losing approximately 23,000 soldiers. Although not a decisive victory, Bennigsen's army retreated in good order, resulting in false expectations and much elation on the part of Alexander I who viewed Eylau to be the first check against French military operations largely because the Russian army remained intact. This was not to be the case after the Battle of Friedland in June 1807 where the Russian army suffered a devastating defeat that resulted in the loss of an additional 20,000 men. The tsar needed to address several pressing concerns that all added up to Russia needing to break off from the Fourth Coalition. Thus, Alexander I agreed to join the Continental System when he signed the Treaty of Tilsit on July 7, 1807, knowing full well that eliminating trade with Great Britain would be a disaster for the Russian economy.

Nonetheless, Alexander signed the treaty for two reasons. The first was that he had run out of soldiers and supplies. Russia needed time to recover from the expenditures of men and equipment resulting from operations in the periods of the Third and Fourth Coalitions. The other concern was the deterioration of relations and the outbreak of yet another war between Moscow and Constantinople in 1806. Although the Russian army had been badly beaten at Friedland, Napoleon so badly wanted Russia to join his Continental System that he went easy on Alexander I when they met in the middle of the river Neman to sign the treaty. The tsar effectively declared war on the British when he agreed to join the Continental System. While Napoleon insisted that Russia withdraw from Wallachia and Moldavia, which they had just occupied at the start of the recent Ottoman conflict, he also promised to support the Russians in their war against the Porte. These terms were light compared to the terms Napoleon imposed on the Prussian two days later on July 9, 1807, when he stripped Prussia of about half of its territory and completely consolidated French control over Central Europe.[41]

While Russia's war with Turkey progressed in southeastern Europe, the tsar formally declared war with the British in October 1807 mainly to demonstrate support for the Continental System. More significantly, in September 1807 Alexander I sent a letter to King Gustav IV Adolf of Sweden to inform him that he had to join the Continental System or he would find himself at war with Russia. Gustav, who despised Napoleon, was put to the test soon after when, as a result of Sweden declaring war, Alexander requested that the Swedish navy prevent the British navy from entering the Baltic Sea. The crisis that ensued was resolved when Gustav decided to disregard Alexander I and enter into a formal alliance with Great Britain on February 8, 1808. This agreement resulted in Russia invading Sweden's eastern territory (modern Finland) with a force of 24,000 men under the command of General Friedrich Wilhelm von Buxhoevden on February 21, 1808. What followed was an eighteen-month conflict in which the Russians ultimately gained control over Finland. While the Russian army dominated on land, the war at sea almost prevented the Russians from achieving victory. Because of Gustav's alliance with Great Britain, the Russian navy could not defend the west coast of Finland because of the strength and looming threat of the British Royal Navy. Concerns about a Swedish invasion of Finland, therefore, prevailed in the thinking of first von Buxhoevden and then later by his successor General Count Nikolai Kamensky. Despite these concerns in November 1808 all Swedish forces evacuated Finish territory. The Russians decided to pursue the Swedes and to spend the winter of 1808 organizing an invasion that featured the tsar's army marching across the frozen Gulf of Bothnia. One expedition led by Barclay de Tolly made it to the Swedish city of Umea and occupied it in March. Tolly's aggressive operational leadership so impressed the tsar that he made him commander in chief of the forces in this theater of war at the beginning of April 1809. With this foothold in Sweden proper, the Russians created a force of approximately 17,000 troops under the command of Lieutenant-General Pyotr Bagration who remained operational in northern Sweden until the end of the war. Meanwhile, with Central Europe at peace, Napoleon turned his attention to the Iberian Peninsula and invaded Spain. After the popular uprising of the Spanish people, the British became entangled in what became known as the Peninsular War, hence their support to Sweden waned resulting in the end of the Baltic conflict. Gustav IV would be overthrown, his uncle the new king Charles XIII agreed to the Treaty of Fredrikshamn on September 17, 1809, and all of Sweden's eastern empire was ceded to Russia. This territory became known as the Grand Duchy of Finland and would remain a part of the Russian Empire until 1918. The conclusion of this war also marked the demise of Sweden as an imperial power as she joined the Continental System and no longer controlled the Baltic region on any level.

While the conflict in the Baltic was a clear danger for the Russian Empire, the real challenge to Russia during the period of the wars of the Third and Fourth

Coalitions was the developing situation in Wallachia and Moldavia. Once again, a Romanov tsar found himself at war with the Ottoman Empire and this time in the midst of the enormous conflict on her western frontier. This war was simply known as the Russo-Turkish War of 1806–12. While a costly war for the Russians, its impact was far greater in the Ottoman Empire as in its course two sultans, Selim III and Mustafa IV, would be assassinated and, in the end, the Russians would annex the eastern half of Moldavia and create a newly controlled territory renamed Bessarabia. This war broke out in the aftermath of Russia's defeat at Austerlitz because in 1806 Selim III, with Napoleon's encouragement, sought to depose the pro-Russian Hospodar in Wallachia and Moldavia. Although both territories were considered Ottoman vassals, the Sublime Porte had been slowly losing control on the ground since the last Turkish conflict against Catherine the Great. At the same time, the French occupied Dalmatia and their forces represented a threat to the Danubian principalities, which Alexander I could not ignore despite the pressing danger of Napoleon's armies on his western frontier. Thus, and with much reluctance, the tsar ordered the composition of a 40,000-man force that advanced into the two provinces, which prompted Selim III to block the Dardanelles to Russian shipping and to declare war on December 30, 1806.

The war that followed actually took place on three fronts, the first being in Wallachia and Moldavia, otherwise known as the Danubian principalities, the second in Armenia, and the third in the Dardanelles itself. Initial movements occurred in June 1807 when the Russians checked a much larger Turkish force outside of Bucharest and again a much larger Turkish force failed to defeat the Russians in Armenia later in the month. While Napoleon imposed peace between the Russians and Turks as a part of the Tilsit treaty, Alexander I used this development as an opportunity to transfer a large number of troops from his now "peaceful" western front to the Danubian provinces. The tsar then made his course of action clear when he ordered the Black Sea fleet to challenge the Ottoman navy in the Dardanelles, which it did beginning in February 1808. Under the command of Vice Admiral Dmitri Senyavin, the Russian fleet fought two major battles, the Battle of the Dardanelles in May and in June the Battle of Athos. Both battles were tremendous victories for the Russian navy that resulted in the opening of the Dardanelles to their ships and effective control over the Aegean Sea for the rest of the war.[42] The naval defeats and the ensuing blockade of Constantinople resulted in the ousting and assassination of Selim III. These victories, combined with the peace engineered at Tilsit, emboldened Alexander I to double the size of his force in the Danubian principalities and to make an

Map 3.2 Expansion into the Caucasus.

all-out effort to gain complete control over them. Initially the campaign went nowhere largely because of the poor leadership of the operational commander Field Marshal Alexander Alexandrovich Prozorovski. In an effort to gain some success on this front, the tsar sent Prince Pyotr Ivanovich Bagration, fresh off of his success in the Swedish War to the Turkish front where he was Prozorovski's assistant until he (Prozorovski) died in August 1809. Upon taking over command of the army, Bagration instilled an offensive spirit and launched assaults capturing Turkish forts at Macin, Constanta, Girsov, Cavarna, Bazaedjik, and Rassevat in August and September 1809. He continued this operation with the defeat of a superior Turkish army at Tataritsa in October and by the end of the year defeated them yet again at Ismail and Braila. This magnificent string of successes, however, did not lead to a decisive victory in the war and this failure led to Bagration and Alexander I having a falling out in March 1810. This paved the way for the final stage of the war.

Under mounting French pressure, Alexander I needed to end the war with Turkey. By 1810 informed people in Europe knew it was only a matter of time before Napoleon would once again confront Russia. The Russian nobility never endorsed the Treaty of Tilsit; they believed it beneath their tsar agreeing to meet with Napoleon at all because, after all, he was nothing more than a Corsican peasant. The real issue, however, was economic. Simply put, Russia's commercial operators were not interested in losing all of their business with Great Britain. The Russian Empire therefore did not adhere to the regulations of the Continental System and, much to Napoleon's angst, continued to trade with Great Britain. Still, conflict with the Sublime Porte loomed and had to be resolved as Napoleon gathered forces to address his Russia problem. With the Caucasus front largely dormant, the resolution of yet another conflict brewing with the Ottomans would have to be resolved in the Danubian principalities. To accomplish this, Alexander I appointed Mikhail Illarionovich Kutuzov commander of the Russian army of the Danube. Kutuzov was actually enduring a period of exile for disagreeing with Prozorovski earlier in the war. He was brought back after Bagration had been dispatched for disagreeing with the tsar over the strategy of the war against the Turks. After a brutal campaign between March and November 1811, Kutuzov bottled up the Turks at Ruse and Silistra for which Alexander I conferred on the general the title of Count. Kutuzov then orchestrated the Treaty of Bucharest that was signed on May 28, 1812, about three weeks before the invasion of Russia proper by Napoleon's grande armee. The timing was critical to Russia's future as it gave the army a brief window in which it started to transfer troops from the Balkans to central Russia where they would participate in the campaign of 1812.[43]

Ending the war against the Ottoman, however, became imperative in the spring of 1812 because Napoleon was in the midst of making his final preparations for the now expected invasion of Russia. Alexander I expected the invasion because by the spring of 1812 it was blatantly clear that Russia was not adhering to the terms of the Treaty of Tilsit. In clear violation of the Continental System, Russia continued to conduct trade with Great Britain. Russia, rich in natural resources, had built an economy dependent on trading raw material with Great Britain for manufactured goods. Eliminating trade with Great Britain, therefore, would cause a devastating blow to the Russian economy and as a result Russia never completely participated in the blockade of trade with their British partners. True to his self-perception as an enlighten despot, Napoleon developed propaganda claiming that the French army needed to invade Russia to defend the rights and liberate all of Poland from the threat of Russian power. He had, after all, created the Duchy of Warsaw and seemed to have the goal of reconstituting the Polish-Lithuanian Commonwealth. When generating a political agenda for his military actions Napoleon composed his *grande armee* of some 400,000 French and 285,000 European soldiers. The composition of the army, his forcibly inducting the Europeans to serve under the French flag, did much to undermine what was left of the enthusiasm initially generated for the

Corsican when he "liberated" Europe in the 1805–7 period. This simmering opposition combined with formation of huge military units, perhaps the largest army ever composed up to that time, moving toward Russia along with all of their supplies made it plain that the French emperor was on the move once again. Moreover, the Russians had developed a sophisticated spy network across Europe that reached all the way to Paris and the numerous and various reports it generated eliminated any doubt about what Napoleon was planning for world history in the spring of 1812.[44]

Bonaparte envisioned fighting a war in which he would strike hard in an effort to destroy the Russian army before it could gain any traction to repel the invaders. In this regard, Napoleon had defined his 1812 Russian campaign in classic strategic terms: first, destroy the enemy's armies and then force the defeated empire's political leaders to acquiesce to France's demands. He divided his *grande armee* into five columns and crossed the Russian border in numerous spots along the Neiman River on Wednesday, June 24th. Their line of march took them first to Vilna and then on to Vitebsk. Since the Russians kept up a steady withdrawal the French marched on Minsk where they arrived on July 8th. The campaign, less than a month old, was taking its toll on the French yet they persisted and kept up the pressure and forced the Russians to give battle at Smolensk on August 16–18. Both armies lined up on opposite banks of the Dniepr River on the 16th and that night Napoleon assaulted the Smolensk Kremlin. Prince Barclay De Tolly, fearing encirclement, withdrew from the city the next day and once again the Russians eluded the French. What followed was the only major battle of the campaign, the Battle of Borodino on September 7th. Napoleon's marched end when he rode into Moscow on September 14, 1812. French occupation of the ancient Russian capital lasted for five weeks when his retreat into the winter resulted in his defeat in the East and the eventual collapse of his empire. Ironically, Napoleon either underestimated or simply dismissed the potential power of the people of Russia should they decided to stand unified behind their tsar.[45]

While the unity of a people against any threat is difficult to measure, at the very least Russia's nobility did support their tsar, which was absolutely critical to the successful defense of the realm. Alexander I, at the urging of his war minister Barclay de Tolly and other military advisors, adopted a war plan that depended on taking advantage of Napoleon's largest weakness, which was maintaining a supply train that would keep his troops equipped as they further marched away from its base in France and Central Europe. This of course meant that Russia's war plan was based on a strategic retreat designed to draw the French along a

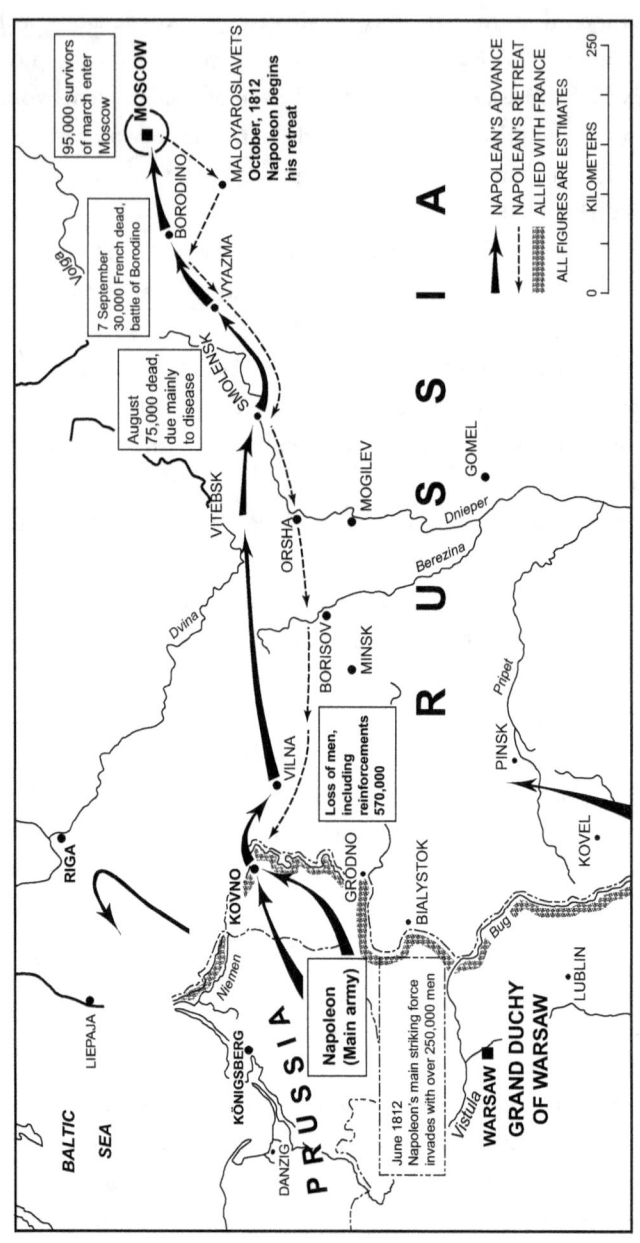

Map 3.3 The Campaign of Napoleon in Russia.

projected route before launching a decisive counterstrike to defeat Napoleon. A necessary consequence of such a plan was the implementation of a scorched-earth policy. Everything that could be of value to the French army was ordered destroyed—burning cities and villages, burning crops and killing animals, even poisoning water wells fomented a disaster on the countryside.[46] In addition to the physical damage wrought on the landscape and lives of humans and animals, the invasion displaced people resulting in the mass movement of refugees fleeing the French army. Sanitary conditions collapsed as the invasion route became flooded with large numbers of wounded and sick soldiers along with rotting bodies and dead animals.[47] Russian conduct throughout the course of their retreat stupefied the French because of their willingness to destroy their country. The strategy, however, worked just as expected as it slowly deprived Napoleon of essential war fighting supplies such as munitions, horses, and fodder as well as rations for his soldiers. The supply situation turned critical as the seasons changed from summer to fall. With the French lines already seriously overextended, moving supplies forward started grinding into slow motion because the army was simultaneously confronted with attacks from partisans and Cossacks on a road network that was slowly disintegrating into a muddy mess.

The estimated size of the Russian army in June 1812 exceeded 400,000 men when De Tolly set up his forward command post in Vilnius. Napoleon expected to defeat the Russian army in short order, and at first his strategy seemed to be working. Initially he met little resistance and reached Vilnius on June 28, possibly thinking the lack of opposition was a signal from the Russians that they intended to capitulate. De Tolly, however, retreated, thus starting Russia's long march into the interior of the country. Although the tsar and Barclay agreed about Russia's strategic retreat, both men were under tremendous pressure to halt the advance of the French. The situation became an open controversy when General Peter Ivanovich Bagration, commander of the 2nd Western Army, developed a reputation for evading Napoleon's enveloping maneuvers throughout July before forming up with Barclay and his 1st Army in front of Smolensk at the beginning of August. After much agitation, Bagration prevailed and convinced Barclay that they must hold their ground in front of Smolensk, thereby halting the strategic retreat. For the battle of Smolensk, Napoleon was able to concentrate 175,000 men to Barclay's 50,000. Over the course of August 15–18, Napoleon was able to dislodge the Russians from the Smolensk Kremlin, and although both sides lost around 10,000 men, Barclay's flight from the battlefield left the impression that the French had won the battle. The loss at Smolensk was disturbing for the Russians because the city marked the halfway point to Moscow from Vilnius. The outcome of this battle, however, was in fact a strategic victory for the Russians. With the tsar's army still intact, Napoleon had the stark choice of remaining in place and occupying western Russia, thereby billeting his troops in Russian winter quarters, or continuing the offensive in the hope of destroying the Russian army and occupying Moscow.

Meanwhile, the controversy over the implementation of the Russian war plan had undermined Barclay De Tolly's authority throughout the army and society in general. This loss of faith in the army's leadership combined with tremendous pressure from the nobility over the destruction of their land and property resulted in Alexander I's decision to relieve his commander in chief and replace him with General Kutuzov of recently fame for bringing the 1806–12 Russo-Turkish War to its successful conclusion. Kutuzov continued the retreat and chose the village of Borodino some 70 miles west of Moscow to turn and make a stand against the French in an effort to spare Moscow from being occupied. Borodino was an ideal place for the Russian army to make a stand because a river protected their northern or left flank and to the south field fortifications and woods protected their right flank. To further strengthen his right flank, Kutuzov regrouped and then redeployed his Cossacks fresh from their two-and-a-half-month scorched earth mission in which they had persistently harassed the French army and its supply lines. On the morning of September 7, 1812, approximately 133,000 French troops struck the center of this battlefield, the actual village of Borodino, and what ensued was a bloody day of battle that ended some twelve hours later with the Russians losing 40,000 men and the French losing some 33,000 soldiers. The day ended with the Russian army still intact at a second line of defense and Napoleon wondering if this had been the battle when his army had achieved a decisive victory. By dawn on September 8, he realized that his victory had been pyrrhic at best because the Russian army, still intact, continued its retreat toward Moscow. Napoleon and his army would now indeed occupy Moscow but only after taking a serious beating and with supply lines that were impossibly overextended. His best hope was that when the army arrived in Moscow, the French would find provisions that could sustain them through the winter.[48]

A week later Napoleon entered Moscow after it had been largely evacuated of its citizens. In the course of this evacuation the city governor, Count Fyodor Rostopchin, ordered the destruction of the Kremlin and all major public buildings including churches. While it is logical to conclude that Moscow was burnt by the Russians as they evacuated the city, no hard evidence has been produced to prove this conclusion. As their army retreated eastward toward Kazan, large numbers of civilians followed them. Smoke from small fires were seen rising from the city center. The next day Napoleon arrived at the Kremlin but quickly found himself surrounded by a growing conflagration; he would have to flee the flames when they engulfed the Kitai Gorod part of the city, allegedly having to skirt the flames as he went down the Arbat, he got to the Moskva River and followed it to the northwest until he reached the Petrovsky estate where he resided for two days before returning to the city. While he was gone, civil and military order completely broke down, which resulted in the French troops rioting, raping, looting, and pillaging throughout the city. Upon his return to the Kremlin, Bonaparte would spend the next month waiting for a plea for peace from Alexander I. The tsar, however, had no intention of surrendering or pleading for terms of any type from the occupiers of Russia's former capital. Having executed a war plan that mobilized the national wealth and faith in the Fatherland, and especially after enduring the loss of life and destruction of property that had occurred as a consequence of the plan, Alexander, with his army regrouping to the east and south, had no intention of surrendering. In strategic terms, the tsar had the French emperor in a very difficult spot. The destruction in Moscow was so widespread that the city could not serve as the winter quarters for the French army. Napoleon had neither the logistical support to supply his army nor could he depend on gaining anything from the Russians that could sustain his officers and soldiers for any length of time.[49]

With no offer of negotiations of any type forthcoming from Alexander I, and with inadequate provisions and insufficient housing for his troops, Napoleon's options were limited. As he pondered whether or not to set out in the direction of St. Petersburg to force the issue on the tsar, his troops grew increasingly malnourished and subsequently a variety of illnesses started to weaken his soldiers. Thus just thirty-five days after their arrival, or on October 19, 1812, the French army abandoned Moscow. Realizing that his army was too weak to engage in offensive operations in the direction of St. Petersburg, Napoleon optioned to retreat to the southwest with the goal of gaining access to the resources of Ukraine to resupply his army as it marched back to the Central European frontier. Kutuzov anticipated this move and gave battle to the French at Maloyaroslavets, 75 miles southwest of Moscow on October 24, 1812. While a French and Italian force of approximately 24,000 troops got to Maloyaroslavets first and therefore controlled key bridges into the city, a similar sized Russian force spent the day trying to dislodge their enemies from the town. At the end of the day Marshal Kutuzov arrived and true to the operational conduct of the entire campaign, he ordered the Russians to redraw to the south of the city to block the road to Kuluga. While the French had held on as they did at Borodino, they had once again earned a pyrrhic victory. The Russian army was still intact and even worse the French were cut off from their nearest base of supplies, which was in Kuluga. Not wishing to fight to another draw, Napoleon was forced to turn north and march down the same route as he had used in the summer's invasion. Maloyaroslavets was therefore a strategic disaster for Napoleon! Instead of being able to claim he was conducting a strategic retreat into Ukraine, Napoleon now had a retreat on his hands that was on the verge and ultimately would actually become a route. A combination of partisans and Cossacks kept the *Grande Armee* within the confines of the invasion route that had been devastated the first time the armies traveled over the landscape. The French retreat crossed over the Borodino battlefield; seeing it did much to undermine French morale. Even worse, at the beginning of November the weather turned bitterly cold, complete with snow that slowed down the movement of the army. At this stage of the retreat the remnants of his army dissipated into the Russian winter suffering from hunger, disease, and frostbite. Then, when the French arrived in Smolensk, much to the emperor's chagrin, he learned that the supplies he was counting on did not exist as they had been consumed or used up by the garrison troops. After resting for a few days, the retreat continued as the army headed for Vilnius on November 13th. Three weeks later the exhausted and decimated army arrived in Vilnius on December 8th where Napoleon learned that his throne was under threat of a *coup d'etat*. Pleading that he needed to return to rebuild France's army to confront the oncoming onslaught, he left his army in Vilnius under the command of Marshal Joachim Murat who decided to avoid battle and abandon all of his heavy guns along with everything the French had gathered as war trophies, especially from Moscow, as he and his troops retreated into Western Europe. When they crossed the river Nieman on December 14, 1812, he had 40,000 soldiers under his command, most of whom were too ill to be called effective warriors.[50]

What followed was the formation of the Sixth Coalition in March 1813. Led by the Russians, armies from Austria, Prussia, Great Britain, Portugal, Sweden, Spain, and a number of the lesser German States engaged in battle with French forces as they retreated toward Paris. Notable battles included action at Lutzen and Bautsen in May where Napoleon's troops prevailed but such French victories strengthened the resolve of the allies and ultimately culminated with the Austrians committing 300,000 troops to the cause. While the summer of 1813 featured a formal Armistice of Plaswitz between all belligerents, both sides used this period to reinforce their military forces. The Austrian reinforcements combined with an infusion of Russian reserves meant that in August 1813 the allies had combined over 800,000 troops to confront Napoleon in Central Europe. As Prussia was regaining control over all of its sovereign territory—the campaigns of 1813 are often referred to as the period of German liberation—members of the Sixth Coalition continued to muster troops and, as a result, built a reserve of troops that would grow to become an international force of over 350,000 soldiers. Although now completely outnumbered, Napoleon maintained his mastery of the battlefield with a decisive defeat of the allies at Dresden at the end of August. This victory emboldened him to aim to reconquer Prussia, but these efforts failed due to a lack of cavalry and the inability of Napoleon's subordinates to prevail on the battlefield. The autumn campaign culminated with the Battle of Leipzig or the so-called Battle of Nations that occurred on October 16–19, 1813. Here the allies finally coordinated their efforts under the overall command of Alexander I to organize a force of over 430,000 troops against a French army that numbered under 200,000 soldiers. The Battle of Leipzig became the breaking point for the French army. They had lost in excess of 500,000 troops in 1813 and this combined with their losses in 1812 made their military's future untenable. Complicating his situation Napoleon lost the support of his allies as the losses mounted, thereby making any attempt to replace the lost troops impossible. Military defeats across Central Europe set the stage for the invasion of France in the spring of 1814. The French army could not stop the combined strength of the Sixth Coalition, which resulted in Alexander I's army leading the allied forces into Paris on March 31, 1814. Military defeat combined with the occupation of his capital forced Napoleon to abdicate on April 11, 1814.[51] While the Russian army played a decisive role in terms of providing manpower for this invasion, it did not provide much decisive leadership for two reasons: first, with the death of Kutuzov in April 1813 Russia lost its most effective battlefield commander, and second the role Alexander I played as his army invaded Europe. Never being the best judge of military leadership and always believing that he could command armies in battle, the tsar acted with increasing authority in operational matters. Then, as a harbinger of his future conduct, Alexander I increasingly turned to religion and while he was supreme commander of the allied forces when they invaded France, his steady drift toward guidance from scriptures would undermine his effectiveness, not only on the battlefield but also throughout the peacemaking process.[52]

Subsequently, as the world was being restored and, as the Russian army was acknowledged as the largest and most powerful force on the Eurasian landmass, their tsar was increasingly losing his place as the leader of the Sixth Coalition. By November 1814 when the statesmen, diplomats, and military leaders met at Vienna, Alexander I in addition to brokering a hard-earned peace also had become interested in overseeing some type of evangelical revival of the continent.[53] Nonetheless, there is no denying that by 1815 Russia had reached the pinnacle of success; since Peter the Great had created the military system, the empire had acquired the north shore of the Black Sea, the Crimea, and Bessarabia. In the north, Russia had gained control over the Baltic provinces, all of Finland, and had a strong maritime presence in the Baltic Sea. To the west, Catherine had eliminated the Polish problem, something that had bedeviled the Romanovs since their 1613 rise to power. Paul's 1801 peaceful annexation of Georgia allowed the Russians to become a fixture of power in the Caucasus, which also started the period that would lead to its complete conquest. The stage was set for continuous eastward expansion that would culminate with Russian settlements in Alaska that extended as far south as northern California. The Russian Empire would continue its eastward expansion into Central Asia for the balance of the nineteenth century. By 1815 Russia had emerged as the strongest of the Great Powers with an army of some 700,000 men. More significantly, when Paul got involved in the Second Coalition all of Europe respected Russian military strength, but no one believed that the Romanovs could confront Napoleon without the assistance of allies. This belief held true throughout the wars of the Third Coalition up to the Treaty of Tilsit. While the Russian army had developed its own style of warfare, it had been used most effectively against the Ottomans and other foes on her southern frontier. No one expected the Russians to hold their own against a Western enemy until they defeated Napoleon in 1812 without the military aid of anyone.[54]

Russia's military victories had been stunning and not at all expected when Napoleon invaded in June 1812. Seeking to establish exact numbers in the Russian environment is tricky business because of the ever-changing request for troops through the annual levy. This combined with the paucity of accurate records results in every number regarding the composition of the army to be an estimate at best. Janet M. Hartley, largely using Beskrovnyi whom she states does not completely reveal the sources of his numbers, notes that in 1768, the annual levy for soldiers was 50,000. This number increased to 100,000 men by the early 1790s; as Catherine the Great waged war, she constantly needed more troops. Because of the Napoleonic threat, the annual levy increased to the point where in 1812 the empire inducted some 420,000 recruits into the ranks. In addition, beginning in 1806, in an unprecedented move, Alexander I ordered the creation of a militia that was composed of men who fell prey to a pseudo draft of sorts that temporarily liberated serfs to serve in the army based on the principle that once the emergency was over, they would return to their lord's estate.[55] Free men could also enlist in the militia and the numbers of such enlistees grew throughout the period reaching an apex in 1812. While the intent was for militia men to be used in the defense of their own region, many stayed with the army during the 1813–14 invasion of Europe.[56] Such emergency measures demonstrate the extent to which Alexander I mobilized Russia to confront the most significant invasion of Russia's homeland since the Mongols got on their horses and rode out of Asia! In the end Hartley estimates that between 1796 and 1815 the army required the induction of 1,616,199 men to eliminate the French threat.[57]

Manpower needs, however, were just one of the challenges of the Napoleonic period. Destroying the land, however, caused the Russians enormous losses in people and subsequent tax collections. Moreover, the expense of mobilizing the army and fighting the French brought the budget to the brink of bankruptcy.[58] In the aftermath of the invasion, while the Russian army was still campaigning against the French in Western Europe, the Russians started the huge process of repairing and rebuilding the damage to their empire. Taken together the Napoleonic invasion cost Russia hundreds of million rubles.[59] Paul I sought to limit the army to 200,000 men because of the persistent deficit spending that the empire's military establishment required to maintain its strength throughout the reign of Catherine the Great. The only reason the state could remain afloat was due to population growth that increased the number of tsarist subjects from 28.4 million in 1782 to 41.7 million in 1811.[60] This not only increased the tax base of the Russian government but it also meant that the army would have an endless supply of troops. The huge size of the military establishment also necessitated that its leadership reconsider its organizational structure, which led to its first fundamental overhaul since Peter the Great's reign. In 1810, realizing that the Continental System was failing and that war with France would be inevitable, Alexander I teamed his newly appointed war minister General de Tolly with Mikhail M. Speranskii, Russia's most powerful reforming voice of the period and a confidant of the tsar, to reform the military's administration. The following reforms actually concluded the work of Paul I as a War Ministry had been created right after his assassination, which was a broad effort to transform the military colleges created by Peter the Great into a modern administrative organization. In the end the War College was eliminated so that all components of the military's administration could be centralized into the hands of an all-powerful war minister.[61] Then, to oversee the operational aspects of the army, still under the leadership of deTolly and Speranskii, a committee of experts and senior statesmen, ironically largely acting on the research gathered by

P. M. Volkonskii when he went to Paris and studied the French army and its organization, drafted the "Regulation for the Administration of a Large Active Army," which became the basic governing document for the army until after its defeat in the Crimean War (1853–6). This document was far reaching in that it provided instruction on all aspects of the Russian army from the chain of command and training of troops to their billeting and supply both in peace and in war.

The combination of Russia's success on the battlefield and the adoption of organizational and administrative structures that culminated in the recruitment and supply of a huge army at the end of the Napoleonic epoch had rendered the Russian Empire supreme among all the Great Powers. Since Alexander I believed it would be Russia's responsibility to maintain European peace in the post-Napoleonic period, before he left France in September 1815 he oversaw the creation of the Holy Alliance.[62] At the tsar's urging, Francis I of Austria and Frederick Wilhelm III of Prussia agreed to the alliance, which aimed to reassert the principle that kings had a divine right to rule and that they should let Christian values guide their decisions about governance. Everyone else rejected the alliance because the underlying principle of peacemaking in 1814–15 was to create a balance of power among all nations based on political expediency. While the connection to Christian values fits well into the motif of Alexander's growing mysticism, the tsar's drift from real politics did not undermine his power. The existence and potential of the Russian army remained paramount in the thinking of all European leaders until the Crimean War.

When Alexander I returned to St. Petersburg in October 1815 much hope existed within Russian society that the tsar would return with a burning desire to return to the liberal reform agenda that he tried to pursue at the start of his reign. Whether it was from his growing religiosity or his new-found role as the most powerful emperor in Europe in charge of maintaining the peace, there would be no liberal reform in the last ten years of Alexander I's reign. What followed was the tsar slowly distancing himself from matters of state and turning over governance to one of his father's loyalists, Aleksei Andreivich Arakcheev, who had a reputation for being brutal and disliked but highly efficient in everything he sought to accomplish. Arakcheev gained the tsar's attention in the midst of the Napoleonic conflict not only because he measured up as a top military administrator but also because Alexander I had put him in charge of developing a reform idea that predated Napoleon's invasion. In an effort to generate more productivity out of soldiers, Alexander I ordered the creation of military colonies where soldiers could live with their families while engaging in agricultural pursuits. A combination of factors sparked the initiative that led to the creation of these settlements. Their origin can be traced to a 1793 decision by Catherine the Great to limit the term of soldiers in the ranks to twenty-five years as opposed to them serving until they died.[63] While most soldiers would not survive twenty-five years in the ranks, the reform nonetheless necessitated some consideration about where a man would go if he did survive his term of service. The fate of retired troops, however, was a mere consideration for the regime as the real aim of creating military colonies was to put soldiers to work to simultaneously make the army more self-sufficient and in the best of all possible worlds generate more income for the empire. The tsar aimed to make crown lands more productive by creating a class of peasant-soldiers. The colonies, however, did nothing of the sort. At the time, and usually attributed to Arakcheev's arrogance and ruthlessness, the colonies devolved into a sort of retirement village for those soldiers who did survive a twenty-five-year term in the ranks. More significantly, within the colonies the harsh discipline and soldierly duties and responsibilities were maintained to the point where men were supposed to respond to the sound of the bugle for the rest of their lives. Such treatment of veterans resulted in the emergence of a level of dissatisfaction with the regime itself.[64]

The last ten years of Alexander I's reign, the period after he returned from France until his death, were fraught with first his erratic conduct and then his long absences from his capital when he left the hated general (Arakcheev) in control of the state. The period was largely peaceful between the Great Powers but the Russian Empire still had unstable borderlands to contend with in the Caucasus and while the Ottomans had clearly slipped as a Great Power, they remained a threat to Russian security. Alexander I's detachment from his people and his giving seemingly unlimited authority to Arakcheev combined with the demise of any type of reform agenda led to the growth of friction between the autocracy and its subjects. To be sure, throughout Europe the departure of Napoleon sparked the emergence of national movements that gained political traction no matter what any king, emperor, or general sought to impose on people to maintain their power and authority. Surprisingly and alarmingly this unrest struck at the core of Russian power when the soldiers in the Semenovsky guard's regiment rebelled in November 1820 over the harsh disciplinary demands of Colonel R. E. Schwartz who had been recently posted to the unit by Arakcheev with orders to impose rigid discipline on troops to command their obedience. This mutiny would have a profound effect on Alexander I as he considered the Semenvsky to be his own regiment. The tsar's angst over this incident resulted in him disbanding the regiment, disciplining its leaders, and then reassigning the rest of its troops to units across the empire, which in turn enhanced levels of dissatisfaction throughout the rest of the army.[65] The officers who were dispersed were posted largely to the south where there were always serious threats of either bloody action or diseases such as plague, smallpox, typhoid, and a host of undefined viruses. In the south disenchanted elements of the officer corps found solace through organization, and their dissatisfaction contributed to the unification of men and ideas into the "Southern Society" where ideas matured into a part of the rationale that prompted the Decembrist revolt.

The Decembrist revolt was initially a protest by army officers in reaction to the confusion that clouded the succession process after the sudden death of Alexander I on November 19, 1825. Confusion reigned over the process because Alexander had no surviving children. In such circumstances, according to Paul I's succession law, the deceased tsar's next eldest brother then became the new emperor of Russia. The next brother Constantine, however, had removed himself from the line of succession because he married a Polish woman (Joanna Grudzinska) of lesser noble status. This meant that the next Romanov brother Nicholas was about to become tsar, but no one, including Nicholas, knew about this arrangement. Nicholas's status as tsar was not revealed until Alexander's body was returned to St. Petersburg for interment with the other Romanovs in the cathedral at the Peter and Paul fortress. Since Alexander I had died in the south of Russia and since Grand Duke Constantine remained silent and did not offer to abdicate as family members expected on the day that it became known in St. Petersburg that Alexander I was dead, Nicholas immediately swore an oath of allegiance to his brother. Constantine had not abdicated but letters left by Alexander I to be opened upon his death revealing his intention that Nicholas was to be the next tsar had circulated around the State Council and the Holy Synod. Believing that enough of Russia's political and religious leaders understood his claim to the throne was legitimate, Nicholas made his claim to the throne on December 13, 1825. Nicholas I acted swiftly once all the pieces of the claim to his throne were in place because he was privy to information that indicated that a revolt was brewing within the army's officer corps. Such news was disquieting for the newly minted tsar because his deepest and darkest fear was that the opposition was rooted in the guard's regiments because of Arakcheev's imposition of rigid and unforgiving military discipline over them. Regardless of Nicholas's popularity or lack thereof among guard's officers, there are other long-term causes for the attempt by a cohort of Russian noblemen to overthrow the Romanov regime in 1825. Decembrism was a product of the post-Napoleonic quest for educated Russians to demand access to social and political freedoms that had been learned about as a result of the army's occupation of France. These ideas had been suppressed in Russia once the Restoration had been imposed on the rest of Europe. In this regard the Decembrist revolt was an expression of the same type of sentiment that led to the Greek rebellion against Ottoman rule in 1821 and other assorted national revolts that occurred across Europe in the 1820s. Although the Greeks sought their separation from the Ottomans, the Decembrists, as best as their politics can be understood, sought to infuse a degree of social justice into the empire by advocating for the freedom of the serfs and by suggesting that some degree of political participation should be infused into the Empire's political franchise.[66]

Nicholas I

Nicholas I was outraged that elements of his nobility within the officer corps had rebelled and saddened that he had to spill the blood of Russian soldiers on the day he became tsar. Even worse, his first major task as tsar was to investigate the entire officer corps of the army to root out all those who had collaborated with the Decembrists. Nicholas oversaw the prosecution of all of the Decembrist, five of whom were hanged, thirty-one sent to prison, and over one hundred and twenty were exiled to Irkutsk and its environs to spend the rest of their days in Siberia.[67] Then, as a genuine heir to the parade ground mentality of his father Paul I, he took over the political leadership and commanded the Russian Empire as if it were an army regiment until his death in 1855. After all, he was born and spent the early years of his life in Gatchina where he developed a lifelong affinity for the lifestyle of the military.[68] The empire that he inherited from his brother was unlike anything any previous Romanov and arguably any Russian ruler had ever ruled. The Russians had contained the Ottomans, the Persians, and assorted nomadic peoples across the southern reaches of the empire. More significantly, defeating the French and maintaining Russian power in Europe had resulted in the Imperial Army growing to over 700,000 soldiers. Nicholas I asserted his authority as tsar by imposing a firm grip over the empire, and he constantly formed committees of trusted officers to examine all of Russia's social and political problems. In the course of developing his own style of leadership, he adopted an "Official Ideology" that was formulated by his minister of education, Count Sergey Uvarov, which made conservative concepts of Orthodoxy in religion, autocracy in government, and the predominant role of Russian nationality throughout the empire as the guiding principles of his regime. As a result of his attitudes toward governance, he emerged as Europe's foremost conservative leader who diligently formulated policies designed to prevent progressive reforms because he feared such activity would ultimately pose a challenge to legitimacy of the Romanov autocracy. The price Russia paid for Nicholas I's conservative extremism was that the state failed to industrialize at the time when the products of the industrial revolution were transforming military capabilities on every level—from weapons to logistics. Perhaps because of the devastation of the Napoleonic campaigns or perhaps because of the success of peacemaking at the Congress of Vienna, no major conflict broke out between the Europeans until the Crimean War. As a result, while the Western Great Powers used the products of the Industrial Revolution to enhance the power and strength of their military establishments, the Russians did little to modernize any aspect of Russian life until after their shocking defeat in the Crimea.

The Caucasus

Russians did not enjoy a prolonged period of peace during Nicholas I reign. Russia's western front was relatively quiet, but the situation in the south and in the east remained in a state of constant warfare that can be traced as far back as the sixteenth-century reign of Ivan the Terrible. While every Romanov tsar/tsarina fought a war with the Ottomans except for Paul I, these conflicts centered on control over the northern laterals of the Black Sea and the Danubian provinces of Moldavia and Wallachia. Over time this conflict became identified within Russian foreign policy circles as the "Eastern Question" and its ultimate goal was to gain control over the Turkish straits so that Russia could establish a permanent presence in the eastern Mediterranean Sea.[69] While this would ultimately pit Russia against the great European powers, perpetual conflict occurred on the other side of the Ottoman Empire. Ever present in the thinking of Russians when they considered eastward and southward expansion of their empire, the other side of the Romanov-Ottoman conflict occurred in and over the Caucasus. Peter I and Catherine II both engaged in struggles over the Caucasus, but the region gained greater significance in the early nineteenth century because of Catherine's military successes that had finally resolved control over Russia's southern frontier. The elimination of the threat of the invasion of southern Russian by irregular steppe and Ottoman armies provided Russia's leaders with the opportunity to refocus their attention on the Caucasus. Further bringing the region into focus in St. Petersburg was what proved to be the last gasp of the Persian Empire that held influence over the assorted tribal societies that populated the area. Competition between the Russian, Turkish, and Persian empires over controlling territory and resources also sharpened the religious conflict that existed between Christians and Muslims that continues to this day.[70]

Conflict in the region escalated in 1804 during the reign of Alexander I when the new Persian king Fath Ali Shah Qajar challenged the recent annexation of the modern day Georgia by Paul I in early 1801. At the time of this annexation no one in St. Petersburg understood that Paul had opened up a zone of conflict that would persist until the 1850s. Bringing Georgia into the empire was seen as an effort to protect Christians who lived in the Caucasus, which created a complicated scenario for Russian imperial design. While warfare in the Caucasus is not as well-studied as almost every other aspect of Russian military history, this region of the world where the Asia and Europe met turned into a zone of conflict where the conventional style of warfare that the Russians had developed throughout the eighteenth century would be tested to its limits in a way the Napoleonic wars did not. Alexander I made his thinking about the Caucasus clear in 1803 when he appointed General Paul Tsitsianov commander of Russia's forces in the region. In January 1804 he stormed and captured the Persian citadel at Ganja. Fath Ali Shah correctly viewed this as a direct threat to the northern reaches of his empire and a conflict would ensue that would last until 1813. Russia, however, could not dedicate overwhelming resources to this conflict due to the Napoleonic threat, which loomed throughout the duration of this Caucasian engagement. In the course of fighting the Persian Empire, Alexander I also simultaneously waged a war against the Ottomans from 1806 to 1812 not only depleting more resources but also demonstrating that the Russian army could fight more than one conflict at the same time. At best, Tsitsainov had command over 10,000 troops in the early part of this conflict in the Caucasus, but the Russian army was a far better military organization than anything the Persians could muster, which would ultimately assure success for the Romanovs by the end of this conflict. Despite contending with the French and simultaneously fighting the Ottomans between 1806 and 1812 the Russians prevailed in this conflict.[71] The scope of this victory was spelled out in the 1813 Treaty of Gulistan, which acknowledged Russia as the controlling power over the south Caucasus. The Russians, however, did not seek to occupy this territory and instead withdrew to what was now recognized as the Caucasian line that consisted of a series of fortresses and fortified positions in the north that had been constructed along the Kuban and Terek Rivers during the reign of Catherine the

Great. While the aim of St. Petersburg at this point was to build up the means of transportation and communications to integrate Georgia into the empire, the Romanovs instead encountered a slowly strengthening resistance movement composed of native tribes, largely from Chechenia and Dagestan who opposed growing Russian power that was based on religious and nationalistic reasons. This opposition would in turn teach the Russian army that their style of warfare was not going to successfully defeat what turned out to be an unconventional army, thus making this theater of operations a laboratory that ultimately solved the challenge of fighting irregular troops on their own territory.

The Persians, however, were not done in the Caucasus. Once Napoleon was defeated, in an effort to contain the further expansion of the Russian Empire, the British convinced Fath Ali Shah to strike one more time with his army in the Caucasus. What ensued was Nicholas I's first war as tsar, the Russo-Persian War of 1826–8. This conflict started when the shah ordered his army at the end of July 1826 to invade eastern Transcaucasia. The immediate impact of this strike was the Persian cavalry overrunning the Yerevan Khanate. The Russian response to this threat to her position in the Caucasus was twofold: first, a force under the command of General Valerian Grigorievich Madatov liberated Yelizaveta Pol, which had just been occupied and then the tsar's trusted friend and confidant General Ivan Fyodorocvich Paskevich commanding elements of the Caucasus Corps launched operations that pushed the Persian forces toward the Aras River. In the spring of 1827 Persian troops under the command of Prince Abbas Mirza attempted once again to seize and maintain control over the Yerevan Khanate but the effort was thwarted by troops under the command of General Afanasii Ivanovich Krasovsky. Shortly after Prince Mirza retreated back to Persia, Paskevich's main force captured Yerevan on September 28, 1827, and laid siege to the Sardarabad fortress located on the Hrazdan River. The commander of the fortress, Gassan Khan, at first intended to hold out until reinforcements arrived from Persia, but his plans were foiled when the people of Yerevan so strongly protested against being in the middle of siege that all resistance collapsed on October 1, 1827. Then, General G. Ye. Eristov chased the remaining Persian troops into southern Azerbaijan and seized its capital of Tabriz where he met up with Paskevich. With the sovereignty of Persia now threatened, the shah sued for peace and what followed was the February 10, 1828, Treaty of Turkmenchay, which eliminated Persian control over any part of the Caucasus and ushered in the annexation of the Yerevan Khanate with Yerevan as its capital. Russia had now gained complete control over the Caspian Sea and the Aras River was declared the new border between Russia and Persia. While Persia had been

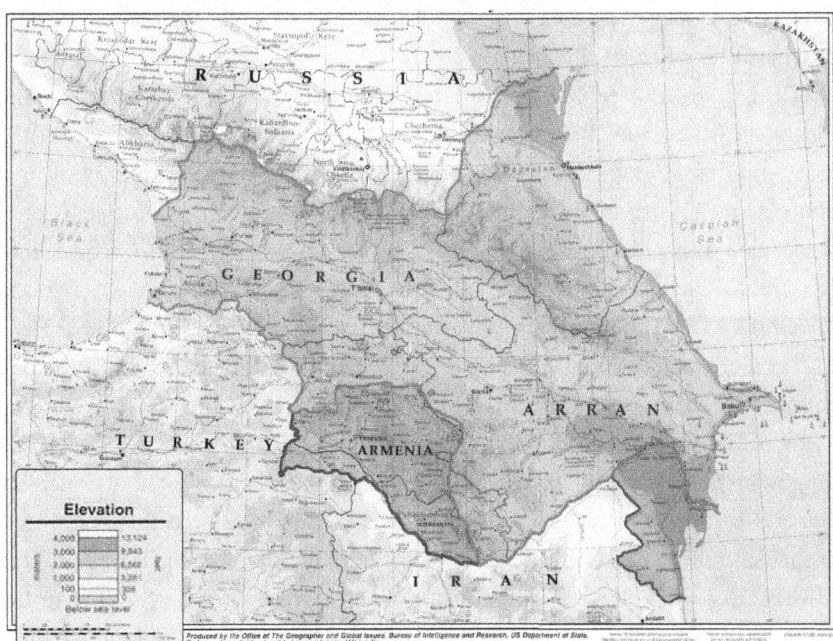

Map 3.4 The Caucasus after 1828.

removed from the Caucasus, Russia still had to contend with the Ottomans and their remaining plans for the region.

Russo-Turkish War, 1828–9

As the war in the Caucasus was winding down, the Greek War of Independence boiled over and sparked the outbreak of the 1828–9 Russo-Turkish War. Relations between Russia and the Ottomans took a turn for the worse when the Russians allied with the French and the British in defeating a combined Turkish and Egyptian fleet at the Battle of Navarino on October 20, 1827. The Greek War of Independence had reached its apex, and by the time of the battle even the Russians had decided to support the Greek nationalist drive for independence over the continued hegemony of the Ottomans over the Peloponnesian peninsula. Sultan Mahmud's response to this turn of events was to close the straits to the Russians, which prompted Russia to declare war on April 26, 1828. While French and Greek forces were removing the Ottomans from the Greek archipelago in

1828, the Turks also had to contend with a Russian invasion of Moldavia and Wallachia. Under the direct command of Nicholas I and Russian commander in chief Prince Peter Wittgenstein, 100,000 Russian troops crossed the Danube and laid siege to three Ottoman fortresses at Shumla, Varna, and Silistra. The Black Sea fleet under the command of Admiral Aleksei Greig supported the army and managed to capture Varna on September 29, 1828. Operations against Shumla and Silistra failed as the Turkish troops wore down the Russians after a summer of aggressive campaigning. The Russian army withdrew back into Bessarabia, Nicholas I returned to St. Petersburg, and Wittgenstein was relieved of command and replaced by another of the tsar's favorites, Field Marshal Hans Karl von Diebitsch. He invaded with 60,000 troops and by the end of June had conquered the fortress at Silistra rendering Shumla irrelevant.

In addition to operations in the Balkans, the Russians and the Turks also fought in the Caucasus. Having just defeated the Persians in the Caucasus, General/Prince soon to be Field Marshal Paskevich mustered Russian troops available to him and confronted the efforts of the Pasha of Akhaltsikhe and the Muslim Georgian Beys to gain control of the territory recently added to the Romanov Empire. First Paskevich captured the fortress at Kars on June 23, 1828, and on July 24 his army overran the garrison at Akhalkalaki. Then in August Paskevich led his troops on a march through the wilderness and emerged west of Akhaltsikhe where he confronted 30,000 troops loyal to the Ottomans and under the command of Kios Pasha. Outnumbered three to one, with the enemy on two sides of his forces, the Russians viciously turned on the Turks and forced them to retreat to the fortress at Akhaltsikhe. A siege ensued and on August 17, 1828, the fortress surrendered, which then allowed the Russians to consolidate their holdings over the Black Sea coast with the tsar's soldiers occupying Guria on September 30, 1828. The level of violence escalated in the spring and summer of 1829 as irregular troops mustered throughout the Caucasus turned on the Russians. Paskevich, after receiving reinforcements from European Russia, launched operations from Kars on June 13, 1829, and by June 27 he had conquered and occupied Erzerum. Major warfare in the Caucasus effectively came to a halt after the Russians won at Erzerum as Paskevich had achieved two major goals. Russia now had control over the Caucasus, which included a strong naval presence on both the Caspian and the Black Seas. Moreover, Paskevich had effectively tied up major Ottoman forces, thereby preventing the Sultan from using them in the Balkan theater of operations.[72]

Meanwhile, in the Balkans theater, Diebitsch launched an invasion of the region on July 2, 1829, with a force of 35,000 troops. By August 22, the Russians had taken Adrianople causing a direct threat to Constantinople. After losing on every front and with his empire's existence in question on September 14, 1829, Mahmud II agreed to the terms of the Treaty of Adrianople. This treaty delivered a major victory to the Russian Empire as Moldavia and Wallachia became protectorates of the tsar. It extended and strengthened the tsar's grip on the Eastern shore of the Black Sea and also acknowledged that Russia would control the mouth of the Danube River where it flowed into the Black Sea. The sultan also gave Nicholas I control over the fortresses at Akhaltsikhe and Akhalkalaki and recognized all of Russia's gains in the Caucasus as a result of the treaty of Turkmenchay. In addition, Mahmud II recognized the independence of Greece and Serbia. Perhaps most importantly, the treaty opened the strategically vital Dardanelles to all commercial traffic, which finally meant that Russia could bring its harvest of grains, cereals, livestock, and lumber out of the Black Sea to trade on global markets. The success of this war allowed St. Petersburg the luxury of concluding that Russia no longer needed to gain control of the Turkish straits. In the course of concluding the war, Nicholas I came to believe that regular trade with the West meant that, at least in 1829, the Russians had met the spirit of the original goals and aspirations in regard to their struggle with the Ottoman Empire. In the course of the two wars—the Russo-Persian 1826–8 and Russo-Turkish War 1828–9—St. Petersburg had to acknowledge that both the British and the French were taking on an unusual interest in the Ottoman Empire. Even as far back as Peter the Great, the Russians had come to understand that if they were ever going to control the vital entrance into the Black Sea, they would have to completely defeat the Turks and oust the Ottomans from power. After signing the Treaty of Adrianople, Russian policy shifted because of the realization that if the Ottomans disappeared from world history, then in all probability, the British

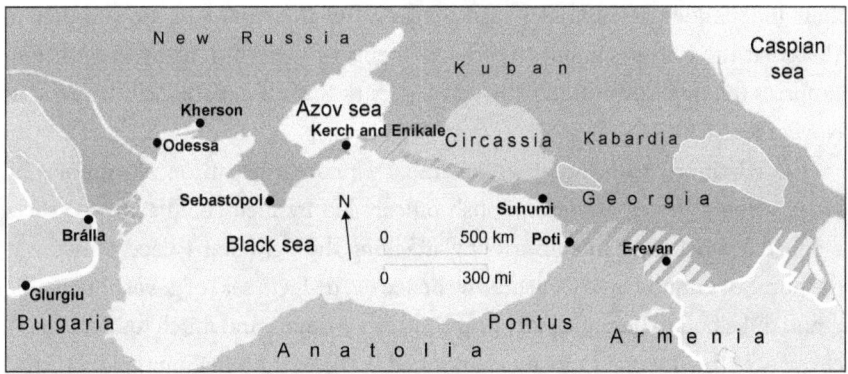

Map 3.5 Treaties of Tukmenchay and Andrianople.

and French would seek to control as much Ottoman territory as they possibly could. As a result, Nicholas I adopted a policy of normalizing relations with the Porte so that he could regroup from the cycle of constant warfare that had greeted his rise to power and determine his next move as tsar and emperor of Russia.[73]

The Gendarme of Europe

Nicholas I, however, had no time to reflect on the situation in his empire because of another major challenge to his authority, this time from Poland. The situation in Poland reached a boiling point in the summer and fall of 1830 largely because the dream of the restoration of Polish independence had received an infusion of energy during the Napoleonic period. Poland as a country remained partitioned, but after 1815 Polish upper classes believed that they could exercise a degree of internal autonomy through a political institution formed at the Congress of Vienna entitled the Congress Kingdom of Poland, which had its own constitution. The creation of the Congress Kingdom that featured what was considered the most progressive constitution in Europe combined with the widespread knowledge that Alexander I favored progressive reform resulted in a spirit of optimism among Poles after 1815. Alexander I, however, largely ignoring this constitution appointed his brother Grand Duke Constantine Pavlovich the Viceroy of Poland, which gave him command of the Polish army. Although Constantine literally gave up the crown of the Russian Empire because he married a Polish woman, he was never well-liked by the Poles largely because he systematically prevented them from gaining power and autonomy on any level in their country. No doubt the success of the Greeks in achieving their independence inspired Polish patriots, but the rumor in the summer of 1830 that the tsar was about to order elements of the Polish army to France to suppress the July Revolution provided the spark that culminated with a revolt in November 1830.

The rebellion, known as the November Uprising, began on November 29, 1830, when a group of young Polish officers led by Lieutenant Piotr Wysocki rebelled against Russian authority by attacking the Belweder Palace, which was the home of Grand Duke Constantine hence the de facto seat of government. The grand duke had to flee, allegedly disguised as a woman, and much to Nicholas I's chagrin, as the Russian garrison abandoned Warsaw, the rebellion rapidly spread into what is today Lithuania, Belarus, and western Ukraine. While the Poles themselves were caught off guard by this uprising, by the end of January they had formed a national government after the reconstituted Sejm passed an Act of Dethronement of Nicholas I on January 25, 1831. Then, under the political leadership of Jerzy Czartoryski and Michal Radziwill and the military leadership of General Jozef Chlopicki, the Poles braced themselves for the tsar's reaction to Poland's latest drive for Independence. Nicholas I's reaction to the Poles and their rebellion is known to history as the Russo-Polish War of 1831, which commenced on February 4 when Nicholas ordered von Diebitsch, fresh off of his victory in the Balkans, to invade Polish territory with 115,000 troops. Some initial successes combined with marginal support from the British, French, and the United States energized the Polish cause, which carried them into the late spring. But then Nicholas I's younger brother Grand Duke Michael Pavlovich arrived in Poland with reinforcements when roughly at the same time the Austrians and Prussians closed their borders with Poland making it extremely difficult to gather further supplies for the fledgling Polish army. Even worse, fearing a reawakening of a spirit of independence based on nascent nationalistic ideas, the British and French governments decided not to support the Polish Rebellion.[74]

The fate of the rebellion was put on hold because of Diebitsch's death from cholera on June 10, 1831. With the Ottoman front secure, Paskevich arrived in Poland to replace Diebitsch at the end of June. He took over command of the Russian army and started a slow but steady offensive drive on Warsaw. All along Polish military leadership first under Chlopicki and then, after he was wounded in the spring his replacement, General Jan Skrzynecki knew that in the long run they would not prevail against the Russian army. Yet, they had been swept away by the moment and by the enthusiasm of their compatriots, which energized them through the summer. Nonetheless, there was no stopping Paskevich as his army was composed of 180,000 men and at best the Poles mustered 70,000 soldiers at the height of the rebellion. Paskevich reached the gates of Warsaw at the beginning of September and by October 5, 1831, all Polish resistance had been eliminated, thereby ending the rebellion. Any hope of some degree of Polish autonomy was over and would not rekindle for another generation. Nicholas I imposed the Organic Statute of the Kingdom of Poland from occupied Warsaw on March 13, 1832, which abolished the Congress Kingdom of Poland that had emerged from the Congress of Vienna. Moreover, the Statute oversaw the incorporation of Poland into Russia, the Sejm was abolished and outlawed, and the Polish army was merged into the Russian army. The last injury and insult forced on the Poles in the wake of their rebellion's failure came when

Nicholas I named Paskavich the viceroy of Poland. He would rule Poland with an iron fist until his death on February 1, 1856.[75]

With the conclusion of hostilities in Poland, Nicholas I's reign that started with the Decembrist revolt in 1825 had finally gained a period of relative peace that provided him with the opportunity to consider the future of the Russian Empire and its armed forces. In this period, Nicholas I emerged as the *gendarme* of Europe and of the world. To act as the leader of the world, the tsar formed commissions composed of officers whose loyalty to himself personally and the autocracy in general were beyond reproach. These assorted commissions were charged with the tasks of studying every social, political, and economic problem facing the Russian Empire. Nothing concerned the tsar more than the status of his army. While the army had delivered victory after victory after it marched into Western Europe, the Balkans, and the Caucasus in the first quarter of the nineteenth century, the combination of Russia's changing security environment and the task of managing such a huge military force had created problems such as the one that confronted Nicholas I and his military leaders at the outbreak of the 1828–9 Turkish War. Despite having an army that approached 800,000 soldiers, when the tsar planned to invade the Danubian principalities in the spring of 1828, the most troops he could muster were 100,000. This situation highlighted the challenges that had been mounting as the empire's military forces succeeded in most every campaign they participated in dating back to at least the reign of Catherine the Great, arguably even earlier, to the reign of Peter the Great. As the empire grew in size, so did its security needs. As a result, in 1828, the bulk of the Russian army was stationed to defend a vast space against security threats from the Finnish frontier in the Baltic, to their western border with the Austrians, Prussians, and Poles, to its vast southern frontiers and the Caucasus. Moreover, as the tsar steadfastly avoided discussion about modernizing his regime on any level out of the fear that economic development based on industrialization would undermine the status quo, the army found itself to be a slow-moving, hard-to-supply organization that generated exorbitant expenses and caused financial shortfalls every year. In addition to the lack of revenues, the army endured annual struggles in meeting its manpower requirements for both its officer and its soldier cadres.

The irony of this emerging situation is that while Nicholas's commissions did a wonderful job of determining the source of the empire's problems, little was done to resolve them. Most of Russia's modernization challenges related directly to the enserfment of the peasantry, and while many schemes for eliminating serfdom were examined, nothing would be done until later. In fact, the end result of the tsar's examination of all of the empire's woes did not culminate until after the disastrous defeat in the Crimea. What became clear in the aftermath of the Crimean defeat was that all of Nicholas I's studies about Russia provided an environment in which a generation of bureaucrats emerged who laid the groundwork for the reforms that followed in the 1860–70s.[76] Nonetheless, the tsar sought to maintain his army as best as he could, so he addressed the shortcoming of officers by trying to maintain the corps through the system of military education that he inherited from Cadet Corp Academies. The Academies became the main source and preserve of the nobility who, to Nicholas I's way of thinking, were the core of his officers' cadre. While they had been in existence since the 1730s, Nicholas would insist on the modernization of their curriculum and increased the number of them from eight to sixteen over the course of his reign.[77] More significantly, the mere size of the army required a higher level of planning and organization that simply did not exist within its ranks. Nicholas I recognized the problem and much to his credit understood the solution rested in creating a higher staff organization that could oversee all of the army's needs from the planning of campaigns to the education and training of men, to the supply of soldiers in peace and war. To this end, the tsar invited the Napoleonic era Marshall Antoine-Henri, Baron Jomini to Russia when in 1832 he fostered the creation of the Imperial Military Academy that would train officers to serve on a Russian General Staff until the collapse of the Romanov regime.[78] While the Russians learned about general staff work as a result of the French revolutionary experience, they never accepted the notorious Prussian model that allowed their chief of staff to become all powerful. Instead, the Russian army followed the administrative model that first emerged during Alexander I's reign when the Russian war minister became the all-powerful force behind all things involving the empire's armed forces. Throughout the 1830s assorted commissions would concoct various schemes to try to address perpetual shortfalls in providing soldiers for the rank and file, indeed there would be a major reform in 1832 designed to create a trained reserve that could be called to duty in case of national emergency. The aim of this reform was an attempt to reign in the army's budget by limiting its size. No such effort succeeded because of the institution of serfdom, which offered no flexibility for men to rotate from a trained reserve to an operational army—either the Russian peasants were serfs or they were soldiers. As Nicholas struggled with reform limits imposed on his army by Russia's social organization, his efforts did ultimately produce the *svod voennykh postanovlenii* (Digest of Military Regulations) that remained the standard with revisions until the collapse of the Romanov dynasty.[79]

The Caucasus Still

The Russian Empire during the reign of Nicholas I, therefore, while projecting a powerful profile based on the size and success of the army during the Napoleonic period, was in fact weakening as it failed to overcome its internal challenges. Serving in the Russian army during this period offered little in the way of opportunity to engage in combat and subsequently further the careers of its officers and soldiers. One exception in this period of noncombat operations was the unconventional war that the Russians fought in and over the Caucasus. While detached from the rising tide of nationalism in Western Europe during this period and, despite being largely conquered and occupied after the last Russo-Persian War, the region featured holdout groups of clans and tribal groups such as the Chechens and the Ingush who were centered in the northeast region of Dagestan. The most famous of the rebels who resisted Russian occupation and annexation was Iman Shamil who withstood repeated efforts by the Russian army under the command of Caucasian Viceroy and Prince Mikhail Semionovich Vorontsov to defeat and destroy his movement.[80] His resistance would not be extinguished until after the Crimean War. As a result, officers in search of military action in a prolonged period of peace would seek to be assigned to the Caucasus. One of the most famous to serve in the region was D. A. Miliutin who would be Alexander II's war minister and who developed many of his ideas about the needs of the Russian army while campaigning in Dagestan and the Caucasus. More significantly, campaigning in the Caucasus formalized ideas of and about unconventional warfare into the operational thinking of the Imperial Army. Shamil in particular presented the army with the challenge of defeating a feisty, less numerous force that gained significant advantage because they better understood local topography. While serving in the Caucasus Russian officers learned about the importance of maintaining adequate supplies so their soldiers had the capability to project power in the midst of a hostile environment. These lessons would not be lost on military leaders, especially later in the century when they would become the basis for the thinking and planning of campaigns in the conquest of Central Asia.

The other action that materialized for Russian soldiers during this period of prolonged peace was their invasion of Hungary in 1849. Nicholas I's hard-core opposition to all things modern that might challenge the status quo throughout the Russian Empire seemingly paid off in 1848 when the agitation of nationalists that had slowly been simmering since the Restoration exploded across Europe.

As is common with most revolutionary outbursts, economic downturns affecting the cost and supply of foodstuff had provided the spark of revolution in the West. By the time the revolt had spread into Central and Eastern Europe, the numerous ethnic groups living in empires, especially the Austrian Empire, revealed their strident opposition to the monarchs of Restoration Europe in the course of making their demands for some degree of autonomy. Not surprisingly the Austrian and Prussian armies squashed most of these revolutionary outbursts by the force of arms. The Hungarians, however, through a combination of their own determination and with foreign support emanating from several sources managed to prevail into 1849. While the new Austrian emperor, the very young Francis Joseph, was mustering his forces in the spring, Nicholas I, who naturally considered such revolutionary activism to be abhorrent to the status quo he enforced, authorized the use of his army to suppress the Magyars. As a result, Paskavich mobilized over 30,000 troops and marched into Hungary, invading through the Carpathian Mountains in May/June 1849 and defeating the Hungarians in August.[81] The campaign strengthened Nicholas I's status as Europe's gendarme but would not bode well for his future relations with Great Britain, France, and Turkey as events in the Crimea would shortly reveal.[82]

Disaster in the Crimea

The defeat in the Crimean War (October 1853–February 1856), the worse debacle in Imperial Russian history since Peter the Great was surrounded at Purt, exhibited how Nicholas I's abhorrence of modernizing practices such as industrialization or emancipation of the serfs at once shattered the perception of the empire as being all-powerful. Ostensibly started over the rights of Christian minorities in the Ottoman Empire, the war was in fact another episode in the series of conflicts that revolved around the Eastern Question.[83] What made the Crimean situation different was the Ottomans had formed an alliance with the British, the French, and Sardinia, all of whom came to their aid once hostilities commenced. During the summer of 1853 Nicholas I became incensed with Napoleon III's claim as the guardian of Christians throughout the Ottoman realm. Nicholas responded to French posturing by accepting British efforts to negotiate a settlement that appeared to be working until Sultan Abdulmecid I balked, which culminated in the tsar invading the Danubian principalities in July 1853. Under the command of Field Marshal Ivan Paskevich and General

Mikhail Gorchakov, Nicholas I ordered the 4th and 5th Army Corps to invade Moldavia and Wallachia with 80,000 troops to protect the rights of the orthodox Christians in the Balkans. The tsar considered this move to be the least hostile action he could take. Expecting the support of the Austrians in remuneration for supporting the Habsburgs against the Hungarians, Nicholas I miscalculated when he also concluded that no one would object to Russia's occupation and his demand for the right to annex a couple of long contested Ottoman principalities on the northwestern edge of their empire. Instead, the Austrians, fearing their own weaknesses, remained neutral throughout the war and the British, concerned about Russian power expanding into the eastern Mediterranean, sent a naval task force into the Dardanelles. Napoleon III, promising to make France great again, matched the British move and sent a French task force into the Dardanelles as well. The Porte, emboldened with the knowledge that in this latest chapter of the Russo-Turkish conflict they would have Western support, declared war on Russia on October 16, 1853.[84]

In the meantime, as all diplomatic efforts failed, the conflict rapidly became a multifront war as hostilities broke out in western Armenia. While the Turkish Black Sea's fleet was inferior in size and firepower to what the Russians had deployed, the sultan slowly concentrated some 100,000 troops along their Caucasian frontier. The Russians, after two decades of maintaining military forces in the Caucasus largely to pacify rebellious Muslims throughout the region but especially in Dagestan, needed to sort out their forces as their long-time commander Prince Vorontsov had retired at the beginning of 1853. As the Turks sent a relief force via sea to the besieged fortress at Kars, Omar Pasha led a gallant defensive action in the Balkans in the late summer and into the fall of 1853. The British and French responded to this escalating conflict and sent their own expeditionary forces to Gallipoli where they stood ready for action in case the Ottomans collapsed on either front. As the British and French completed their deployment, the Russian Black Sea fleet under the command of Vice Admiral Pavel Stepanovich Nakhimov fought the Turkish relief force at the end of November 1853 on the Ottomans' northern coast at Sinop, which ended any hope for the Turks to prevail at Kars.[85] The failure of the Turkish navy at Sinop resulted in the British and the French sending their respective task forces into the Black Sea on December 22, 1853. This set the stage for a formal declaration of war on the Russians by both the British and the French on March 28, 1854. Much to the angst of Nicholas I, Austrian neutrality was illusionary as they now took a keen interest in the status of the Danubian provinces and started to concentrate troops in the southeastern region of their empire threatening to

From the Wars of the French Revolution to the Crimean Disaster 149

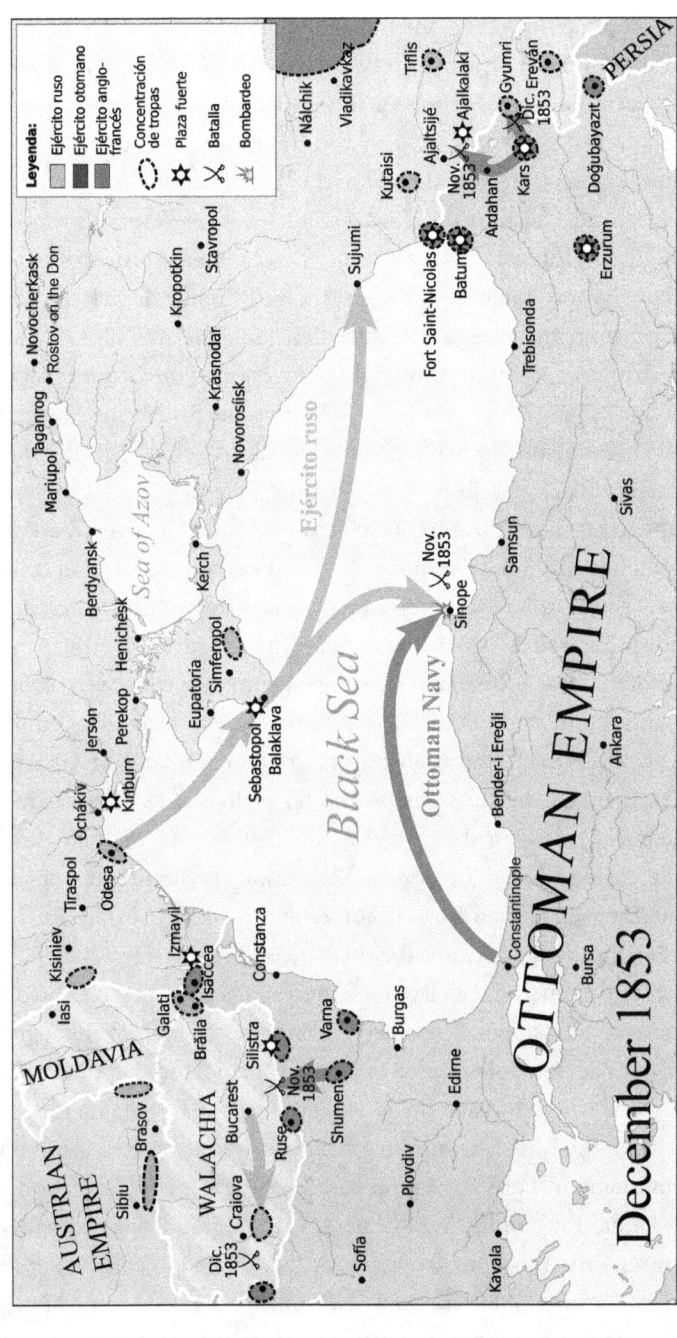

Map 3.6 Operations in the Crimean War (Ottoman Empire).

respond to Russia's invasion of the territory where the tsar's army remained embroiled against stiff Turkish defenses. To avoid going to war with another European power, in July 1854, the tsar ordered the evacuation of his army from Moldavia and Wallachia, which the Austrians would occupy in August 1854. This chain of events left Nicholas I feeling betrayed by his brother monarch Franz Joseph, an embitterment with the Habsburgs that remained for every subsequent Russian tsar. It would be a part of the equation that would culminate in the First World War wartime alliances.[86]

Although the Russian evacuation of the Danubian principalities sparked a hope that the war could end, the British and French, largely responding to the demand from their respective societies, took the war directly to Russian territory. The result of this decision was the invasion of the Crimea that occurred in September 1854. With a fleet of over 400 ships, the British and French invaded the Crimean Peninsula on September 14, north of Sevastopol, the major base of the Russian Black Sea fleet. While it took four days to get organized, the allies managed to land close to 60,000 troops under the overall command of General Jacques Arnaud. In response to this invasion, the Russian commander in chief of Crimea Adjutant General and Admiral Prince Alexander Sergeievich Menshikov mobilized 30,000 troops and marched northward to meet the enemy. By September 20th the Russians were dug in, complete with over 100 field guns on the high ground south of the river Alma. While Russian guns pinned down the British, the French 2nd division under the command of General Pierre Bosquet outflanked the Russians on the far right where Menshikov had not set up defenses believing that the cliffs on that part of the battlefield would act as a defensive barrier. This opened the door for the British and French to coordinate their assault on Russian forces and by 4:30 p.m. the Russian army uncharacteristically fled from the battlefield in disarray. Lacking cavalry, the British and French did not pursue the Russians as they retreated into the fortifications at Sevastopol. The allies, fearing the strength of Russian defenses to the north of Sevastopol, decided to encircle the port so that they could attack from the south where Russian defenses were weaker. To prepare for a long war in the Crimea, the British set up their headquarters at Balaclava and under the overall command of Lord Raglan prepared for the next confrontation with the Russians. Under the command of General Pavel Liprandi approximately 20,000 Russian troops tried to force the allies off the Crimean Peninsula at Balaclava at the end of October but to no avail. All controversies aside, one of this battle's turning points was the famous charge of the light brigade that unnerved the Russians. Through this charge, combined with the effective use of their infantry, the British were able to prevail but again could not follow up and defeat the Russians. As a result, shortly afterwards, on November 5, 1854, the commander of the Russian 10th division Lt. General Fedor Ivanovich Soimonov launched a heavy attack on the right flank of the allies in what is known as the Battle of Inkeman. Despite outnumbering the allies almost 3 to 1, the Russians had 42,000 to the allied 13,239 troops, the tsar's army did not prevail and by the end of the battle had given up on trying to remove the British and French from Crimea.[87] The siege of Sevastopol then ensued.

As the Battles of Alma, Balaclava, and Inkeman unfolded, French and British engineers started directing the work for the construction of a line of trenches, gun battery positions, and assorted redoubts from their base at Balaklava. The result of their work was that by the time of the Battle of Balaklava the allies had around 120 guns lined up to lay siege on Sevastopol. After the trio of defeats Menshikov was removed from command and replaced by General Prince Mikhail Dmitrievich Gorchakov, who was an artillery specialist. He in turn placed Vice Admiral Vladimir Alexeievich Kornilov in command of the fortress. Unfortunately, he was killed on October 5, 1854, just as the siege commenced when British shells set off the magazine at Malakoff redoubt where the admiral was observing the artillery fire of the allies. His replacement was Admiral Nakhimov, of Sinop fame, who took over command of a garrison under siege with some 35,000 men and close to 400 heavy field pieces to withstand the allied effort to destroy the Russian positions in and around the fortress. In addition to enduring the siege from land, the Russians were assailed from the sea by a mixed allied force that was composed of both steam- and sail-driven ships, thus combining two eras of naval architecture in one campaign. More important, the combined bombardment (from land and sea) became a repeated pattern that would last throughout the siege. But, a severe winter storm at the end of November halted operations and led to a long and at times desperate winter for the besiegers who struggled to bring supplies to the front. Then, in a harbinger of future conflict, the rest of the winter became a race to see which side could do a better job of supplying their armies in the field, which the allies won without question. By mid-summer, especially after the combat death of Admiral Nakhimov on June 28, 1855, the allies overwhelmed Sevastopol with a series of bombardments that forced the Russians to evacuate their positions on September 9, 1855.[88]

While the Russian debacle at Sevastopol effectively concluded the war, there remained the many other theaters of operations that were a part of this conflict. In the Caucasus, for example, the Ottomans would spend a good part of 1854 trying to get Shamil to launch large operations and at the same time attempting to negotiate an alliance with Persia. While nothing became of these efforts, the threat was clear and present and tied down Russian forces that were needed elsewhere. Throughout the war the fortress at Kars was contested and while costing some 8,000 casualties, the Russians prevailed and occupied the position on November 8, 1855. This victory, however, came too late as Sevastopol had already fallen. The allies attempted to seize Taganrog in the summer of 1855 when they sent a naval expedition into the sea of Azov in an effort to disrupt Russian supply lines. Thanks to the steady leadership of the city's governor Yegor Petrovich Tolstoy and military commander General Ivan Ivanovich Krasnov, both of whom had the support of the Don Cossacks and local loyalists, they withstood the assault and the British and French withdrew in September 1855. Meanwhile, an Anglo-French fleet entered the Baltic in April 1854 and presented a direct threat to St. Petersburg. Although the allied force outnumbered the Russian Baltic Fleet, the Russians kept the allies out of the Gulf of Finland effectively using naval mines for the first time. Allied maritime operations in the Baltic, however, disrupted Russian trade, causing economic damage as rubles were bleeding from the state's coffers because of the war. Then adding further damage to Russia, the allied fleet remained active in the Baltic and in August 1854 the allies captured the Russian Bomarsund fortress on the Aland Islands and then launched a massive assault on the Russian dockyard at Sveaborg outside of Helsinki. The assault lasted for two days and the allies reportedly fired over 20,000 shells on the Russian fortifications. But the tsar's army and navy prevailed, which left the allies determined to build a stronger fleet to sortie into the Baltic in 1855. Before that occurred, the war ended.[89]

Almost one year later, on March 2, 1855, before all of the belligerents assembled to broker a peace, Nicholas I died of pneumonia. At the time of his death the war's outcome was not in doubt. Fortunately, there was no controversy or even question about succession. After a period of transition, Nicholas I's oldest son acceded to the Romanov crown on January 15, 1856, just in time to negotiate an end to the war. The March 30, 1856, Treaty of Paris that formally ended the Crimean War marked a watershed not only in Russian history but also in modern international history. The devastating strategic loss for the Russians was their forcing to surrender the Black Sea Fleet, thereby eliminating their naval presence in this vital region. The allies evacuated Crimea returning control to the Russians, and the Russians gave Kars back to the Turks. Losing a naval presence in the Black Sea, however, resulted in Russian trade from its southern regions being under constant threat of intervention from one of the

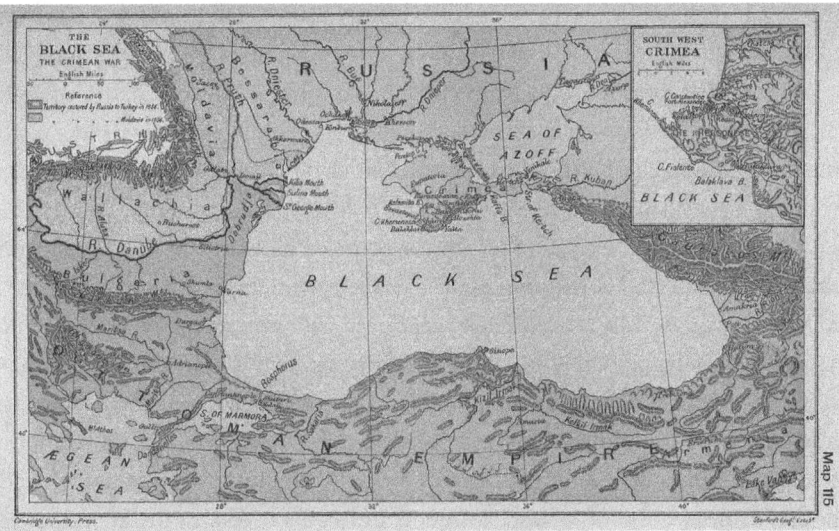

Map 3.7 The 1856 Settlement Map of the Crimean War.

Great Powers. In addition, the British and the French welcomed the Ottomans into the community of Great Powers as a way to insure them from being further threatened by Russian expansionist tendencies. Moldavia and Wallachia, while returned to Ottoman control in fact, were recognized as all but independent, which served as a prelude for emergence of an autonomous Romania in the wake of the next 1877–8 Russo-Turkish War. The war and the peace that followed all but destroyed the Concert of Europe that had been constructed after the Napoleonic epoch. Russia was defeated, Austria was isolated, British imperialism spread globally for the rest of their century, France was on its way to reestablishing its First Empire, and the Ottomans were now the weakest member of the family of Great Powers. Yet the Eastern Question still lingered in the minds of Russian policymakers and rising Slavic nationalism was transforming the Balkans into a region fraught with tensions always threatening to escalate into conflict.[90]

The war furthermore exhibited the failure of Nicholas I's decision to prevent the modernization of his empire. It laid bare the shortcomings of every state institution in the Russian government. The military command had not measured up to the task because of the dual existence of corruption and incompetence. The lack of technological development resulted in the army and navy not having the equipment necessary to win in any theater of the war, which was a major embarrassment that had not been suffered by the Russian state since the Times of Trouble. Simply put, the allied powers outclassed the Russians in the arms from their Minie rifles to their steam-driven ships. No rail network combined with medieval road conditions prevented the state from moving troops and supplies to the assorted fronts in a timely fashion. This contributed to the poor physical condition of the troops who were illiterate serfs but who were smart enough to take note that the world of the battlefield was rapidly changing. Indeed, all the Great Powers learned on the Crimean battlefields that industrialized warfare resulted in casualties on a level unknown to previous conflicts. While the Russian troops expected either terrible or no medical treatment, the British and the French expected something better for their soldiers. Thanks to journalists following troops onto the battlefield and even more importantly, their having access to the telegraph, reports of the atrocious sanitary and medical conditions reached London and Paris before going through any level of military censorship leading to the founding of the international Red Cross. The Russian Empire that had experienced well over a century of military success was bankrupt and its serf economy could no longer support the state's needs. In the aftermath of the Crimean War, therefore, no educated Russian could deny that the empire needed to reform almost every aspect of its existence if the Romanov regime was going to survive into the future.[91]

The Way Forward

Defeat in the Crimean metaphorically and literally turned a page on Russian Imperial history. The fiction of Russian military might embodied in the image of the gendarme of Europe was exposed for all to see. Losing a conflict on its own territory, albeit a regional backwater, opened up the military establishment to accusations that ranged from unpreparedness to incompetence. Even worse, any thinking person saw that restoring the empire's security and international status was not going to be easy, since its challenges were being caused by self-inflicted wounds. Nicholas I, fearing the future, deliberately promoted state policies that prevented the development of the means needed for the military establishment to have the capability to defeat an invasion such as the one that occurred in Crimea. Resolving the threats to the empire, however, meant uprooting deeply embedded features in the social, political, and economic status quo of the Romanovs' realm. The stunning military defeat clearly laid plain that the tsar's decision not to embrace and adopt the new-found technology and subsequent products of the Industrial Revolution rendered the army poorly armed compared to its foes. To put it another way, Russian soldiers were carrying small arms from the Napoleonic era while western armies and even the Ottomans had superior weapons because their troops carried breech loading rifles. Russia's deficiencies in small arms was just the tip of the iceberg! Her military preparedness did not measure up to its enemies' in any aspect—from logistics to care for the wounded. The reign of Nicholas I, arguably the most pro-military Romanov tsar with the exception of Peter the Great, came to grief because while he insisted on maintaining an exceptional military establishment, he failed to comprehend the challenges of the world in which he lived. Thus, he left his realm in desperate straits and in need of immediate reform if the Imperial project had any hope of surviving into the next century.

The defeat in Crimea did not entirely discredit the military; the teachings emanating from Suvorovian experience formed the basis of Russian military doctrine well into the twentieth century and the defeat of Napoleon remains an example of how the army once conquered all of Europe.[92] What the defeat in Crimea called into question was if Russian society could be reorganized to respond to the challenges the nineteenth century imposed upon it—from the industrial revolution to the emergence of national groups who populated the empire's borderland and sought the type of recognition that comes with the adoption of liberal ideas and participatory political franchises. Ironically, for all of his opposition to change, Nicholas I arranged for his son Alexander II to have the education and mentoring that allowed him to grasp and respond to the challenges that confronted Russia in the aftermath of the disaster in Crimean. Almost from the moment he came to power he planned for and ushered in an age of reform that offered Russian society both a path and a process to transform the military establishment from an institution dependent on serfs—subjects of the tsar—who were drafted into a standing army for the rest of their lives to one composed of a cadre who became soldiers because of universal conscription. This transformation from feudal knights to citizen soldiers was the way forward! But the path was strewn with numerous obstacles starting with the essential basic reform of Alexander II's great reforms—the emancipation of the Russian serf. Not only the struggle to adopt progressive reforms but more critically the implementation of the reforms became the central challenge for the Romanovs for the remaining time they were in power. Modernizing Russian society and economy had to occur for the military to defend the empire. In addition to continuing the process and expanding the size of the empire, the new tsar, Alexander II, also had to respond to the challenges of modernity and reform Russia from the bottom up and the top down. His task was enormous, but it was the way forward.

4

Expanding the Empire in the Wake of Defeat

The defeat in the Crimean War revealed the shortcomings of the tsarist military establishment in a dramatic and undeniable fashion. Military failure on the battlefield acted as a catalyst that ushered in an age of Great Reforms that sought to transform Russia on the same scale as the reforms of Peter the Great. The Crimean defeat necessitated prompt action to address Russia's newly revealed weaknesses if the empire was to remain a great European power. The single greatest accomplishment of this reform period was the emancipation of the serfs. Creating a free class of laborers was a prerequisite for Russia to industrialize, and industrialization had become vital to the empire. The recent loss in Crimea demonstrated that Russia needed the products of an industrialized economy to satisfy national security needs. Alexander II, moreover, came to understand that to support the transformation of his subjects from serfs to free people, all of Russian society would need to be restructured. Indeed, the era of the Great Reforms represented a period of the restructuring of all of Russian society from the practice of law, to the creation of local government (the Zemstvos), to the emergence of public health care and educational institutions on a local level unprecedented in Russian history. The Great Reforms touched most every aspect of Russian society and would have a broad and lasting impact on the empire that in some cases survived into the Soviet period.[1] For the Russian military, the central challenge was to reform itself from a serf-based army commanded by aristocrats into an armed force of mass conscripts commanded by officers whose capabilities, as opposed to social standing, propelled them to the top of the command establishment. Or to put it another way, the army needed to transform from its traditional praetorian makeup into a modern national, citizen army. And, this transformation had to take place in the midst of the crisis that followed military defeat and the effective bankruptcy that was paralyzing state finances.

Alexander II infused great energy into the Russian state and government, which was instrumental to the success the empire enjoyed during his reign. Ironically, thanks largely to his father's persistent investigation of all state issues, he was assisted by a small but dedicated group of bureaucrats who understood and therefore contributed to the reforming process of the 1860s and 1870s. By the time of his March 1881 assassination Alexander II had lived to see his military establishment recover from the disgrace that marked the beginning of his reign and defeat the Ottomans in the 1877–8 Russo-Turkish War while engineering the acquisition of Central Asia as a substantial and significant addition to the empire. These two events demonstrated that Russia's armed forces had regained their operational capabilities and could once again carry out the dual mission of securing the empire on its western and southern frontiers while pursuing imperial conquest in the east. This chapter seeks to exhibit how Alexander II Great Reforms restored the luster of the Russian military establishment by focusing on how the army adapted to its new environment and slowly, indeed in most cases begrudgingly, accepted that for the Romanovs to remain in command of Russia's empire, the state would have to modernize and accept the challenges that industrialism and emerging nationalism foisted upon it. After assessing the impact of the Great Reforms on the composition, organization, and administration of the army, and at the expense of assessing other activities such as the Polish rebellion of 1863–4, this chapter will first exam first the last great Romanov-Ottoman War in 1877–8 and then the conquest of Central Asia. As the struggle for modernization impacted the army in European Russia, the conquest of Central Asia required the military to continue to develop further the unconventional capabilities that it learned in the Caucasus during the reign of Nicholas I. Taken together the military establishment was as well poised to lead Russia into the twentieth century as any other institution of the tsarist empire.

The extent of the national crisis caused after the defeat in Crimea that confronted Alexander II when he came to the throne should not be underestimated. Understanding that emancipation of the Russian serfs was the best way to start to revive his empire, Alexander II had to respond to crushing questions that demanded immediate answers. How could emancipation occur without alienating the empire's nobility, the autocracy's traditional base of political support? How would the state finance the emancipation when its treasury was empty largely because of the expenditures made to fund the army during the Crimean War? Could these bold reforms be managed in a fashion that would not result in the alienation of the nobility and the laboring classes from the crown? Little question existed among the tsar and his advisors that modernizing Russia's economy and society started with emancipation. The challenge for the young tsar was that reform on all levels urgently had to be addressed not only to reestablish Russia's international standing, but also to reassert the primacy of imperial objectives in the policies, aims, and goals of the Romanov dynasty. The defeat in the Crimea forced the tsar and his advisors to consider the future of the empire as the Ottoman threat, while not as prevalent as it had been in the eighteenth century, clearly persisted. Meanwhile, the Russians were gaining the upper hand in the Caucasus by the end of the 1850s. At the same time, Central Asia and the Far East required attention to achieve the long-term goal of dominating the Eurasian landmass. The Russian political and military establishments needed to reform and to reorganize quickly to restore the empire's security. The Nicholaevan traditions that had institutionalized appearance and spiffy parade ground drill as the apogee of the imperial army were no longer going to maintain the power and authority of the army inside or outside of Russia.

The Great Reforms and the Russian Army

While not alone in his outlook, when D. A. Miliutin was appointed war minister on November 9, 1861, he joined the ranks of a small but well-embedded group of men who had been preparing for this moment since they had emerged as reform-minded civil servants during the reign of Nicholas I.[2] The enduring results of his reforming activities ascribed a legacy to Miliutin as one of the seminal reformers who accomplished much in his efforts to modernize Russia's military establishment through the Great Reform period. At the very least by the 1877–8 Russo-Turkish War he had restored the luster to the imperial army despite staunch aristocratic opposition. While Miliutin's early biography is available elsewhere in great detail, it is important to note that his military career was atypical for officers of his generation. Miliutin stood out among his peers because of his ability to envision the big picture, to understand that the military's administrative and command structure needed to be reformed just as much as the technological and operational capabilities of the army when it confronted the enemy on the battlefield. While his father was not wealthy, his family had sufficient means and connections to launch him in a military career as a Junker in a Life Guard's Regiment, and his intellect propelled him to be one of the Imperial Military Academy's early graduates in 1836 when he was thirty years old. Between 1837 and 1845 he served two tours in the Caucasus, the continuous theater of operation where soldiers of Nicholas I's army received combat experience, and after being wounded during the first tour, he spent ten months on recuperative leave in Europe when he learned much about the relationship between industrialization and military capabilities. This early period of his career culminated with his promotion to the rank of lieutenant colonel and his 1845 appointment to the faculty of the War Academy as professor of military geography. While always on the fast track, Miliutin gained notoriety in intellectual circles for his studies of the relationship between resources and military potential, in which he pioneered the application of statistical analysis to military geography. His statistics-based study of an adversary's resources in relation to theaters of operation not only represents the birth of modern military intelligence gathering in Russia, but it also created an enduring tradition that became a significant component in the education of future Russian and Soviet staff officers. During the Crimean War, he served on the Imperial Suite and, as the conflict's outcome became clear, found himself to be in a position to offer suggestions for reform.[3]

Soon after the defeat of the Russians in the Crimea, Miliutin linked the emancipation of the Russia peasant to any effort at military modernization, which made him an outspoken advocate of major reforms. As a result, he rejoined the operational army in the Caucasus until the dialogue on reform reached a point where his views had become acceptable. He therefore spent the next four years in the Caucasus where he put his theories into practice as General Alexander Ivanovich Bariatinskii's chief of staff.[4] Together the two men ultimately oversaw the pacification of Caucasian rebels who had fought tsarist troops for the balance of Nicholas I's reign. When Miliutin returned to St. Petersburg in 1860, he joined a cadre of imperial bureaucrats who were well-prepared to reform every aspect of life in Russia. His military career had instilled reform ideas based on solid research and teaching at the academy and extensive service in the field. Upon his appointment as war minister, he started the process of completely overhauling Russia's military establishment with a series of far-reaching reforms. Through this outburst of reforming activity, Miliutin revealed a unified plan that was designed to oversee comprehensive military improvement in Russia. First, he created military districts that were designed to simplify and streamline the authority of the war ministry throughout the empire. Miliutin's second significant reform simultaneously revamped the entire military educational and training system. Here, he sought to reestablish the Petrine concept of advancement through the ranks based on merit, a principle slowly compromised over the course of the eighteenth century. The crowning achievement to his reform efforts, however, occurred when he convinced Alexander II to enact the universal conscription act of 1874. If mass conscript armies were the wave of the future, if for no other reason than financial, then Miliutin had paved the way for Russia to reassert its supremacy in military affairs because of the size of her population compared to any other European power.[5]

Shortly after becoming war minister Miliutin began to oversee the transformation of the army's administrative structure. He foresaw that the way forward was to transform the army's ponderous administration into a better organized and hopefully more efficient organization. Military district commanders under Miliutin became responsible for overseeing the education and training while providing all necessary supplies for the soldiers under his command. While it had the impact of the gathering of command powers into a central command on the local level, it also decentralized the authority of the war ministry that until this point oversaw all of these activities from St. Petersburg. Such a system suffered from duplication of efforts throughout the military causing tremendous wastage of everything on all levels in the army. Nicholas I's scheme of concentrating all power into the hands of the war minister, in Miliutin's opinion, was a central cause for the failure of the army in Crimea. Army bureaucrats/administrators in St. Petersburg who made decisions without complete information from the operational army lead to inefficient operations on all levels—from supplying the army to the use of troops in the field. Responding to gathering unrest in the empire's Western Borderlands, properly understanding the growing agitation of the Poles for greater autonomy as a harbinger of the 1863 Polish rebellion, Miliutin experimented with his new administrative concept by establishing proto-military districts in Warsaw, Vilno, Kiev, and Odessa in 1862.[6] The efficiency exhibited by these organizations paved the way for the broader military district reform of 1864, which added the St. Petersburg, Moscow, Finland, Riga, Kharkov, and Kazin military districts to the list. By the end of the decade more districts were established in Turkestan, Western Siberia, Eastern Siberia, the Caucasus, and the Orenburg region. If nothing else, the fifteen military districts resulted in a substantial reduction in the duplication of supplies distributed throughout the army, which helped to contain expenses. Perhaps of greater significance, in one form or another, the administrative structures Miliutin created in the 1860s still exist in Russia at the time of this writing.[7]

The creation of military districts transformed the Russian military not only in the way it managed its forces in peace and war times, but also in the way it conducted business as an institution. W. Bruce Lincoln notes that between

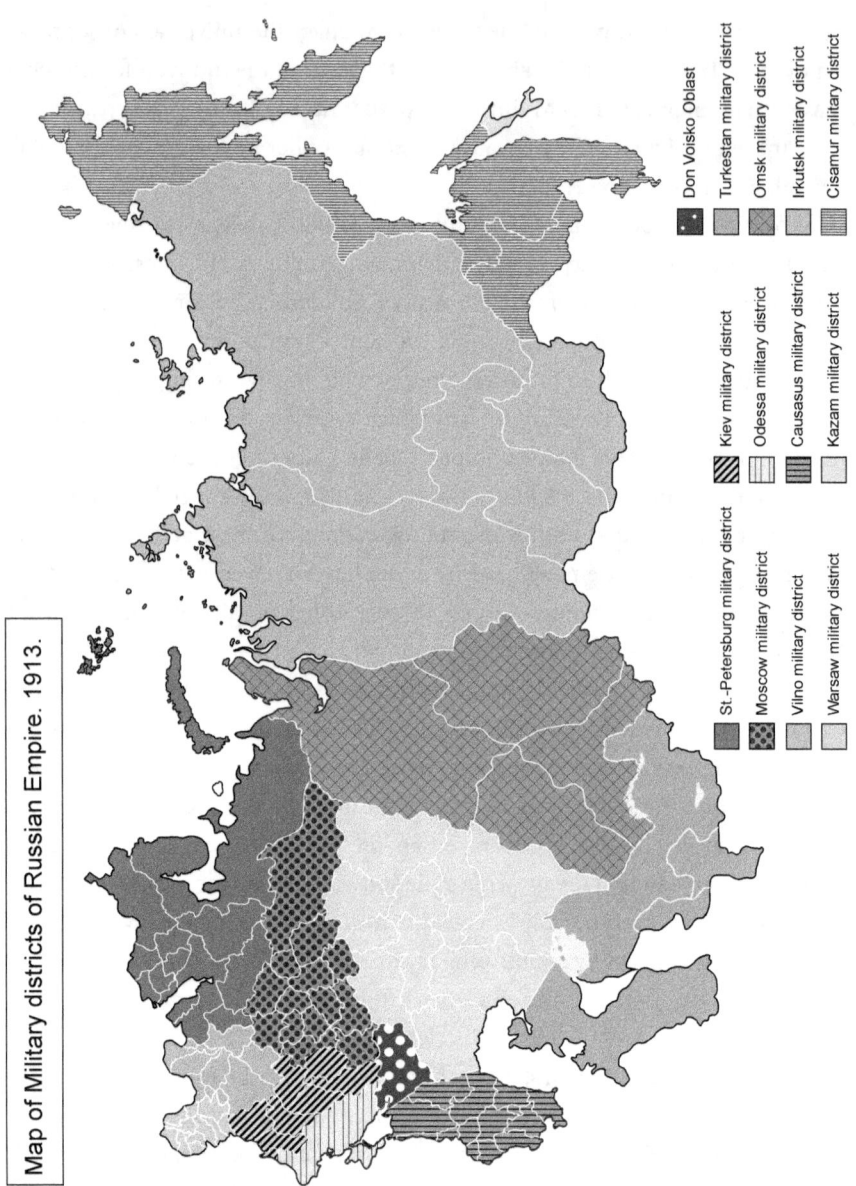

Map 4.1 Miliutin's Military Districts.

1863 and 1875 the number of documents processed up and down the chain of command dropped from 446,044 to 244,291, largely because Miliutin broke the back of the Nicholaevan system that required all matters great and small to be reported to the war minister.[8] The elimination of such redundancies throughout the system not only meant that fewer officers were needed to maintain the army, but it also allowed officers to focus more on the military's operational concerns. This shift prompted a cultural transformation within the officer corps. It restored the Petrine principle that advancement could occur for anyone who worked to develop the capabilities that they merited the right to promotion. The power of one's birthright and connections did not simply go away, but a process had been put in place that would challenge them for the remaining years of the Romanov dynasty. When he became war minister Miliutin took advantage of the journal his predecessor launched *Voenny sbornik* (*Military Digest*) that steadily became a platform in which the idea of military reform was discussed and debated. Through *Voenny sbornik*, Miliutin first put forward his ideas that the basis for the rethinking of the duties and responsibilities of an officer rested on reforming the military educational system throughout the empire. Not surprisingly, as with all of his reforms, the war minister desired to recast military education so that it touched on every aspect of a rising officer's career.

As the war minister was restructuring the army's administration he simultaneously initiated the process of overhauling the empire's military educational system. Here, Miliutin would encounter stiff opposition because a free military education had become entrenched as a birthright of those born into the empire's noble classes. That education had paved the way for Russia's nobility to enter the ranks and rise to the very top of the army's command structure, especially if the tsar noticed them, which most often happened on the parade ground during maneuvers or other such drills. This tradition had woven its way into the fabric of the Russian military. Unfortunately, by the mid-nineteenth century the military education officers received had been institutionalized so that being outfitted smartly in imperial regalia while demonstrating superior horsemanship on the parade ground had become more significant in the promotion of an officer than developing military leadership skills. Even worse, with the exception of the very small cadre that were selected to attend the Staff Academy that opened its doors in 1832, Russian officers of the early nineteenth century were not taught even a rudimentary knowledge about the world. Few Russian officers understood how the growing military capabilities of the industrial powers were transforming the battlefield into a far more lethal environment than it had ever been in the past. Miliutin was keenly aware of the shortcomings of officers' education and training because of his own educational experiences. His social status barely allowed him an education at all which meant that because of his low standing, he did not attend an elite Cadet Corps Academy. Instead, Miliutin attended the Boarding School for the Sons of the Nobility at Moscow University before entering the army.

Upon being commissioned as an ensign, he soon discovered that his education had better prepared him for the world in which he served than those who attended the prestigious Cadet Corps Academies. Miliutin fortunately had superior reading, writing, and critical thinking skills. His intellectual prowess, not his social and political connections or his appearance, propelled him to the top of the military establishment. This became strikingly clear to him after he attended the General Staff Military Academy that did little to prepare him for command. Instead he developed his thinking about the art of command while serving in the army in the Caucasus and then spending a year observing the military forces of Western Europe. In addition to knowing that education standards had to be redefined, Miliutin also envisioned that the future of Russian military power rested with the creation of a mass conscript as opposed to standing army. Such an army would require not only better trained officers but also more of them. Thus, he linked his redesign of officer's education to his main goal of transforming the army into one populated through mass conscription.

What Miliutin sought in the 1860s was to create a military educational system that would focus on military training for any young man who had the desire to serve as an army officer. As early as 1862 the war minister advised Alexander II that the old system, dependent on the nobility sending their sons to Cadet Corps Academies when they were as young as seven years old, needed to be redesigned so that military education did not begin until students were well into their teenage years. The war minister advocated for large numbers of Russian youth, ultimately from all social classes including emancipated peasants, to have access to a broad liberal arts education to obtain the skills needed to read, write, and think while they decided if serving in the army as an officer was going to be their choice for a career. Miliutin's plan was for subjects of the tsar to gain access to military education after they had become literate in civilian-run schools. To accommodate them, the war minister sent a shock wave through the nobility when he proposed transforming the Cadet Corp Academies into specialized branch training schools. Contributing to the shock, he further imposed a meritorious system of admissions based on a selective process that required officer candidates to pass a battery of tests that revealed what they knew and how well they could think. As these reforms started to transform Russia's military educational system, Miliutin's intent gained greater clarity. True to his form, over time the war minister sought to create a unified educational process designed to provide all Russian men with the opportunity to serve their tsar as an officer in his army. In his vision, regardless of social standing, a young man was supposed to go to school to gain an elementary education before joining the army. While in these schools young Russians also received information that cultivated a spirit of patriotism that would result in them having a burning desire to serve their empire as soldiers in the tsar's army. The budding soldiers then would have the knowledge to take entrance exams and earn admission into a branch training school known as military colleges (*voennye uchilishcha*) where they became experts in the requirements of their chosen service branch, be it infantry, cavalry, artillery, or engineering. Along the way the rising officers would learn the nuances of tactical operations and command through persistent peacetime training exercises, maneuvers, and summer camps. All of the education and training aimed not only to provide them with the military skills needed to prevail on the battlefield but also to inculcate a professional identity within a rapidly modernizing officer corps. Officers who excelled in this environment could next set their sights on attending one of the Empire's Staff Academies, of which graduating from the Nicholas Academy of the General Staff opened up a new path to the high command of the army.[9]

Opposition to the military education reforms remained relentless throughout the twenty years Miliutin was war minister. In many ways this opposition exposed the basic cause for the inability of Russia's armed forces to modernize at a pace that would allow it to keep up with the rest of the world. Miliutin understood that the way forward was to educate and train with the aim of professionalizing the army's officer cadre to prepare them to command an army composed of citizen soldiers who also were educated and trained to the point where they wanted to enthusiastically serve their tsar in his army. Traditional servitors, however, opposed any such thinking. When Miliutin commanded the transformation of Cadet Corps Academies into either a new type of school renamed as military gymnasiums or as the newly conceptualized military colleges in 1862, the old nobility was so appalled that the reform was never completely realized. In fact, upon his being relieved as war minister after the assassination of Alexander II, his successor P. A. Vannovski immediately restored the name and the role of Cadet Corps Academies into the roster of Russian military schools so that they could continue to serve the nobility as they always had. But what this wave of counterreform could not change was the impact Miliutin had on the curriculum offered throughout the military educational establishment. Students and officers would henceforth encounter a rigorous education that blended core educational offerings with military topics and themes regardless of their stage of education. While the aristocracy reasserted its status and prerogative, he oversaw the standardization of Junker schools throughout the empire. These schools had existed in a helter-skelter fashion throughout the empire for volunteers from lower social class (but not serfs in pre-reform Russia). Miliutin encouraged their creation in each military district sometimes attached to army regiments to provide more educational opportunities and a path into the officer corps for nonaristocrats. Another aspect of Miliutin's educational reforms that could not be completely short-circuited was the introduction of rigorous entrance exams for all military schools, and likewise, a battery of exams that had to be passed and in some cases research projects completed before students graduated and received commissions, higher ranks, and plum appointments throughout the tsar's armed forces. In this fashion Miliutin fused a level of professionalization based on merit into the ranks of the Russian officer corps that had an impact on its overall composition and capabilities by the end of the nineteenth century when anyone who held a commission in the army had also graduated from these reformed schools.[10]

Miliutin was not done with his reforms once he overhauled the empire's military educational institutions. What remained defined his efforts to transform Russia's military as an institution and agency of social change during the period of the Great Reforms. Overcoming much opposition, Miliutin lobbied for and successfully achieved through the Universal Military Training Act of 1874 what amounted to conscription into the ranks for all able-bodied males.[11] The intent, from this time forward, was for all males to serve in the ranks for a specific period and then muster out of the active duty army into first the reserves and then the militia. Through such practices Miliutin sought to have ready trained soldiers who could be called up in times of national emergency. The aim of this reform ran even deeper as it was designed to eliminate Russia's use of the dreaded lifetime service requirement that depended on a haphazard process that sometimes had young men being selected by chance based on the decisions of village elders who may or may not have acted in the best interest of their community. Eliminating a standing army and replacing it with one composed of conscripts was modeled after Western European practices and used to great effect by the Prussian when they unified their German nation in 1870–1. The time had come for Russia to transform its standing army into a conscript army to send the clear message that she was joining the European powers in the business of creating, maintaining, and fighting with a nation in arms, thereby possessing an army that represented the empire, not just the regime. In the end, Miliutin convinced Alexander II to agree to universal conscription by demonstrating how adopting a military system in which all men served in the ranks would provide the empire with the capacity to mobilize as many men, if not more, than all of the Western European powers combined all while saving funds and resources especially during peacetime.[12]

The Russo-Turkish War, 1877–8

The improved capabilities of the imperial army were plainly revealed when it went to war against the Turks in 1877–8. The 200-year-old conflict between imperial Russia and the Ottoman Turks remained rooted in two issues: geographic hegemony over the strategically vital entrance into the Black Sea (The Dardanelles, the Sea of Marmora, and the Bosporus Straits), otherwise known as the Eastern Question and religion. Since the Ottoman conquest of the Byzantine Empire, all of Europe's Great Powers used the status of Christian subjects under the sultan's control as a reason to meddle in Turkish affairs. The fate of the Christians living in a Muslim-dominated world took on heightened significance in the age of imperialism as Europeans conquered the world while claiming they were doing it to spread the faith. Looming over Russian-Ottoman relations was a perceived need to redress the terms of the 1856 Treaty of Paris that concluded the Crimean War to which Alexander II agreed as a young tsar in great distress. In the post–Crimean War period, the question of national self-determination in the Balkans further inflamed relations between Constantinople, St. Petersburg, and the Western Europeans. Mainly born out of agitation by the Serbs, Romanians, and Bulgarians against Turkish tax policies, tensions over religion and taxes had been growing since before the Crimean War and they reached a boiling point in the 1870s. This combined with increasing nationalistic sentiment that was sweeping across Europe by mid-nineteenth century had made most of the territories in the Balkans hot spots of dissent against the Turkish yoke. Long-term and new grievances combined with growing Pan-Slavic sentiment, that all Slavs should be united under Russian leadership, provided Tsar Alexander II with cause to consider fighting his own Turkish conflict. There was more, however, to the origins of this war. As a result of the unification of Germany, the European strategic situation underwent a transformation that started the process of realigning the Great Powers for the first time since the 1815 Congress of Vienna. After the wars of German Unification, Prussia, now Germany, replaced Austria-Hungary as the dominant Central European power. Russia had supported the Germans in their drive to unify but now had to consider the presence of a new power in terms of how the Germans would seek to spread their influence, especially in the Balkans where Ottoman power waned. Thanks to Alexander II's appointment of Alexander Mikhailovich Gorchakov as his foreign minister, relations between Russia and the new German nation started off well. In the aftermath of France's defeat and with the support of Russia's new ally, Germany, the tsar gained international support for the reestablishment of its Black Sea fleet for the first time since losing the right in 1856.[13]

Germany's initial support of Russian ambitions in the realm of foreign affairs was based on the principle of the formation of an alliance between Alexander II, Wilhelm I, and Francis Joseph known as the Three Emperors League, which had one source of unity—the isolation of France. The alliance, however, was fraught with conflicting imperial ambitions over the Balkans that grew stronger as the Ottomans became weaker. In this diplomatic environment Gorchakov crafted a Balkan alliance composed of Bulgarians, Romanians, Serbians, and Montenegrins. Activities on the ground culminated in the outbreak of hostilities including a series of uprisings by Christians who lived under the Ottoman yoke in southeastern Europe beginning in Herzegovina in the summer of 1875. As the Ottomans sent troops to quell the revolt, resistance spread into Bosnia. By the next spring, a group of Bucharest-based Bulgarians gained support across Bulgaria, which prompted the Ottomans to react viciously as regular and irregular troops from the Portal committed atrocities against civilian populations that resulted in international condemnation from across Europe. At the same time with Ottoman troops marauding throughout Bulgarian lands, the Serbs and Montenegrins declared war on Turkey, which resulted in them, with Russian support, repulsing an Ottoman invasion of their respective territories. These Ottoman actions in the Balkans prompted a meeting between Franz Joseph and Alexander II with their foreign ministers in Bohemia that resulted in an agreement that Austria would occupy Bosnia and Herzegovina and in return the Russians would regain Bessarabia, which it had lost after the Crimean debacle. The Russians also got to annex the Black Sea port of Batum, which further made the loss of influence in Bosnia Herzegovina acceptable. Both leaders recognized that the time had come for Bulgaria to be declared autonomous. The Ottomans did not recognize these agreements and continued to fight in Serbia. When in the fall of 1876 the Russians started to mobilize troops aimed at the Balkans, the sultan agreed to meet with all of the European powers in December 1876 in Constantinople. The Europeans at this Constantinople conference tried to force the Ottomans to accept the autonomy of Bulgaria, Bosnia, and Herzegovinian. When the sultan refused these terms and, with European opinion outraged over Ottoman atrocities, the Russians stood on the brink of declaring war. In the early winter of 1877 Alexander II decided he could go to war against the Ottomans once the Austro-Hungarians assured Russia that they would remain neutral in a future Balkan conflict. Once his military leaders informed him that they were ready, the tsar declared war on the Ottoman Empire on April 24, 1877.[14]

This latest version of the Russo-Turkish conflict revealed that Miliutin's reforms had resulted in improvements in the army's organization and administration that, thanks to a modern war plan, gave Russia's army's leaders a set of aims and goals to pursue against the Ottoman military forces. Having a war plan that factored all aspects of military capabilities from the mobilization of forces to a guide for operations represented a coming of age of Russian staff work. It was the product of Nicholas I's decision to professionalize his general staff through the creation of its own academy—the Nicholas Academy of the General Staff—and Miliutin's tireless effort to promote the role of staff officers and their work throughout the military establishment. The plan was based on the premise that Turkish naval superiority on the Black Sea combined with geographical constraints limited the army to a two-prong invasion of Ottoman territory—one in the Caucasus and the other in the Balkans. The main theater of operation was the Balkans because the political agendas of nationalists along with calls by the orthodox Christians of the region to break out from being under the Ottoman yoke had been the cause of the war. The Caucasus campaign, while a secondary theater of operations, tied up Turkish troops and, in the end, gave the Russians more opportunity to expand their control. The war plan first emerged from a series of lectures written by General Nicholas Nikolaevich Obruchev who was one of Miliutin's key reformer allies, chief of the main staff, and sometimes referred to as Russia's Moltke.[15] The lectures were delivered by Lt. Colonel N. D. Artamonov of the main staff to the officers of the St. Petersburg military district in the spring of 1876. Concerned that the western Europeans could choose intervention in the Balkans at any time, Obruchev planned a rapid strike on the Ottoman capital Constantinople with 250,000 troops that he wanted to concentrate in Bessarabia before the outbreak of hostilities. Once war was declared, these troops would march directly across Romania and then cross the Danube River all while protecting the flanks of the invasion force with defensive cordons to the east and west. After invading Bulgarian territory, the Russian army would aim for the Shipka Pass to cross it before the Turks could mobilize their defenses and make such passage costly in men and equipment. If all went according to plan, the Russians would spend at most four months campaigning from the period of the invasion until they broke out of the Balkan Mountains and marched on Adrianople and then Constantinople. Thus, Obruchev, together with officers on the main staff, planned a lightning campaign striking the Turks through the Balkans before they could respond. According to the aim of this plan, the Russians were going to knock the Ottomans out of southeastern Europe and present them and the rest of the world with a *fait accompli*.

Through the mobilization period and the initial stages of operations, the General Staff maintained control of the movement of supplies and troops thus exhibiting a higher level of professional skills than in prior conflicts. Once the Russians invaded Bulgaria, however, their poor understanding of their operational environment and interference from the tsar and top aristocratic military leaders combined with stiffer than expected Turkish resistance compromised the Russian initiative and transformed the war's pace from a lightning campaign to a slog through the Balkans.[16] A professional understanding of duties and responsibilities was indeed emerging among command elements in the army, but they had a long way to go before they controlled operations. This campaign started when upon the April declaration of war the Russian army of some 185,000 men started marching through Romanian territory under the overall command of Grand Duke Nikolai Nikolaevich (the elder). It reached the northern bank of the Danube by the end of June. The march had been arduous and suffered from delays largely due to flooding in the Danubian provinces, which fortunately did not compromise the war plan. Subsequently, on the night of June 14–15, using a pontoon bridge system Major-General Mikhail Ivanovich Dragomirov ordered the four army corps under his command (VIII, IX, XII, and XIII) to cross the Danube. With little opposition they successfully established a beachhead by the next morning on the southern shore. Based on extensive intelligence gathering, the Russian chose Zimnicea, a small town between two large Turkish garrisons at Nikopol and Ruschuk, as the place to cross the Danube because it was in direct line with the Shipka Pass, a vital route that each side needed to control to maintain their lines of communications and supply. In addition, in the buildup for the invasion, artillery batteries were positioned opposite Nikopol and Ruschuk to harass and contain each position once the crossing started. Engineering troops contributed to the preparations for the invasion by constructing pontoon bridges and five mine barriers were laid in the Danube east and west of the invasion site, thereby rendering Turkish ironclad river patrol boats useless. Dragomirov was without question the right person in the right place and the right time as he was bold, confident, and above all else had the most knowledge of any officer in the army at that time. He exhibited courage and cunning by being with the vanguard of his troops, which gave him a bird's eye view of the battlefield. These observations and his

Expanding the Empire in the Wake of Defeat 171

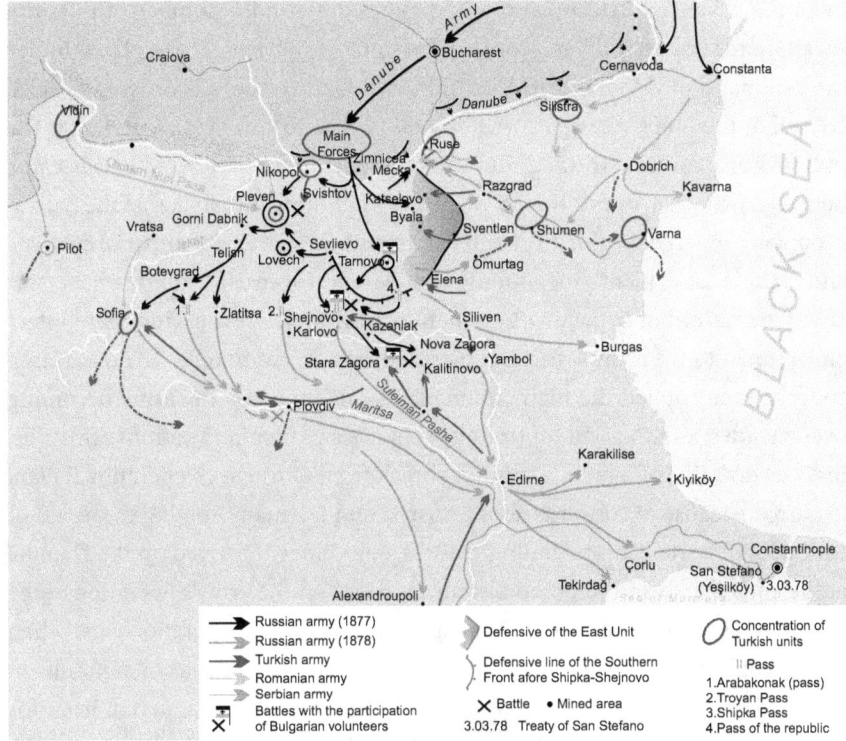

Map 4.2 Campaign Map of Russo-Turkish War, 1877–8.

ability to explain his ideas and goals for the invasion with his unit commanders during operations resulted in Dragomirov exercising decisive control over small unit operations after the army entered Bulgarian territory. His enthusiasm led to success as within 24 hours—a beachhead existed that the Ottomans could not contain. Dragomirov's leadership through this operation imbued confidence in everything the army was doing. As one of the war minister's collaborators and supporters through the reform period, Dragominov's performance offered strong evidence that Miliutin's reforms had found solutions to the malaise from which the army had most recently suffered.[17]

As it deployed into Bulgaria, the army was organized into three main columns. The grand duke remained in command of the western column as it moved on Turkish positions at Nikopol and Plevan (Plevna). An eastern detachment, under the command of Tsarevich Alexander Alexandrovich advanced on Ruse and it was assigned the task of protecting the invading army's flank. The third group was modeled after J. E. B. Stuart whose US Civil War accomplishments had been studied at the Russian General Staff Academy. This group, sometimes referred to as the advanced detachment, was organized around a number of infantry, cavalry, and support units and consisted of some 16,000 men. It was placed under the command of General Iosif Vladimirovich Gurko who was ordered to seize control of the Shipka Pass, a corridor vital to the Turkish war effort. So far the prewar war plan was working. But then the operation floundered and became bogged down when opposition to Obruchev's lightning thrusts across the Balkan Mountains emerged within the High Command. Supporters of imperial customs and traditions, evidently beginning with Miliutin himself, cautioned the tsar about the hazard of bypassing Ottoman fortresses, thereby leaving them intact and a threat to the army's rear as it marched on Constantinople. The overriding concern that gripped the high command at this time was the army becoming overextended and thus cut off from its supplies and communications. This shift in the army's line of march, a stunning break from Obruchev's operational plan, occurred because of concerns about Austria and Germany coming to the aid of the Sublime Porte. Compounding matters, Alexander II arrived on the Danube at the end of June and imposed a strategic pause on the army's operation at the worst possible moment in the campaign. Besides halting operations just when Gurko could have broken out of the Balkans, it set up a long-term conundrum that affected the operations, indeed the capabilities of the imperial army for the rest of its existence. Without question the Romanovs had always been deeply connected to their armed forces. Yet, one of the products of Miliutin's reforms was the emergence of a new breed of professionalized officers who were educated, trained, and prepared to command and administer the army based on knowledge and merit, not customs and traditions. In addition to its immediate impact on the course of the war, the decisions of the tsar and grand duke in July 1877 to derail Obruchev's war plan set up a long-term struggle between the emerging military professionals and the traditionalists who populated the army's high command over which cohort was going to command the army in war and peace. This issue was never resolved as long as a Romanov remained on the throne.

The decision to engage in a dubious battle in Balkan passes against Ottoman fortified positions resulted in the collapse of prewar schedules and much bloodshed. The decision to revise the war plan and not advance headlong toward Constantinople was also based on growing concerns about the strength of the enemy forces. Once the invasion was underway, the Russian High Command came to realize that prewar estimates of Ottoman strength may have been incomplete. For example, prewar estimates determined that the Ottomans had no more than 150,000 troops in the theater of operations at the beginning of the war. What was missing from this information was that the Turks could easily mobilize 400,000 soldiers from across the Balkans and western Anatolia. The Turks' prewar strategic thinking on the Balkans was based on having absolute control of the Black Sea and stationing large and powerful troop formations in the quadrilateral fortresses network formed around battlements at Rushchuk, Silistria, Varna, and Shumen. While the names of these fortresses may not mean much to a western audience, the point is the Ottomans had built numerous fortresses throughout the Balkans and that they were not going to be easily removed from an area they had occupied since the sixteenth century. By July 7th when Gurko had occupied the Shipka Pass, it had become clear that the Ottomans were reinforcing their armies at a pace more rapidly than the Russians had anticipated. The concern of both the grand duke and the tsar was that a headlong advance through modern-day Bulgaria would leave them stretched too thin, thereby creating vulnerabilities that could become fatal to the campaign. Hence their surrendering of the operational initiative resulted in three efforts to reduce, and then they failed to besiege the fortress complex at Plevna. The fortress at Plevna became the focus of operations between July and December 1877 because an Ottoman army under the command of Osman Nuri Pasha, considered the best Ottoman commander in the theater of operations, was transferred from Serbia where he had been confronting and containing nationalist activists who sought their liberation from Ottoman tutelage. At first, he was ordered to reinforce the garrison at Nikopolis, but it fell to the Russian IX Army Corps under the command of Lt. General Baron Krudener on July 4th. With the Russians occupying their objective, the Turks descended on Plevna some 25 miles from Nikopolis because it featured many redoubts and was at a vital crossroads in the Balkans.[18]

The siege of Plevna became the center of operations, therefore, and turned into the best-known campaign of the war largely due to newspaper reports from the British Press. The Russians did not plan for a siege at Plevna. Obruchev's plan had hinged on avoiding a prolonged siege operation because of the costs in men and materials along with the loss of time, which worked against the Russians in the court of international opinion. The Ottomans turned it into a center of resistance by accident that the Russians could not ignore because it threatened the western flank of the army; if the Turks prevailed, they could cut off Russian supplies and communications. After an initial foray into Plevna at the beginning of July—one in which Gurko briefly occupied the town on July 8th, Osman Pasha took advantage of the Russian distraction with the conquest of the Shipka Pass (see below) to rush troops into Plevna and to fortify the position with all the resources available to him. Once Gurko had pacified the Turks in Shipka, the Russians became acutely aware of the growing threat to their western flank at Plevna and subsequently shifted their attention to that position. Pasha's efforts to rush troops to Plevna first paid off on July 9th when Lt. General Yuri Ivanovich Schilder Schuldner lost half of his troops—some 3,000 casualties—in a poorly executed attempt to oust the Turks from their position. The failure of this first battle of Plevna forced the Russians to do a proper reconnaissance of the position—a task that should have been completed before launching any attack. This defeat combined with the information gathered in its aftermath made clear both the extent of Pasha's re-enforcement efforts and the threat to Russia's war effort. Plevna now emerged as the focal point of Russia's war effort in the Balkans. As the Russians learned about and better understood their situation, they reinforced their troops and by July 18th had concentrated some 35,000 troops who launched a second assault on Plevna that also failed despite having at least 10,000 more troops than the Turks. The Turks had not wasted time after their success in the first battle of Plevna and had spent the ten days between battles fortifying their positions and setting up fields of fire that gave their superior assault weapons, the Martini-Peabody Rifle, a decisive advantage over the Russians. Although suffering from sagging morale after the second Plevna battle, the Russians regained their composure because of successes in Shipka Pass and the arrival of Romanian reinforcements. At this point the Russians used allied Romanian troops to reinforce the size of their forces to over 90,000 combatants who had at their disposal close to 450 heavy weapons. Then, after some advanced reconnaissance and planning, the Russians launched a third attempt to capture Plevna that started with an artillery barrage that lasted four days beginning August 22nd. The attack would persist until the end of the month before it collapsed due to poor command and control that resulted in failed coordination between Russian and Romanian units. Even worse, after the third Plevna the Russians could not ignore the devastating effect of controlled rifle fire on their troops as they assaulted Turkish fortified positions in open formations. This failed assault resulted in approximately 20,000 additional casualties. At this point the tsar called on General Franz Eduard Graf von Todleben, hero of the Crimean War for his command of sappers, to command the reduction of Plevna. Upon arriving on the field of battle and assessing the course and outcomes of the three prior battles, Todleben concluded that an old-fashioned siege offered the best path forward. In late November Osman Pasha ordered what proved the final attempt to break out of his position due to a lack of supplies and when that failed, he capitulated and surrendered to the Russians.[19]

The outcome of the siege of Plevna was linked to the other operation that occurred simultaneously at Shipka Pass. Supporting General Gurko as he marched toward Shipka Pass was the ninth infantry division under the command of Major General Prince Mirsky. He arrived at the pass a day before Gurko who was delayed by Turkish resistance. Mirsky nonetheless with inferior forces attacked the Turks on July 17th and while his attack was ultimately turned back, he did occupy some mountains on both sides of the pass. The next day Gurko arrived in force and used these positions that were north and south of the Ottoman army to launch his assault on the Turks. By the end of the day the Russians, using frontal assaults, exposed their men to withering Turkish fire and had been turned back. Suleiman Husnu, commander of the Turks in the Pass, who had been wounded the previous day, nonetheless decided that his forces stood no chance of success with Russians to his north and south and therefore sought an armistice. Husnu, however, used the subsequent negotiations to buy time as his forces slipped away from their positions in small units to the west and east. In this fashion the Russians gained control of the pass by the end of the month. Then, in an effort to maximize their resources, the Russians sent the bulk of their army in the pass to re-enforce their efforts to reduce Plevna. To replace the troops sent back to Plevna, the tsar approved the deployment of Bulgarian volunteers known as *Opalchentsi* to help occupy and defend the Shipka Pass. The *Opalchentsi* viewed this war as the moment in history when they would gain their liberation from the Ottoman yoke. The Bulgarians volunteers proved their metal in August when approximately 5,500 of them together with some 2,000 Russians held back an assault of some 40,000 Turks that started on August 9th and lasted for six days. By the end of the battle, the Russians and the Bulgarians were out of ammunition and allegedly threw rocks and other debris at the Turks but did not yield their positions. Suleiman Pasha would try one more assault on September 13th but by this time the Russians and Bulgarians had built solid defensive redoubts. Turkish forces using their own version of a frontal assault failed to dislodge the allies, and this third attempt by the Ottomans to seize control of the pass ended in failure as well. The forces remained stalemated with the Russians and their Bulgarian allies never being ousted from the positions.

Meanwhile, at the outbreak of war and according to Obruchev's original plan, the Russians were supposed to mobilize 125,000 men to send to the Caucasus to tie down Ottoman forces and with some luck reduce their fortresses at Kars, Batumi, Ardahan, Bayazid, and Erzerum. Under the command of Grand Duke Michael, the Russians managed to dispatch only 50,000 troops in April, and they were divided into four detachments. The grand duke ordered his chief of staff, General Adjutant M. T. Loris-Melikov, to orchestrate a campaign designed to achieve his mission's goals. The Russians enjoyed some early success, but by the beginning of May the Turks had managed to mobilize close to 100,000 men under the command of Mukhtiar Pasha who first slowed the Russian offensive and by the end of the May had forced the tsar's armies in the Caucasus into a defensive posture. Despite the Caucasus being a secondary theater of operations and regardless of the situation in the Balkans, the high command decided that action had to be taken to remedy the army's malaise. Thus, at the beginning of July, on the orders of Alexander II, Miliutin mobilized more troops to send to the theater of operations and perhaps most importantly transferred Obruchev and attached him to Grand Duke Michael's staff. Obruchev went right to work in planning a new campaign and when reinforcements arrived, he managed to isolate Mukhtiar outside of Kars and fight a three day battle from September 20 to 22. Although the outcome of this confrontation was indecisive, the Pasha inexplicably withdrew to static defensive lines in the heights outside of Kars. Obruchev, recognizing an opportunity, ordered his troops to maneuver for an assault on Mukhtair Pasha's position that occurred on the morning of October 3rd when the grand duke ordered a frontal assault. By the end of the day the assault had developed into a battle of annihilation as the deployment of the Russian army allowed it to attack from the front, the rear, and the flank. But in the general confusion of the day, the Pasha slipped away and made his way to the fortress Kars and prepared for the forthcoming siege. The Russians clearly had gained the initiative and spent the next month reinforcing and concentrating troops for the final storming of the fort, which occurred on the night of November 5–6. Again, and most likely because of Obruchev's presence, elaborate preparations were made to execute a complex plan that depended on deception and surprise and by mid-day on November 6th the Russians had reduced and occupied Kars. There would be a final drama to this campaign as Mukhtair Pasha once again escaped from certain capture and made for the fortress at Erzerum where the war devolved into another siege, but outbreaks of typhoid and cholera prevented either side from prevailing before the war ended in March 1878.[20]

The situation in the Caucasus notwithstanding, the turning point in the war came with the surrender of Plevna on December 10, 1877. With the western flank secured and with control of the Shipka Pass, the grand duke finally executed the end stage of Obruchev's plan when he ordered his army to march on Constantinople. Of course, Obruchev meant for this to happen before the dead of winter, yet the army marched through the Balkans despite the cold and ice and while slow and ponderous the Russian army became an unstoppable

Map 4.3 Russo-Turkish War in Caucasus, 1877.

juggernaut. By January 20th the Russians occupied Adrianople and stood at the gates of Constantinople and prepared to lay siege to the Ottomans' capital. This threat to the Sublime Porte was too much to bear for the Western Powers and in response to it the British sent a task force into the Sea of Marmara. Fearing a broader European conflict, the Russians agreed to an armistice on January 31, 1878. Once hostilities concluded, the Russians and the Turks negotiated what became the Treaty of San Stefano that was signed on March 3, 1878. The treaty was a far-reaching affair that transformed the political status of the Balkans as it recognized the independence of Romania, Serbia, and Montenegro and created a "Greater Bulgaria," that Alexander II envisioned as a Russian satellite state. The aim in creating this state, in addition to gaining influence throughout the Balkans, was to have an overland access from the Black to the Aegean Seas, thereby resolving Russia's long-standing eastern question. The "Concert of Europe," however, could not accept this treaty because it gave Russia too much power and authority throughout the Balkans. Seeking to balance the interest of all the Great Powers in the Balkans, Bismarck emerged as the Metternich of his time by organizing a Congress of Berlin that met in June and July 1878. With representatives of all the Great Powers present, the Congress revised the amount of territory Russia dominated down to granting the tsar gains in southern Bessarabia and control over former Ottoman fortresses at Batumi,

Artvin, Ardahan, Olti, Bayazid, and most importantly Kars. More significantly the Russian idea of a "Greater Bulgaria" was revised into a smaller principality with an elected king who still needed the approval of the sultan. And most importantly, Russia was allowed to restore its naval presence in the Black Sea for the first time since the Crimean War. The Russians therefore won the war but lost the peace and became so outraged with Bismarck's heavy-handed conduct that irreparable damage was done to the Three Emperors' League, thus paving the way for the Franco-Russian alliance of the 1890s. The Russians emerged from this bruising experience so disenchanted with the Europeans that they separated themselves from the mainstream of European affairs and shifted the main focus of their empire building activities from Europe to Central Asia and the Far East.[21]

In the war's aftermath, everyone from Tsar Alexander II through Miliutin on down the chain of command understood that the recent conflict needed to be studied and assessed to interpret the successes and to learn from the failures of the army's performance in the conflict. Without question the army's execution of its

Map 4.4 The Balkans before and after 1878.

mobilization plan and its early performance after crossing the Danube indicated that its capabilities had improved since the Crimean debacle. Yet the operational doctrine of the imperial army failed to lead to overwhelming battlefield success in a timely manner. The Russian army was still fighting Napoleonic-type battles with soldiers lined up in ranks before being ordered to charge openly into Turkish defenses. When they deviated from their mobilization plan, however, three shortcomings slowed down operations and almost caused the entire campaign to end in failure. The first was for all of the successes of the Miliutin reforms, the army did not universally execute on a tactical level either with the initiative or with vim and vigor. There were some tactical successes on the regimental level but more occurred in the Caucasus than in the Balkans and they were always the product of individual commanders who gathered intelligence, thereby arming themselves with the information needed to retain the initiative when their command engaged the enemy. The other problem was technological, that is, Russia too often found itself outclassed in small arms although not as grievously as during the Crimean War. The doctrinal challenge combined with the technological shortcoming meant that in the face of withering Turkish fire, Russian infantry still marched in linear formations, thus presenting themselves as exposed targets. The Turks, therefore, better armed with repeating rifles outmatched the Russians in this aspect of fighting. The result was mass casualties that reached levels never before seen nor anticipated. While accurate numbers are difficult to assess, casualties totaled tens of thousands of combatants and civilians.

The lethality of modern infantry weapons would have an especially devastating effect on the Romanovs as one battle after another turned into repeated bloodbaths. Winning the war in the face of these technological challenges created an immediate need for a careful assessment of the army and its operations in every aspect. Unfortunately, such a study caused huge challenges for the Russians because all of its conclusions ultimately called into question the leadership of the imperial army. Conducting a thorough investigation of operations was complicated because the army's commanding elements, despite Miliutin's best efforts, were still heavily dependent on the Romanovs' personal leadership as well as that of members of the high nobility. In other words, to question the military's performance was also to question the capabilities of the tsar's relatives and his main political supporters. After all, the overall commander in chief of the army that invaded the Balkans was Grand Duke Nikolai Nikolaevich, the tsar's brother, and his son, Tsaravich Alexander, nominally commanded the army's eastern detachment or the left wing of the invading force. With some 70,000 men under his command, the future Alexander III oversaw the initial assault of the fortress of Rushchuk. From this experience he came to despise war, hence he earned the reputation as being the "Tsar-Peacemaker." Yet, specifically because of the intervention of the tsar, Miliutin, and Grand Duke Nikolai Nikolaevich, Obruchev's plan for a lightning campaign was discarded in favor of a slow and cautious march through the Balkans. Dislodging the Turks from their various redoubts and fortresses resulted in the Russians suffering frightful losses. Casualties amounting to estimates of 25 percent of its officer corps and 23 percent of its rank and file cast a long shadow over the Russian army.[22] Nonetheless, and because of the tsarist and imperial system of governance, efforts to study the war immediately became bogged down in a quagmire heavily influenced by concerns over the image of the Romanov family and its relationship to the military's successes or failures.

Regardless of the political difficulties inherent in assessing the job performance of the military's leadership, Miliutin formed a military historical commission in 1879 and charged it with the task of collecting documents related to the campaigns of the army for the purposes of learning the lessons about the recent experiences of the Russian army throughout the empire during its last conflict. The commission's existence barely survived the transfer of power that occurred in the wake of Alexander II's assassination. Miliutin was ousted or forced to resign as war minister on May 5, 1881, and his replacement, P. S. Vannovski, gave definition to the term "counterreform" in his efforts to return the army to its prior customs and practices, especially in the realm of officer's education. In his efforts to appease the higher nobility's wounded pride over their loss of power within the army's command structure as a result of Miliutin's reforms, Vannovski set back the cause of reform and arguably irreparably damaged the ability of the tsar's army to complete its transformation from king's to a citizen's army by the beginning of the twentieth century. Alexander III supported Vannovski in his counterreforming efforts. Seemingly because of his negative attitude toward conflict, Alexander III expressed little interest in the work of the historical commission and its mission of teaching Russia's future military leaders about the lessons of the war. In the end, the Historical Commission would not publish its first volume until 1898. They kept publishing until 1911; when they had finished, they had published ninety-eight volumes of mostly books of documents without analysis or assessment.[23] The controversy over what could and could not be said about the role of and actions of members of the royal family and other high command elements continued to stifle meaningful discussions about the war until the collapse of the regime. A generation of officers, therefore, did not learn about their army's most recent conflict just as Europe's armies were whole-heartedly adopting the new, ever increasingly lethal weapons and weapon systems that rendered eighteenth-century operational practices obsolete. Simply put, ignoring the lessons of the 1877–8 Russo-Turkish War stunted the development of Russian operational and tactical doctrine, which resulted in tsarist military forces being poorly prepared to fight the Japanese in Asia or the Central Powers in Europe at the beginning of the twentieth century.[24]

Because of the postwar controversies whatever positive results that did occur were often overlooked. While prewar planning was ultimately abrogated in the heat of the campaign, the common understanding that emanated through the army was that such planning yielded worthwhile results. To develop such a plan, the army would from this time forward need a trained cadre that could not only create the plan, but also execute it. To this end what was understood was that the army needed to redouble its efforts to educate officers and train soldiers to be prepared for future battles. Indeed, the army knew and had been attempting constantly and persistently to achieve such goals at least since the time of Peter the Great. What emerged in the postwar period, therefore, was a reinvigoration of the entire training establishment under the tutelage of the redoubtable General Dragomirov. In all aspects Dragomirov was the perfect person to step into the role of the army's foremost tactician if he had not been that already before the war. An 1856 graduate of the Nicholas Academy of the General Staff, after serving in the Semenovski Guard's Regiment, he emerged in the 1860s as professor of tactics at the academy and became a confidant of Miliutin's while serving at the same time on the War Minister's Special Committee on the Structure and Training of Troops. As a result of this service he concluded that all troops' preparation needed to be divided into two categories—indoctrination (*vospitanie*) and training (*obrazovanie*). By the time he was done commanding troops at Plevna and Shipka Pass, Dragomirov had learned that the key to success on a battlefield that featured modern "industrialized" weapons was to first shatter the army's custom of training soldiers to be marching marionettes and then train men to be prepared for ever changing conditions, especially once live fire started. Because of his being wounded in the knee on August 12, 1877, at Shipka Pass, Dragonmirov's operational career effectively ended. Instead, he devoted the rest of his life to education and training first as commandant of the Nicholas Academy and then as commander of the Kiev military district. He endlessly strove for the rest of his life to teach soldiers to be loyal to the tsar, patriotic to the state, and courageous on the battlefield. His training routine focused on physical training and marksmanship. But, his major shortcoming for the era of modern warfare was he clung to the idea that, in the end, battles were decided because the troops with the superior training possessed the morale and the courage to force the outcome on their enemies with the cold steel of the bayonet. Despite commanding in modern combat and being painfully wounded in the knee at Shipka Pass, Dragomirov still insisted that well-trained and indoctrinated troops could overcome the lethal challenges of the industrialized battlefield. He therefore went into the post-Turkish war period firmly believing that the cold steel of a bayonet was more effective than any modern breech loading assault weapon because of the impact the former had on the morale of soldiers on both sides of a frontal charge. While still acceptable in this conflict with the Turks, "Bayonets before Bullets" was a doctrine that did not serve the Russians well in the Russo-Japanese War or the First World War. The continuing development of weaponry would make the battlefield too lethal for the teachings of General Dragomirov by the beginning of the twentieth century.[25]

The Conquest of Central Asia

Mikhail Dmitrievich Skobelov, one of the commanders who emerged from the Russo-Turkish War, epitomized the Miliutin era transformation of the army and specifically the emergence of a new breed of officer. After graduating from the General Staff Academy in 1868, he put in for and was sent to serve on the steppes of Central Asia to learn the art of war fighting in an active theater of operations where the Russian Empire continued its endless efforts to expand its boundaries. By the time of the 1877–8 Russo-Turkish War he had emerged as a rising star after playing a leading role in the 1873 capture of Khiva, commanding troops at the 1875 Battle of Makram, and then seizing the fortified city of Andijan 1876, which was defended by over 30,000 Muslims, with only 2,800 troops. Thus, by the outbreak of the Turkish War, Skobelov had a well-earned reputation for fighting Muslims and prevailing against overwhelming odds. As a result, he was attached as an aid to General Dragomirov's staff and saw heavy action from the invasion of Bulgaria until troops under his command stormed the fortress of San Stefano in February 1878, which signaled the final stage of the war. At the time the armistice was signed, he had reached the rank of adjutant general, was in command of the IV Army Corps, and had literally gained the reputation of being the White General on horseback thanks to favorable reports in the press of his command exploits while riding a white horse while dressed in white uniforms. Upon the conclusion of the war, at the age of thirty-six, Skobelov returned to

Central Asia poised to lead the Russian army in the final stages of its combat operations in the conquest of the region.[26]

In geopolitical terms the move into Central Asia was the logical extension of what had become an Anglo-Russian realm of competition that stretched from the Turkish straits through the Caucasus, that touched on northern Persia and extended to what is modern Afghanistan.[27] As he completed the conquest of the Caucasus, General A. I. Bariatinskii suggested that the next step in imperial conquest would be constructing a railway from the eastern shores of the Caspian Sea to the Aral Sea. But most commentators link the start of Russian expansion into this region to the founding of the city of Orenburg on the northern edge of the Kazakh steppe, which emerged as a trading center in the 1730s–40s. For the next century, the Russians built trading networks that penetrated the steppe but were preoccupied with the more lucrative trade of western Siberia and with consolidating strength and power on its frontiers with the Ottoman Empire. Beginning in the 1840s, the Russians started to focus on pacifying the Kazakh steppe. By the mid-1860s Russian forces had enveloped the steppe and beginning in 1864 started the process of subjugating the three Central Asian Khanates of Bukhara, Kokand, and Khiva. The military phase of this conquest would conclude in 1881 with the defeat of the Teke Tukhomans, which brought Russian power to the borders of northern Persia and Afghanistan. What ensued from the 1880s onward would play out in large part in the press and became known to history as the Great Game. While there was without question a journalistic flair that went with this moment in history, most issues after the defeat of the Turkoman were resolved through diplomacy. The boundaries between Russian and British interests in this region were ultimately resolved through a series of accords and treaties of which the Anglo-Russian convention of 1907 finally brought resolution to this confrontation between the two great imperial powers.[28]

Bariantinskii would not participate in the conquest of Central Asia, but many officers who served under him in the 1850s would move on to that theater of operation after the Caucasus had been pacified. His longtime chief of staff, D.A. Miliutin would be war minister during the decisive phase of the conquest. The unconventional warfare of the Caucasus conquest proved to be a training ground for the expansion of the empire into Central Asia. The greatest lesson learned in the Caucasus was how to prevail against a stubbornly entrenched enemy who was fighting for their home territory. Both operations depended as much on developing the logistical infrastructure needed to project military power to places far from their base of supply as on the war-fighting capabilities of the opposing forces. The huge expanses of the steppes required the Russians to further develop their thinking about logistics from what they had learned in the Caucasus. In the best tradition of using creative solutions to confront new challenges, the Russians solved their logistical needs by using camels and caravans to move soldiers and equipment to proper locations. The Russians were usually vastly outnumbered in their operations but had become masters at siege warfare. And, while their enemies had fortresses and superior numbers, the Russians responded by concentrating superior firepower that overwhelmed their enemies who were neither well trained nor well equipped.[29]

While the Russians would ultimately prevail in the conquest of Central Asia, they did have to contend with native opposition, which, while never well unified, started to coalesce against Russian expansion in the 1820s. Orenburg became a focal point in the Russian effort to contain some of the native opposition, in this case the Kazakhs. A Cossack host was stationed in and around the city that secured the area so that the tsarist soldiers and bureaucrats could oversee the construction of a string of fortified settlements that defined the extent of their expansion. By the middle of the century, the Russians had succeeded in creating what became known as the Orenburg and Siberian lines of fortifications, thereby emulating a strategy that had been used first on the Pontic steppe and then in the Caucasus. In this fashion, the Romanovs continued the policy of building fortified settlements to contain nomadic tribesmen who threatened the smooth operation of their trade routes while also providing personal security for all Russians in the area. Once the northern end of the steppe was secured with the construction of fortified lines, the Russians sought to push their forces southward to gain hegemony over the entire region.[30] In the 1840s, a Kazakh chieftain named Kenisary Kasimov organized sporadic but brutal attacks on Russian caravans trading between settlements with no more than 1,000 warriors. Even though the focus of attention in the 1840s was on pacifying the Caucasus, these attacks necessitated a response and over the course of the next three years Kasimov taught the Russians about the challenges of unconventional warfare. Mounting expeditions of approximately 2,000 men, the Russians intended to draw the chieftain into open battle and eliminate the threat. Kasimov did not cooperate as he became a master of deploying in a hit-and-run tactic and then drawing Russian troops into a pursuit across the open steppe, operations that left them exhausted and exposed not only to the elements but also to the hostile response of the natives. Kasimov, who at the height of his success would be known as the Kazakh Shamil, would ultimately perish in a struggle with rival tribesmen, thereby eliminating the threat and providing the Russians with false claims of victory.[31]

Meanwhile, at roughly the same time, the Central Asian theater kept drawing more resources as raiders from the Khivan and Kokand Khanates harassed Russian traders, thereby threatening not only their security but also making them look inferior to tribesmen on horseback. Campaigns were mounted which at best resulted in the construction of more fortified settlements as the Russians continuously moved southward in an effort to secure their position on the southern part of the steppe. The fortifications that the nomads built were primitive compared to those that existed in Europe. Usually constructed out of mud as opposed to stone, they symbolized the power of local khans and chieftains. Disciplined troops, especially if they had any heavy weapons at their disposal, did not find these structures to be much of an obstacle to their movements. By 1845 Nicholas I had approved a strategy for operations that involved the deployment of flying detachments that had a mission of enveloping and eliminating steppe raiders, thus paving the way for the construction of more Russian fortified settlements at the expense first of Khivan and later Kokand Khanates. Nothing symbolized the success of these operations more than the 1847 founding of the fortress at Aralsk on the mouth of the Syr River. Aralsk then became the home base of the Aral Sea flotilla, which helped facilitate southward expansion until the outbreak of the Crimean War. By 1853 the Russians had constructed Fort Perovsk further south on the Syr River and in the next year they built a fortified outpost at Vernoe that has become modern-day Alma Ata. Thus, by the Crimean War, the Russians were well on their way to encircling the steppe, but there was still much native opposition that would challenge their presence for the next thirty years or so.

Once the war ministry found its bearings after the Crimean debacle, Miliutin in particular paid closer attention to continuing operations in Central Asia where a new phenomenon emerged perhaps as a by-product of his reforms but more likely due to the distance from the central command center. Colonel M. G Cherniaev took charge after this development when in 1864 he led a column out of Vernoe and with little effort captured a Kokandian fortress at Aulie Ata while simultaneously another column under Colonel N. A. Verevkin commanded a separate detachment that captured the city of Turkestan. The two forces then linked up and under the overall command of Cherniaev laid siege to and captured Chimkent. As a result of this campaign, the Russians were able to establish a line of fortified garrisons across the southern boundaries of Kokand and Bukhara.[32] From this campaign, a style of warfare emerged that would be used throughout the 1870s and into the 1880s. Although not entirely new, the Central Asian theater offered opportunities for commanders to demonstrate local initiative because distances and primitive means of communication prevented them from receiving orders from superiors. Moreover, the style of warfare that developed as the Russians pushed further and further into Central Asia necessitated the composition of self-sufficient expeditions aimed at laying siege to fortified positions usually manned by irregular troops who were effective as warriors on horseback but not trained in the art of static warfare. Because of this it was not uncommon for the Russians to defeat their foes with vastly smaller forces if for no other reason than their superior firepower. The effectiveness of Russian firepower improved as Russians adopted rifled weapons across their armed forces in the 1870s and 1880s. Although the growing power of Russian arms cannot be discounted in this tale of conquest, the factor that cannot be overlooked is logistics—moving supplies across Central Asia remained a permanent challenge for men and camels alike as the Russians persistently pushed east and south.[33]

While Cherniaev's initiative strengthened Russia's position in the region, it also brought unwanted international attention to the conquest and ultimately resulted in the Emir of Bukhara organizing a coalition of indigenous peoples to resist the expansion of the Romanovs. These developments set the stage for the events that unfolded on the ground in the 1870s and ultimately defined the competition between the British and the Russians that is known to history as the Great Game.[34] The origin of this well-known diplomatic entanglement was the combination of Russia's push into Central Asia and the British viewing these expansive efforts by the Romanovs as a threat to the British Empire in India. While Foreign Minister Mikhail Gorchakov made clear in his famous 1864 memorandum that Russia merely sought to establish a border with a stable state as opposed to pursuing a policy of endless expansion, the British remained wary of his explanation.[35] As a result, into the twentieth century the testing ground of the aims of each empire became the land that is now contemporary Afghanistan, thus propelling that tortured region into an important front of world history not for the first nor the last time. Despite the efforts of Russia's foreign ministry to smooth over the expansion of Russian power across Central Asia, the military's operations told another story. In the aftermath of Cherniaev's move against Turkestan, Miliutin concluded that like many commanders in Central Asia, he as war minister could not depend on him (Cherniaev) to follow orders.[36] Cherniaev was therefore replaced with General D. I. Romanovskii who immediately used the forces at his disposal to occupy Khodzhent in 1866. This move challenged the authority of the Khanate of Bukhara and effectively gave the

Russians control over the resource rich Fergana Valley. In short order they then laid siege to the fortress at Ura-Tiube and had little trouble reducing what was the most important fortified position in Bukhara. Again, however, Romanovskii had followed in Cherniaev's footsteps and acted on his own initiative because the situation provided the opportunity that only the commander on the ground could ascertain. And still, Miliutin sought to find a way for St. Petersburg to maintain firmer control over the army in the field even when commanders delivered victories to their tsar and empire.

While the capture of Ura-Tiube meant that Russians had penetrated deeper into Central Asia than any other Europeans, it did little to assuage British concerns and even more significantly for the forces on the ground, it mobilized indigenous opposition to Russian expansion. As the Russians persistently threatened to undermine his power in 1868, the Emir of Bukhara organized the region's clerics to support a broad coalition with representatives from Kokand, Khiva, Kashgar, and Afghanistan. In an attempt to reign in the conduct of the army, Alexander II had appointed General Konstantin Pavlovich von Kaufman governor general of Turkestan in 1867, and he was the official who responded to the threat of the emir's coalition. What followed was a column organized and under the command of Kaufman launching an assault on Samarkand, the ancient commercial trading city that was also the center of the emir's power. By the end of 1868 Russian force's vastly inferiority in numbers but overwhelmingly superior in training and firepower routed the forces of the emir's coalition forcing him to cede commercial rights over his territory and leaving him as a puppet of the Romanovs. Kaufman's success subsequently set the stage for the rest of the conquest of Central Asia in the 1870s, and it offered further evidence of how the major issue of the conquest of the region was supplying Russian forces in the field. If Russian troops were well supplied then their superior firepower and training would prevail against overwhelming force numbers that their Central Asian adversaries could muster. Counter to all other Russian combat experiences, the casualty rates in campaigns that stretched from the 1850s to the 1880s did not exceed 2,000 men, an incredibly low number given the huge amount of combat that occurred throughout this region at this time.[37]

Gaining control over Bukhara emboldened von Kaufman and Miliutin to take on a long-time nemesis Khan Seid Mahomet-Rakhim, the khan of Khiva, in an effort to gain control of the Amu-Darya River valley up to the Afghan border.[38] The khan of Khiva was a formidable foe because he maintained a large standing army composed mainly of Uzbek infantry and Turkoman cavalry. Although poorly equipped and trained, they were, unlike the Russians, accustomed to desert warfare. This provided an important advantage because the Khanate was surrounded on all four sides by scorching deserts. In addition to having geography on his side and a large number of troops, the khan also had a tax-paying population estimated at 400,000 souls and thus had access to resources that could sustain his operations. In the meantime, the movement of supplies remained a significant issue in this campaign and to this end the Russians established a forward base on the eastern side of the Caspian Sea at Krasnovodsk in 1869 after the subjugation of Bukhara. Von Kaufman then spent the winter of 1872–3 organizing a campaign that featured expeditionary forces being organized in the Caucasus, in Orenburg, and in Turkestan. While Kaufman struggled to build his invasion force, he also encountered stiff competition from each side from other Russian commanders seeking their own fame and glory by commanding troops in battle. Moreover, the khan was not blind or ignorant to the plans of the Russians, especially since they did a poor job of securing their communications. With the knowledge that the Russians were preparing a large-scale operation against him, he spent the winter using all of his power and connection to limit, if not prevent, von Kaufman from gaining access and control over the camels he would need to cross the desert.

Hoping to avoid the worst of the summer heat, the campaign was launched in the spring of 1873 and, as expected, the biggest challenge for all the Russian columns was crossing broad desert expanses ranging from 700 to 1,000 miles. As they crossed the desert the major concern, of course, was having enough water for the troops and animals carrying supplies. The aim was for all columns that together consisted of approximately 13,000 men to converge on the Amu River, which was largely accomplished by the middle of May. Reaching the river naturally solved the water crisis that all columns encountered as a result of the desert crossing. While all columns survived the crossing, they had become scattered and the troops suffered from exhaustion, so von Kaufman needed to spend some time for his troops to rest and recuperate from their arduous encounter with the desert. The columns therefore straggled to the rendezvous point at different times, so von Kaufman used the interregnum to appeal to the local inhabitants with an offer for all people to go to work for the tsar as peaceful laborers. He warned that anyone who fled from the Russian army would be considered an enemy and would forfeit their property. The appeal garnered some success, which resulted in a contingent of native guides and procurement agents who contributed to the overall success of the campaign. Once von Kaufman had concentrated his forces on the Amu, he had not only overcome his most challenging task—crossing the desert—but he also effectively won the campaign. After he crossed the river, forces loyal to Khivan Khan engaged in some asymmetrical battles, but they could not halt what for them had become the Russian juggernaut. By the end of May all forces under von Kaufman's command had assembled outside of Khiva leaving the khan no choice but to seek an armistice. While there was some adjustment to boundaries, the main aspect of the ensuing peace was to give Russian merchants extensive rights to conduct trade throughout the region. The significance of von Kaufman's command of this campaign can be measured in terms of the model it created for Central Asian warfare at this time in history. The Russian army had an easy time dispatching all armed opposition in this and in all its campaigns across the region because of its superior use of concentrated firepower. For them the question of success could be measured in how well they mastered operating in the climate and on the tricky topography of any desert. Von Kaufman exhibited that these challenges could be mastered if careful attention was paid to the question of supply, which he did by permanently establishing well-positioned garrison posts and by gaining the support of locals who supplied them with draft animals. The other key to Kaufman's success was developing a system of reconnaissance and communication that allowed for the coordination of the disparate parts of his armies that inevitably occur when engaged in large troop movements as well as having accurate and current information about the disposition of his enemies.[39]

After the defeat of Khiva, the conquest of Central Asia entered into its final stage that actually occurred as a two-part process. In the aftermath of the march across the desert, the big issue for the Russian army was one of governance. The tsar and his army after all were a small group of European Christian conquerors who sought to dominate a region both for all the benefits they could reap from commercial activity and to contain the spread of the British Empire from its outposts in India. At first, von Kaufman, recognizing that the Russians were vastly outnumbered, pursued a policy of tolerance and accommodation as he sought to use native peoples to administer the territory. The presence of the Russians and their attempts to control Central Asia not surprisingly led to rebellions among native people. The first sign of rebellion occurred in July 1875 when Khudoiar Khan of Kokand, unpopular in his own right, fled to the security of the Russian army for protection. Rebels led by the khan's son Nasr-Eddin then attacked the Russian garrison at Khodzhent. While under siege, von Kaufman, headquartered in Tashkent, organized an expedition to respond to this rebellion. This action resulted in the emergence of a young colonel M. D. Skobelev, who commanded three squadrons of Cossacks, attacked the flank of a rebel mob that sent them into flight. Von Kaufman then followed up this victory with a march on the rebel base at Margelan, and this campaign forced Nar-Eddin to sue for peace. Subsequent negotiations culminated with the Russians gaining control over the Kokand territory up to the right bank of the river Syr. This "peace," however, did not end the rebellion as another relative of Khudoiar Khan, Pulat-bek, made a stand at Andizhan on the eastern edge of Kokandian territory. Here the rebels put up a well-organized defense that withstood the initial Russian assault. Von Kaufman turned this operation over to the recently promoted General Skobelev, who, using his forces at the outposts of Tiurakurgan and Namangan, employed an operational technique that started with heavy bombardments before using his infantry to launch an overwhelming assault on these positions. Successful action by the Russians in these operations paved the way for Skobelev to bombard the defenders of Andizhan into submission by the end of the year.

Skobelev's success in Kokand, combined with the persistent rebelliousness of the native population, resulted in a change of policy in St. Petersburg. Instead of trying to accommodate the local population on any level, Skobelev received orders to occupy Andizhan, which served as a prelude to Alexander II proclaiming in February 1876 that he was annexing the entire region to his empire. To disseminate this information across Kokand, the young general led a small expedition, much to the trepidation of the British because of the proximity to their empire, into the mountainous southeastern region of Kokand to inform the Kirghiz tribal peoples of their newfound status in the Russian Empire. In this fashion, the Russian army demonstrated that it had the power to reach across the entirety of the territory. But, as had been the case in the Caucasus, the tsar's servitors discovered that achieving military dominance did not guarantee long-term political control over any occupied territory. And, since the Russians had already given up on inducing locals to govern themselves, von Kaufman, as governor general of Turkestan, was charged with the task of implementing a functional administrative system. To his credit, and based on past experiences, he sought to create a military administration that still respected local customs and traditions in an effort to quell future unrest. His major challenge then became finding Russian bureaucrats willing to move to Central Asia to help him administer the territory. Such service was not wanted or desired by civilian tsarist officials for two reasons. First, such a posting was viewed as a dead end for an official career because of its remoteness … out of sight … out of mind! Perhaps even more vexing were the split signals being sent from the Capital. While conquest for the sake of containing the British and developing commercial connections were viewed as cause for expansion, Central Asia was not viewed as a territory worth colonizing because of the expense of such an operation versus potential return.[40]

As von Kaufman grappled with the opportunity to establish a Russian-style administrative apparatus across Central Asia, he still had the challenge of local elements who stubbornly resisted Russian expansion. Efforts to address this issue were delayed as a result of the 1877–8 Russo-Turkish War. The outcome of the war, especially the effort by the Great Powers to impose their idea of a peace settlement on the Balkans, specifically Bulgaria, reenergized Russia's imperial designs across Asia in general. In the period after this war, the group that presented the greatest challenge to the Russians were the Turkoman tribes of the Teke oasis in Transcaspia or what is modern Turkmenistan. The point of resistance for this group became a great earthen fortress at Geok Tepe, which was near the Persian frontier. An 1879 campaign launched first under the command of General I. D. Lazarev (who died of an infection while campaigning at the end of July) and then under General N. P. Lomakin failed because both generals ignored what had proven to be the keys to success in Central Asian campaigning. They both underestimated the main lessons learned about operations in the region when they decided to invade without adequate planning for supplies and conducting proper reconnaissance of their enemies. Even worse, while Lomakin reached the fortress at Geok Tepe, he did not utilize superior Russian firepower and training and, without understanding that the Turkomen had gathered some 15,000 defenders, stormed the fortress in September 1879, which exposed the Russian troops to hand-to-hand combat. Greatly outnumbered, the Russians suffered high casualties of some 500 men, which alone was unusual based on their previous experiences in Central Asian, but of greater embarrassment, Lomakin's troops melted against the sabers and pikes of the Turkomen and withdrew in complete disorder.[41]

Christian colonialists could not tolerate such a defeat at the hands of any native population anywhere in the world during the age of imperialism. The response to this defeat started in St. Petersburg where Miliutin urged a rapid response to this disgrace with the organization of another expedition that had a goal of reducing the fortress at Geok Tepe to completely defeat the Turkomen. At the tsar's insistence, the recent hero of the Russo-Turkish War, now Adjutant-General Skobelev was given command of this operation. As a veteran of Central Asian campaigning, he understood the value of proper preparations before launching any operation in the region. He, therefore, set up bases of supply along his invasion route. In the course of assembling his forces, he developed and applied the so-called "Turkestan proportion" in which his goal became to plan for companies consisting of 200 men available to confront 1,000 Turkomen.[42] Then, in the late summer, allegedly riding his white horse, Skobelev led a small 1,000-man reconnaissance force deep into the region, even reaching the fortress at Geok Tepe before he withdrew after gathering the intelligence he needed to launch his decisive campaign. In November he invaded with a force of 7,000 men and his first goal was Iangi-kala because all water that supplied Geok Tepe went through this village. Careful planning of this campaign meant that well-supplied Russians stood before their enemies and the stage was set for the final assault on Geok Tepe after they gained control of the water vital to survival in the desert environment. Skobelev dictated the terms of battle when he informed his troops that their enemy was a brave, indeed formidable foe if fought one on one. Their weakness, however, was they did not follow orders, which meant that they did not fight as a unified force. Not wishing to repeat the failure of Lomakin by attempting to storm the fortress and realizing that he did not have sufficient forces to endure a prolonged siege, Skobelev ordered his forces to set mines under the walls of the fortress beginning in December. Again, the intelligence he gained as a result of his reconnaissance of the position, plus his careful logistical preparations, meant that he had the forces in place who had the supplies they needed so that when those mines were detonated on January 12, 1881, Turkomen resistance melted away. Once the walls had been breached, the Turkomen fled to the north while Skobelev's forces pursued their enemies, the fate of Transcaspia was now sealed as it too was annexed into the Russian Empire.[43]

Conclusion

Once Skobelev defeated the Turkomen, the military conquest of Central Asia was essentially completed. With this victory, and because of the way the Russians were manhandled by the European diplomats after the 1877–8 Russo-Turkish War, the Russians started to pay greater attention to their far east. What followed in Central Asia was two decades of diplomatic negotiations often viewed through the prism of "The Great Game." This catch-all term was used throughout the nineteenth century to describe the rivalry that existed between Russia and Great Britain over the territory of modern Afghanistan and its environs. As the Russians pushed their empire eastward, the British became concerned that the Russians ultimately would threaten their position in South Asia. This concern was not without justification as the Russian army conquered Central Asia, thus

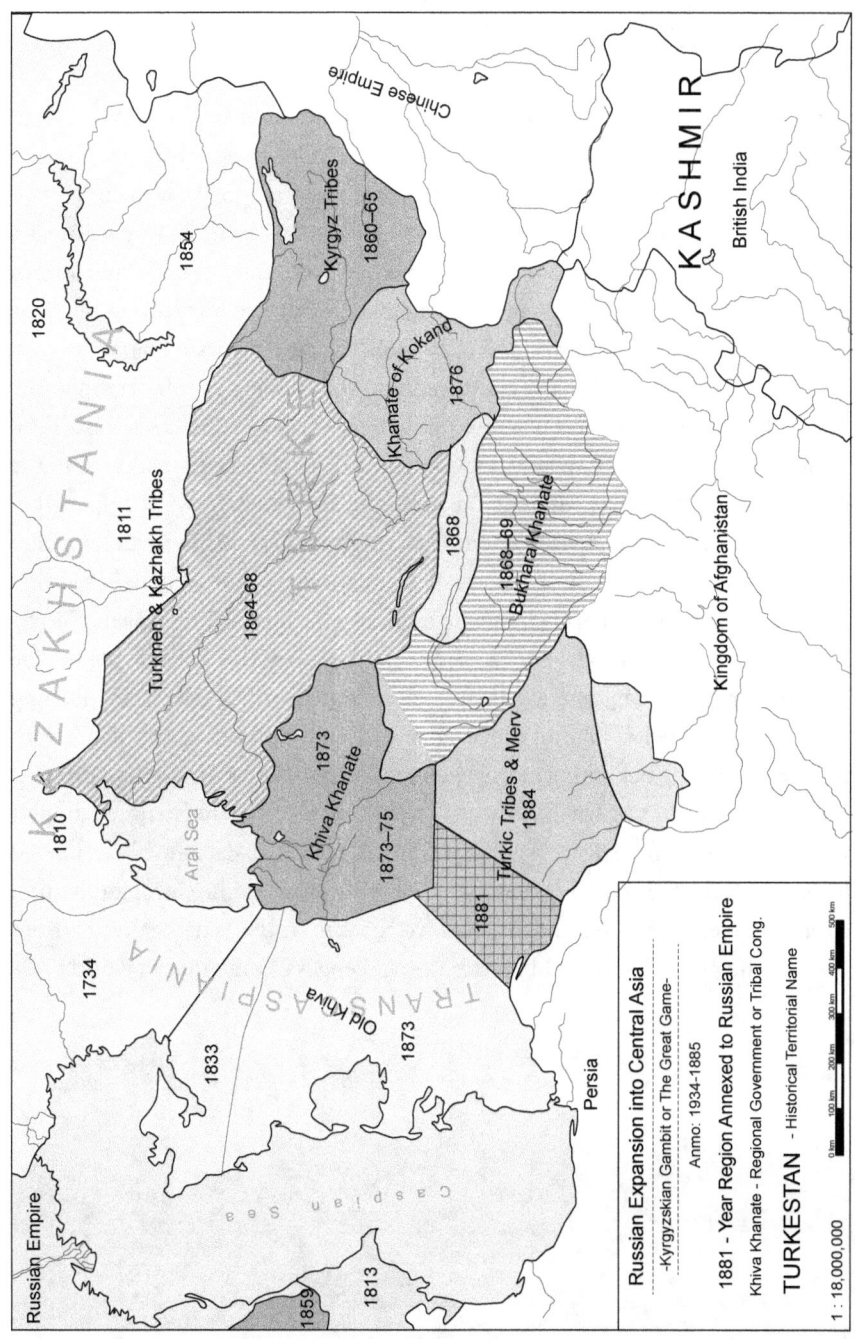

Map 4.5 Conquest of Central Asia up to 1881.

developing the capability to station forces on the extreme frontiers of the British Empire in India. As history demonstrates, however, "The Great Game" was more a legend than a reality, the brainchild of politicians, journalists, and adventurers rather than military leaders. In fact, neither the British nor the Russians had the logistical capability to confront each other in south or Central Asia and thus choose a diplomatic path as opposed to conflict to establish a status quo in the region. As a result, a series of agreements were signed between the two empires beginning as early as the 1870 and culminating with the Anglo-Russian Convention of 1907, which not only aimed at preventing the Germans from building their proposed Berlin to Baghdad railway, but also normalized relations over the frontiers of southwest and south Asia between the rival empires.

At the beginning of the twentieth century, the Russian Empire stood at the brink of an abyss that, of course, was little understood by the tsar's most loyal subjects. Reasons for optimism about the future no doubt existed because of the successes of the military. After all, the defeat of the Ottomans was completed in 1878. Most of the controversy about the army's failings during that campaign were not widely known. In the war's aftermath, it was commonly believed that while Russia's reformed army had won a decisive victory, the Europeans, led by the Germans, had deprived Russia of the spoils of war. This belief provided the seeds for the huge diplomatic shift that culminated with the Russians turning away from their fellow central European monarchs and forging an alliance with the French. By the beginning of the twentieth century, the Russians had directed much attention to the Far East, which would result in their fateful encounter with the Japanese in 1904–5. And, that conflict, the Russo-Japanese War, proved to be the event that plainly revealed that the Russian Empire, despite the best efforts of every reformer and progressive thinker in the tsar's realm, had not reached the point that it could master the challenges of the modern world.

5

The Far Eastern Disaster

It would be hard to prove definitively that the Romanovs sought to reconstruct a Eurasian Empire comparable to what had once been controlled by the Mongols in a bygone era. Yet the history of the growth of Russia during their reign (1613–1917) reveals that once the Romanovs came to power, they adopted a security policy designed to, at the very least, prevent the state from being overwhelmed and subjugated by anyone as the Mongols had once done. Peter the Great, therefore, built a state designed to sustain an army capable of defending his realm against all of his enemies. His successors continued strengthening their military forces so that, by the beginning of the nineteenth century, the Imperial Russian army reached the apex of its power when its soldiers occupied Paris in March/April 1814 and ousted from power Napoleon Bonaparte—who is still considered one of the greatest military leaders in history. Perhaps because of the geographic proximity and the power of the Western threat, the drama of this history, the history of the Russian army against the Great European Powers, has long directed historians to inordinately focus their work on these feats of arms. The explanation for the focus on the West also emanates from the Russian belief that their future as a Great Power was inherently linked to their developing diplomatic recognition and extensive trade networks with the Europeans. Yet, as exhibited throughout this book, the Russian state, beginning at least with the reign of Peter the Great, came to terms with its need for two styles of armies—one that could meet European armies with their overwhelming firepower, the other being capable of defeating the cavalry armies that operated throughout the Pontic steppe. The tsarist military, moreover, entered the post-Napoleonic period confident that it could confront and defeat any force that threatened its realm. This confidence was further strengthened due to their experiences in the Caucasus. While it took fifty years, the suppression of all opposition in the Caucasus provided the army with a laboratory to study, practice, and finally prevail against a well-embedded enemy that was determined to defend its home territory. The lessons learned about unconventional warfare in the Caucasus were then applied, albeit not at all seamlessly, to the conquest of Central Asia, which occurred mostly after the disastrous Crimean War, thereby demonstrating the relentless efforts of the Romanovs to pursue their Imperial project.[1]

Throughout this period of growth, the Russians always had an eye on the Far East.[2] Yet, the conquest of this part of the Eurasian landmass did not involve the use of large-scale military forces until the end of the nineteenth century. Predating the Romanovs, Yermak Timofeyevich, for example, marched into Siberia in 1582 with a Cossack host that numbered some 500 men. Not much organized opposition greeted him and the conquest of Siberia started what became a vital commercial enterprise that contributed largely to the financing of the empire. In this fashion, the exploration of Siberia became a story of expeditions organized to construct outposts and forts that established what became an extensive trading network that stretched so far that at its furthest extent Russians were setting up outposts in Alaska and northern California. With the exception of a few brief encounters, Russia's relations with China were largely maintained via diplomatic means. After a series of encounters over the Amur River basin, the Romanovs signed the 1689 Treaty of Nerchinsk with the Manchus, which calmed tensions emerging over their mutual border. The aim of these early encounters was not only to resolve questions about frontiers but also to establish harmonious relations that would be conducive to constructing a trade network across the Middle Kingdom. Neither Peter the Great nor Chinese Emperor K'hang Hsi were entirely satisfied with the outcomes of Nerchinsk, so they engaged in further relations that ultimately resulted in the Treaty of Kyakhta in 1729 after both emperors had died. Nonetheless, Nerchinsk and Kyakhta regularized relations between the two countries for over 100 years before growing imperialistic encroachment on China in the nineteenth century transformed the status quo.[3]

Nothing symbolized the fusion of imperialism and industrialism more than railroads; railroad construction symbolized progress and modernity as they fostered global industrial economic development, thereby contributing to the spread of the power of imperialists. Not surprisingly, Russia's position in the Far East became a matter of far greater concern not only in St. Petersburg but throughout the world in the 1890s when the Russians started building the Trans-Siberian railway. While the railway was conceptualized as a project that would promote economic development, its political ramifications were not well thought through in St. Petersburg when the decision was made to start building it.[4] As Russian railway designers struggled with the enormous engineering challenges, Alexander III, the tsar who ordered the construction of the railway in 1891 suddenly died in 1894 and his son Nicholas, soon to be Nicholas II, found himself to be tsar long before he or anyone else thought it would happen. Nicholas II's naiveté and ineptitude toward seemingly everything would hugely complicate Russia's efforts to extend its power and influence to the Far East if for no other reason than his inability to develop and apply consistent state policy toward anything. Then, a new player, the Japanese emerged in the second half of the nineteenth century, which set the stage for the confrontation that would start the process of the collapse of the Romanov regime. When Commodore Perry "opened" Japan in 1853, its modernization followed far more rapidly than anyone envisioned as being possible. The Japanese agitation for their own empire put them on a collision course with Russian ambitions in the Far East. The first event that led to their fateful encounter was the work of Count Sergei Witte as the broker of peace at the end of the first Sino-Japanese War in 1894–5. The resulting Treaty of Shimonoseki set Russia on a collision course with the Japanese that would not be resolved until the Treaty of Portsmouth in September 1905 that brought an end to the Russo-Japanese War.[5]

This chapter aims to focus on the Romanovs' encounter with the Japanese Empire in northern China, Manchuria, and Korea at the end of the nineteenth century and the beginning of the twentieth century. While the Russians had been engaged in Siberia and then the Far East since at least the sixteenth century, until the end of the nineteenth century, the Russian military's role in these expansive efforts was limited as diplomacy and commercial concerns primarily managed this eastward drive. Russia's entanglement in the Far East represents a chapter in the history of imperialism as it reached its apogee. China, in a prolonged state of decline, had become the last remaining prize in the minds of Western and Japanese imperialists who endlessly sought to expand their power, influence, and control. While Russia viewed its expansion to the east as another chapter in their Imperial project, the Japanese viewed the status of China and especially gaining control over Korea as vital to their achieving their own imperial ambitions.

From the Treaty of Shimonoseki to the Outbreak of War

Nicholas II had visited Japan in 1890 on a world tour that he was taking as tsarevich and, as a result of an assassination attempt outside of Kyoto, he did not have a positive impression of the Japanese. This event turned out to be the first in a series of events for Nicholas II that foreshadowed his relationship with the Japanese and the Far East. His inability to establish consistent policy on any state affairs combined with surrounding himself with a host of self-styled adventurers and entrepreneurs who had little understanding of international affairs or national security concerns resulted in practices that first destabilized and eventually inflamed Russia's relations with Japan, thus setting the Far East on fire at the beginning of the twentieth century.[6] Constructing the Trans-Siberian railway provided the Russians with the means to not only to promote economic development but to also transport military assets across the empire. But the entanglement with the Far East actually started when the Russians brokered the peace between Japan and China after the first Sino-Japanese War in 1894–5. This conflict occurred because the Japanese were seeking to wrest control of Korea from China. When war broke out in July 1894, no one considered that the Japanese might prevail, but after a series of successive defeats the Chinese sued for peace in February 1895. Negotiations occurred in the Japanese city of Shimonoseki, and it was here that the Japanese learned that you can win a war but lose the peace. With the oversight of all of the Western powers, the Japanese initially negotiated a favorable treaty that included China recognizing the independence of Korea, while also ceding control of Taiwan, the Pescadores, and the eastern portion of the bay of the Liaodong Peninsula including all fortifications and arsenals. In addition, the Chinese ceded a series of ports to Japan. At the same time the Japanese were elevated to the status of a most favored nation for all future economic transactions with the Western powers. Finally, as was the custom of the period, the Chinese agreed to a reparation's payment of some 16,534,500 pounds of silver.[7] The terms of the Shimonoseki Treaty set off the first important foreign policy decision, some called a crisis, for the young Nicholas II. The issue for all of the imperial powers in the immediate aftermath of Shimonoseki was whom to support—the emerging Japanese or the old stalwart of the crumbling Middle Kingdom. Thanks largely to the machinations of one of Nicholas II's most competent ministers, Sergei Iul'evich Witte who held the portfolio of finance minister, Russia firmly supported the Chinese in the immediate aftermath of the treaty signing that occurred on April 17, 1895.[8]

Witte's rise through the tsarist bureaucracy started in the 1870s when he gained recognition for his efforts in transporting the army and its supplies to the operation theater in the Balkans during the 1877–8 Russo-Turkish War. For this service he was recognized by Grand Duke Nikolai Nikolaevich (the elder) and such recognition emanating from the imperial family paved the way for Witte to work his way to the top of the tsarist bureaucracy. When he was appointed minister of finance in 1892 by Alexander III, he emerged as the foremost advocate and activist of Russia's industrialization process. From this position he vigorously supported the construction of the Trans-Siberian railway, and this enthusiasm drew his attention to Far Eastern affairs in the wake of the signing of the Treaty of Shimonoseki. All of the Great Powers took notice and opposed how the Japanese had gained control over large tracts of mainland Asian territory as a result of the treaty. Their reaction became known to history as the triple intervention of 1898. Witte, however, took matters into his own hands, which prompted negotiations between Russia and China that culminated with a secret agreement signed in June 1896 by Foreign Minister Alexei Borisovich Lobanov-Rostovsky and the Chinese viceroy Li Hong Zhang who was in Russia to attend the coronation of Nicholas II. In the period immediately before this encounter, Witte, at the request of the Chinese for loans to finance the treaty's indemnities, established a Russia-Chinese Bank and, using French monies, made loans to the Chinese. The secret agreement of 1896 then offered the Chinese Russian guarantees to defend China from any further hostile action from the Japanese. In return for the loans and the guarantees, the Russians gained the concession that gave them the right to construct the Eastern Chinese Railway across northern Manchuria, which substantially shortened the distance it would take to link Vladivostok (the terminus point) to the Trans-Siberian Railway. This agreement was followed by another, not so secret convention signed in March 1898 that granted the Russians a lease to use the Liaotung Peninsula and, most fatefully, control the Port Arthur fortress and port that immediately gave them a warm water port in Asia. To complement this lease, the Chinese also granted the Russians the right to build a southern link to the Eastern Chinese Railway that connected the city of Harbin in northern Manchuria to Port Arthur and the southern tip of the Liaotung Peninsula.[9]

These agreements effectively gave Russia control over northern Manchuria to the point just short of annexing the territory. The Russians then sought and achieved their goal of getting the Germans and the French to support their heavy-handed policy over China. All of the European imperial powers, already weary of Japanese encroachment in Asia, sought to carve out their own zone of influence at China's expense. After all, by 1898 the Europeans had effectively shared Africa as a reflection of their endless desire to expand their imperial power, and they expected to do the same with China. The triple intervention that followed in April 1898 was designed to impose both diplomatic and military pressure on the Japanese to back off of territorial claims and extraordinary control over Korea in exchange for more indemnities. The Japanese and the Chinese now both believed that they were the victims of unequal treatment by the Western powers. In the end, the British, in the wake of the intervention, also joined the Germans and the French in establishing treaty ports on China's northeast coast, all in a gambit to expand their power and influence in Asia. For the Japanese, this was another in a series of diplomatic encounters with the West where, in the end, they believed that regardless of what they did, they would never be treated as equals. This contributed to their estrangement from the other imperial powers and started them down a road that would culminate with their decision to go to war in 1904. After the triple intervention, the Chinese had to accept that their dealings with the Russians were not working to their advantage, but their situation was such that they could do little to stop their decline. Even worse, Russian encroachment in Manchuria alienated parts of the Chinese population because of the inability of their government to contain the spread of Western influence. This opposition would coalesce in two years into the Boxer Rebellion that became another point in a series of moments where the Qing dynasty lost its political footing and would eventually collapse.[10]

The Boxer Rebellion exploded into a full-blown international crisis once the rebellious elements of the Chinese population threatened foreigners, largely Christian missionaries who had started to embed themselves across the Middle Empire after the 1860 conclusion of the Second Opium War. The catalyst for the outbreak of what turned into a period of extreme violence, however, was the persistent encroachment of the Western imperialists after the defeat dealt to the Chinese by the Japanese in 1894. Heavy-handed Russian action aimed primarily to gain concessions for railway construction had turned Manchuria into their zone of influence. The situation became far more upsetting especially to the Japanese after the period when the Russians gained control of the Liaotung Peninsula after the three powers' intervention because of how rapidly the tsar's military had become ensconced at Port Arthur, thereby giving them a naval presence in the Yellow Sea, which threatened the viability of the emerging Japanese Empire. When the Quig dynasty's stability waffled in the face of the agitation of imperialists, the countryside exploded in violent rebellion aimed at Westerners throughout the spring and summer in 1900. In the summer of 1900 over 200 missionaries would lose their lives to the violence of the Boxer movement. As their situation became more threatening, they sought security by moving to their respective embassies in Beijing. This set the stage for the 55-day siege of the foreign legation in Beijing as missionaries, diplomats, assorted civilians, and Chinese Christians waited for relief from the threat imposed by the Boxers and by Chinese imperial troops.[11]

In response to this imminent danger to foreigners, a military force composed of soldiers from eight nations invaded China. The Boxer Rebellion, therefore, resulted in the invasion of Manchuria. Before it was over the Russians sent 200,000 troops into the region ostensibly to protect Russian Christians but mainly to protect their interests all along the Chinese Eastern Railway. While it would never be called an occupation, the Russians would not leave the region until after their defeat in the Russo-Japanese War. The focal point of the rebellion, however, became the June to August siege of the foreign legation in Beijing. While eight nations composed the force that relieved the legation, the Japanese took a primary role and this in turn resulted in a large presence of Japanese troops in China. By the end of the summer 1900, the Boxers were defeated, the Chinese empress Cixi, who had demonstrated a lack of consistency in her application of policy throughout, had been seriously weakened, and northern China and Manchuria were overrun with foreign troops, which resulted in the occupation of region primarily by Russian and Japanese troops. According to the Boxer protocols that were designed to restore the status quo, the Chinese were charged reparations and the foreigners were supposed to withdraw their forces from the region. In fact, none of them left! The US Marines, for example, did not leave China until 1949. More to the point, Manchuria was now occupied by Russian and Japanese forces that set the two nations on a collision course that would result in the outbreak of hostilities in 1904. The source of conflict between the two powers now clearly became the question of who would control Korea. The Russians strove to cut off Korea from China by land with their railroads and by sea with their having control of Port Arthur and Vladivostok. The Japanese viewed this situation as entirely unacceptable as they considered Korea vital to their strategic interests because of its geographic relationship to control over the entrance to the Sea of Japan. Thus, the military/diplomatic events that occurred in the period between the first Sino-Japanese War and the Boxer Rebellion set the Russians and the Japanese on the path that ended with the outbreak of the Russo-Japanese War.[12]

The period between the Boxer Rebellion and the outbreak of the Russo-Japanese War exhibited how all the imperialists struggled to gain concessions from China that were designed to subjugate the Middle Kingdom by reducing its control over vital territory and resources. Regardless of China being the object of imperialist exploitation, the conduct of Russia in its efforts to spread the power of its empire from the heart of Europe to the Pacific Ocean reveals the weaknesses of Nicholas II as tsar. His failure as a ruler resulted in his government being divided, especially ready to fracture when the tsar attempted to apply firmness or force his will on the application of policy. In this period, while the Japanese consolidated their thinking, planning, and preparations to respond to the encroachment of Western imperialism on China, Manchuria, and Korea, Russian policy failed to consolidate into a unified strategic plan. Instead, a bitter rivalry engulfed Nicholas II's government with Witte on the one hand continuing to pursue a policy based on expansion of empire through railroad building and on the other a clique of court insiders, adventurers, and entrepreneurs whose leader became Alexander Mikhailovich Bezobrazov who sought to ruthlessly exploit the resources of the region. Using his control over timber on both sides of the Yalu, Bezobrazov formed a circle of supporters composed of court insiders such as Grand Duke Alexander Mikhailovich, Rear Admiral Alexei Abazov, and Prince Felix Yusupov, among others. Bezobrazov and his circle gained inordinate control over Russia's Far East policy by promising immediate returns on the millions of rubles invested in the region whereas Witte's plans counted on huge payoffs in the long run. Meanwhile, Nicholas II fancied the idea of controlling Korea as a means to spread the glory of his empire, which by definition enhanced his personal power. In 1903, therefore, the tsar sided with the Bezobrazov group, thus forcing Witte from his powerful position as finance minister. Losing the best minister he inherited from his father was sheer folly, but it was true to the tsar's mismanagement of most policy decisions that he made at the beginning of the twentieth century. And, true to form, Nicholas made the situation worse by appointing Admiral Yevgeny Ivanovich Alexeiev, an illegitimate son of Alexander II, as viceroy of the region. From this position Alexeiev, who identified himself as a member of the Bezobrazov circle, had supreme command of the region, which effectively gave free reign to Bezobrazov and his clique to do as they pleased without interference from St. Petersburg. Their activity, especially their harvesting of timber according to their interpretation of the Yalu Concession, served to antagonize the Japanese and alienate the Russians from the Chinese population throughout northern China and Korea. The activities of Bezobrazov circle therefore heightened tensions across the region but especially on the Liaotung Peninsula at the same time when the Russian state was building the southern branch of the Eastern Chinese Railway from Harbin to Port Arthur. If the Russians had withdrawn their troops from Manchuria, as they had agreed to do in the aftermath of the Boxer Rebellion, war most likely could have been avoided. Instead, the massive construction of railroads combined with the exploitation of the resources of the region necessitated the transfer of more Russian troops to Manchuria, thereby contributing to the overall militarization of the region.[13]

Expansion into the Far East served as a flashpoint between interest groups in Nicholas II's government. Beginning in 1898, however, the tsar had a good moment when he appointed Alexsei Nikolaevich Kuropotkin war minister. Born in 1848, he was a very young fifty-year-old when he became the most important military leader in the empire. He represented the new breed of officers whom Miliutin envisioned as the future of the army—well educated and well trained to command and administer the army in both peace and war. Kuropatkin's family was not a part of the old Russian elites; in fact, his father retired from the army as a captain in the midst of the Great Reforms and spent the rest of his life serving in the Zemstov of his native Pskov region. The family's status nonetheless gained him admission into the 1st Cadet Corp Academy and upon completion he entered the newly reformed Pavlov Military School that now focused on advanced infantry training. He graduated in 1866 receiving a commission and rank of second lieutenant and was posted to First Turkestan Rifleman's Battalion. His biography then becomes linked to the conquest of Russia's Central Asian Empire. His service in Central Asia would be interrupted when he attended the General Staff Academy in 1871 where he excelled and was rewarded with a tour of Europe. While in France he managed to get himself attached to an expedition that crossed the Sahara Desert. His extensive report comparing operations in the Sahara to the Russian army's activities in Central Asia exhibited his emergence as a military intellectual and also garnered attention from none other than D. A. Miliutin. Such recognition resulted in an 1876 appointment to the post of senior adjutant of the Turkestan Military District, which was a very big job for a 28-year-old junior staff officer. His ascent to the commanding heights of the army received a boost because of his service as chief of staff to General M. O. Sokobelov, the "White General" in the 1877–8 Turkish War. Kuropatkin personally led an assault on Plevna and then marched to the gates of Constantinople, thereby establishing himself as an effective operational commander. In the war's aftermath he was decorated, promoted to the rank of colonel, and returned to Central Asia where he remained under Sokobelov's command. His leadership during the assault at Geok-Tepe along with his continued campaigning led to his promotion to major-general. He then became the empire's foremost expert on the region as he traveled, wrote reports, and drew maps. His repeated exploits combined with his gathering of intelligence while on active service resulted in him being posted to the Main Staff in 1883 where he served as adjutant to N. N. Obruchev. This posting provided the opportunity for Kuropatkin to hone his administrative skills on every aspect of military establishment—education, training, planning, logistics, intelligence gathering, and so forth. Now a lieutenant-general, in

1890 Kuropatkin was appointed military governor of the recently acquired and strategically significant Trans-Caspian region when he remained until he was appointed war minister in 1898.

Kuropatkin's career trajectory therefore embodied the vision that Miliutin sought to inculcate throughout the ranks of his officer corps: he was well educated and had completed a broad assortment of administrative tasks all while gaining invaluable leadership experience throughout his service in the operational army. He was appointed war minister because he merited it; his education, training, and experiences made him the rising star of the military establishment. Upon becoming war minister, he was inundated with a variety of challenges that encompassed every aspect of the empire's status and security. As had been the case throughout the Imperial period, one of Kuropatkin's biggest tasks was managing the military resources of an empire that was constantly expanding yet always suffering from financial limitations. This situation was acute at the beginning of the twentieth century largely because of pressure mounting from the West. While the Russians had been pressing eastward after their plans for the Balkans, following the 1877–8 Russo-Turkish War, and had been squashed by Bismarck and the rest of Europe, the Europeans continued to build up their military establishments. The root of confrontation in the west remained the bitterness lingering from the way Germany unified itself in 1870–1. Unified Germany's peace terms and the annexation of the French provinces of Alsace and Lorraine planted the seeds in the French imagination for the need to fight a war of revenge. In an effort to isolate the Germans, the French sought and the Russians agreed to the establishment of an alliance that grew from the French and the Russians agreeing to an unlikely partnership that started with the French lending money to the tsar for purposes of economic development throughout the 1890s. This détente of sorts evolved into a relationship based on military commitments in the first decade of the twentieth century. Besides exhibiting that politics truly does make for strange bedfellows as the most liberal and the most conservative empires in Europe found common ground, this relationship had one aspect that exacerbated Russia's financial struggles. While accepting French loans, the Russians became overwhelmed with the rapid pace of technological modernization that was occurring within the European military establishments and specifically the impact the Industrial Revolution was having on the weapon systems. Kuropatkin sought to contain the heightening of costs associated with technologically sophisticated systems, such as rapid-fire artillery, by suggesting to Nicholas II that he try to negotiate a halt to further weapon's development with the Europeans. What followed, at the urging of Nicholas II, were the Hague Peace Conventions of 1899 and 1907, both designed to foster peaceful relations among Europeans that may have delayed the outbreak of the First World War.[14]

While Kuropatkin offered his tsar naive ideas aimed at containing the threat from the West, he also found himself embroiled in the split that had developed in Nicholas II's government over Far Eastern policy. He supported Witte's plans for the systematic expansion of the Russian Empire to the shores of the Pacific Ocean. Moreover, he facilitated the militarization of Manchuria during and after the Boxer Rebellion. Then, however, he did what he did best—a systematic examination of the region that culminated with a comprehensive tour of the Far East in the spring of 1903 that included a visit to Japan. From his observations he drew two conclusions that were largely ignored in St. Petersburg. This first was that reckless activities of the Bezobrazov group were not only alienating the Russians from the Chinese across Manchuria but were also leaving the empire dangerously exposed to military threats. Keying on the newly constructed port of Dalnii, just north of Port Arthur, Kuropatkin complained that while business interests saw the need for and therefore created this port, nothing was being done to secure it from attack. The war minister's main point was that without securing it, the Russians could effectively be building a port that an enemy such as Japan could easily occupy if war broke out over Manchuria and Korea, a possibility that grew with each passing day. In addition, while Kuropatkin can be linked to all the propaganda that identified the Japanese as the "Yellow Peril" that threatened Western civilization, he was also the first Russian to accurately assess their military capabilities. While the rest of Europe, indeed the majority of the subjects of his own empire, viewed the Japanese as an inferior enemy that could not represent much of a challenge to any Western military power, Kuropatkin, especially after his visit to Japan in 1903, knew the case to be something very different. From his own personal observations, the war minister understood that as a result of the westernizing efforts of the men of the Mejii Restorations, the Japanese had transformed their military into a formidable army and navy that would not be a pushover in future conflict. Not surprisingly, just as Kuropatkin was making his astute assessment of the situation, Witte lost power, Alexeiev became viceroy of the Far East, and the entrepreneurial adventurism that defined the activities of Bezobrazov gained control of the politics of the region. With that, the path toward war became unstoppable. Simply put, the Japanese did not believe they could sit by as the Westerners, led by the Russians, gained control over Far East territories but especially Korea.[15]

The Russo-Japanese War

The significance of the Japanese navy's surprise attack on the Russian battle fleet moored at Port Arthur on the night of February 8–9, 1904, far outweighed any of the damage that was absorbed by either fleet. The opening salvo of this war marked a major starting point for the age of global conflict that defined

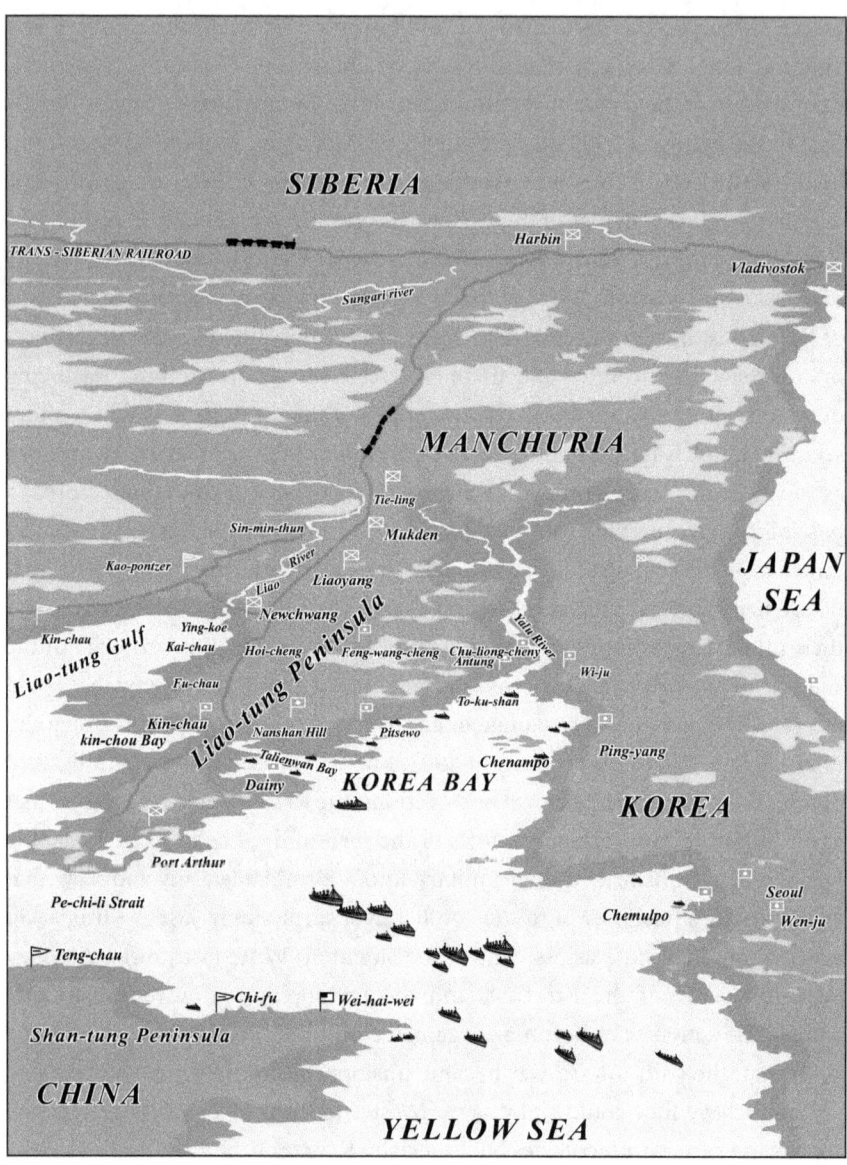

Map 5.1 Russo-Japanese War Theater of Operations.

the twentieth century. The rising Japanese empire exhibited that it intended to expand its authority onto the Asian continent and no power, not even the huge and powerful Russian Empire, was going to deter them from pursuing their goals. The use of a naval assault displayed the Japanese as a rising power that had adopted sophisticated industrial technology to back up their colonial ambitions. It also fit well into the thinking of the military leaders of the Great Powers about the significance of naval power at the time as the colonial powers strove to construct navies that would provide them with control over the world's oceans and by extension international trade. Once the Russians got past the outrage of being victims of a dastardly sneak attack, they flooded their media with stories about the threat of "yellow peril" to the rest of the world. They grossly underestimated the military potential of their adversaries. Beginning with Nicholas II, the attitude that prevailed in St. Petersburg, despite the warnings of Kuropatkin a year earlier, was that the Russian military establishment would handily destroy their Asian foe. The actual damage to the Russian fleet as a result of the attack, however, was minimal and could have made questionable the risk the Japanese taken in undertaking it. Strategically, however, the attack on Port Arthur was a phenomenal success. It unnerved the Russian navy so that the Russian military did nothing the next day to confront the Japanese landing of an expeditionary force at Chemulpo (Inchon). The invasion paved the way for the Japanese army to march up the Korean peninsula in the dead of winter to position themselves for the assault they launched against the Russian forces in northern Manchuria in the spring of 1904. The attack on Port Arthur and the invasion of Korea also demonstrated that one of the factors that would determine the outcome of the war would be control of the sea. If the Russian battle fleet had sortied on February 9th and blocked Japan's invasion of Korea, and if the Russians had maintained control of the Yellow Sea throughout the war, then the Japanese would have been unable to confront the tsar's army on the ground in Manchuria. The Russians, however, stumbled over their response and found themselves reacting to Japanese actions as opposed to controlling any aspect of the growing conflict.

Sometimes referred to as World War Zero, the Russo-Japanese War was also at the very least a harbinger of the First World War.[16] In addition to modern navies engaged in what ultimately became a culminating battle that determined control of the sea—the May 1905 Battle of Tsushima Strait—the Russian and Japanese armies engaged in numerous battles that lasted for days, even weeks toward the end of the war. The war featured both a war of maneuver as the Japanese pushed the Russians up the Liaotung Peninsula and a prolonged fortress battle at Port

Arthur. These battles featured an unprecedented level of lethality because of the use of industrialized weapon systems that ranged from machine guns to rapid-fire artillery on land and torpedoes and mines at sea, resulting in a dramatic rise in casualty levels that overwhelmed medical corps with desperately wounded soldiers in need of immediate life-saving medical assistance. Both nations mobilized resources—human and material—that overwhelmed their finances and resulted in each belligerent borrowing money leading to the emergence of complex financial transactions that involved international bankers backing each side. While defeat on the battlefield—both on land and on sea—was the major cause for the Russians to agree to engage in a peacemaking process, the Japanese needed to make peace even more urgently in the spring of 1905 after a cabal of Wall Street bankers withdrew their financial backing after the Battle of Muken. In addition to widespread military failure, by the end of the war, the Russian Empire was engulfed in a revolution—the Revolution of 1905—that would, in the end, undermine the authority of the regime. While his grandfather Alexander II was able to overcome the disastrous outcome of the Crimean War, Nicholas II did not have the intellectual capability, the practical skill, or the interpersonal skills to survive his Far Eastern disaster over the long term.

These outcomes, of course, were still unknown in February 1904. In fact, in addition to the propaganda campaign, there was cause for optimism in St. Petersburg after the Japanese attack of the Russian fleet in Port Arthur. In addition to the commonly perceived Russian advantage based on her huge advantage in size and resources, the tsar possessed a military establishment that had been modernizing since the Miliutin's reforms in the 1860s. The army had a professionalized officer corps of which at least 50 percent did not achieve their rank and status based on social status. Instead they earned their positions within the army based on merit that they proved through education, training, and operational experience. Nicholas II's navy, moreover, possessed completely modernized ships designed and built to compete with the other navies of the Great Powers. Moreover, the rank–and-file cadre had progressed two generations beyond being serfs inducted, usually against their will, into the Russian army. Instead the army was supposed to be composed of soldiers who now viewed themselves as subjects of the tsar who wanted to defend their empire. As the course of the war would demonstrate, however, neither the officers nor the soldiers proved to be the modern force everyone expected to take the battlefield. The officers usually did not support each other when they found themselves engaged in battle and by the end of the war large numbers of soldiers chose mutiny in support of the revolutionaries throughout the empire.

Indeed, the fact that the soldiers' mutiny took place in the Far East rather than St. Petersburg—as it did in 1917—is a significant reason the regime was able to restore order and persevere for another decade or so. The Russo-Japanese War, therefore, demonstrated that the Russian military establishment had not become the lethal weapon that represented the nation-in-arms that Miliutin had envisioned as his goal.

With their attack on Port Arthur, the Japanese were able to seize the initiative in the war and the Russians never recovered. The Russian war effort suffered from a level of confusion from the moment the Japanese attacked. After all, at the very least, the Russian Far Eastern Fleet should have been on high alert in February 1904 as tensions over Manchuria and Korea were at a very high level. Nonetheless on the night of February 8th most of the officers of the fleet were at a party that was thrown by their commander Admiral Oscar Viktorovich Starck. On a systemic level the Port was not well defended as funds to shore up coastal defenses had been diverted to be used for the further development of Dalnii, the port located north of Port Arthur that was being developed for commercial reasons. The Japanese commander Admiral Togo intended to use the main strength of his fleet, six pre-dreadnought class battleships led by himself on his flagship the Mikasa and a second division of five battle cruisers. Adding to the strength of his forces, Togo had at this disposal fifteen destroyers and twenty smaller hybrid ships classified as torpedo destroyers. With this large force and surprise on his side, Togo intended to deliver a crushing and decisive blow to the Russian naval presence in the Far East. But it was not to be, despite the overall incompetence of the Russian navy on both a technical and leadership level. Two factors saved the Russians from complete destruction on the night of February 8-9, 1904. The first was the natural topography of Port Arthur that featured a shallow draft entrance into the port itself. Without dredging the entrance—something the Russians did not have the equipment to do—entering and exiting the port could only occur at high tide. While some controversy exists over Togo's timid use of his capital ships during the attack, the limitations over the entrance to the port meant that he would only send his smaller ships into harm's way when the attack actually occurred. Then, while the Japanese launched an estimated sixteen torpedoes during their attack, only three hit targets and only one ship—the protected cruiser Pallada—was significantly damaged. Here the second factor came into play; many of the Russian ships, while not at all prepared to sortie and engage with the main Japanese fleet lurking outside of their main base of operation, were protected by torpedo nets that did their job of thwarting the weapons aimed at their ships. Damage did occur to other Russian ships from shellfire but the results were not the overwhelming success the Japanese hoped for. The attack, which started just after midnight, was broken up by 2:00 a.m. largely because the Russian officers had found their way back to their ships and had organized a defense by turning on huge search lights that illuminated the Japanese navy. Togo, always in fear of losing his fleet because it could not be readily replaced, withdrew and prepared for the next day's operation.[17]

As is usually the case in conflicts, the immediate results of the attack were not clearly understood by either side. The Japanese had no idea if the Russians were about to sortie and turn the Yellow Sea into their lake or if they would be able to land their army in Korea the next day. The worst failure of the opening salvo of the war occurred because of the leadership of the Russian navy. Not only did they fail to be prepared for a pending conflict, in the aftermath of the attack they suffered from a strategic and operational paralysis that set the tone of their conduct for the rest of the war. In addition to a lack of combat readiness, the leaders of the Russian navy had failed to take any steps to transform Port Arthur into a naval base that could act with a high degree of autonomy in the period leading up to the war. While dredging the entrance to the port may well have been beyond their capabilities, nothing was done to modernize the base's repair facilities. This meant that there was not one functioning dry dock in Port Arthur, and the fleet had little capability to perform regular maintenance let alone repair battle damage to its ships. For the Russian navy to perform at a level that would allow it to compete with the Japanese, the command structure of the fleet had to be completely overhauled from the top down. How well either side understood the shortcomings of Russia's navy in February 1904 is not clear but for a war that would depend on which side would control the sea between Manchuria, Korea, and Japan, the early indications did not bode well for the Russians.

Could it be that the level of dysfunction for the Russians was even worse within the empire's army? In February 1904 it was not clear who was in overall command of Russian land forces in Manchuria. As noted, one of the by-products of Nicholas II policy machinations was his appointment of Admiral Evgeni Ivanovich Alexseiev as viceroy of Russia's Far Eastern provinces in 1903. The admiral considered himself to be the overall military commander of the region and immediately began to implement his strategy for fighting the war after the attack on Port Arthur. Yet, also typical of the layers of confusion that emerged from the tsar's clumsy efforts at policymaking, the lines of authority within the high command of the army were not well defined, which greatly complicated all efforts at responding to the Japanese attack. Even worse, Alexseiev was an admiral in name only, that is, his rank and status existed because of his distant familial relationship to the tsar and were not the product of any formal military training or experiences. Further compounding the situation, the admiral was a factor in the Bezobrazov cabal who did not understand the scope of the Japanese threat. In fact, Alexseiev subscribed to all of the racists' "yellow peril" thinking of the period and, therefore, did not take the Japanese as a serious challenger to Russian power. As a result, his strategy was based on the principle of letting the Japanese come to Russia's prepared positions because, when conflict would occur, the Russian army would be able to handily dispatch the enemy without much trouble. The other half of the command drama that became a part of the early Russian efforts at this war played out in St. Petersburg. Wanting to secure his place in the pantheon of great Russian operational commanders, Kuropatkin lobbied the tsar for and successfully convinced Nicholas II to appoint him overall commander in chief of Russian military operations in the Far East right after the outbreak of war. Resigning as war minister and becoming the overall commander of Russia's armed forces in the theater of operations became the biggest mistake of Kurpotkin's career as his efforts to command the war effort failed on almost every level, especially when it came to the operational conduct of the army in the field.[18]

From the start, Kuropatkin's efforts suffered from a lack of overall coordination of the war effort. His understanding of the military potential of the Japanese resulted in his developing a strategy based on limiting engagements with the Japanese and then, when confronted with battle, fighting a defensive action. Such thinking and subsequent planning was intended to buy time for the Russian military to build up its strength in Manchuria. This type of operational conduct became known as "Kuropatkin's Strategy," and it ran counter to Alexseiev's plan and thinking about the Japanese. The two men, Kuropatkin and Alexseiev, had opposing views on how to contain and confront their enemy with the former ordering troops to fight defensive battles and the latter insisting on striking the enemy with bold offensive actions. Much to the detriment of the course of the war for the Russians, no one sorted out this conflict until the Japanese forced the issue in campaigns in the late winter and spring of 1904. The Japanese invasion of Korea occurred according to plan and made plain what their strategy was from the beginning of the war; the Korean invasion ultimately placed the Japanese army in the position to attack entrenched Russian positions in the hills of northern Manchuria. After Togo successfully gained command of the sea by bottling up the Russian fleet at Port Arthur, the Japanese landed their First Army under the command of General Kuroki Tametomo at Chemulpo (Inchon) and they marched unchallenged up the Korean peninsula to the Yalu River that to this day remains the border between North Korea and Manchuria. An important and not well-studied aspect of this campaign emerged from the march in that a group of international military observers accompanied the Japanese and their reports attracted the attention of military establishments across the globe. Many of these observers (e.g., John J. Pershing and Ian Hamilton to name only two) would become senior leaders in their armies during the First World War. The product of the reports of the hundreds of military observers who accompanied both armies onto the Manchurian battlefield was the publication of numerous volumes of operational studies written either by professional officers or by journalists. Every aspect of the conflict would be studied—from the maneuver of troops to the use of artillery and cavalry to studies of logistical challenges and how the requirements of modern warfare transformed the needs of and care for soldiers in battle. These publications made this war an instantly studied conflict that clearly laid out the parameters of what it would take to fight a modern conflict. Sadly, for the fate of millions, the lessons of this war would not be learned by the outbreak of the First World War.[19]

Meanwhile, as soon as he was appointed commander in chief, Kuropatkin got on the Trans-Siberian railroad and headed to the theater of operations. Kuropatkin, no doubt, must have spent much time thinking about the logistical challenges of the coming military operations. While the war could not have been possible for the Russians without the Trans-Siberian railway, in February 1904 it was still not completed. Famously, the war started with no clear means for the trains to work the way around Lake Baikal and there were still some stretches of track that had not been completed, thus reducing traffic to a single rail thereby causing long delays as trains had to spend idle time on sidings to let traffic going in the opposite direction pass. Kuropatkin made it to the Far East by the middle of March only because his train received high priority, which meant that other traffic across the line was shuffled onto sidings to make way for his train. Such practices meant long delays for soldiers and war fighting materials as they endured a long journey on an almost completed railroad. While much has been written about these shortcomings, the railroad still would not have been sufficient for the war effort even if it had been completed because it had no surge capacity. As the war unfolded Russian logicians planned for a minimum of thirty days to move one regiment of the army from European Russia to the Far East. Compared to the three days the Japanese planned to move one regiment from Japan to the theater of operations is a telling clue about the outcome of the war. The Russians needed to control the sea as the best way to hold off the Japanese if Kuropatkin's strategy of delay and reinforce until he had overwhelming force in Manchuria had a chance of succeeding. How well the Russians understood this is not clear. They lacked a naval leader with strong strategic thinking skills; none had ever gained favor at court. Even more vexing, the Russian navy had very few aggressive operational commanders. Arguably, the lack of aggressive military leadership throughout the military establishment in 1904–5 would be one of the legacies of the entire wartime experience for the Russians. While the military had become completely embedded in Russian society, by the beginning of the twentieth century it still did not have the operational leadership capable of prevailing on the battlefield. Miliutin's reforms had upgraded the administrative and educational side of the army, but the army had lost its way as a war fighting machine.[20]

Regardless of Russia's confused situation, the war proceeded largely according to the Japanese plan of operations. Kuroki's First Army, some 42,000 strong and composed of the 2nd, 12th, and Imperial Guard's Division, relentlessly marched through a Korean winter to reach the banks of the Yalu by the end of April. There with his headquarters in the town of Wiju he paused to give his soldiers time to rest after their long march and to carefully reconnoiter the Russian positions on the other side of the Yalu. The Japanese had been cultivating intelligence assets in Korea and Manchuria since the end of the 1894–5 Sino-Japanese War, and in addition to having accurate topographical maps of the theater of operations, they had also cultivated relatively harmonious relations with the indigenous population. As a result, and most importantly for the initial battle in the war, they had found laborers who helped them establish and maintain a logistical capability that supported their soldiers in the field.[21] For the Russians the situation was just the opposite. For starters, when the war broke out, all command elements in St. Petersburg and in the Far East lacked suitable maps of the region. Moreover, the Russians treated the native Chinese population of the region as an occupied colonial population of inferior people and did not cultivate a workable relationship with them. The Russians therefore went to war in a region they had been occupying for a number of years without adequate intelligence about the terrain in which they were about to fight populated with people they had been alienating through their systematic conduct as colonizers. And, to make matters worse, the soldiers who were about to engage the Japanese enemy suffered the ultimate failure of their command establishment by receiving two sets of orders. Thus, going into the battle, the Russian commander Lt. General Mikhail Zasulich, vastly outnumbered with approximately 18,000 effectives under his command, officially identified as the Eastern Detachment, had to contend with receiving different orders from Kuropatkin's and Alexeiev's headquarters. Kuropatkin, in what became typical for his conduct, told Zasulich that it was vital to prevent the Japanese from achieving a decisive victory as it would raise their morale and likewise compromise the attitude of the Russian combatants. Despite such a warning, in the end, Kuropatkin told his general to avoid engaging and instead prevent the enemy from crossing the Yalu. If necessary Kuropatkin told Zasulich to retreat in good order toward the ancient city of Liaoyang. Zasulich, unhappy with Kuropatkin's orders to hold and retreat, appealed to Alexeiev's headquarters for a different set of orders. The admiral, believing inaccurate information about the strength and capabilities of the Japanese army, ordered Zasulich to hold the enemy at the Yalu and if he saw the opportunity to advance into Korea with an aim to force them off of the Asian mainland. The fractured nature of the Russian command system that arguably reflected the weakness of the Russian political establishment starting with the tsar was now compromising the military effort in the midst of a major conflict. Indeed, having a commander who can appeal a set of orders between command establishments in the course of a battle is not a formula for victory at any level.[22]

The folly of Russia's conduct became clear when Kuroki unleashed the might of his forces on the night of April 30–May 1. A spot in the Yalu where a tributary called the Ai River branched off and caused two islands, Kintei and Kyuri, to emerge in the middle proved ideal for their plan. In the days leading up to this engagement, Japanese engineers, much to the amazement and chagrin of the Russians, built a series of ten bridges at this spot using some steel beams that they had carried during their invasion while finding the rest of what they needed from local resources. The Russians did not have enough artillery to render the bridges ineffective and while the Japanese suffered heavy casualties, they did force their way across the river by the end of the day. Moreover, the Japanese moved their artillery onto the mid-river island of Kintei and, because of their careful reconnaissance, peppered the Russian positions with well-aimed howitzer fire. By 10:00 a.m. the next morning Zasulich evacuated his headquarters at Chuliencheng, the town on the western bank of the Ai River directly across from Wiju. From this point Zasulich's army withdrew into the hills of Manchuria in disarray and demoralized as a result of their failure on the battlefield. The psychological impact of this loss cannot be overestimated in understanding the future of the conflict. At once the Russians learned that they were now fighting a determined and ferocious enemy and that their (the Russians') command establishment was suffering from a lack of cohesion that emboldened operational commanders to appeal orders if they did not like them.[23] And, as the Russians struggled to gain control over their operations, the Japanese landed their Second Army at Pitzuwo 60 km north of Dalnii on May 5th under the command of General Oku Yasukata, which set the stage for the Battle of Nanshan.[24] The Battle of the Yalu was relatively minor in terms of troops engaged and damage inflicted. But it was huge in global terms for the Russians—the myth of the Japanese enemy being a pushover and that the war would be short was exposed as false. For the Japanese, victory on the Yalu meant that they had control over Korea and with their territorial concerns addressed; they now sought to destroy the Russian army.

The landing at Pitzuwo further demonstrated the recklessness of Russia's conduct in the Far East both before the war and once the conflict started. The empire's military and political leaders failed to connect their capabilities to the potential consequences of their actions, and they would pay a huge price for their shortcomings as the war unfolded. The unopposed landing of an entirely new army, the Second Army using a fleet of around eighty transports and additional warships, exhibited the complete control the Japanese had of the sea. It further revealed that the influence of the Bezobrazov clique at court prevailed in such a fashion that little regard or concern was paid to the development of defenses to protect commercial development while the Russians had poured resources into the Liaotung Peninsula in the prewar period and despite the warnings of then War Minister Kuropatkin. Russia's efforts to control any aspect of the naval war, already in chaos from the moment the first Japanese torpedo was launched on February 8, suffered what turned out to be an overwhelming setback in the weeks leading up to the Battle of Nanshan. While Admiral Stark may well have been deeply engaged in improving every aspect of Port Arthur's facilities, training the fleet to enhance its combat effectiveness was not one of his priorities. As a result, the fleet failed to respond to the attack in a meaningful manner and, even worse, the Russian navy effectively surrendered control of the sea to the Japanese upon their firing the first shot of the war.

St. Petersburg responded to the admiral's shortcomings by replacing him with their best leader Vice Admiral Stepan Osipovich Makarov who arrived to take over command of the fleet on March 8, 1904. Makarov earned his reputation as a charismatic fighting leader during the 1877–8 Russo-Turkish War and as a progressive innovator in subsequent years because of his persistent efforts to get the Romanovs to dedicate ever-increasing financial resources to building a fleet that could defend and help the empire expand during the age of imperialism. His arrival signified renewed energy throughout the fleet especially when he made it clear that he would emphasize combat readiness through intensive training. The impact of his arrival and the implementation of his ideas and plans resulted in morale soaring to new levels. Then, however, tragedy struck the fleet and Russia's war effort when he sortied on his flagship, the battleship Petropavlovsk on April 13, 1904, in response to sightings of Japanese ships off the entrance of Port Arthur. Seeking battle, the Petropavlovsk sailed into a newly laid Japanese minefield and struck one or two mines, which resulted in the ship's forward magazine igniting. Two minutes later it sank with the loss of over 600 sailors including Admiral Makarov. This tragedy was hard for the Russian public to accept; the Imperial Russian navy, especially its Far Eastern flotilla, never recovered from the loss of Admiral Makarov during the war. Makarov represented the best chance for the Russians to, if not gain outright control of the sea, then make the Yellow Sea a very difficult and costly place for the Japanese to operate. With his passing, the Russians had no other naval leader who came close to replacing him.[25] Instead, in the wake of the defeat on the Yalu and the landing of the Japanese at Pitzuwo, Viceroy Alexeiev abandoned Port Arthur on May 5th and traveled to Mukden for further consultations with Kuropatkin. He left Port Arthur's commandant General Baron Anatoli Mikhailovich Stoessel in charge of land operations and Admiral Wilhelm Witgeft in command of all naval forces in the theater of operations, which was unfortunate because neither man was up to the task of command especially against an aggressive and determined Japanese enemy.[26]

The Japanese, therefore, landed unopposed at Pitzuwo at the beginning of May, which launched what became known as the Manchurian war of maneuver. This invasion of the Liaotung Peninsula not only represented the beginning of the next stage of the conflict, but it also defined Japanese strategy for the rest of the war. With Kuroki's First Army pressing the Russians in northern Manchuria, Oku's army offered the Japanese the opportunity to pressure the Russians with a second operational army, menacing the tsar's armies with a two-prong threat. In the period building up to the invasion of the second prong of the attack (Oku's Second Army), the Japanese navy devised a plan to sink old ships in the channel leading into Port Arthur to blockade the Russian Far Eastern Navy in its own home facilities. Japanese planning for this blockade predated the war and ultimately failed in real terms to physically bottle up the Russian navy. Nonetheless, naval planners moved forward with their idea about containing the Russian fleet when Togo's attack of February 8–9 failed to destroy it. Thus, the Japanese would attempt to sink ships in the channel connecting Port Arthur to the Yellow Sea on the nights of February 23, March 26, and May 3. A combination of ships and shore batteries thwarted all of these attempts, but when the Russians did not give chase to the Japanese on May 3rd, Admiral Togo correctly deduced that the Japanese effectively had control of the sea in the theater of operations. Togo, along with all of Japan's military leaders, remained keenly aware that their war effort would be untenable if they lost control of the sea. While the Russians had ships and sailors that could have reversed the Japanese advantage at sea, they did not have the leadership after the death of Admiral Makarov willing to sortie their fleet to threaten their enemy's rapidly growing hegemony over the naval aspect of the war. Thus, after the May 3rd attempt to blockade Port Arthur, Togo believed he had effective control of the sea.[27] This cleared the way for the landing at Pitzumo, which provided a base of operation for a two-prong attack of which the most vital aspect in the spring of 1904 was laying siege to Port Arthur to eliminate any possibility of a future Russian naval threat. At the same time, the Japanese used additional forces to launch the Manchurian war of maneuver designed to link up with Kuroki's forces in the north who were chasing the Russians after dislodging them from their positions on the Yalu with additional Japanese forces who had landed at Pitsuwo. The first step in this operational plan, however, was to lay siege to Port Arthur, which meant assaulting fortified Russian positions in what became known as the Battle of Nanshan.

Nanshan was located at the southern tip of the Liaotung Peninsula and marked the northern edge of the Kwantung Peninsula on which Port Arthur was located at its southern end. The central part of the position was on a 116-m-tall hill that was 2.5 miles across at high tide and would double in size at low tide and covered the most significant land approach to Port Arthur. Moreover, it was 12 miles north of Dalnii, which was 23 miles north of Port Arthur. Its strategic importance was recognized by both sides, and the Russians began to heavily fortify Nanshan after the Boxer Rebellion and with greater intensity after 1903. By May 1904 the position appeared as something akin to a First World War–fortified position with a trench marked by barbed wire replete with machine gun emplacements, minefields, modern communications links, observations balloons, and powerful searchlights made famous in Japanese woodblock prints that depicted the battle. Because of the landing at Pitzumo, the Japanese Second Army was able to concentrate some 38,500 soldiers who were supported with 216 assorted artillery pieces and 48 machine guns. In addition, four gunboats stationed in Chinchou Bay offered fourteen more heavy guns that would provide vital firepower at the climactic moment of the battle. While the Japanese viewed the coming engagement as an all-out effort designed to set the stage for them to gain control of Dalnii so that they would have a readymade port to supply their siege of Port Arthur, the Russians viewed the battle as something very different. Lieutenant General Anatolii Stoessel, commander of Port Arthur, did not think

Nanshan was vital to the overall defense of his naval base and therefore ordered his subordinate Major General Aleksandr Viktorovich Fok to withdraw from the field of battle after inflicting as much damage as possible to the Japanese. In the end Fok would give the task of defending the Russian positions at Nanshan to Colonel Nikolai Aleksandrovich Tretyakov who had under his command 3,500 troops of the 5th East Siberian Rifle Regiment. Tretyakov went into battle with some sixty-five heavy guns, ten heavy machine guns, and fifty light machine guns and the belief that when the battle heated up, he would be able to draw reinforcements from other units composed of approximately 18,000 soldiers who stood ready for action just south of the battlefront.

Oku launched his assault on the position by shelling and attacking the town of Chinchou that served as the location for Tretyakov's headquarters. While the town was defended by only 400 men, the Russians held firm against the onslaught. Their situation benefited from extreme thunderstorms that slowed the Japanese assault, thus taking the battle for the town into the next day. The next day the Japanese, supported by enfilading fire from their gunships, marched through the shallow waters of Chinchou Bay, thus outflanking the Russian position at Chinchou and allowing them to launch what turned into nine attempts to take the 116-m hill at the center of the position. One measure of the ferocity of the battle was how Oku's artillery expended some 34,000 shells, more than they used in the entire Sino-Japanese War of 1894–5. While Tretyakov's meager forces put up a strong defense, by the end of the day his troops were out of ammunition, and he ordered a retreat to a second line of defense where he thought that reinforcements would be made available. What followed on the night of May 26–27 provides another example of how the Russians were going to fight this war. Fok, whose background was all in police work, ordered a general retreat without Tretyakov's knowledge. While the colonel was appealing to Stoessel for reinforcements, his local commander (Fok) had already lost his nerve, leading to the complete collapse of the Russian position and turning any opportunity for an organized retreat into a rout.[28] The Japanese did not follow in hot pursuit for two reasons. First, they had suffered over 6,000 casualties in the course of the battle, which caused them to pause to reconsolidate their forces. Such a high number of casualties overwhelmed the capabilities of their medical services and was a clear harbinger of the number of combat wounded that modern weapons imposed on the force structure of armies. The second reason the Japanese did not launch an immediate assault on Port Arthur was because of some Russian success at sea. While the Far Eastern Fleet lacked suitable leadership, the Russians had deployed mines, which caught and sunk the Japanese battleships Yashima and

Hatsuse, which represented one-third of their total number of battleships. Again, the issue of command of the sea returned to make the Japanese concerned about their overall ability to prevail in this conflict. Despite the concern raised by the tremendous success of mines, the Japanese occupied Dalnii on May 30, which the Russians had abandoned without any opposition. Thus, the Japanese now had a functioning port, built as a result of the Bezobrazov clique's machinations that would serve as the main supply point for the siege of Port Arthur, which commenced later in the summer.[29]

Kuropatkin received the news about Nanshan while he was at his headquarters in Mukden most probably with much angst as he predicted in 1903 Dalnii would end up being a Russian-made port for the Japanese if it remained undefended. Even worse, in the aftermath of the defeat at Nanshan, he was about to learn that Nicholas II had little confidence in his (Kuropatkin's) strategy. With the Japanese firmly possessing the strategic initiative after Nanshan, Alexseiev's and Kuropatkin's opposing ideas on how to conduct operations reached a boiling point after they had a heated meeting in Mukden immediately after the Battle of Nanshan. While Alexseiev wanted to launch an aggressive offensive in response to the recent setback, Kuropatkin adamantly wanted to maintain the army's defensive posture while continuous streams of reinforcements and supplies were sent to the theater of operations via the Trans-Siberian Railway. Lacking the ability to resolve their differences, Alexseiev appealed directly to Nicholas II for intervention in the war on an operational level. The tsar consulted with a newly formed Supreme War Council and his old mentor M. I. Dragomirov then ordered Kuropatkin to follow orders and launch an offensive operation aimed at thwarting Japanese efforts to lay siege to Port Arthur. This setback for Kuropatkin, who believed that General Stoessel and Port Arthur could hold out for an undetermined and prolonged period, did much to undermine his ability to run the war. As a loyal soldier, however, he obeyed his tsar's orders, but his conduct toward the operation revealed that Kuropatkin's priority was to avoid all major confrontations with the Japanese until he was confident that he had the forces that could launch an operation that would remove them from China and Manchuria.[30] Against his better judgment, but in an attempt to satisfy his critics in St. Petersburg, he ordered the movement of troops that would culminate with Baron General Georgi von Shtakel'berg concentrating some 27,000 soldiers of the First Siberian Army Crop combined with 2,500 cavalry troops and ninety-eight artillery pieces to give battle to the Japanese. Nevertheless, Kuropatkin undermined the operation when he ordered Shtakel'berg to prevent the Japanese from consolidating their armies into a siege force while avoiding any major combat. Shtakel'berg correctly interpreted these orders to mean that it would be better to lose any engagement than to lose any significant number of his soldiers in the coming battle.

This force met the Japanese in another deadly encounter at a rail junction called Telissu or Vafangou on June 14–15. Located 129 km north of Port Arthur, the battle unfolded over a 12-km front across rolling hills. The Russians arrived and started to dig in around the railroad station at Vafangou and found themselves in their fortified positions as Oku approached the position with his force of 36,000 men, 2,000 cavalry troops, and 216 artillery pieces in three columns and started the battle with what became a continuous artillery barrage on the morning of June 14. As the morning progressed, it became clear that the Japanese had learned much about the deployment and concentration of artillery as a result of Nanshan, while the Russians still needed to study and learn lessons from their recent combat experiences. In short, the Japanese fired to greater effect as the Russians still had not learned to conceal their artillery positions. In the fury of battle, with his movement undetected because of the sound of artillery, in the early afternoon Oku sent a fourth column of infantry into an attack of Shtakel'berg's right flank. As the sun was setting, the Japanese were outplanning and outmaneuvering the Russians at every stage of the battle. Even worse, Shtakel'berg had little information on the disposition of the Japanese, which highlighted the overall weakness of Russian intelligence gathering abilities that would plague the military effort throughout the war. As a result of these shortcomings Shtakel'berg went into the night of June 14–15 believing that he could commit his reserves and reverse the course of battle the next day. He, therefore, spent the night sending orders to his commanders to attack the Japanese on the Russian right flank in the morning. At this point, and in the confusion of the battle, the Russian operational commanders utterly failed to seize the initiative as they spent the night seeking greater clarity or definition into what they should do, often blaming breakdowns in communications links for their confusion. What they in fact did was not follow orders if they disagreed with them, which is no way to run an army in the midst of a war! Thus, throughout the night of June 14–15 Shtakel'berg's immediate subordinates, Generals A. A. Grengross and F. F. Glasko, failed to unify the forces under their command into an effective reserve that would strike Oku on the morning of June 15th. Instead Shtakel'berg had to accept at midday that he was being enveloped. Heavy rainfall in the late afternoon saved his forces from being routed from the battlefield yet again; even so, the Japanese decisively prevailed in combat!

What became clear as a result of the Russians' conduct at Vafangou was that their army had lost its way on the battlefield. Regardless of a history replete with two centuries of military success highlighted with the teachings and experiences of a host of great captains starting with Peter the Great and featuring legendary names such as Suvorov and Dragomirov to name only two, the Russian army could not and would not prevail in any engagement in this conflict. The outcome at Vafangou meant that Kuropatkin would now implement his strategy of maintaining a defensive posture until he built up the overwhelming forces that he intended to use to launch a decisive offensive against his foe. The strategy would be very unpopular up and down the chain of command, beginning in St. Petersburg with Nicholas II and members of his Supreme War Council and going through the members of the officer corps and ultimately trickling down to a lack of confidence in leadership at the unit level. The slowness of the Russians to adapt to and to learn about using modern weapons that rapidly transformed capabilities and lethality on the battlefield compounded the shortcomings of the Imperial Army.[31] Meanwhile, as the Russians retreated northward up the Liaotung Peninsula after the drilling they received at Vafangou, the Japanese implemented the next stage of their operations in this conflict. General Oku with his Second Army advanced northward seeking out the Russian army for the purpose of destroying it. At the same time, General Nogi, in command of the Japanese Third Army, started concentrating forces to lay siege to Port Arthur. Strategically, the most significant outcome of the Vafangou engagement was the Japanese had cut the East Manchurian railway line that connected Port Arthur to Muken. Ironically, the Russian cruiser squadron stationed at Vladivostok, while patrolling in the Sea of Japan caught and sank the Japanese transports Hatichi Mura and Sado Maru on June 15th. The Japanese lost 2,000 men of the 1st Reserve Guard's Regiment and along with a battalion of railway engineers and, at the same time, lost an entire siege train of 11-inch howitzers meant for the assault on Port Arthur. This event did more to slow down the Japanese military effort in Manchuria than any action taken by the Russian army to date.[32]

The next stage of the war unfolded with the Japanese firmly in command. While their Second Army marched northward in pursuit of Kuropatkin's retreating forces, their Third Army gathered its strength to launch a land-based assault on Port Arthur. This was all made possible when the Russian Far Eastern Fleet, suffering from a lack of leadership, had become paralyzed and was therefore ineffective in halting the saturation of the Liaotung Peninsula with men and supplies by the Japanese navy. In fact, mines, an old weapon that had been greatly enhanced in the age of technologically sophisticated warfare and far cheaper than the cost of any naval vessel, did more damage to the Japanese navy than any action of the Russian fleet from this stage of the war until its climatic battle at Tsushima. Nogi was chosen to lead the assault on Port Arthur not only because of his rank and status within his army, but also because he had been one of the commanders who conquered Port Arthur in the 1894–5 Sino-Japanese War. While he may have been familiar with the terrain, nothing had prepared the general, or anyone else in authority, for the slaughter that ensued in Port Arthur and its environs in the second half of 1904. First the assault and then the siege opened a page in modern warfare that can serve as a harbinger of future twentieth-century conflicts. Both belligerents were well stocked with heavy artillery and rapid-fire light artillery. The Russians had spent time and resources building fortified positions that formed defensive lines around the hills that surrounded the port. These positions featured the construction of strong points that utilized maxim machine guns and extensive trench networks fortified with barbed and electrified wire. Both sides were equipped with modern small arms that included soldiers having bolt action rifles and hand grenades. Officers also had at their disposal assorted forms of powerful searchlights to expose their enemies in night battles and radio communications to coordinate their activities. Taken together, the battle for Port Arthur turned into a bloodbath that shocked the sensibilities of all involved parties. Yet despite widespread reporting and extensive follow-up reports by the numerous military observers, the same parties failed to learn the lessons of this battle, thereby setting the stage for armies to suffer the same fate in the First World War.

The Russians, some 50,000 men strong under the command of General Stoessel, spent the period after the Battle of Nanshan preparing their outer defenses while Nogi concentrated his forces that, by the end of July, reached a total of around 150,000 soldiers. Nogi ordered the shelling of Port Arthur to commence on August 7th and in this first stage of the battle the shelling continued intermittently until the end of August with the support of the Japanese navy. In unison with the shelling and revealing the crafty use of his intelligence-gathering capabilities, Nogi ordered his troops to assault two lightly defended hills known as big orphan and little orphan on the northeastern side of the Russian position. The hills were lightly defended but their approach was very steep. This topographical feature combined with support from the guns of the Russian cruiser Novik stalled the Japanese assault and exacted a terrible cost in casualties. Nogi, determined to take the position to start the encirclement of the Russians, pressed on throughout August 8th. On August 9th the Russians finally relented and withdrew in the direction of Port Arthur. Taking these two hills cost the Japanese over 1,200 casualties. Heightening the tension of the moment, Viceroy Admiral Alexeiev had been watching the battle unfold from his new headquarters in Mukden from where he persistently agitated for the fleet to engage the Japanese navy in battle. He made his feelings clear not only in Mukden, but also in Port Arthur and in St. Petersburg. And, while not immediately clear who possessed the upper hand in the battle in the aftermath of the action of August 7–9, the ability of the Japanese to prevail in their assault rattled nerves in St. Petersburg. Nicholas II, responding to Alexeiev's messages, expressed his thinking when he ordered the fleet to evacuate Port Arthur, which it did the next day.[33]

What followed is known in naval history as the Battle of the Yellow Sea. Receiving orders from his high command in St. Petersburg to leave Port Arthur and sail to Vladivostok and combine forces with the squadron stationed at that location, Admiral Vitgift dispatched his fleet composed of six battleships, four cruisers, and fourteen destroyers from Port Arthur on the morning of August 10th. As noted earlier Vitgift was not an aggressive leader and had managed to sour his relations with Viceroy Alexeiev because of his lack of activity after he took over command of the fleet. Vitgift preferred to wait for reinforcements which he hoped would come in the form of the Baltic fleet, thereby seeking to implement a naval version of Kuropatkin's strategy.[34] What followed was the first fleet engagement between two navies that were equipped with modern steel hulled ships as Togo was waiting with a force of five battleships, fourteen cruisers, eighteen destroyers, and thirty torpedo boats. The two forces engaged in a day-long running battle with each fleet causing battle damage to the other. At the end of the day Vitgift was killed by a shell that struck the bridge of his flagship, the Tsesarevitch. The same shell also jammed the ship's rudder so that it started a circular maneuver that other ships of the fleet followed at first believing their commander was executing a maneuver designed to confuse the Japanese. While Togo's ships had suffered their fair share of damage, the death of Vitgift effectively ended the Russian effort to break out of Port Arthur and the Yellow Sea. Most of the fleet returned to Port Arthur and its effectiveness as a naval force capable of waging war was over! Instead the guns of the fleet would eventually be removed from their ships and used in the later stages of the siege of the port. Effective August 11th the Japanese had complete control of the Yellow Sea. While they were still mindful of the potential threat of the Vladivostok squadron, they had little problem maintaining their supply chain to their forces in Manchuria. More importantly, the outcome of the Battle of the Yellow Sea resulted in Admiral Togo having all the evidence he needed to conclude that the Russian Far Eastern fleet presented no threat to Japanese naval operations.[35]

Meanwhile, General Nogi, under extreme pressure from Tokyo for immediate results, after a brief pause in operations, continued his assault on Port Arthur. At noon on August 13 Nogi launched a reconnaissance balloon from the Wolf Hills north of the city where his intelligence experts observed a distinct lack of preparedness of the Russians at 174 Meter Hill. Against the advice of his immediate subordinate, yielding to pressure from his commanders, Nogi ordered a direct frontal assault on Russian positions by advancing through the Wantai ravine. The attack was launched six days later on August 19 when Japanese forces collided with the 5th and 13th East Siberian Regiments reinforced with sailors from the fleet and under the command of the redoubtable Colonel Tretyakov. The ensuing Battle of 174 Meter Hill mirrored the earlier Battle of Nanshan in that Tretyakov's soldiers put up a stout defense throughout the night of the 19th/20th but when no reinforcements were sent on the morning of August 20th, the Russian position on the hill crumbled. Yet the Russians withdrew further into the Wantai ravine where their line held, forcing Nogi to give up on this attack on August 24th. Since the siege of Port Arthur had started, Nogi's forces had suffered in excess of 16,000 casualties. Frontal assaults were proving too costly and, as a result, the Japanese shifted operations from reducing Port Arthur with frontal assaults to engineering a protracted siege.[36] Nogi was afforded this luxury for two reasons. First, the siege train lost in June when the Hatchi Mura was sunk by a Russian cruiser was replaced with massive 11-inch howitzers that could fire 500-pound shells over 5 miles had reached the theater of operations. Second, now under the constant threat of shelling, the Russians could do little to stop Japanese sappers from engaging in the long-term process of digging trenches and tunnels into and around the defensive battlements of Port Arthur. While the siege commenced, the Manchuria war of maneuver reached a critical turning point when the Japanese and Russian armies collided in a massive engagement known as the Battle of Liaoyang.

After Nanshan and Vafangou, as General Nogi was converting his operations from frontal assaults on fortified positions to the siege of Port Arthur, the Russian army started implementing Kuropatkin's strategy. This meant that the Russian army retreated northward up the Liaotung Peninsula in a maneuver designed to buy time for Kuropatkin to concentrate overwhelming forces in Manchuria. This was a fighting retreat that featured a couple of small-scale engagements at Tashihchiao and Hsimucheng at the end of July. These battles failed to slow the relentless advance of the Japanese under Marshal Oyama Iwao

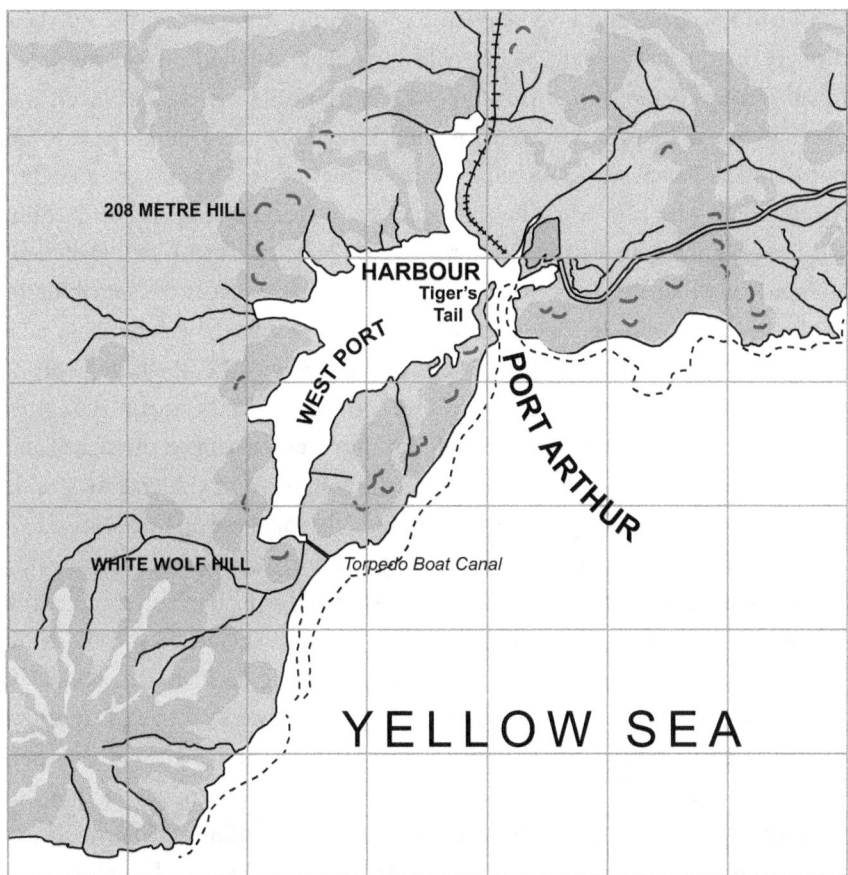

Map 5.2 Port Arthur.

who had been given overall command of all Japanese forces for their march up the Liaotung Peninsula. He sought to concentrate the three armies under his command as they converged in front of a massive Russian defensive position being prepared by elements of five different Siberian army corps at the city of Liaoyang. The battle shaping up would ultimately define a pattern of operational conduct for the rest of the war. Both armies sought to imitate the Prussians at Sedan by enveloping each other in an attempt to destroy their respective armies. The Russian positions featured three circular fortified lines of defense that stretched across a radius of 70 km. What followed was the first massive land engagement of the war. Both armies went into this battle presuming that its outcome would be decisive and perhaps lead to a conclusion of hostilities. By the end of August, although not clear to him at the time due to poor intelligence gathering, Kuropatkin had amassed a numerical advantage over Oyama's forces.

With two European and Five Siberian Army Corps concentrated, the Russians brought to the battlefield 158,000 effectives that included 30,000 mounted cavalry troops. Supporting these forces were 600 artillery pieces deployed and dug into the series of three defensive lines throughout and around the Russian position. The Japanese had mobilized three armies under Oyama's command to march north with him when he split apart from General Nogi at Port Arthur. His three highly motivated armies consisted of 125,000 men with 10,000 of them as mounted cavalry troops that also had 400 artillery pieces to contribute to the battle. Thus, over 280,000 soldiers engaged in this the largest battle to take place since the 1870–1 Franco-Prussian War. On August 22, 1904, elements of Kuroki's First Army under the immediate command of Lt. General Hasegawa Yoshimichi marched out of the hills of Manchuria and assaulted the right flank of the Third Siberian Army Corps under the command of General Aleksandr Aleksandrovich Bilderling whose artillery held the Japanese up but did not halt their overall effort to encircle his position. While the Japanese retired in disarray by the evening of August 22, at this decisive moment in the battle, Bilderling found himself without effective communications or intelligence and therefore could not count on anyone coming to his aid. Being in such a position left Bilderling at a loss about what to do next. The problem was Kuropatkin's strategy. Instead of encouraging officers under his command to pursue the enemy when advantages occurred, Kuropatkin ordered his officers to defend all positions to the breaking point and then retreat northward to the next line of defense, always deeper into Manchuria. Officers in the field therefore acted with such tactical conservatism that they hesitated to seize the initiative even when it obviously presented itself. Such hesitancy resulted in a devastating lack of confidence throughout the army's entire command structure, which descended into the rank and file. This type of conduct on the battlefield had come to epitomize Russian war fighting capabilities. Even worse, the Japanese recognized this, and it served to embolden them for the rest of the war.

The second phase of the battle started on August 25 when the First Army still under Kuroki's command started a push against the Tenth Siberian Army Corps east of Liaoyang. By the morning of August 26th the Japanese had captured the high ground at a point called Suribachi-Yama, and the next morning Kuropatkin did what he became famous for doing—he ordered his troops to abandon their most outer line of defense in favor a of second line that was closer to the city. Oyama, recognizing that Kuropatkin intended to defend the city of Liaoyang itself, took this moment to maneuver his troops to be in position to achieve his objective, which was to envelop and destroy the Russian army much as Moltke had done to the French at Sedan. To achieve his goal he ordered his Second Army under the command of General Oku Yasukata and his Fourth Army under the command of General Nozu Michitsura to march southward to prepare for an assault on the Russian positions. The Japanese effectively concealed their movements with the help of the tall stands of kaoliang, a grain grown in the region that could easily reach heights of six feet as it matured. At the same time Kuroki on his own initiative crossed the Taitzu River with the specific goal of cutting the Eastern Chinese Railway north of Liaoyang. This series of maneuvers set the stage for the decisive period of the battle. The Japanese launched an all-out assault on the Russian second defensive line on the morning of August 30th. By the end of the day Kuropatkin could have been pleased with the outcome as his troops had maintained a stout defense and had held the line. Moreover, he ordered the execution of a preplanned maneuver to withdraw to his third line of defense. By the morning of September 2, Kuropatkin was in a prime position to launch a counterattack as he had roughly six divisions or half of the troops under his command held in reserve. He hesitated, however, for a host of reasons of which the most prominent was he did not understand that he held an advantage over the Japanese in terms of men and materials. Again, the Russian intelligence service had failed him. Far worse, the Battle of Liaoyang made the shortcomings of Kuropatkin's strategy clear. His idea of remaining on the defensive to buy time to reinforce and concentrate had in practice undermined the effectiveness of the army because his repeated orders to retreat did not encourage any single commander to take a risk or to engage in aggressive and decisive operations. Instead officers and soldiers throughout the army started to think and believe that they could not defeat their enemy on the battlefield. The conclusion to the battle exhibited a level of dysfunction that, in the end, prevented the army of the Romanovs to ever win a war again. As Japanese artillery started to pound the city of Liaoyang in the early morning of September 2nd, their infantry launched an assault from the southern end of the Russian position and applied intense pressure in a northward direction for the rest of the day. Kuropatkin, meanwhile, intended to shift his forces from his left to his right flank in an effort to dislodge Kuroki's army and regain the initiative. The maneuver, however, proved to be too complicated for the Russians to manage, thereby setting the stage for the battle to reach its climax on the night of September 2nd when the Japanese seized Manjuyama, a hill on the eastern edge of the position that provided an overlook of the entire battlefield. Kuropatkin's plan then unraveled because he knew the Japanese would position artillery on top of Manjuyama and use it to cut off the railway. The next day Kuropatkin made one last attempt to prevent defeat when he ordered General N. A. Orlov to hold the center of the Russian position in front of the Yentai mines. Orlov, however, retreated by evening claiming he had lost touch with General A. V. Samsonov's cavalry screen. As a result, the Russians folded and Kuropatkin ordered a general retreat northward for his entire army up the Mandarin Road toward Mukden. At this point Nicholas II was being pressured, especially by General M. I. Dragomirov, to fire Kuropatkin and put a fighting general in command who would inspire the army to engage in offensive and aggressive warfare. Nicholas II, however, demonstrating his usual lack of decisiveness in everything he did, decided to let Kuropatkin remain in command believing that he could change the course of the war once he had concentrated an overwhelming number of troops along with all the supplies needed to deliver on his promise to throw the Japanese off the Asian mainland. In other words, at least for the moment, the tsar was buying into Kuropatkin's strategy. While the victory for the Japanese represented a great feat of arms, it came at a cost. Oyama's forces suffered 23,000 casualties against 16,000 for the Russians.[37] More significantly, the Japanese were fatigued from the march northward and, although they controlled the battlefield, they did not have the strength to pursue and defeat the Russian army as it retreated. In operational terms, as the Russians retreated northward, the Japanese found themselves supplying two massive operations—Oyama's maneuvering army and Nogi's siege at Port Arthur—at opposite ends of the Liaotung Peninsula. Of equal concern for the Japanese, the conflict was evolving into a war of attrition, and they did not have the men, the materials, or the finances to endlessly continue the conflict.

Kuropatkin's position, on the other hand, can best be described as embattled. His "strategy" was broadly questioned by everyone in St. Petersburg. Despite some limited support from the tsar, the Supreme War Council, under the influence of General Dragomirov and his supporters along with numerous members of the officer corps in the field, had lost confidence in Kuropatkin's operational leadership. Although he did his very best to claim that the Battle of Liaoyang had been a Russian victory, the retreat of the army toward Mukden revealed just the opposite. While Kuropatkin may not have understood that he had more soldiers in the field than the Japanese in August, with the continued arrival of reinforcements from European Russia via the trans-Siberian railway, there was little question as the Russians reorganized after Liaoyang that they had achieved numerical superiority. Such calculations combined with pressure from St. Petersburg resulted in Kuropatkin deciding that the time had come for his army to go on the offensive. What followed was another exercise in frustration for the Russian army in the form of an operation known to history as the Battle of Shaho. From his base in Mukden, Kuropatkin reorganized his forces into Eastern and Western Detachments with the Western force still under the command of General A. A. Bilderling and the Eastern Detachment now under the command of General von Shtakel'berg. With 210,000 men under their command, they marched south to confront Oyama's army, still organized as it was at Liaoyang but now totaling 170,000 men. Kuropatkin's plan was to block the Japanese advance at the Shaho River south of Mukden and then launch a counteroffensive with Shtakel'berg's force attacking the Japanese right flank. At the same time, Bilderling's force was ordered to assault Kuroki's 1st army on the other side of the Japanese army. Because the Kaoliang had been harvested, the battlefield, which stretched across a 37-mile front, was flat on the right and in the center but gave way to hills on its left. The grain that had provided vital cover for the Japanese in August at Liaoyang no longer was a factor in the movement of troops.

A ferocious battle ensued beginning October 5th that would last until October 17th. Again, the Japanese would outmaneuver the Russians and force them on a northward march toward Mukden. Two aspects about the effectiveness of Russian military operations became clear as a result of the Battle of Shaho. First, the Russian way of war was flailing due to the confusing and contradicting orders. This practice that had existed at the top of the army high command since their first engagement with the Japanese on the Yalu River had now permeated the ranks of the Russian officer corps at most every level. Officers throughout the ranks then developed the self-defeating habit of selectively choosing which orders to follow, which served to undermine the ability of the army to operate as a unified force at any point when it was engaged in hostilities. Thus, as Shtakel'berg and Bilderling marched against their enemy, their actions were not well coordinated and the situation, as is the case in the midst of combat, became more confused as the battle unfolded. Even worse, Kuropatkin had no faith in telegraphic communication and as the war progressed he lost confidence in couriers delivering messages in a timely fashion. Due to his own angst about these capabilities, Kuropatkin did the worst thing possible to try to resolve the army's failure to communicate with itself; he left his command and went into the field in search of units engaged in battle. The commander in chief, therefore, effectively took himself out of communications at the key moment when he needed to remain at his command post. The second aspect of Russian military operations that doomed the Russian army to fail in this conflict was a by-product of Kuropatkin's "strategy." Simply put, the general did not understand when best to commit his reserves in the heat of battle. This aspect of his command had developed into a predictable trend by the time of the Battle of Shaho and would haunt his every effort for the rest of the war. For example, in addition to having two detachments on the march at the Battle of Shaho, Kuropatkin had three army corps and a Cossack brigade in reserve. He did deploy his reserve to patch a gap that emerged in the center of his forces as the Japanese outmaneuvered them in the course of the battle. But, this was a poor use of reserves that should have been in position to strike at the Japanese in order to carry the army to victory in a battle as opposed to protecting it from disintegrating on the battlefield. While using the reserve for defensive purposes may have saved the day, it did not deliver the victory in battle that the Russian so sorely needed. Nonetheless, instead of recognizing that the Russians had just squandered their last opportunity to relieve Port Arthur, Kuropatkin would sell the idea to Nicholas II that the Battle of Shaho was a victory because his army remained intact and was preparing for future operations. Despite suffering over 40,000 casualties, the tsar, believing his commander's "strategy" was now working, rewarded Kuropatkin by ordering Admiral Alekseiev to return to St. Petersburg, thereby giving him (Kuropatkin) complete and unchallenged command of the Russian army in Manchuria. The Japanese found little consolation in this victory because they had to absorb over 20,000 casualties and the course of the war, as a war of attrition, was becoming clear to them. Realizing that their position would weaken the longer the war was fought, they placed a renewed emphasis on the siege of Port Arthur.[38]

The Japanese High Command had never de-emphasized the struggle at Port Arthur. Rather, General Nogi and his superiors had agreed that the Russian defenses were too strong for the Japanese infantry to succeed with frontal assault without proper preparations. Thus, the siege of Port Arthur started to look like the siege of Sebastopol because in August the Japanese resupplied and enhanced their force at the outer edge of Port Arthur. In an effort to adapt to the power and the lethality of modern ballistics, Nogi ordered his sappers to dig trenches that zig-zagged their way to the edge of the Russian defenses and then to dig tunnels to plant mines at key points that would be detonated at the beginning of the next offensive effort. All of this was occurring as Oyama was maneuvering his armies to victory at Liaoyang and Shaho—a magnificent feat of arms for a very young and emerging empire. Some controversy exists as to whether it was General Nogi or Oyama's chief of staff General Kodama Gentaro who recognized that the Russian fortifications at 203 Meter Hill had become the key to the position. From 203 Meter Hill all of Port Arthur could be observed and, more importantly, from this position the entirety of the port could be shelled once artillery had been placed. By mid-September, Nogi's sappers had dug over five miles of trenches, and he therefore launched his first assault on 203 Meter Hill. The Russians, recognizing the significance of 203 Meter Hill, heavily fortified it and Colonel Tretiakov of Nanshan fame was in command of the position. Unwilling to challenge the stiff Russian defenses at 203 Meter Hill, Nogi spent the rest of September and October ordering his troops to assault different Russian strongpoints in an effort to get their entire defensive network to collapse. Not finding any success in these efforts, Nogi under tremendous pressure from not only Oyama and the High Command in Tokyo, but also from the Press and by extension the entire nation, ordered the assault to begin on 203 Meter Hill on November 28th. Starting with a massive artillery barrage and ending with the critical wounding of Tretiakov on December 5th, the Japanese fought valiantly and, with much blood spilled, finally took control of the position.

As far as General Stoessel, the embattled Port Arthur commandant was concerned, the loss of 203 Meter Hill meant that it was only a matter of time before he would have to capitulate to the Japanese. He was not wrong, as the Japanese started to shell Port Arthur at will as soon as they took over control of 203 Meter Hill. From 203 Meter Hill the Japanese shelled all of Port Arthur including the Far Eastern Fleet, which had been sheltering in place since the August Battle of the Yellow Sea. By the end of the month, the entire Russian fleet had either been sunk or so severely damaged that it could not sortie to escape. This set the stage for the Russians to surrender Port Arthur to the Japanese on January 2, 1905, much to the chagrin of Nicholas II. Stoessel, ultimately, would be court martialed for his failure to maintain resistance as the Baltic Fleet was well on its way to relieve the base. For Nogi, however, the end of the battle did not represent a victory for himself or Japan. Personally, his second son was killed in the final assault of 203 Meter Hill; his first son was killed earlier in the battle. These losses combined with the over 90,000 casualties, of which almost 60,000 had been killed in action, signified failure in the mind of the general. So distraught was Nogi that he asked the emperor Meiji for permission to kill himself at the end of the war. In addition, the conduct of the Japanese infantrymen at Port Arthur gave birth to the myth of them being human bullets; that is, that Emperor Meiji's soldiers would stop at nothing to have the honor to die while serving in the name of their emperor.[39] Such a legacy that centered on the fierceness and obedience of Japanese soldiers would prevail throughout their actions in the Second World War. More significant to the moment, however, the surrender of the Russians at Port Arthur meant that after being resupplied with men and materials, Nogi's army would march north toward Mukden and join Oyama's efforts to defeat the Russians in total and end the war.[40]

Capitulation at Port Arthur, therefore, signified the beginning of the final stage of the land war in Manchuria. The situation had become dire for the Russians! Until this point in the war, nothing had worked—with the exception of sinking a few Japanese ships. Russian military forces had lost every engagement that they had fought against the Japanese. Yet, there was still cause for hope among elements of the Russian High Command. After all, the entire point of Kuropatkin's strategy was to transfer troops from European Russia to the Far East, which due to the limited capacity of the trans-Siberian railway had occurred at a slow, indeed, plodding pace. By the late summer of 1904 the troop numbers had decisively and overwhelmingly turned in Russia's favor. Although the numbers had started to turn in Russia's favor by the Battle at Liaoyang and, despite the losses at Liaoyang and Shaho, reinforcements continued to arrive in Harbin and Mukden so much so that by the early winter of 1905, Kuropatkin's excuses for delays and retreats no longer existed; he could no longer claim a need to wait for additional reinforcements to launch the long awaited offensive operation. In fact, in the aftermath of Shaho, in addition to Viceroy Alekseev being relieved and removed from the theater of operation, Kuropatkin also benefited from the arrival in Manchuria of the VIII and XVI Army Corps as well as three reinforced rifle brigades. Without Alekseev muddling up operations and as supreme commander, Kuropatkin divided his army into three field armies. The disposition of these forces started to his east with the First Army under the command of General Nikolai Petrovich Linevich, in the center position of his forces General Alexander Vasil'evich Kaul'bars commanded the Third Army and to the west General Oskar-Ferdinand Kasimirovich Grippenberg rapidly formed a Russian Second Army. As these forces oriented to the theater of operations, Kuropatkin had to cope with three sources of intense pressure that would ultimately determine the final stage of the war on the ground in Manchuria. First, and despite the weaknesses and failures of Russian intelligence-gathering capabilities, there could be little question among and within the tsar's defense establishment that the next Japanese move would be to move Nogi's army north to join in their march up the Liaotung Peninsula. More vexing, however, was the second source of tension, the performance of the Russian army on the battlefield. Simply put, Kuropatkin was out of excuses. He had numerical superiority in men and materials as he now had 372 battalions, 172 cavalry squadrons, 1,156 artillery pieces of all calibers, and too many machine guns to count. The time had come for the Russian army to seize control of the battlefield if it was ever going to do it during this war. The third source of tension was the most dangerous of all. The impact of Bloody Sunday (January 9, 1905) and the outbreak of the 1905 Revolution in St. Petersburg would spread to Manchuria in January/February. The breakdown of civil order and the subsequent political unrest that was spreading throughout Russia, however, could not be ignored and would eventually, as Kuropatkin and his subordinates feared, have a negative impact on the combat effectiveness of the tsar's army at war.[41]

Taken together, all three of these developments provided the spark Kuropatkin needed to resume the offensive as soon as possible if for no other reason than to stop the Japanese onslaught before Oyama was reinforced with Nogi's army. Fearing that a frontal assault would be too costly, Kuropatkin ordered Grippenberg's Second Army to deploy and seize the village of Sandepu, some 53 miles south of Mukden, which it attempted to do in numbing cold and freezing rain early on the morning of January 25, 1905. The supreme commander was pinning great hopes on this operation not only because of the fresh troops but also with the reorganized command structure he believed that his officers would begin to do a better job of collecting information and receiving and following orders. The aim of the operation was to seize Sandepu and then use it as a focal point to launch an enveloping operation that would encircle all of Oyama's forces and force the Japanese from the battlefield and ultimately from Korea and Manchuria. But it was not to be! Four days later and with Oyama correctly assessing the situation, the Japanese launched a counterstroke that negated all Russian progress in and around Sandepu and once again sent them retreating back to their positions at Mukden. Even worse for the fate of the Russian war effort, the army was becoming completely infected with a level of defeatism that started at high command levels. Even more alarming, the revolutionary turmoil from European Russia was having an impact on the operational army as soldiers throughout the theater mutinied in support of the revolt. Officers managed to suppress these rebellions, yet the combination of failure on the battlefield and the challenge to the tsar's power were taking a toll on the army's effectiveness on all levels. For example, in the aftermath of Sandepu, Grippenberg resigned his commission claiming ill health. By the time he arrived at Harbin, he had decided to reveal to journalists that he considered Kropotkin to be the army's biggest source and cause for its repeated failure on the battlefield. His critique was scathing in that he revealed how the commander in chief had no confidence in his subordinates, which became clear when Kuropatkin would leave his command post and go into the field to try to micromanage operations. Even more vexing was his communications directly with staff officers, which usually resulted in operational commanders such as Grippenberg not knowing what was taking place within his own command. Such conduct created a poisonous atmosphere within the headquarters staff because different elements found themselves working at cross-purposes in what was an already a difficult environment as they were seeking to remain one step ahead of a very determined enemy.

Such acrimony set the stage for the final anticlimactic battle of the Manchurian war of maneuver that occurred at Mukden from February 20 until March 10, 1905. Anticlimactic because despite being the largest land battle fought between the two belligerents in the war, the outcome was entirely predictable. The sum effect of Russian offensive action at Shaho and Sandepu had been to slow the Japanese invasion but to do nothing to stop their persistent and determined drive up the Liaotung Peninsula. Over 600,000 men from both sides fought at Mukden making it the largest concentration of soldiers to gather on a battlefield since the Napoleonic wars. Kuropatkin deployed his army along a 90-mile front in a defensive posture without any plans or considerations to launch a counteroffensive. Oyama, on the other hand, did what he had done throughout the war. Beginning on February 20 he ordered a newly formed fifth army to attack General Linevich's army on Russia's right flank. As Linevich's forces held their ground, Oyama ordered General Nozu's Fourth Army to attack General Baron von Kaulbars (Kaulbars was Grippenberg's replacement) Second Army on the Russians' left flank. In this fashion, Oyama's plan of enveloping the Russian army started to unfold. Predictably, Kuropatkin lost confidence in his army, communications broke down, and any sense of initiative was lost, thus dooming the Russians to their fate. Although the outcome was determined, arguably before the first shot was fired, the battle devolved into another bloodbath, which above all else offered the most obvious evidence about the brutal nature of industrialized and highly lethal early twentieth-century warfare. By the end of Mukden, the battlefield would be littered with over 165,000 casualties of which 24,000 would be killed in action. The Japanese marching through the gates of Mukden on March 10, 1905, signified the end of the land war but not the end of the war as there were still large armies in the field and one last weapon that Tsarist Russia had at its disposal.[42]

In the aftermath of Mukden, Kuropatkin was relieved of command and replaced by Linevich. The army itself retreated northward and established its forward base of operation at Harbin.[43] The irony of the moment was the Russian army now clearly had an overwhelming advantage in men and equipment over the Japanese. Not only were the Japanese facing a dire shortage of soldiers after Mukden but equally challenging to their war effort at this moment was the decision by their financial backers, largely Wall Street bankers, to withdraw their lines of credit that were absolutely essential to their paying for the war effort.[44]

The moment that Kuropatkin's strategy actually rendered positive results, however, was completely compromised by persistent failure on the battlefield and revolutionary turmoil on the home front. Then, from the theater of the absurd, Nicholas II refused to consider all overtures to sue for peace because he romanced the idea that he could turn the tide of the war once his Baltic fleet reached the theater of operations. The saga of the Baltic fleet captured the attention of the world from the moment it was renamed the Second Pacific Squadron and sortied from St. Petersburg with thirty-eight capital ships and numerous auxiliaries in mid-October, 1904, under the overall command of Admiral Zinovi Petrovich Rozhestvenski. The idea first entered into the minds of Russian naval planners after the defeat of the First Pacific Squadron in the August 1904 Battle of the Yellow Sea. The aim of sending another fleet to the Far East rested on the goal of regaining control of the sea and thereby preventing the Japanese from having the unchallenged capability of moving troops and supplies from their homeland to Korea and Manchuria. The tragedy of the saga started immediately when it attacked British fishing trawlers off Dogger Bank, sinking one and damaging six others while killing several fishermen and some of their own sailors on the night of October 20–21. This incident at once transformed the journey of this fleet from a military operation to a series of encounters that became rich information for the international media. Most likely French diplomatic intervention prevented the British from declaring war over Dogger Bank but, from that moment on, the media tracked the Russian fleet as it split up with slower ships given permission (by the British) to join up with ships from the Black Sea and sail through the Suez Canal. This Third Pacific Squadron joined up with Second Squadron that had sailed around Africa at Nossi Be, Madagascar, after the first of the year. Before pressing on, Rozhestvenski learned that Port Arthur had surrendered, which further complicated his task as it meant that he was going to have to sail to Vladivostok. And, no matter what the Russians did, they attracted media attention especially over the question of refueling. Without control over any bases on their route and unable to obtain coal in neutral ports, the fleet became wholly dependent on the colliers of the Hamburg-Amerika Line for the numerous refueling sessions that were needed to get the fleet to Asia.

Even worse was the fate of the sailors in the Second and Third Pacific Squadrons. They spent the journey surrounded by mountains of coal as it was crammed into every nook and cranny of the ship creating a constant state of tension. The officers could not maintain any semblance of drill and training; they had no means to replenish munitions, which prevented gunnery drill.

Moreover, once word of the Bloody Sunday and the 1905 Revolution reached the fleet, the morale of the sailors plummeted; the trip became exhausting and, as they got closer to their destiny, sailors progressively lost all confidence in their officers, their tsar, indeed their empire. In addition, the ships themselves endured a journey of some 18,000 miles without any means to perform maintenance and thus, by the time they sailed into battle, their coal-burning, steam-driven power plants were worn out and in need of major overhaul. In comparison, Admiral Togo had been able to return his fleet to Japan after the August Battle of the Yellow Sea where he had ample time to perform all major and minor maintenance on all of his ships. His crews would engage in battle well rested and, unlike the Russians, battle tested. Moreover, the Japanese sailors did not question their officers or the reason why they were about to engage in battle. For them the coming engagement was being fought to defend the honor of their emperor and for his emerging empire. The final and most decisive advantage that Togo had was superior intelligence. Either through the international press or through Japan's own operatives throughout Asia, Togo knew where the Russian fleet was and, as a result, he predicted where and when the Russians were going to enter his home waters. Thus, with all the odds stacked against the Russians and in favor of the Japanese, one of the last great naval battles between ships of the line occurred in the straits of Tsushima on May 27–28, 1905.

In Mahanian terms, the Battle of Tsushima was a decisive engagement that once and for all determined control of the sea in the Far East. It culminated with an unmitigated disaster for the Russian navy and a glorious victory for the Japanese. The Japanese had all of the advantages going into the battle. Their ships were in top battle condition, and the training of their crews was vastly superior to the Russians. Moreover, while the Russians outnumbered them in capital ships, the Japanese made up for this disparity by outmanning the Russians in smaller, more versatile vessels ranging from destroyers to torpedo boats. Further adding to their mastery of the moment, the Japanese ships could operate at a speed of 15 knots while the Russians, with their overused hence rundowned power plants, could only manage 10–11 knots. The Japanese fleet therefore was better trained and possessed tactical and operational advantages that meant they could sail as a unified force, thereby delivering its firepower in a unified way that culminated in a forceful result. Even more significantly, Togo had viewed his challenges and opportunities in a coherent fashion and thus planned for all eventualities. As a result he decided it would be best to station his fleet at the southern edge of Korea due west of the straits of Tsushima, otherwise known as the Korean straits, in the Chinhae Bay and use the Kadok Channel to sortie directly into the straits. From here Togo had a decisive strategic advantage. While he presumed Rozhestvenski would try to slip through these straits, he was also well positioned to respond to the Russians if they decided to remain and operate out of the Yellow Sea. Rozhestvenski might have decided to sail around the east coast of Japan to reach Vladivostok by sailing north of Hokkaido. Yet Togo deduced this an unlikely option since it would add days and an arduous navigational challenge at the end of a long journey with worn-out ships. Nonetheless, if the Russians choose such a path, Togo's pickets would alert him with plenty of time for his fleet to sail up and confront the Russians in the Sea of Japan. Togo indeed had outplanned and outthought the Russians down to having his ships painted a light gray so they blended into the sea. Russian ships had black hulls and yellow funnels that stuck out like perfect targets for the better trained Japanese gunners. While Togo and the Japanese were trained and prepared to strike with effect, Rozhestvenski and the Russians enjoyed no such planning. Instead, he led his fleet into the Tsushima Strait with the goal of somehow evading Togo and reaching Vladivostok without being detected.

One other advantage that the Japanese utilized to great effect for the first time in naval history was radio communications. While Rozhestvenski ordered radio silence out of fear of detection, on the morning of May 27th the Japanese wireless was alive with chatter confirming that the trajectory of the Russian ships had them aimed directly for the Tsushima Strait. Togo sortied from his safe harbor a little after 6:30 a.m. and spent the next six hours first finding and then positioning his fleet to be in an optimal position to strike. Shortly after 2:00 p.m., he demonstrated that the Japanese navy was the master of the sea on this day as Togo positioned his ships some 5,500 m from the Russians with their battle line in full effect. While the Russians stumbled through a maneuver in which they had to put the engines in neutral to avoid colliding with each other, the Japanese brought to great effect their superior gunnery and over the next hour inflicted heavy damage on their foe. While the battle would continue for another 24 hours, the outcome was largely determined by 3 p.m. At that time Rozhestvenski lay wounded on the deck of this flagship, the Suvorov, which was steaming out of control in a circular cloud of black smoke. Togo had so outmaneuvered the Russians that he had forced them to turn away from Vladivostok, thereby trapping the Russians in the Sea of Japan with no option to seek shelter. The battle, however, was not over. Instead it entered into a period of confusion only to witness the Russian battle line reform and run northward as it emerged from the fog of battle at 1800. At this moment the Russians had actually gotten in front of the Japanese, but Togo was able to use his superior speed to run down the Russians, and what followed was a punishing exercise in gunnery for both sides, but again Japanese superior training and high-velocity ammunition prevailed and they broke up Russia's battle line. After this engagement, Togo broke off with his major ships and headed for a prearranged rendezvous point for his fleet off of Ullung Island while turning night action over to his destroyers. They harassed the Russian fleet through the night and by the morning of May 28th the Japanese were mopping up the remnants of their enemy as the ships that were still seaworthy either surrendered or found sanctuary in neutral ports where they were interned for the rest of the war. Of the thirty-eight ships that Rozhestvenski had at the beginning of the battle, thirty-four had been sunk or lost to the Russian fleet through battle damage or internment in neutral ports. Thus ended the decisive naval battle between two modern battleship fleets so envisioned by naval planners throughout the world. Largely because of developments in naval aviation, there would never be another like it. More important to the moment, after suffering this annihilating defeat at sea, Nicholas II, embattled with a still threatening revolutionary situation, finally agreed to sue for peace two days after learning of the outcome at Tsushima.[45]

Peacemaking

Both the Japanese and the Russians agreed to US President Theodore Roosevelt as the mediator of peace in June 1905. Roosevelt, in turn, invited Japanese and Russian diplomats to Portsmouth, New Hampshire, to negotiate a settlement. The Russian lead diplomat, former finance minister Sergei Witte held firm to the tsar's hard line of refusing to pay reparations because Russia's defeat had not been total. Nicholas II based this conclusion on the failure of the Japanese to invade Russia proper after the Battle of Mukden, hence Japan's victory was not total. And, while the tsar was just as adamantly opposed to any territorial concessions, he did have to yield on this point. Japan's chief negotiator, Foreign Minister Komura Jutaro, stuck to his demands based on his military's stunning and overwhelming victories on the battlefield and at sea.[46] The Japanese expected to gain complete control over Korea, thereby achieving their strategic goal for going to war. The question of reparations, however, became a serious sticking point in the negotiations because the Japanese were counting on receiving substantial funds from the Russians to pay off the loans that they secured largely from a cabal of Wall Street bankers to finance the war. President Roosevelt worked diligently behind the scene to work out a compromise between the Russians and the Japanese.[47]

After doing their best to avoid the summer heat while remaining civil toward each other, a compromise was finally reached at the beginning of September.[48] When the treaty was signed on September 5, 1905, Russia recognized Japan's control over Korea, promised to evacuate Manchuria, return Port Arthur and the Liaotung Peninsula to Chinese control, and in a major concession ceded the southern half of Sakhalin Island that was considered sovereign Russian territory to the Japanese. Roosevelt was able to sell the concession of this territory to the Japanese as the compromise that warranted their acquiescing to Nicholas II insistence that he would not pay reparations. Begrudgingly Nicholas II did agree to pay indemnities to the Japanese for the cost of maintaining Russian prisoners of war in Japan during the course of the war.[49]

In retrospect, the Russo-Japanese War was a precursor of future conflict. It demonstrated the lethality of modern firepower, and this alone entirely transformed warfare killing and wounding soldiers in unimaginable numbers and in brutal fashion. No one was prepared to care for the wounded on the battlefield nor did societies have the infrastructure in place to care for long-term invalids. In addition, Tsushima notwithstanding, this war ended because both sides were exhausted politically and economically—1905 found Russia in revolution. Witte would return immediately to St. Petersburg where he would negotiate the October Manifesto that at once turned the tide of the revolution and paved the way for the emergence of the Duma or Russia's first attempt to create an institution that represented the will of the people. After appointing Witte as his new prime minister in November, Nicholas II would come to resent and blame him for the emergence of political franchise based on limited suffrage in his empire. Without question one of the greatest statesmen in late imperial Russia and after years of saving Nicholas II from all of his follies, Witte was fired in April and spent the rest of his life in retirement.[50] The tsar continued to incompetently rule his empire, which set the stage for the events of February 1917 and the overthrow of the Romanov dynasty after 304 years of rule. More important to the moment, the Russians, with the plans for an empire in the Far East shattered, went home and refocused their foreign policy concerns on the Balkans and European affairs.[51]

Peacemaking left the Japanese on the cusp of bankruptcy. They would spend the next decade capitalizing on the timber concessions they gained in Korea and Manchuria to pay off the money they borrowed to finance the war.[52] The level of dissatisfaction over the terms of the Treaty of Portsmouth in Tokyo resulted in the outbreak of major riots that started in Hibiya port the night of September 5th and spread across the city. The failure to collect reparations after all of the sacrifice and loss on the battlefield started the Japanese public Japanese drift toward a belief in militarism since civilian politicians kept giving away the army's victories at the peace table. The Japanese became further alienated toward the United States in response to its role in the peacemaking process.[53] Although Theodore Roosevelt was awarded the Nobel Prize for peace for his role in negotiating the treaty of Portsmouth, there was little peace in the Far East or in Russia proper in the aftermath of the Russo-Japanese War.[54]

6

The First World War and the End of Tsarism, 1905–17

Reforming the tsar's army in the aftermath of defeat: 1905–14

Russia lost the Russo-Japanese War after a series of defeats that exposed shortcomings and weaknesses throughout both the Imperial Army and Navy at the beginning of the twentieth century. Failure on the battlefield combined with long-term social, political, and economic grievances culminated with a high level of domestic unrest beginning with Bloody Sunday (January 9, 1905) that resulted in the 1905 Revolution. To quell the revolt Nicholas II granted the October Manifesto that authorized the creation of a representative political body, the Duma. The creation of a legislature formed and legitimized by elections transformed the political foundation of the empire. Further destabilizing the power of the tsar were widespread soldiers' revolts throughout the army in Asia that compromised its effectiveness subsequently endangering the security of the empire. Enhancing the level of rebelliousness, the sailors on the battleship Potemkin mutinied, and their actions sparked sedition throughout the Black Sea Fleet, the only element of the Imperial Navy that did not fight, hence was not destroyed in the Far East. Russia found itself in far worse shape after its defeat in the Russo-Japanese War than she had been after the defeat in the Crimean War. In Crimea, Russia lost to the combined might of three great powers (Great Britain, France, and the Ottomans) as opposed to an "upstart" Asian nation. Unlike Alexander II who sparked the modernization of the empire beginning with the emancipation of the serfs, after the Japanese defeat, Nicholas II had a difficult time embracing his own reforms. He neither wanted nor was prepared to understand how to govern in a world where civilian politicians held him responsible for his actions. Even more confusing for the tsar, he could not tolerate the efforts of political parties and politicians to impose a reform agenda upon the regime. In addition, much to the tsar's chagrin, officers within Russia's armed forces also chose this moment to adopt their own reform agenda. The war taught them that their army needed to transform on every level from the weapons used to the doctrine that governed operations. Reform, however, regardless of how necessary or essential it might be, represented a challenge to traditional elites, many of whom populated the army's high command coming from the world of the nobility and from the ranks of the imperial guard's regiments. Regardless of who attempted reform or who endeavored to prevent it, efforts to transform and modernize the military establishment in the aftermath of the Asian debacle suffered from the polarization of ideas and opinions, which made accomplishing anything difficult to achieve. Nevertheless, reform did occur in two waves that enhanced the capabilities of the military establishment as it prepared for the First World War. There was no other option than to reform because in the post-1905 period, the Russian military establishment had not been in such a weakened condition since the early seventeenth-century period.

The empire's standing in the international community was equally alarming for Russian patriots of the post–Russo-Japanese War of the period. While Sergei Witte maintained Russia's dignity throughout the peacemaking process that ended with the signing of the Treaty of Portsmouth, the international perception of the empire was one of weakness. No amount of rhetoric could portray Russia through a lens that projected strength and optimism. In need of allies, Nicholas II turned to France and sought to strengthen the relationship that his father had started in the 1890s. Alexander III turned to France after the Germans thwarted Russia's designs for the Balkans at the 1878 Congress of Berlin. In 1878, therefore, the Russians learned that even after her army had marched to the gates of Constantinople, the Concert of Europe had the strength and unity to impose their will on international affairs. The heavy-handed action orchestrated by Bismarck prevented Russia from achieving its long-term aim of gaining access to year-round access to warm water ports. Beginning with the tsar, Russia's political leadership emerged from this diplomatic afront embittered and subsequently redirected its empire-building efforts to Central Asia and the Far East. Despite this estrangement from the Concert of Europe, by 1905 the Franco-Russian alliance had become a relationship by which the French received strategic agreements that were in their best interests but not necessarily in Russia's. Nicholas II and his ministers nonetheless continued the relationship because the French persistently offered the cash-strapped Russians seemingly endless access to loans. Especially in the aftermath of the military defeat in Asia, Russia's political and military leaders could not risk losing access to this international source of finance. The alliance complicated Russian strategic thinking because over time shrewd French negotiators linked their loans to slowly yet methodically drawing the Russian Empire into agreements that aided Paris's determination to fight their "war of revenge" against Germany. This meant that in exchange for the loans, the French extracted commitments that would help them achieve their goal of encircling Germany with belligerent forces when war broke out between them. The French war aim was clear—encirclement and annihilation of Germany—so they could reclaim their lost provinces of Alsace and Lorraine. After two decades of the French first gently and later bluntly linking loans to military commitments, the Russians had become committed to a war plan that promised an invasion of East Prussia fifteen days after a mobilization declaration. While French loans were vital to the continued industrialization and reconstruction of Russian military forces, the problem was that Russia's vital interests were not in East Prussia.[1]

The defeat in the Far East revealed serious defects in every realm of the military from its system of recruiting to the training of troops, to its planning, supply and mobilization process. Reforms, therefore, first addressed changes needed from the top of its high command to its troops in the field. An immediate measure was the creation of the Council of State Defense in 1905 in an effort to emulate the Germans' use of a War Council. Placed under the command of Grand Duke Nicholas Nikolaevich, the only Romanov of his generation to attend the Nicholas Academy of the General Staff, its main purpose was to decentralize the responsibilities of an all-powerful war minister. Then, the purpose of the Council was to provide a bureaucratic entity charged with creating a decision-making process capable of overseeing a unified defense system. At the same time, Russia's chief of the general staff no longer remained under the direct control of the war minister and instead would report directly to the tsar about all matters related to preparedness for war. Here the aim was to create an all-powerful chief of staff modeled again after the Germans.[2] While designed to unify decision-making involving all questions pertaining to the empire's security, it in fact confused and complicated efforts to plan for future conflict. What emerged because of this reform was a three-headed system in which the grand duke as chief of the Council of State Defense, Aleksandr Fedorovich Rediger as war minister, and Fedor Fedorovich Palisyn as chief of the general staff all reported separately to the tsar, thereby providing Nicholas II with too much and often conflicting information. Commanders of each military district also reported directly to the tsar, thereby further undermining the goal of creating a unified decision-making apparatus. Each service branch—infantry, cavalry, artillery, engineering, plus the department of military educational institutions—had its own inspector general who operated independently of the war ministry. They too reported directly to

Nicholas II, and he made certain to appoint his relatives (mostly grand dukes) to these positions. Moreover, inspector generals also maintained a path for the old guard to maintain influence over Nicholas II at the expense of progressive thinkers. Further decentralizing the decision-making process, as the Duma gained traction in Russia's infant civil-military system, politicians also, albeit slowly, gained influence through the Council of State Defense in as many aspects of the armed forces as possible, but especially in financing it. Once the army had returned to its peacetime footing, the Council of State Defense created its most significant and lasting reform through the creation of the Supreme Certification Commission. This Commission's work entailed examining the service records of the entire officer corps for the purposes of judging capabilities. Their conclusions resulted in the early or forced retirement of approximately 7,000 officers who were too old, superannuated, or simply incompetent.[3]

The urban and rural unrest of the 1905 Revolution combined with an undermanned domestic police or militia forces resulted in the state being largely dependent on the army's soldiers to restore order to the land. Widespread revolutionary outbursts persisted, resulting in a prolonged two-year period before the army restored order to the realm; after that, by the end of 1907, it returned to its peacetime footing. At the same time a small but diverse group of officers affiliated with the General Staff Academy loosely known as the "Young Turks" sought to reform the war-fighting capabilities of their army. The Young Turks served as the sharp edge of a drive to reform that spread throughout progressive elements in the officer corps. They took advantage of the Duma-Monarchy period to share their ideas by publishing their works in books, which did everything from assess the course of the war to the condition of the empire's armed forces, and in the journals, *Razvedchik* and *Obshchestvo revnitelei voennykh znaii*, and the newspaper *Voennyi golos*. William C. Fuller identified at least 1,500 such publications in the five years after the war. This corpus of literature combined with seminars and troop training exercises were defined by General Anton I. Denikin as a "Military Renaissance."[4] While coping with the pain of the defeat in the Far East, this group inundated the military, indeed the empire, with a wave of publications calling for a total overhaul of Russia's armed forces written by officers who just served in Asia.[5] The most informative of these books was Major-General Evgeny Ivanovich Martynov's *Iz pechal'nago opyta Ryssko-Iaponskou voiny* (*From the Sad Experience of the Russo-Japanese War*). Martynov, a former professor at the General Staff Academy, had first-hand experiences of the army's performance in Asia having commanded the 140th Zaraisk Regiment in the war. Based on his operational experiences in the Far East, he called for a complete overhaul of the military establishment on par with what occurred after the Crimean War. The "Young Turks" picked up on this theme, led by Colonel Nicholas Nikolaevich Golovin, professor of tactics at the General Staff Academy. He used his position to develop and deliver a set of lectures designed to cast off the eighteenth-century doctrinal thinking of Aleksandr Vasil'evich Suvorov and the nineteenth-century teachings of Mikhail Ivanovich Dragomirov and Genrikh Antonovich Leer. The Russian army subsequently marched onto the twentieth-century battlefield still wedded to an operational doctrine that instructed soldiers and officers to think that the cold steel of a bayonet still dominated warfare, hence bayonets before bullets. Golovin and his cohort understood that such thinking overlooked new technological capabilities available as a result of the industrialization of warfare. His ideas, therefore, centered on the adoption of new "applied" tactics and strategy developed from the lessons learned from recent conflicts, especially the Russo-Japanese War. Golovin's concept of "applied" tactic and strategy evolved into the art of combined operations, eventually adopted in one fashion or another by all the First World War military establishments. Nevertheless and not surprisingly, the "Young Turks" did not have universal support and, as the reaction set in, they were dispersed to postings throughout the army.[6]

Regardless of the struggle between traditionalists and progressive reformers, early reform efforts made little practical progress because of financial constraints. The Russo-Japanese War had cost the empire the equivalent of one year of its annual budget. As the Duma-Monarchy system evolved, the point of conflict with the tsar became how and where to dedicate the limited financial resources available to the military establishment. The bureaucratic system that emerged in the wake of Nicholas's October Manifesto also suffered from poor organization and the birth pains that inevitably accompany a significant effort to reform the empire's political franchise.[7] The Council of State Defense, the entity created to unify the numerous elements needed to create and adopt rational practices in all security matters, did not include the finance minister or for that matter the foreign minister. Without these two ministers in the mix, the chance of forming a cohesive decision-making process in all matters related to the empire's security were minimal. Then, the tsar's government was overwhelmed by two events—one international, the other domestic—that led to the demise of the first post-Japanese war reform period. In international affairs, the revelation of the extent of the army's weakness during the Bosnian Crisis of 1909 combined with the embarrassment of being able to do nothing to prevent the Austria-Hungary from occupying Bosnia-Herzegovina discredited the leadership of the Grand

Duke, Rediger, and Palitsyn and directly led to their dismissal from their posts.[8] Domestically, within the Duma a group of its representatives, led by Alexander Ivanovich Guchkov, sought to impose their views over defense matters, especially over the defense budget. Beginning in 1908 they expressed strong opposition to the efforts of Nicholas II to rebuild the empire's navy because it was still commanded by the same admirals whose leadership resulted in defeat after defeat in the Japanese War. This attempt to create a discourse between the autocrat and its fledgling representative assembly infuriated Nicholas II; it touched his rawest nerve. In a demonstration of his thoughts about reforms and reformers, Nicholas II exercised his supreme authority and eliminated the Council of State Defense in early 1909. The activities of civilian politicians combined with the natural resistance among the system's most traditional and ardent supporters had led to the collapse of the Council of State Defense and with it the best chance for the Russians to create a unified military system before the outbreak of the First World War. Unfortunately, the Council of State Defense failed in its mission to unify all of the moving parts that composed the Russian defense establishment.

Although the military leaders who oversaw the initial reorganization of the military in the Russo-Japanese War's aftermath had been relieved of command, the reformers of the period of "military renaissance" did not relent in their efforts to address the military establishment's shortcomings. What followed was the second wave of reforms that started with the reestablishment of the war minister as the power broker over the entire military establishment. Between 1908–1910 the general staff and, most significantly, its chief returned to being a department within the war ministry, as it had been before the Russo-Japanese War. All of the inspector generals became subordinate to the new war minister who also was designated the chairman of the Supreme Certification Commission.[9] Appointed in March 1909, the new war minister Vladimir Aleksandrovich Sukhomlinov, a veteran of the 1877–8 Russo-Turkish War, had spent the balance of his career serving in the Kiev military district under the command of M. I. Dragomirov. Sukhomlinov emerged from Dragomirov's tutelage as an opponent to almost any type of modernization of the army that would undercut the role of the traditional service elite. Yet his actions clearly revealed that he understood the tsar's army needed to modernize at a doctrinal and technological level. To this end, he did much to reorganize and expand the army's size while doing his level best to prepare for the next war. One of his major innovations was to abolish reserves and garrison troops, to shift their numbers into the active army so that by 1914 the peacetime strength of Russia's armed forces reached over 1.4 million men. More importantly, this reorganization led to troops training together as unified units, thus enhancing the overall effectiveness of training exercises. He also reorganized infantry divisions so that they had a complement of one artillery brigade (forty-eight guns) while at the same time seeking to introduce more heavy artillery to his forces. In addition, he made a point of strengthening both in size and in capabilities the engineering, railroad, and signal corps troops. While financial considerations thwarted many of Sukhomlinov's efforts, he did manage to reequip the army with more advanced weapons, such as heavy artillery and machine guns, while also enlarging its numbers of trucks and automobiles. He was also responsible for introducing an aviation corps to the army's force structure so that by the outbreak of the First World War Russia had the third largest air force in the world.[10]

In the meantime, Sukhomlinov did try to link his reorganizational efforts with a plan to redeploy troops based on a program developed in 1908 under Palitsyn by Major General Mikhail Vasil'evich Alekseev, attached at the time to the war plans and operations section of the general staff. Alekseev, one of the most talented general staff officers of the period, envisioned the redeployment of the army originally based on a defensive line that connected Vil'no, Belostok, and Brest that fell roughly along the Vistula and the Narew Rivers to a new line further east formed by the rivers Niemen and Western Bug. The main goal of this shift was to reduce the number and the significance of old fortresses, built in the second half of the eighteenth century, to form a new defensive network based on fortified positions across the empire's western frontiers. Shifting troops further east eliminated their vulnerability in Poland while strengthening the army's position in central Russia. Moreover, it gave the army the capability of deploying forces in multiple directions based on needs and threats. With the new defensive line, the army would stop sinking funds into a fortress system that no longer had the impact it once had due to the advent of industrialized warfare. The shift in lines, however, was put on hold when the State Defense Council collapsed and Nicholas II insisted on rebuilding his navies regardless of questions about costs and leadership. Beginning in 1910, however, Sukhomlinov started to redeploy troops by quietly transferring 128 battalions from the Kiev and Vilna military districts on the western frontier and placing them in central military districts. This put them closer to their territorial base, which facilitated better transit times for mobilization considerations and, perhaps more significantly, reduced the cost of peacetime training simply because trained reserves did not have to travel as far for summer maneuvers. In addition, it created greater flexibility so that the army could indeed mobilize if the empire was threatened not only from the Central Powers but also from Asia where there was still great concern about the rising Japanese Empire.[11] The redeployment of the army consequently deemphasized the role of the western fortress network in the army's strategic thinking and war planning. Often overlooked in the assessment of Sukhomlinov is how he worked within the Duma-Monarchy political franchise to bring about a series of legislative initiatives that culminated with the passage of a huge reform bill in 1914. Known as the Big Program, Sukomlinov had pushed through a reform that sought to provide the resources to meet strategic needs. While he essentially accomplished what the Council of State Defense failed to achieve, he also benefited from the empire's finances being restored, which resulted in a 33 percent increase to the army's and navy's budget between 1909 and 1914. The increase in military spending fostered an economic boom especially throughout the arms and allied industries beginning in 1910 that lasted until the outbreak of the First World War.[12]

Meanwhile, general staff officers who considered the teachings of N. N. Golovin and other Young Turks as solutions to winning on the modern battlefield had been dispersed throughout the empire after the fall of Grand Duke Nicholas, General F. F. Palitsyn, and General A. F. Rediger. They sought to introduce to the troops the application of their theories of applied tactics. This resulted in a heightened effort to enhance the peacetime training exercises throughout the army, which fortunately occurred as Sukhomlinov's reorganization of the army's force structure also had resulted in additional attention being paid to these vital exercises. The initiative met with mixed results. Since the reign of Paul I (1796-1801), peacetime training exercises had been the place where the army's aristocratic elite appeared in full regalia replete with pomp and ceremony in front of their tsar. The aim and goal of such performances was not to train for military operations on any level. Rather what guard's officers sought for their efforts during maneuvers was to attract the tsar's attention and perhaps gain access to further power and wealth—careers were made and broken based on appearance rather than merit or capabilities. This custom would not die as long as the Romanovs were in power. Maneuvers, however, that could be orchestrated without the participation of the army's traditional elite—especially that of the tsar and his suite—resulted in progress in troop training and capabilities. Unfortunately, such progress was limited as the army ran out of time before the First World War was upon them. Nonetheless, in August 1914 the army did respond to the call to colors with the same enthusiasm as the rest of Europe's armies.[13]

Prior to their response to the call to arms in the summer of 1914, Russia's military leadership had spent the short period starting in 1905 seeking to solve operational challenges and material shortcomings. General staff offices also sought to create a war plan that represented both the empire's military capabilities and overall war aims. Developing, possessing, and, in the end, utilizing a practical war plan had become a vital goal of all the European Great Powers in the period leading up to the First World War. In the end, the Russians never had a well-defined war plan. The closest they got to formulating a mobilization plan was to do their very best to coordinate the movement of troops and supplies to a series of launching points in the northwest to invade East Prussian and in the southwest to invade Austrian Galicia. In other words, Russia's mobilization plan amounted to a series of railway schedules that they were constantly modifying practically until the outbreak of war. And, when war came, even before the first shot was fired, the tsar learned that his mobilization plan was inflexible and incapable of responding to the developing situation that unfolded in July 1914. Before condemning the Russians to poor preparations for war, it should be noted that the greatest war plan of the era, the Schlieffen plan, failed and when it failed, Germany had no contingency plan. The result of the greatest war plan of the period was four years of stalemated warfare. The planning challenges of the pre-war period proved overwhelming for the consummate professionals throughout pre–First World War Europe because they all underestimated or did not fully appreciate the lethality of the weapons of the industrial revolution. The root of the problem was weapons ranging from machine guns to rapid fire artillery had an insatiable appetite for munitions, a factor that was not recognized until everyone ran out of artillery shells after the war's opening campaigns. Far worse, the political and military leaders of all the great powers poorly understood the new operational environment in which the soldiers of mass armies became the carnage that fed an endless war of attrition. And, while they had the lethal weapons at their disposal, their leadership had little remedy for the men they commanded to defend themselves beyond ordering them to dig deeper and more complex trenches.[14]

Historians have been analyzing and assessing the chain of events that culminated with the outbreak of the First World War since the summer of 1914. Perhaps the only universally agreed-upon aspect of the "July Crisis" is the June 28, 1914, assassination of the Habsburg archduke Franz-Ferdinand that prompted it.[15] After that, the history of the origins of the First World War focuses on questions of causation that devolve into accusations aimed at fixing blame on someone or one empire or another. During the summer of 1914 Europe's drift toward war was the product of a catalyst (the Arch-Duke's assassination) sparking a series of long-term grievances related to persistently strengthening nationalist aspirations and diplomatic entanglements. At the beginning of the twentieth century all the Great Powers suffered from a deeply embedded Imperialist mentality that guided them to develop policies designed to provide them with additional avenues to expand the extent of their control over territory and people. Complicating the machination of the Great Powers was the growing appeal and strength of the nationalistic goal of self-determination so desired by the assorted national groups who were long suppressed inside empires and in emerging nations such as Serbia, Bulgaria, and Romania. For Russia, the July Crisis reached its climax at the end of the month when Nicholas II concluded that the threat he needed to respond to was Austria-Hungary's insistence that the assassination of their heir to the throne was the product of a conspiracy engineered at the hands of the Serbian secret service. The tsar, sticking to his foreign policy of defending his brother Slavs in Serbia and realizing the absurdity of invading East Prussia in fifteen days, as had been promised to the French in 1912, ordered his chief of staff, General N. N. Ianushkevich, to only partially mobilize Russia's armed forces in a fashion designed to meet the Austrian threat to Serbia. In a revelatory moment, the tsar learned that a partial mobilization was not possible without leaving the empire exposed to German invasion because of the limitations of his railways. The lack of flexibility in Russia's war planning and subsequent mobilization schedule limited Nicholas II's options and, therefore, compelled him to honor his commitment to the French and invade East Prussia more rapidly than his logistical network could support his army in the field. Being caught with few options, the Russians proclaimed their mobilization before anyone else on July 30, 1914, with the rest of Europe following in short order. And, in a world where the military controlled the mobilization process through the timetables of railroads, mobilization meant war!

The Russian army found itself marching into the lake country of East Prussia ill-equipped for the challenges that followed in August 1914. Despite the best efforts of Russia's most intelligent and progressively minded military leaders, time, or the lack of it, turned out to be the limiting factor of all the reform and planning efforts of the post-Japanese war period. Nine years, the first two of which were lost to suppressing civil unrest, was not enough time for the army to overcome the defeat in Asia, restore its financial base, reorganize its force structure, develop a military doctrine appropriate for twentieth-century industrial war, adopt new weapons, enhance logistical capabilities, and train for their next great challenge. Nonetheless, many officers throughout the army, regardless of their social or professional background, struggled to improve their cadre's operational capabilities on every level. Their efforts contributed to the ability of the army to mobilize in two directions to engage the German and the Austro-Hungarian armies at the beginning of the war. The work completed in the interwar period (1905–14) contributed to the ability of the tsar's army to survive the extremes of the First World War until the 1917 Revolution. Moreover, their attempts to introduce new ideas to their military doctrine and to modernize their armories with advanced and new weapons such as the airplane indicated that their thinking was progressive and making the tsar's army stronger with each passing day. The mobilization of the armed forces in August 1914 demonstrated that Russia could use her railroads and move troops to her western frontiers more rapidly than anyone, especially the Germans and Austro-Hungarians, thought possible. But it was not enough! Just like in the Far East, Russian soldiers went to the battlefront wondering why they had been inducted to fight a war for a regime that had lost much of its popular support. Despite the best efforts of some of the brightest Russian leaders to modernize their army through the adoption of mass conscription, the democratization of the officer corps and recognition of excellence in leadership through promotion by merit was still a work in progress. The indecisiveness of Nicholas II exacerbated the problem at the highest levels of the defense decision-making process. The tsar's weakness resulted in confusion when the guns of August sounded across Europe. Two Russian armies marched into East Prussia without adequate intelligence or logistics to support the offensive until it achieved a decisive victory, only after the Nicholas attempted to stop the invasion because he realized his long-term interests gaining control of the Balkans and gaining access to the Mediterranean and his short-term interest, coming to the aid of Serbia, would not be achieved in East Prussia.

The First World War

Nothing symbolizes warfare on the Eastern Front in the First World War more than book titles such as Winston Churchill's *The Unknown War* or Sir John Wheeler-Bennett's *The Forgotten Peace*, his study on the Treaty of Brest-Litovsk. The 1917 Russian Revolution, the rise of the Bolsheviks, and the West's decision to ignore the infant Bolshevik State at Versailles combined to relegate the First World War's Eastern Front to an "unknown" and "forgotten" status. Warfare in the east featured long periods of prolonged battles that included large-scale maneuvers and ultimately movement that military leaders and soldiers in the west envied. As in the West, industrial capabilities combined with emerging technologies to produce weapon systems with rapid-fire capabilities that consumed ammunition and soldiers alike. On all the First World War fronts, military leaders little understood the effect industrial warfare had on their armies. They either willfully choose to ignore or were ignorant of the deadly battlefield environment over which they commanded. Also, as in the West, successfully waging industrialized warfare demanded and wholly depended on logistics. Little excuse existed among the Great Powers for their failure to understand the dynamics of the modern battlefield because of the many conflicts ranging from the Boer War to the Russo-Japanese War to the Balkan Wars that had been studied and written about by the press and military observers from each great power (including the United States). The tragic irony of Russia's First World War being an "unknown war" resolved by a "forgotten peace" is that the four empires—the Romanovs, the Habsburgs, the Hohenzollerns and, the Ottomans—fought a brutal conflict for control over the vast territories of central, eastern, and southeastern Europe and in the end none of the empires still stood—they all lost their struggle to gain control over each other's borderland and collapsed in the wake of their failure. As the imperial monarchies disappeared, independent nations emerged and with that the old nationality problem of the borderlands became the unsolvable minority problem that plagued international politics from Versailles to the outbreak of the Second World War in Europe.[16]

Opening Battles

While Imperial Germany deployed slightly under one million men in their Schlieffen plan invasion of Belgium and France, war exploded across the borderlands of Russia, Germany, and Austria-Hungary in August 1914, resulting in the mobilization of millions of men by all of the belligerents in the first weeks of the war. The front's geographical parameters were defined by the town of Czernowitz on the Romanian border to Memel on the Baltic Sea. To defend a space of some 1,600 kilometers (990 miles), the Russians upon mobilization expanded the size of their army from 1 to 3.5 million men and divided this territory into two operational fronts—northwestern and southwestern. A central premise of Germany's war plan was that it would take the Russians six weeks to mobilize their massive yet lumbering army universally known as the steamroller. But, as is well known, the Russians invaded East Prussia on the fifteenth day after mobilization out of respect to their treaty obligations with France. The ensuing battles of Tannenberg and Gumbinnen culminated in the destruction of the

Russian 2nd Army and a decisive victory for the Germans that set the stage for the conflict between the Germans and the Russians for the rest of the war. The battles in August 1914 featured rapid movement of troops into East Prussia. This operation was doomed from the outset, firstly because the Russians advance outstripped its logistical capabilities, but there were other significant causes for Russia's East Prussian disaster. The Russian army failed to gather useful battlefield intelligence, thereby leaving commanders in the field blind to the disposition and movements of German forces. As a result, the ability of commanders in the Russian army to effectively control the movement of the armies in the field was weak to nonexistent. Just as vexing, the failure of command and control within the Russian army permeated to the top of its command structure. The front commander, the man responsible for coordinating the movements of two armies composed of fifteen divisions each, General Iakov Gregorevich Zhilinsky had no business being in command of an active theater as he had no operational experience. He was, in fact, an administrator who did not have a good track record at anything he did.[17] Criticizing the Russians for depending on non-cryptic or open communications, as most commentators have done since 1914, misses the key point that German intelligence assets, led by aviators flying over the front line, actually provided the reports that the Germans used to out maneuver the Russians at the outset of the Battle of Tannenberg. For the Russians, the failure of its high command elements to work in unison with commanders in the field resulted in command and control shortcomings that amounted to officers not following orders. Instead, they conducted operations as they best saw fit. In the end, this meant that Russian army groups of most any size did not mutually support each other in the midst of battle. This defined the operational conduct of the tsar's army throughout the war.

Initially, General Pavel Karlovich von Rennenkampf's 1st Army marched into East Prussia on August 17th and inflicted defeats on the Germans at Stalluponen and Gumbinnen on August 20, 1914. General Maximilian von Prittwitz und Gaffron commander of the VIII army composed of approximately 150,000 men panicked and ordered his forces to retreat behind the Vistula River. In effect, he chooses to surrender East Prussia to the Russians. As Prittwitz melted down under the strain of battle, Helmut von Moltke (the younger), as chief of staff of the German army who was otherwise engaged on the Western Front trying to preserve the integrity of the Schlieffen plan, responded to this situation by first transferring two army corps from France to the east and then relieving von Prittwitz of his command.[18] Fortunately for the Germans, Prittwitz's chief of staff, Max Hoffman, had the aerial intelligence assets in place to ascertain that the 1st Russian Army had halted in place after the Battle of Gumbinnen. He, therefore, deployed a light cavalry screen in front of the Russians on August 20th and in a logistical feat transferred the bulk of all German forces in East Prussia to the south to confront the 2nd Russian Army under the command of General Alexander Vasilovich Samsonov. The 2nd Army was marching around the Masurian Lakes to the south and had the aim of using Rennenkampf's advancing army as an anvil while his (Samsonov's) army hammered the Germans into submission in the vicinity of the town of Allenstein. Here is where Russian sloppiness in communications and overall command compromised their East Prussian campaign.

Unbeknownst to Samsonov, Rennenkampf had called a halt to his advance at Gumbinnen. In the aftermath of this unfolding debacle, efforts were made to blame Rennenkampf for not supporting Samsonov—even worse, much innuendo emerged claiming that personal animosity dating back to the Russo-Japanese War existed between the two commanders, hence the cause for one not supporting the other on the field of battle. No such evidence exists. Two factors resulted in the halt of 1st Army operations: (1) The aggressiveness of the Germans as they retreated had taken a toll on the 1st Army and (2) the rapid advance had caused the Russians to out run their supply lines, thus causing Rennenkampf to order a halt to rest, refit, and resupply. Of greater detriment to the operation, Zhilinsky lost control of the situation and did not understand that the 1st Army had halted operations and, not only did he fail to alert Samsonov, he completely misinterpreted the situation and ordered him to speed up his advance, thereby preventing both Russian armies from having a chance of supporting each other's operations. This failure in command at the highest level exposed the northern flank of the 2nd Russian Army to the sharp end of the force that Hoffman had transferred from the northern to the southern sector of the theater of battle. The resulting Battle of Tannenberg started when the 2nd Army emerged from the Pripet Marshes on August 23 and marched into the trap set by Hoffman. Prittwitz's replacement, General Paul Von Hindenburg and his chief of staff General Erich Ludendorff arrived just in time to take command of the Germans and execute Hoffman's plan. Using the bulk of the German 8th Army, they enveloped and annihilated the Russian 2nd Army by August 30th. In the end, with the Russian 2nd Army destroyed, the Germans were overwhelmed with Russian POWs—something for which there was no planning. More important to the scheme of history, the decisive German action in East Prussia saved what was considered sacred territory to Prussian aristocrats from Russian occupation. Only 10,000 men out of approximately 180,000 men of the 2nd Army escaped

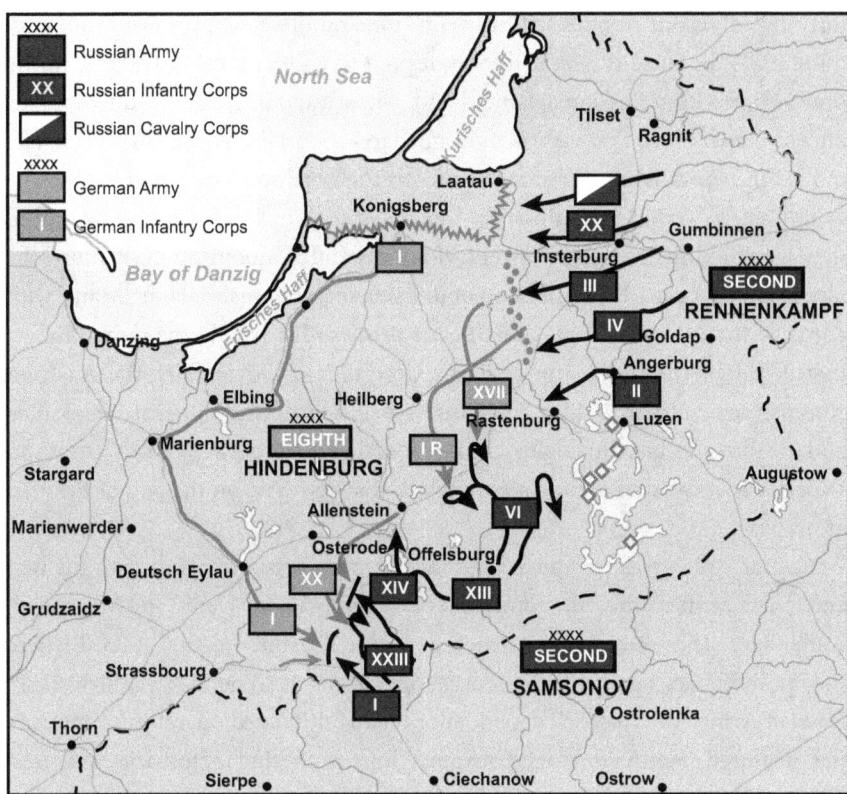

Map 6.1 The East Prussia Campaign, August 1914.

the battlefield to continue their service to the tsar. An astonishing 92,000 men ended up POWs and another 78,000 had been killed or wounded. Most of the army's equipment including 350 artillery pieces were lost. Humiliated Samsonov wandered off into the woods of East Prussia and allegedly committed suicide. Hindenburg and Ludendorff, however, became national heroes and would by war's end be leading the military effort for the Kaiser.[19]

Nonetheless, the Russians were able to endure the defeat in East Prussia and largely cover up the disaster because of their operations against their other main adversary, Austria-Hungary. The Russian war plan, or to more accurately describe the plan that controlled their operational conduct, their mobilization plan, was known in August 1914 as Mobilization Schedule 19 (Variant A) called for the simultaneous invasion of East Prussia and of Austro-Hungarian Galicia. Grand Duke Nicholas Nicholaevich, commander in chief of the Russian army, at his headquarters known as Stavka, took a more active role in operation on the Southwestern Front perhaps because it involved almost twice as many troops, forty-five divisions as opposed to twenty-nine on the Northwestern Front and, more likely, because Russia had long desired to gain control of Galicia. In the prewar period the Russians planned and, when war came, launched two major offensive operations that were not designed to support each other and ultimately moved in two different directions—one to the northwest and the other to the southwest. In Galicia, the Russians mobilized four instead of two armies, and they launched their offensive twenty-four days after mobilization. Perhaps the saving factor for the Russians in all of this was that the Austro-Hungarians, with arguably the weakest of the Great Power armies, did exactly the same thing— that is, under the leadership of Franz Conrad von Hotzendorf, the Austrian commander in chief divided their forces between defending Austrian Galicia and invading Serbia. He deployed his forces on an arc between the Vistula and Dniester Rivers using the fortress network that centered on the city of Przmysl as his base.

Conrad's plan was to launch an offensive into Russian Poland with his first and fourth armies under the command of Generals Viktor Dankl and Moritz von Auffenberg. These two armies struck first near Krasnik on August 23rd where they pushed back against the defensive operations of General Pavel Plehve's 5th Russian Army. The Austria's dependence on an antiquated operational doctrine that featured mounted frontal assaults into withering automatic weapons, however, resulted in 40 percent to 50 percent losses of the attacking forces. What followed was defeat after defeat of the Austrian army. General Alexsi Brusilov, commander of the 8th Russian Army, and General Nikolai Ruzki, commander of the 3rd Army, so soundly defeated the Austrian forces at Gnila Lipa on August 30th that the Habsburg army retreated in complete chaos, which resulted in Brusilov's army capturing the fortress city of Lemberg (Lviv) on September 3rd. Losing Lemberg was a major blow to Austrian prestige in the region as it effectively gave control of eastern Galicia to the Russians. The situation then deteriorated further for the armies of Francis Joseph. The Russians were far better coordinated on the southwestern as opposed to the Northwestern Front. This started with the front commander Nikolai Iudovich Ivanov who, as opposed to his peer Zhilinsky in East Prussia, was a fighting general. Even better, his chief of staff General M. I. Alekseev, of prewar planning fame, was arguably the officer in the Imperial Army who understood best the complex modern battlefield and the nuance of imperial politics. Both of these attributes would serve him and Nicholas II well in the coming years of conflict. Observing the disarray of Conrad's forces, Ivanov ordered the Cossacks attached to General Plehve's 5th Army along with elements of a newly formed 9th Army to pursue the fleeing

The First World War and the End of Tsarism, 1905–17

Map 6.2 The Galician Campaign, August 1914.

Austrians. They chased them to the outskirts of Przemysl where operations paused as both armies needed to rest and resupply.

Gaining control of the fortress network at Przemysl at this moment would have transformed the course of the war. The fortress blocked Russia's ability to traverse across Carpathian Mountain passes and advance across the Hungarian plain to the gates of Vienna and potentially knock the Habsburg's out of the war. The Russians did not knock out the Austro-Hungarians in September 1914, but Franz Joseph's army did suffer over 300,000 casualties (killed and wounded) and had over 100,000 of their soldiers captured and interned as POWs. Nearly a third of their army was lost in this opening campaign. The loss of their professional officer cadre was permanent. In the end, the Austro-Hungarian army would be dependent on German material support and reinforcement for the balance of the war. In the aftermath of their push into eastern Galicia, the Russians isolated the city of Przemysl, which resulted in their laying siege to the fortress network that defended it. As the maneuver period of operations concluded, the Russians too had suffered enormous casualties (approximately 250,000 soldiers killed and wounded) and did not have the force to reduce Przemysl in the fall of 1914. Without question, however, the Russian victories in Galicia allowed Nicholas II and his military leaders to shift attention from the disasters in East Prussia, which bought them some valuable time in their efforts to control public opinion.[20]

Once the Schlieffen plan had run its course and failed, and while the "race to the sea" was occurring on the Western Front, the Germans also maintained pressure on the Russians in East Prussia. After sending reinforcements to the Austrians, the Germans attempted to destroy Rennenkampf's 1st Army using the two army corps sent to the Eastern Front from the Western Front at the height of the panic before the Battle of Tannenberg. The transfer of these two corps from the Western Front contributed to the failure of the Schlieffen plan. They arrived in the east after Tannenberg yet nonetheless reinforced the German 8th Army. Ludendorf and Hoffman did not waste the arrival of these troops and used them to confront the Russians still in East Prussia. While they failed to annihilate the Russian 1st Army, they did cause it to retreat back into Russian territory, thereby liberating East Prussia from a Slavic occupying force by the middle of September. After dislodging the Russians from East Prussia in what became known as the 1st Masurian Lakes campaign, the operations of all three belligerent armies settled down for a period of assessment, rest, and resupply by the middle of September. This lull in the action, however, would not last for long.[21]

At the same time, in mid-September the Russian army was menacing Austrian Galicia with concerns for the defense of Krakow clouding the thinking of Conrad. Even worse, his armies had become bogged down in Serbia due to unexpectedly stiff resistance. Moreover, with the initial campaigns in the history books, Grand Duke Nicholas and his staff at Stavka were eyeing operations in Silesia as the next best possible way to threaten Germany. Accordingly, after the Japanese declaration of war on Germany on August 23 eliminated concerns about war breaking out in the Far East, the Russians started transferring troops from Siberia to reinforce their armies in Poland. These forces were concentrated south of Warsaw. Meanwhile further south and to the west, the Germans concentrated their forces. To better assist the fledgling Austro-Hungarian military, General Erich von Falkenhayn, newly appointed commander of the German armed forces, formed a new army, the German 9th Army under the command of General Richard von Schubert. More fatefully, he transferred Ludendorff to be the 9th Army's chief of staff. Ludendorff promptly suggested to Falkenhayn that Hindenburg should be made commander of both armies, thereby effectively giving him command of all Central Power's forces on the Eastern Front. This organizational scheme of central power forces on the Eastern Front was officially adopted on November 1. Regardless of the transfer of troops and the reorganization of command structures, by the end of September it was clear that the next stage of operations on the Eastern Front was going to occur in Silesia with the fate of the Russian Polish salient at stake.

On September 28th the German 9th Army and the Austrian 1st Army were simultaneously driving on Warsaw from the west and from the south. The Austrians made steady progress capturing Rzeszow on October 7 and Jaroslaw on October 11, but they could not break the back of Russian resistance as the tsar's army retreated across the San river. The tide of battle shifted on October 20th when the grand duke ordered a general offensive, sending Ivanov's 2nd, 4th, 5th, and 9th Russian Armies to cross the Vistula. By October 25th the Germans and the Austrians had to retreat as the Central Power allies started accusing each other of a blatant failure to support their respective operations. By the 30th of the month the Russians reached and occupied Lodz. Nicholas II forces, therefore, had beaten back the drive on Warsaw giving them a victory over both of the Germans and the Austrians. The failure of the German 9th Army led to the promotion of August von Mackensen who, like Hoffman, emerged as a prominent Eastern Front commander for the rest of the war. As the Germans did their post-battle study, they concluded that the battles along the Vistula River had so devastated the countryside that the Russian army would be unable to launch an operation into Silesia anytime soon. Their conclusion was wrong as they underestimated the growing strength of the Russian army.[22]

By the middle of November Nicholas Nikolaevich had decided to adopt General Ruzski's plan for the invasion of Silesia. The plan called for the Russian 1st Army and newly formed 10th Army to maintain pressure on the Germans in East Prussia. The 8th and 11th Armies were to continue the siege of Przemysl while guarding the Carpathian passes. In addition, much to the concern of the Krakovians, the Russian 3rd Army started to advance on their beloved city. This left the Russians with their 2nd, 4th, and 5th Armies to invade Silesia. Again, the Germans, as had been the case in August, were heavily outnumbered in troops and weapons as the Battle of Lodz started in the middle of November. Hindenburg, in complete command of operations and, working closely with Ludendorff, decided to let the Russians seize the initiative while, in a manner of fashion, they repeated history. Instead of meeting the Russian onslaught head-on, they shifted 9th Army troops by rail to the area south of their fortress at Thorn. Once this maneuver had been completed their plan was to turn the 9th Army loose in an effort to cut off Russian access to

Lodz via Warsaw. Mackensen attempted to preempt the Russians when he struck Rennenkampf's 1st Army on November 11th near Wloclawek. Rennenkampf, as he did in East Prussia in August 1914, remained stationary in position to guard the approaches to Warsaw. Fearing another Tannenberg, the grand duke ordered Plehve's 5th Army northward toward Lodz where, after marching some 70 miles in bitter winter conditions, it smashed into Mackensen's right flank on November 18th. For the next ten days the two armies were embroiled in a series of battles while all the soldiers on both sides suffered from the effects of the bitter wintery weather. The approaching end of this battle started when the German 3rd Guards Infantry Division under the command of General Karl Litzmann reached Breziny on November 24th. There he literally caught the Russians sleeping in the early morning, which led to widespread confusion among them as they chaotically retreated and lost all semblance of a combat unit. This success reinvigorated the Germans, which was followed by a series of rapid, hard-hitting engagements that culminated with the Grand Duke ordering the retreat of the Russian army to defensive positions surrounding Warsaw. The Germans then occupied Lodz on December 6, 1914.[23]

The Siege of Przemysl

The bitter Polish winter would finally bring a halt to the maneuver war in December 1914. At this point, the Germans viewed the Russians with contempt for their invasion of East Prussia. More importantly, the die had been cast. The Russian army entered engagements with more troops but kept getting beaten on every level. Hindenburg and Ludendorff in response to the shoddy performance of the Russian army became convinced as they ordered their armies into winter quarters that if they were given enough troops, they could destroy the Russian army in 1915. The end of the maneuver war, however, did not lead to a secession of hostilities in Galicia. Throughout the Battles of the Vistula and Lodz, the Russians did not relent in their efforts to sweep the Austro-Hungarian army out of Galicia and break through the Carpathian Mountain barrier and sweep into the Hungarian plain. By mid-September the four armies under the command of General N.N. Ivanov had pushed the Austro-Hungarian Army back over 100 miles, thus forcing them to retreat to the base of the Carpathian Mountains where elements of the Russian and Austro-Hungarian armies fought a brutal set of battles beginning in December 1914 and continuing throughout the winter of 1915. This series of battles, known as the Carpathian Winter War, were fought in extreme winter conditions. Conrad defined the aim of these engagements as an effort to force the Russians out of Galicia and for the Austro-Hungarian army to reinforce the fortress at Przemysl while seizing control of the region from Krakow to Lemberg (Lviv). This campaign culminated with the two foes lined up for the first major siege of the First World War at the fortress Przemysl in the southeast corner of Austrian Galicia. Here the Russian 3rd Army under the command of General D. R. Radko Dimitriev enveloped the over thirty fortified positions of this fortress network and besieged the city/fortress. The Russians retreated behind the river San in mid-October to wait for the Battle of the Vistula to run its course but otherwise remained engaged against the Austrian through the winter of 1914–15.[24]

The siege of Przemysl has been compared to the Battle of Verdun as all of the elements of fortress warfare in the age of industrialized conflict played out over a long period, in this case 133 days. The siege took on its First World War character because once the war broke out the Austrians immediately began constructing a defensive network that featured 30 miles of trenches and over 650 miles of barbed wire. By the time the Russians arrived the Austrians had constructed seven defensive lines that were heavily fortified with everything from mortars to machine guns to mines. Inside the fortress a force of some 138,000 soldiers served under the command of General Hermann Kusmanek von Burgneustadten; true to the nature of the Austro-Hungarian Empire the men under his command spoke fifteen different languages. Initially the siege went well for the Russians as it was launched by Radko Dimitriev's 3rd Army on September 24th and four days later, on September 28th, the town and its fortress were completely surrounded. Envelopment of the position, however, did not result in it being reduced. Reducing a strongly fortified position required the extensive use of artillery and in the fall of 1914 all belligerents were suffering from massive shell shortages. Everyone underestimated how their armies would expend artillery shells in the First World War.[25] With the Russians lacking the heavy artillery to reduce the fortress, the seven lines of defensive trenches proved invaluable in the ability of Przemysl to hold out against the onslaught of the tsarist assault. Moreover, when the Russians temporarily lifted the siege in October during the Battle of the Vistula, the Austrians enjoyed a brief period to resupply their besieged forces.

Once the Germans and the Austrians had been pushed back from the Vistula, the Russians were able once again to surround the city of Prezmysl and the siege was restored in early November. This time, however, the assaulting army was the Russian 11th Army under the command of General Andrei Nikolaevich Selivanov.

Based on the 40,000 or so casualties of the first siege, Selivanov concluded that frontal assaults served to devastate his troops and waste valuable equipment and munitions. Instead, he adopted an operational strategy of starving the Austro-Hungarians into submission while using the time it took to build up his artillery supplies so that his army could slowly and steadily increase the intensity of its fire on the city and the fortress. Throughout the period from November to February, the Habsburgs repeatedly attempted to relieve their comrades, but all such attempts failed with frostbite and disease taking as large a toll as combat-related wounds. By the end of February Kusmanek von Burgneustadten received word that no further relief columns would be sent to his fortress—the point had come where saving the fortress was not worth the cost. With civilians long evacuated, the general ordered the destruction of anything of value and encouraged units to attempt to fight their way out of the city. None of these efforts succeeded! Finally, on March 22nd, with nothing left to defend his position, Kusmanek surrendered the fort. The loss of the fort was a major blow to Austro-Hungarian prestige. Its defeat represented one of the lowest points in their war effort. After all, Francis Joseph's army failed at everything it had engaged in since the outbreak of the war—it could not gain the upper hand even in Serbia! Operations in Przemysl and those that attempted to relieve the fortress had cost the Habsburgs an estimated one million casualties. When the fortress surrendered, the Russians captured over 2,500 officers and 115,000 soldiers. Moreover, nothing short of men, materials, and leadership was preventing the Russian army from invading the Hungarian plain and threatening Vienna and the very existence of the Danubian monarchy. Indeed, the damage done to the Austrian military in the first year of the war inflicted irreparable damage to their reputation. For the Austrians, the situation was critical. From the outbreak of the war until the spring of 1915, the Austro-Hungarian army had absorbed huge losses. By the end of the war they suffered a 75 percent loss rate of the total number of men mobilized—the highest loss rate of any First World War belligerent. The Danubian army never recovered, which made the security of their empire precariously dependent on German support and did much to lead to the ultimate demise of the Habsburg monarchy.[26]

The Great Retreat

While the situation on the Western Front devolved into a war of attrition over the course of the 1914–15 winter, nothing of the sort had occurred on the Eastern Front.

A continuous front including trenches did coalesce from the Romanian frontier to the Baltic Sea but there would be no Christmas truce. In the southwest the Russian and Austro-Hungarian armies fought brutal engagements often in bitter cold weather in and around Przemysl. The Carpathian Winter War compromised the force structure of the Austro-Hungarian army, and this combined with their failures in Serbia resulted in the emergence of a widespread belief that the empire was teetering on the brink of collapse.[27] Of more concern for the Habsburgs, Italy and Romania loomed as additional threats if they decided to join the Entente. Both nations were tantalized with the thought that their entrance into the war could result in the end of the Danubian monarchy. If the Habsburg Empire collapsed, the Italians and Romanians believed they stood to gain much desired territory populated with people who identified with their respective nation-states.[28] Meanwhile in the northwest, the Russians and Germans dug into Polish territory and planned for future operations in spring 1915. In the interregnum, they had time to reinforce and to resupply their armies. The Russians were believed to be in a much better strategic position than the Central Powers. Although they suffered the humiliating defeats in East Prussia that caused considerable loss of men and materials across the entire front, they had held their own against the Germans in Poland through the winter. Even more promising, they finally reduced the fortresses at Przemysl in March, 1915. Moreover, while the problem of supply would also hamper their operations, the Russians had been able to mobilize sufficient reserves to reinforce their forces across the front for the coming campaigns.[29]

The sheer expanse of the Eastern Front, which after the Ottomans' October 29, 1914, declaration of war ranged from the Baltic to the Black Sea, distinguished it from the Western Front. The most significant difference between the two fronts rested in manpower. Regardless of the total number of twelve million men that Russia ultimately mobilized in the course of the First World War, there were never as many men per square mile on the Eastern Front as there were in the West. The density of soldiers, or lack thereof, combined with its enormity kept the possibility of maneuver warfare alive on the Eastern Front in a way that it could not in the West. Any maneuver warfare, however, had to manage the eternal challenges of conducting military operations in Russia. Indeed, weather and rudimentary conditions, especially in the realm of transportation, hampered the movement of troops but the true limiting factor to any military operations in Russia was the challenge of supply. Russia's supply and transportation challenges were as legendary as they were monumental. The tsar's army struggled with providing everything from weapons to munitions in a timely manner, which always had a direct impact on its ability to conduct operations.[30] For the

Germans, as 1915 would prove, the more successful their maneuvers, the further they pushed the Russian army eastward, the longer their supply lines became, which, in the end, created an unmanageable logistical problem that placed strict limits on their success.

Before the Russians could concentrate the forces and materials needed to launch the anticipated offensive across the Hungarian Plain and threaten the heart of the Austro-Hungarian Empire, the Germans transformed the course of the war in its eastern borderlands when they decided to focus their operations on the Eastern Front in 1915. After becoming mired in the war of attrition in the fields of Flanders, Hindenburg and Ludendorff agitated and prevailed in convincing Falkenhayn to adopt their eastern strategy. Their aim became nothing less than to force the Russians into battle and defeat the Imperial Army, thereby saving the Habsburgs and then allowing them to focus all of their assets on the Western Front. Their struggles with Falkenhayn, in the long run, did much to pave the way for their taking over the German High Command when Falkenhayn's Verdon gambit failed in 1916. The Austrians went into the spring of 1915 badly in need of some type of military success. Much was at stake! Above all else Conrad understood that his armies needed to liberate all territories that the Russians occupied to restore his personal prestige, to demonstrate that the army of Francis Joseph could compete on the twentieth-century battlefield and consequently to provide the Italians and Romanians with cause to remain neutral. Yet to achieve any degree of success, the Austrians and the Germans had to overcome their differences in strategic outlook and form a unified command to direct operations across the front. This was accomplished much to the chagrin of Conrad who spent the rest of the war complaining that he no longer had effective control over the fate of his army. In the end, the Eastern Front strategy provided the Germans with the opportunity to return to maneuver warfare and test and develop methods that might be used to break the deepening stalemate on the Western Front. The lessons the Germans learned from the war of movement on the Eastern Front in 1915 gave rise to what some historians have defined as the birth of the idea of blitzkrieg in German operational thinking that would culminate into the war fighting doctrine of the German armed forces at the beginning of the Second World War.[31]

As the spring thaw occurred, Hindenburg and Ludendorff received authorization to launch what was envisioned as a minor offensive from the line Tarnow-Gorlice just northwest of Przemysl. On May 2nd, the Central Powers under Germany's leadership using a newly formed 11th Army composed of some 220,000 soldiers and 900 heavy and light artillery pieces launched the Gorlice-Tarnow offensive. Under the command of General August von Makenson, an old cavalry general who demanded movement of men and materials and his chief of staff Hans von Seeckt, the Central Powers' army broke through and created a 40-mile gap in the Russian line. General Radko Dimitriev's 3rd Army that consisted of approximately 60,000 men and 150 artillery pieces was all that stood in front of this assault. This despite the Russians having gathered intelligence that revealed the buildup of German forces across the space between Tarnow and Gorlice. Instead of sending reinforcements, however, the Russians choose to concentrate their armies in the territory in and around Przemysl to prepare for their planned offensive into Hungary proper. The Germans beat them to the punch. They started their offensive with a four-hour artillery barrage that decimated Russia's frontline defenses. Despite having dug in over the heights facing Tarnow, the Russians did not have the heavy artillery or munitions to reply with effective counterfire that could have stopped the combined German-Austro-Hungarian force. The Central Powers, therefore, overran the Russians. Lacking the heavy artillery at this point in the line to contain the Germans, the forces under Radko Dimitriev collapsed in front of the onslaught: the rout was on. Eight days later the military effectiveness of the Russian 3rd Army had been compromised to the point that it was all but completely destroyed, which resulted in the Great Retreat of 1915. The Russians had to evacuate Przemysl and then surrender Lemberg (Lviv) on June 22. Losing Lemberg (Lviv) meant that the Russian army had to evacuate Austrian Galicia in its entirety. Their humiliation was complete when the tsar's army and bureaucracy abandoned Warsaw on August 5th. By the end of August, the Eastern Front still ran from Lithuania to Romania, but the Polish bulge in the lines had been removed as a result of the German offensive. Meanwhile, Hindenburg and Ludendorff sought to capitalize on their success by invading Lithuanian territory with the aim of pushing Russian forces into their heartland and in the best of all possible worlds threaten St. Petersburg, now Petrograd and actually cause the defeat of Russia.[32]

Although German offensive into the Baltic region sputtered out in the autumn of 1915, the losses and damage to the Russian Empire proved irreparable. For starters, the Russians had to abandon their hard-fought Galician victories and then had to evacuate the Polish salient, territory they had occupied since the late eighteenth century. In the end, the Russians surrendered 300,000 square miles comprising much of the territory of the western borderlands to the Central Powers. While accurate numbers will never be known, rounded estimates claim that the army lost over one million men either killed, wounded, or otherwise lost

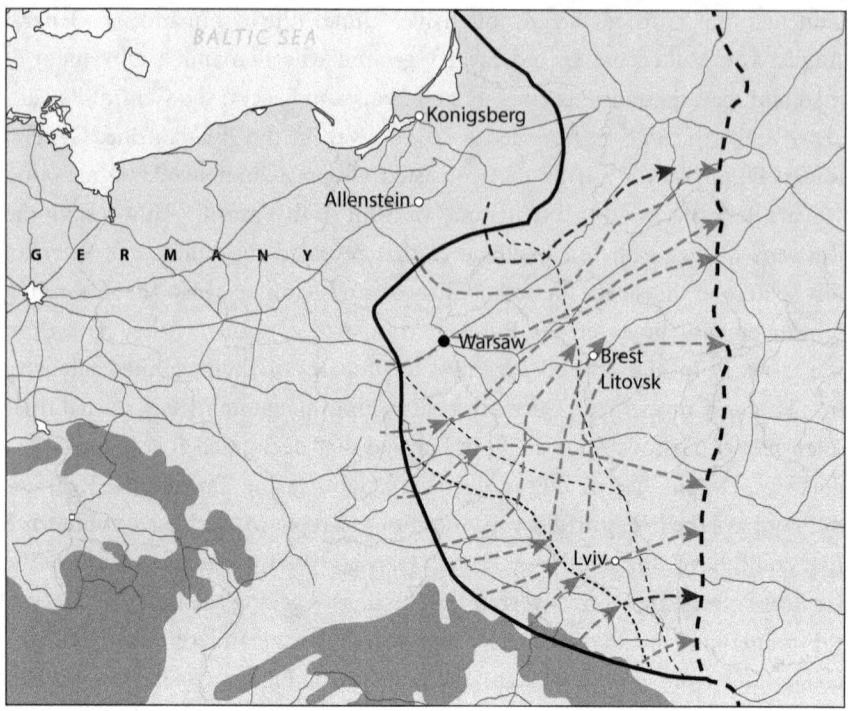

Map 6.3 The Great Retreat, 1915.

to the military effort in the course of their Great Retreat. Notoriously famous for its endless supply of replacement soldiers, the attrition to the professional officer cadre could not be surmounted with wartime replacements. Simply put, officers commissioned during wartime did not have the in-depth training, the battlefield experiences, or the loyalty to the Romanovs as the officers who had been educated and trained to spend their entire lives and careers as servants to the tsar. For the rest of the war, the Russian officer corps struggled to find wartime replacements for the trained and battle-tested officers who were irreplaceably lost to the army in 1914–15. The same scenario played out among the noncommissioned officers as well. The army had traditionally suffered from a shortage of sergeants and corporals. As the people directly responsible for leading soldiers into battle, they endured a level of attrition comparable or worse than their officers. Such leaders could not easily be replaced because they needed to emerge from the ranks after they had demonstrated leadership qualities. Officers rarely had a chance to emerge in the midst of a war that featured high casualties. The lack of fiercely loyal professional officer's corps and the decimation of the army's noncommissioned officers meant that the army's leadership, unlike it did in

1905, was unable to stop the sweeping tide of protest that culminated with the mutiny of the soldiers in February/March 1917.[33]

Another impact of the Great Retreat that undermined the authority of the regime was the emergence of a refugee challenge that was mismanaged or, more appropriately, never managed by tsarist authorities. The First World War generated refugees throughout its operational theaters as civilians fled from the terror and horrors of warfare. Estimating the number of people who fled from their homes because of violence is trickier than generating statistics for military losses due to combat.[34] Fleeing the Central Powers was not the only reason people in the empire's borderlands chose to leave their homes in an effort to survive the conflagration. According to the Field Orders that took effect at the outbreak of the war, the army gained control over the civil administration of any province that was deemed in the zone of combat.[35] Not surprisingly, as the war progressed and especially after the Great Retreat started, the army high command started to target nonethnic Russians who lived in the borderlands as enemies of the state. One of the sad ironies of this situation was that the First World War in the east was largely fought in the old pale of settlements or the region that was largely populated by the Jews in Russia's western borderlands.[36] Thus, starting before and then heightening during the German 1915 offensive, the Russian military authorities started accusing Jews as well as Ukrainians and Poles as enemies of the state, claiming that many of them were spying for the Central Powers. When Makenson's forces overran the homes of these "suspects," civil authority also broke down, and these poor people became victims of the conflict from which they were literally running for their lives. Many lost their homes as their communities were destroyed. Most fled into the depths of Russia, where, unless they had friends or family in the empire's interior, they found little support from the state. Instead, as noted in the memoirs of aid workers, the fate of refugees caught up in the onslaught of the German army was much suffering, hunger, and homelessness.

Much has been written about incompetence, indeed the cruelty, of tsardom toward its Jewish subjects as well as other ethnic minorities in the borderlands throughout the empire. While much of the criticism is warranted, it should come as no surprise as tsarist officials had been trying to Russify its ethnic populations for much of the nineteenth century and had lost its patience with the refusal of non-Russians to assimilate into loyal subjects of the empire. Such criticism should also be taken into consideration as the regime was struggling to maintain its public standing in the midst of another military disaster.[37] To this end the tsar responded to the German invasion by shaking up his high command. The first to fall was War Minister Sukhomlinov who had been under fire since the autumn of 1914. He was largely blamed for the shell shortage and all other failings of Russia's supply efforts. And, in the midst of the Great Retreat, he found himself embroiled in the Miasoyedov affair. Sergei Miasoyedov was a tsarist official, a colonel in the Gendarme, who was accused, tried, and to his surprise, horror, and chagrin, executed as a spy in March 1915. So strong was the force of spy mania at this time throughout the borderlands that his close connections to the war minister could not spare him from a brutal fate that he may or may not have deserved. Nonetheless, the war minister's reputation was flailing before the Great Retreat and battlefield failure sealed his fate.[38] The ultimate response to German success in 1915 was Nicholas II's decision to transfer his cousin the Grand Duke Nicholas Nikolaevich to the Caucasus Front and take over command of the army himself. At this moment in the conflict Nicholas II effectively gave command of his army to General Alekseiev who as commander of the north-Western Front had organized the retreat of the army throughout the summer of 1915. His effort prevented the complete collapse of the army in the face of the German juggernaut. One of Russia's most competent general staff officers now in effective command of the army from this time forward would be considered responsible for the success and more frequently the failures of Russia's armed forces. Even worse, for the fate of the Romanovs, Nicholas II, who had made himself commander in chief of the army, could not both command the army and run his government effectively; the impact of this decision would become clear in February 1917 when the tsar lost his crown.

The Germans, on the other hand, had enjoyed great operational success in the spring/summer of 1915. They developed a new operational technique that exhibited the value of massing troops and artillery at a fixed point and then deploying them in unison. By 1917 the Germans would adopt this type of combined operation to create and then use shock troops as a means to overcome the stalemate that was trench warfare. The outcome was a breakthrough replete with tremendous success that therefore became a model for a new operational doctrine that had potential for use on the Western Front. It did however have one shortcoming—it did not result in a knockout blow culminating in a strategic victory over the Russians. Instead, like many great armies of the past, what the breakthrough of 1915 revealed to the Germans was that Russia was an endless place.[39] The Russian army had a tradition of retreating in good order that dated at least back to the age of Napoleon and most recently practiced and perhaps perfected in the Russo-Japanese War. Nonetheless, as the winter of 1915–16 gripped the Eastern Front, the Russian army had been pushed back and battered; it did not represent an imminent threat to the sovereignty of the Habsburgs or the Hohenzollerns, or the territorial integrity of their respective empires. Despairing over not achieving a decisive victory in the east however, Falkenhayn redirected his energies to the West where he decided to engage the French at Verdun.

The Caucasus

When Nicholas II sent the grand duke to the Caucasus, most observers considered his transfer and elevation to the position of viceroy to be a polite way to push Nicholas Nikolaevich aside as most First World War histories ascribe the Caucasus to being one of the conflict's backwater theaters of operations. The Ottomans, after all, were not taken seriously in the world of the military affairs of the Great Powers. In the July/August 1914 buildup to the war no one was too concerned about the status of the Ottoman Empire. Since the Germans had developed close military relations with the Turks under the guise of the work of Limon von Sanders in the prewar period, it was understood that the sultan was leaning toward the Central Powers. Thus, it came as no shock when the Ottomans entered the war on October 29, 1914, after the British pursuit of the battle cruisers Goeben and Breslau across the Mediterranean Sea ended with Germany giving the ships to the sultan whose navy then started to bombard Russian Black Sea ports. As a result of their decision to go to war, the Ottomans found themselves fighting a four-front war with major campaigns in Mesopotamia, Palestine, Gallipoli, and the Caucasus. The First World War is often overlooked as the last war between the Romanovs and the Ottomans. Every Romanov tsar and tsarina whose reign lasted longer than six months and with the exception of Alexander III fought a major campaign against the Turks. With the exception of Peter the Great's 1710–11 disaster at Prut River and the Crimean War, the Romanovs had steadily pushed back the Ottomans frontiers in the Balkans, Ukraine/Crimea, and the Caucasus. Indeed, much of what the Ottomans hoped to achieve by committing to war in 1914 was to gain back Caucasus territory lost to the Russians in 1877–8 and Balkan territory lost to the Bulgarians and Romanians in the recent 1912–13 Balkan Wars.[40] To accomplish these goals, the Ottomans had a million-man army but an industrial infrastructure that was in worse shape than Russia's. For example, they lacked railroads that had the capacity to rapidly move their troops around their empire. Further, they lagged far behind the Russians in modern artillery, machine guns, all types of small arms, and had not begun to replenish munition stockpiles after their depletion during the Balkan War campaigns. While the Russians outnumbered the Turks in every category, Sukhomlinov treated the Caucasus as a low priority in 1914 and had transferred all Russian forces save for one regular and one reserve army corps to Poland after the disaster at Tannenberg. This meant that the Russians had around 60,000 troops stationed in the Caucasus in the winter of 1914–15.[41]

Before the arrival of the grand duke, the viceroy had been the seventy-seven-year-old Illarion Vorontsov-Dashkov. Due to his age, effective command of the Russian troops in the Caucasus belonged to Vontontsov-Dashkov's next in command Aleksandr Zakharevich Myshelaevskii, a former chief of the general staff. His chief of staff Nikolai Nikolayevich Yudenich (of Civil War fame) actually directed operations in the Caucasus for the first period of the war. After declaring war on the Ottomans on November 2, 1914, the Russians launched offensive operations and invaded their territory on the southeastern side of the Black Sea with the goal of capturing the city of Koprukoy. Once conquering koprukoy, the Russians aimed to construct a defensive line that extended to Dogubeyazit or just northwest of the corner of the world where the Russian and Ottoman Empires met with Persia (Iran). In this opening campaign that took place north of the Armenian cultural center of Van, the Russian army was reinforced with Armenian volunteers. Nicholas II acknowledged their contribution to the Romanov military effort when he visited the region in December 1914 and encouraged all Armenians to join the Russian army. After the initial engagement between their armies, Turkish minister of war Enver Pasha, sensing Russian weakness after the debacle in East Prussia, took command of the front and ordered a winter offensive into Russian territory. What followed became known to history as the Battle of Sarikamish, fought over rough terrain and in harsh winter weather. The Russians prevailed but not until early January when Enver Pasha ordered a retreat toward the fortress city of Erzurum, which turned into a rout and a stunning defeat for Ottoman arms.[42] Enver Pasha's return to Constantinople convinced that the Russians had received vital support in this campaign from Armenian volunteers, which contributed to developing negative attitudes about that minority population that was to have devastating consequences for them in the coming year.

The year 1915 started in the Caucasus with the Russians having the upper hand on the battlefield. As the spring unfolded, the region did genuinely become a backwater of the war as the Russians were all but consumed by events in Poland and the Ottomans faced a similar crisis with the Entente's invasion of Gallipoli. The Russians kept their gains of 1914 along the Caucasus-Turkish frontier. The

Ottomans did not have the forces to prevent the Russians from marching deeper into the territory they controlled in the Caucasus. The status of the Caucasus slowly changed as the year 1914 progressed, largely because of the activities of Yudenich. Yudenich, now recognized as the true operational commander, sought common ground with the Armenian volunteers in an effort to gain control of the city of Van. In the midst of the siege of Van, its Armenian population rebelled against their Ottoman overlords, which compromised the security of their rear and further embittered the attitude of the Turks toward them. By the end of May, Russian forces had forced the Turks out of the city of Van, thus gaining control over the entire province of Van. The success of this operation combined with the support that the Russians received from Armenian volunteers resulted in the Ottoman interior minister Talat Pasha promulgating a law that justified orders to forcibly deport all Armenians out the empire in general and out of the Van province specifically. To accomplish this task, however, the Ottoman army had to reorganize, which it did, thus resulting in heavy fighting throughout the province in June and July. By the beginning of August, the Russians, in response to Ottoman pressure, withdrew from the province, which caused two events that radically transformed the demographics of the region. The first was that over 200,000 Armenian refugees followed the Russians into the Trans-Caucasus creating yet another First World War refugee crisis within the Russian Empire. The second was the removal of all Armenians from the Ottoman Empire, a process that started in May and culminated with their systematic evacuation of the Van Province. To accomplish this task, the Ottomans depended on the support of their Kurdish allies. The removal of these populations has been considered an act of genocide by its victims, something the Turkish government today (2022) still denies. Regardless of how this event is interpreted, there is no denying that the Armenian population including women, children, and the aged who found themselves under Ottoman occupation in the late summer of 1915 were forcibly relocated to the Syrian desert without any supplies to sustain them or shelter to protect them—hundreds of thousands of noncombatants died as a result of this policy.[43] Meanwhile, as the war progressed, the Russians regrouped and launched a counteroffensive that resulted in their pushing northwest of Van and into the interior of Anatolia. The presence of the Russian army in Anatolia unnerved the sultan's political and military leadership in Constantinople.[44]

In the fall of 1915 the grand duke arrived in the Caucasus. While he recognized from the time of his arrival that Yudenich's leadership was the key to Russia's success in the region, he also asserted his presence. First, he visited Yudenich in his headquarters in the fortress at Kars to impress upon his operational commander that he should inform and get his (the grand duke's) approval before engaging the Turks on any level. Then, he set up his personal headquarters at Tiflis in the viceroy's palace where he busied himself with military affairs in the morning and the complex civil affairs of the Caucasus in the afternoon. As a rule, he left Yudenich to his own devices, but as the Caucasus campaign progressed, the army suffered from a lack of unity in its command structure that affected its operation largely because there was no connection between the operational front and the rear. This meant that Yudenich never quite knew when or if he would receive supplies and reinforcements.[45] Since the Gallipoli campaign lingered through the fall leaving the Ottoman's army concentrated on the other side of their empire, Yudenich used this time to reorganize, reinforce, and resupply his army. Meanwhile, the grand duke, learning that German agents had been actively recruiting armed bands in Persia and paying them off with gold, insisted on some response and thus organized an expeditionary force to march into northern Persia, thereby opening up a second Caucasus Front. This force composed of some 14,000 troops landed on the Caspian Sea port of Enzeli on October 28, 1915, and marched across northern Persia with the aim of eventually linking up with a British force that was operating in Mesopotamia with the goal of occupying Baghdad. While a meetup of the two armies did not occur, operations in northern Persia were a success in that they provided the grand duke with the belief that it would be prudent for the regime to develop a plan to recruit the Muslims living in Russia into supporting the war effort. This type of thinking represented a shift in attitude from that of his predecessor's; Count Vorontsov-Dashkov did not trust any Muslims. The grand duke sought to sidestep religious questions in favor of a policy aimed at building trust and support from all the national groups within the Russian Empire.[46]

In the meantime, the Ottomans, in high spirits because of their unexpected victory at Gallipoli, took their time transferring troops to the Caucasus Front. Yudenich, logically concluding that it was only a matter of time before the Turks redirected their attention to the Caucasus, began in December 1915 to lobby for the grand duke's approval to restart operations on the central Caucasus Front. Nicholas Nikolaevich was hesitant at first, largely because of concern over supplies, but he did eventually agree and granted permission. Yudenich ordered an attack in early January that launched a daring campaign aimed at the fortress city of Erzurum. The Russians occupied Erzurum on February 15, 1916, which created fear in Constantinople that the tsar's army was next going to invade Mesopotamia proper. Enver Pasha had returned to the Caucasus Front and he tried to organize a new 2nd Army to liberate Erzurum. Through this effort he

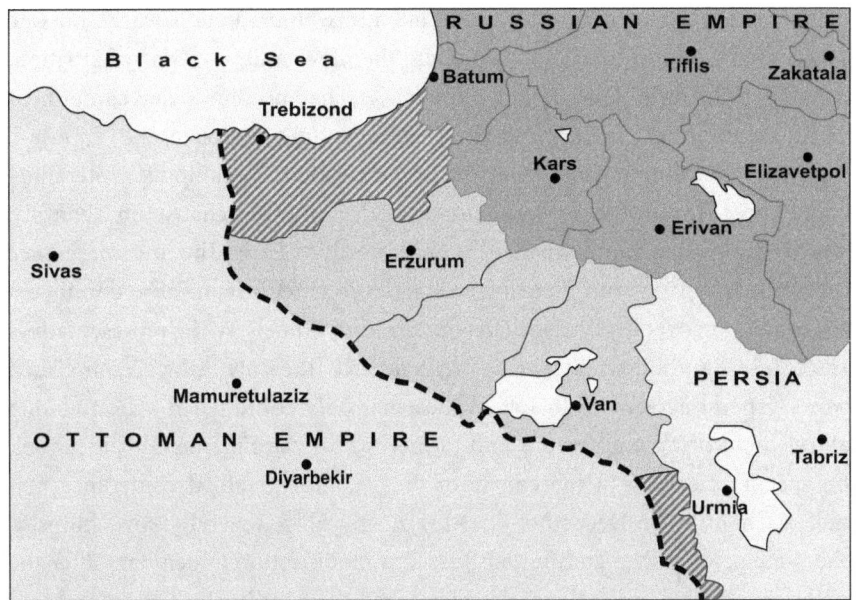

Map 6.4 The Ottoman-Russian Caucasus Campaign in the First World War.

discovered that Yudenich had consolidated his gains and had an impenetrable hold on Erzurum. In addition, the Russian commander had sufficient strength to divide his army into two columns that struck in two directions—one headed north to the shores of the Black sea while the other headed west and attacked Bitlis and Mus in eastern Anatolia. This campaign proved a huge success for the Russian army. By the winter of 1916–17 the Russians, while never completely controlling the Van province again, had extended their frontier into the Ottoman's eastern borderland from Trizond in the north to Bitlis in the south, a distance that covered some 355 km. This extension of the frontier had put the Russian army into Eastern Mesopotamia and left them poised for additional operations that could have threatened the sultanate's existence in the coming year but the February Revolution transpired and the imperial Russian army entered into the final period of its existence.[47]

1916

The steady escalation of the war throughout 1915, which included Bulgaria joining the Central Powers in the wake of the failed Gallipoli campaign, and the success of the German breakthrough at Golice-Tarnow, revealed that all belligerents needed to carefully plan all future operations. Clearly, no one power was going to be able to dominate the other and, in a war of attrition, carefully utilizing all military and human assets had become a vital component of future thinking. To this end the Entente sought to create and impose a higher level of thinking and planning into their effort by calling for interallied conferences. Three of these were actually held; all met at a chateau in Chantilly, which was located approximately 30 miles north of Paris. The first conference met on July 7, 1915, and French commander in chief Joseph Joffre dominated the discussion over his British colleague Sir John French. While representatives from Russia and other allies were in attendance, the only thing accomplished was a general agreement to Joffre's idea that only coordinated action among allies would bring a victorious end to the war for the Entente. This idea took on specific meaning in the course of the second interallied conference that met at Chantilly on December 6, 1915. Inexplicably General Iakov Zhilinsky, the same general who committed Russia to mobilization fifteen days after the outbreak of war and then completely botched the coordination of 1st and 2nd Armies in East Prussia in August 1914, represented the tsar at this conference. While Joffre and the soon to be relieved Sir John French put forth proposals for combined offensive operations among allies, Zhilinsky forcefully insisted on the allies adopting the principle that the members of the Entente must be prepared to come to the aid of the others if the Central Powers attacked as they did to the Russians in 1915. Although in principle the allies agreed to unified action, they remained undecided about what to do next as the French still harbored designs over creating a second front in Salonika and the British envisioned redirecting their efforts from Gallipoli to the fields of Flanders where they could put their newly recruited army to the test. The Germans, however, seized the initiative when they launched their attack against the French fortress city of Verdun in February 1916. From that point on the most salient feature of 1916 was the French appeal to their British and Russian allies to launch some type of counteroperation that would give them relief. Ironically, and despite the devastation its army suffered in 1915, the Russians were the first to respond with an operation at Lake Naroch. Much to the chagrin of the Germans and Austrians, they had underestimated the capabilities of the Russian army to rebound from the previous year's losses.[48]

The Russians were the first to respond to the French call for support as German artillery hammered Verdun. While the British response to the pleas of the French was to slowly implement the plan that became their massive operations on the Somme, which did not commence until July, the Russians attacked the Central

Powers on a spot on the Lithuanian-Belarus border. This operation is known to the First World War history as the Battle of Lake Naroch. General Alexeiev, who controlled Russian operations as chief of staff since Nicholas II took over command of the army the previous autumn, chose this spot because he could order forces to attack from Russia's Northern Army and from its Western Army. On paper this gave the Russians a decisive advantage of over 1.5 million soldiers to a combined German and Austro-Hungarian force of just under 1 million men. Moreover, he came up with a plan based on a pincer movement whereby he ordered the Russian northern group under the command of former war minister General A. N. Kuropatkin of Russo-Japanese War infamy to attack from the northeast toward Vilnius. With this army acting as an anvil, General Smirnov's 2nd Army, which was a part of the Western Army group under the command of General Alexei Evert acted as the hammer as it launched another attack aimed at Vilnius from the east. After a largely ineffective two-day artillery bombardment, the Russia attack started on March 18, 1916, against the German 10th army under the command of General Hermann von Eichhorn. In the end approximately 350,000 Russians attacked 75,000 Germans and managed to decisively lose the battle.[49]

Alexeiev then came to the realization that the Russian army may have been able to recompose its force structure after the Great Retreat of 1915, but that the forces at his disposal suffered inadequacies on every level. The problem started with uninspired commanders such as Kuropatkin and Evert who did not believe they could succeed because of supply and training challenges. The supply challenges were endemic to the entire Russian war effort and therefore nothing new, but nonetheless they posed a problem that compromised operations. Training was also an issue. The question of inadequate training demonstrated that replacing wartime casualties with effective replacement troops took time that the Russian army did not have in the midst of the First World War. Two days into the battle, all forward Russian movement stopped. Soldiers became bogged down in the mud of an early yet rapid thaw and then became exposed to withering German machine gun fire. Poor training resulted in Russian soldiers bunching together, thereby making themselves obvious targets for the Germans. The shortcomings of their commanders and their training in general combined with the failure of the quartermaster's corps to keep them supplied undermined the morale of the Russian soldiers, which can arguably be considered the start of the collapse of the army that came to fruition in 1917. In the immediate moment, however, the Battle of Lake Naroch did not force the Germans to divert forces from Verdun, rendering this engagement a complete failure in strategic, operational, and tactical terms.[50]

What the Entente's military and political leadership could not know was that General Aleksei Alekseevich Brusilov was not going to accept a lack of munitions as an excuse for not conducting offensive operations. While Nicholas II was in title commander in chief of the army, his chief of staff, General Mikhail Vasil'evich Alekseev, was the main force behind all operational decisions, and he was opposed to any further major operations in 1916 because of supply shortages. Being a disciple of orthodox military doctrine, Alekseev believed in the common First World War offensive doctrine that determined that all operations should start with a prolonged artillery bombardment concentrated in one spot in order to cause a major breakthrough such as the Germans accomplished the previous year at Gorlice-Tarnow. Without the heavy artillery and, after appreciating the scope of the army's failure in the Lake Naroch operation, Alekseev was opposed to any operations in 1916 regardless of the urgency of French appeals. General Brusilov, however, being in command of the Southwest Front, realized that the Austrians had transferred large numbers of forces in April and May to aim for what became their summer Italian offensive that commenced in Trentino on May 15. Thus, after the middle of May, the Italians along with the French were making pointed appeals to the Russians and the British for relief in the form of their armies launching some type of operation that would require the Central Powers to divert their resources from Verdun and the Trentino. More importantly, Brusilov believed that the concentration of forces in one spot and then saturating that terrain with a massive artillery bombardment served to alert the enemy of the pending offensive operation. Choosing surprise, and without the endorsement of Stavka (The Russian High Command), Brusilov launched his offensive on June 4th.[51] His plan of invading Galicia with four armies, at least at the beginning, worked in a spectacular fashion. He was able to take back much of the territory lost in Galicia in 1915 and once again threatened to reoccupy Lemberg as Austrian units around Lutsk, Bukovina, and Ocna collapsed prompting widespread retreat along the entire front. While enjoying great initial success, the offensive ran out of steam for three reasons: (1) as General Alexeev foresaw, the army did not have the supply base to provide the munitions Brusilov needed to exploit his initial successes; (2) in addition to material shortages, by the beginning of July, it also became clear to Brusilov that Stavka was not going to provide reinforcements of any type to the ranks that were rapidly becoming depleted due to operational losses; (3) the old problem of commanders in the field refusing to support each other and the High Command not having the ability to change this situation. In this case, Generals Aleksei Evert and Aleksei Nikolaevich Kuropatkin to the north refused to launch diversionary operations

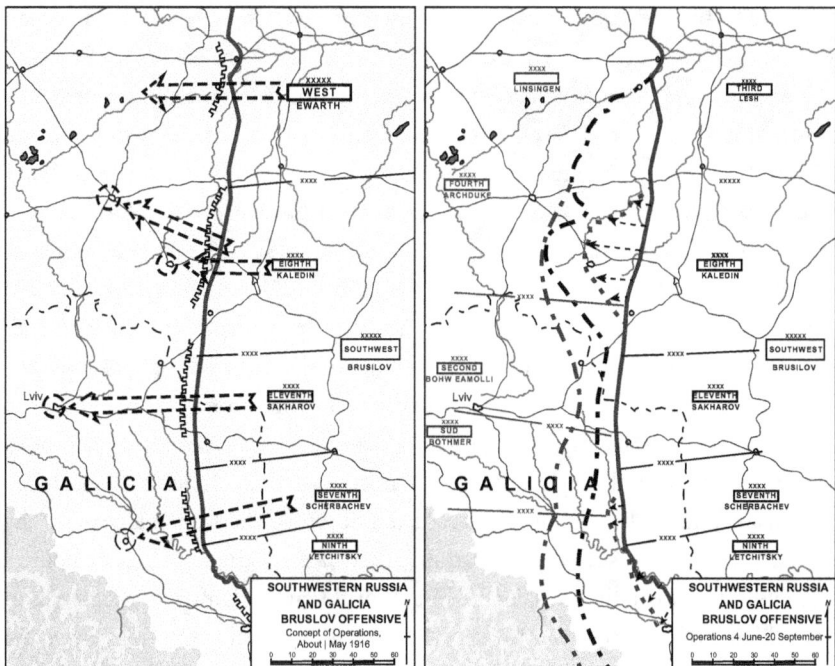

Map 6.5 The Brusilov Offensive.

claiming their armies had not recovered from the battering they received at Lake Naroch. As a result, and as was the case on the Eastern Front, the lack of any other operations gave the Germans a free hand to move forces from the north to the south and in late July a reinforced Austro-Hungarian stemmed the tide and turned back the foe.[52]

The tide of battle had shifted and seemingly once more Brusilov's bold initiative had placed the Russians in the position to decisively defeat Danubian monarchy. Again the Russians did not gain their strategic objectives, thereby failing to provide Nicholas II with a sorely needed military success. Inadequate supplies combined with poor operational leadership doomed General Brusilov's venture to failure. Another retreat out of Galicia marked the conclusion of what turned out to be the last major military operation of the Imperial Army while it was still under the command of its tsar. Nonetheless, the Brusilov offensive did bring relief to the French, arguably saved the Italians from complete collapse, and finally convinced the Romanians to declare war on the Central Powers. But of even greater magnitude, the Austro-Hungarian army never recovered from the losses incurred during the Brusilov offensive, thus rendering their military forces weak, indeed impotent, for the rest of the war.[53]

Perhaps the greatest consequence of the Brusilov offensive was the German demand to unify the Eastern Front command under their leadership to which the Austro-Hungarian emperor Franz Joseph agreed in the months immediately leading up to his December 1916 death.[54] This decision came in time for the Germans to organize a multinational campaign that would sap the military strength of Romania and make it an additional burden on the Russians. On paper, gaining Romania as an ally looked good because of the 600,000+ men in her army. In fact, the Romanian army was poorly trained, badly supplied, and not capable of independent operations.[55] Their declaration of war coincided with the dismissal of Erich von Falkenhyn as chief of the German general staff. He, seeking to restore his reputation, successfully lobbied to command a Central Powers invasion force against Romania once the Brusilov offensive had been contained. Then with an international force consisting of German, Austrian, Bulgarian, and Turkish troops, he invaded and routed the Romanian army. The overwhelming success of this operation served as an example of the capabilities of mobile warfare in the midst of the First World War, a relentless war of attrition for which no end could be found. The operations of the Central Powers in Romania foreshadowed future conflict in that Falkenhyn's leadership provided a model of Blitzkrieg, which the German armed forces had adopted and perfected by the beginning of the Second World War.[56] By the end of the year Romania, save for the province of Moldavia, was completely occupied and the imperial Russian army had another 700 km of front to defend. Of course, more front to defend was the last thing the Russian army needed at the beginning of the 1916–17 winter as it struggled to maintain adequate manpower and supplies across the vast Eastern Front.

1917, the Russian Revolution and the End of the First World War in the East

Ironically, as the 1917 Russian Revolution forced Nicholas II to abdicate in February, the Eastern Front was settling into a static war of attrition as the semblance of a unified trench network, a network comparable to that on the Western Front, was starting to cover the entire length of the front. Some argue that the Russian army was prepared to have its best campaign of the war in 1917 because the question of supplies had largely been resolved, but this assertion is questionable at best. Most importantly it overlooks other salient concerns of which the most prominent was the war-weariness that ultimately compromised the morale of all Russians but especially soldiers. The hardships of the First World War, therefore, resulted in the demonstrations at the end of February 1917 that culminated with the Great Mutiny of February 1917 and the abdication of Nicholas II. Thus, the collapse of the 304-year-old Romanov dynasty was rooted in the family losing the support of the army in the midst of what had become an unpopular war. At first Nicholas II, not surprisingly, did not understand the threat the soldiers' rebellion represented to his regime. After all, soldiers had rebelled against the Romanovs before, and such action had always been contained with troops who remained loyal. No less a commander than General Ivanov of Southwestern Front fame, an officer whose reputation among the soldiers was positive was ordered to launch a countermovement of troops designed to squash the soldiers' rebellion in Petrograd. Ivanov, however, soon learned that revolutionary agitation permeated the landscape, which paralyzed troop movement and, even worse, compromised the effectiveness of organized units as the soldiers succumbed to revolutionary agitation and joined the rebelling masses.[57] In the meantime, moderate politicians led by Duma President Mikhail Rodzianko started to pressure the army's high command to convince the tsar to first accept the creation of a "responsible ministry" to govern Russia through the crisis. But as the revolution deepened, this request switched to a call for the tsar's abdication.

The drama surrounding the abdication of Nicholas II reached its apex on March 1, 1917, when at 6:00 a.m. (Petrograd time) General Alekseev sent a telegram to all front commanders—Grand Duke Nicholai Nikolaevich (Caucasian Front), General Aleksei Ermolaevich Evert (Western Front), General A. A. Brusilov (Southwestern Front), General Vladimir Viktorovich Sakharov (Romanian Front), Admirals Adrian Ivanovich Nepenin and Alexander Vasilyevich Kolchak (Baltic Fleet and the Black Sea Fleet)—informing them of the political situation that had culminated with a request for the tsar's abdication. The critical question Alekseev asked in his message was if the front commanders could guarantee the support of the troops under their command for their tsar. By 2:30 p.m. that afternoon all front commanders had responded, and none had offered the support of the troops under their command for their tsar. Nicholas II, true to his form, had left Stavka at the height of the soldiers' rebellion in an attempt to return to his family in Petrograd and impose his presence in his capital in the hope that he could stabilize the situation. His effort to return to Petrograd, however, failed miserably as revolutionaries took over the railway lines of northwest Russia. Thus, on the morning of March 1, Nicholas II found himself at the headquarters of the Northern Front in the city of Pskov where it fell on the commander of that front, General Nikolai Vladimirovich Ruzskii, to inform the embattled tsar that he had not only a widespread rebellion occurring among his troops but that his top commanders had also lost control of the troops under their command. Even the intensely loyal Alekseev, fearing the complete disintegration of the army in the midst of a world war, advised Nicholas II that abdication appeared to be the best course of action for the future of Russia. Still lost in his own world, Nicholas II's last act as tsar was to break Russian law by abdicating both for himself which was his right and for his son which was not his right. Complaining that he was surrounded by traitors and cowards who had betrayed him, Nicholas II gave up his throne only after it was indisputably clear he had lost the support of both the soldiers and the officers of the Imperial Army.[58] Nicholas II's last act, abdicating for himself and his son, combined with his brother Mikhail Romanov's refusal of the crown, left Russia with no heir to the throne. His final act as tsar effectively killed the autocracy. Russians concerned about their political future scrambled to replace tsarism, and what emerged in the midst of much confusion was the unwieldy system of dual power. Now, two governments emerged with one, the Provisional Government composed mostly of Duma politicians, forming a government designed to represent liberals and conservatives and the other, the Petrograd Soviet of Workers' and Soldiers' Deputies, created by the socialists with the intention of representing Russia's laboring classes. A power struggle of the first magnitude emerged that consumed Russia. Unfortunately, no one on either side understood the scope and the dynamics of the political and military situation in Russia after Nicholas II's abdication.[59]

Simultaneously, as the Imperial Army lost its supreme commander—as Russia lost its tsar and, indeed, tsarism as the source of governance—the army also lost its discipline as command authority collapsed from its highest organizational level (Stavka) down to the lowest unit. At its most basic level, the chain of events that started with Nicholas II's abdication spread across Russia as soldiers decided they were no longer required to follow the orders of officers since their authority was based on their swearing an oath of allegiance to the tsar. The process that culminated in the elimination of imperial command authority while beginning in Pskov received a huge boost when on the same day as Nicholas's abdication the newly formed Petrograd Soviet of Workers' and Soldiers' Deputies issued its mostly misunderstood Order No. 1 to the Petrograd District Garrison. Initially drafted in reaction to a Duma order calling for all soldiers in Petrograd to return to their barracks, Order #1 turned out to be the single document that destroyed the integrity of the tsarist military forces. The Petrograd Soviet first stepped onto the stage of world history by seeking to gain control over the armed forces in Petrograd through a process of democratization. The document called for the election of one representative from each military company to serve as a deputy in this new political organization. It explicitly calls for the maintenance of strict military discipline when soldiers are on duty. But it also notes that soldiers off duty should be granted the rights of ordinary citizens and that above all else soldiers were to be treated with respect especially from their officers. Order #1 did not call for the election of officers nor was it supposed to be in effect throughout the entire army. The intent of the order was to impose some level of control over the soldiers in, and only in, Petrograd. As a result of the tsar's abdication, a political vacuum emerged that was sucking the oxygen out of attempts at legislation or enforcement of rules. Two unintended consequences undermined the intent of Order #1's authors. First, the order spread like an uncontrollable wildfire throughout the army thus necessitating Order #2, which clarified that the intent of Order #1 was to affect the Petrograd garrison alone.[60] Even more devastating, soldiers, encouraged by socialist-revolutionaries, transformed the electoral process into one where they elected both deputies to the Petrograd Soviet and officers to take command of each unit in the army. While not its original intent, Order #1 would, over the course of the revolutionary year, result in the disintegration of the force integrity of the old Imperial Army. Democratizing the army in fact led to the short-lived existence of the Provisional Government's "revolutionary army."

The political chaos in Russia, however, did not lead to an end to the First World War. Naturally, in the aftermath of the fall of the Romanovs, the entire world held its collective breath while waiting to see if the Russians would remain an active belligerent in the global conflict. Likewise, from the moment of Nicholas's abdication, Russia's status as a belligerent became the hot-button issue that consumed much time in the machinations of everyone in Petrograd and throughout the empire. This concern resulted in the last gasp of the old army when it went on the offensive in June 1917—the well-known Kerensky offensive. By this point in the revolutionary year Alexander Kerensky, a prewar lawyer and moderate socialist, had emerged as a compromise politician who for a brief time was an acceptable leader to both the members of the Provisional Government and the Soviet. He emerged as the great communicator who seemingly sold Russia on the idea of using the "revolutionary army" as an offensive weapon that could at once send the message that Russia would not leave the war and, more importantly, build unity among all political elements through fighting for a common cause. But the army that took to the field in June 1917 can only remotely be considered the heir or the legacy of Russia's long and proud military tradition. The army did launch a well-planned operation on June 16th along a 65-km section of the Southwestern Front. For two days the Russians bombarded the Central Powers trenches with over 1300 guns, their largest barrage of the war. While the offensive was expected because of the agitation and troop buildup, the artillery barrage caught everyone off guard. It provides evidence that the supply situation in Russia was the best it had been at any time throughout the war. Two days later, on June 18th over a hundred and seventy thousand troops crossed no-man's land in an effort for the Russian 11th and 7th Armies to break through and reoccupy Lemburg. At the same time the Russian 8th Army was to provide flanking coverage to the north in an effort to pin down the remaining Austrian forces in Galicia.

After two days of forward progress, the "revolutionary army" crumbled against the force of a well-orchestrated German counteroffensive. While the officers of the old army maintained force integrity going into operations, the effectiveness of the Russian soldiers on the battlefield withered in the face of revolutionary agitation that questioned why men were still being ordered to their deaths after the collapse of tsarism. The June offensive, therefore, failed on every level beginning with achieving the operational objective of finally conquering Galicia and ending with a complete failure to build support for the Provisional Government. aimed at keeping Russia in the war. Internationally the failure made it clear to all observers that Russia no longer had an effective military establishment capable of defending the realm from the Central Power enemy. Domestically, Kerensky's aim of translating success on the battlefield to consolidating his own power through the construction of a unified government also failed.[61] For the time being, Dual Power, which progressively became unmanageable as a political system capable of developing consensus on anything, remained in place. In its aftermath the outcome of this military misadventure was to infuse the socialists with future strength and started Russia down the road toward what culminated with the Bolshevik seizure of power.[62]

After the June offensive, as left-wing politics strengthened its hold on the course of the revolution, the military situation, not surprisingly, continued to weaken. After June, the Germans seized the initiative and refocused operations on the Eastern Front from Galicia to the Baltic. The military situation became alarming for the Russians after the complete failure of the army to defend the port of Riga in the middle of August. Here the Russians knew the Germans were planning an attack as they sought to gain control over the entrance to the Gulf of Finland. Petrograd was directly threatened after German armed forces became ensconced in Riga on both land and sea. The failure of the Russian

The First World War and the End of Tsarism, 1905–17

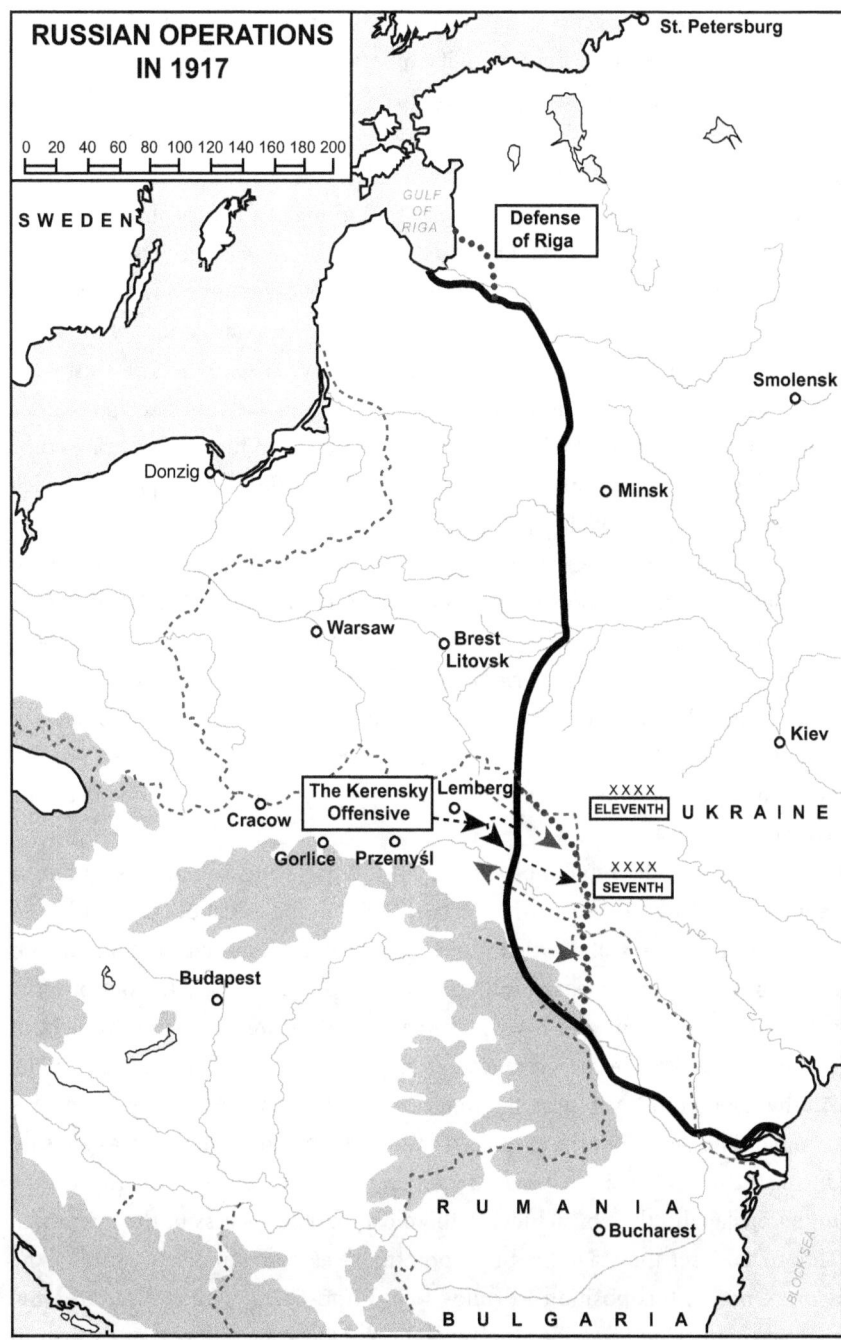

Map 6.6 The June Offensive and the Defense of Riga, 1917.

army to achieve any success in fighting offensive or defensive operations in 1917 served as a prelude to the final act of its imperial existence. As the revolutionary situation deepened, the army suffered from challenges on every level—from defending the empire against a very hostile Germany to keeping soldiers in its ranks—also had a crisis of leadership.[63] After the tsar's abdication and, especially after Order #1, every officer in the army had to make a choice about where to cast his lot in a future Russia. Of course, the situation was very confusing and affected its ranks starting at the very top of its force structure. With its political leadership in question, the chief of staff had become the commander of the army, which meant at the beginning of the revolution M. V. Alekseev was in command. His insistence on maintaining discipline throughout the ranks so that Russia would have an army to confront its enemies resulted in his being dismissed by the Provisional Government right before the June offensive. Hoping to repeat past success A. A. Brusilov became overall commander of the army, but his failure to deliver in June resulted in the rise of Lavr Georgievich Kornilov to commander in chief of the Russian armed forces. In the wake of the defeat at Riga, everybody—especially Kerensky—became alarmed about the military situation. There was little to stop the Germans marching from Riga to St. Petersburg and putting an end to the Provisional Government, the Soviet, indeed the revolution itself. Confronted with an extreme military threat, Kerensky turned to Kornilov, his commander in chief, in search of his support to preserve Russia's fledgling democracy.

Kornilov had the reputation of being a fighting general despite spending a year of captivity as an Austro-Hungarian POW in the midst of the First World War. After the tsar's abdication the Provisional Government appointed him commander of the Petrograd military district, but he quickly fell out of favor with the Soviet because of his determination to restore discipline throughout the army's ranks. He was removed from the capital and transferred to the Southwestern Front when he became commander of the 8th army. From this command he developed a rapport with his soldiers and officers and, as a result, during the June offensive forces under his command overran the Austrians in the initial onslaught, thereby achieving the most notable success of the operation. This success set the stage for his appointment as commander in chief of the army. Once in this position Kornilov found himself in command of an army that was withering away into the revolution's landscape. He remained firm in his belief, as did most officers of the army, that disciple had to be restored to the ranks, which meant imposing military law starting with the restoration of the death penalty for soldiers who deserted from the ranks while on active duty.

Meanwhile moderates and conservatives turned to him seeking his support for some type of undefined action that would contain the growing power of the left-wing socialists. Any tsarist-era general would have been ill-prepared to become an active participant in the chaotic political situation that had engulfed the empire. For military leaders the events of 1917 proved overwhelming. The failure of the June offensive and the collapse of the defense of Riga provided ample evidence that the military was rapidly becoming a nonfactor in the fate of Russia—a situation that had not been the case since the Mongols overran Rus in the thirteenth century.

Military failure combined with the chaos of revolutionary politics was the main cause for Kornilov to revolt. The revolt itself, however, constituted a confusing series of events that occurred at the end of August/beginning of September 1917. Intrigue and conspiracy surround the history of this event, which further complicates the efforts of historians to sort out its details. The chain of events that caused the revolt to occur began sometime after the military defeat at Riga. In the midst of a crisis atmosphere prompted because of concerns about the security of St. Petersburg, Kerensky dispatched his deputy war minister Boris Viktorovish Savinkov to Stavka to initiate discussion with Kornilov about forming a unified government that would replace the unwieldy dual power political system. It remains unclear if Kornilov ever envisioned himself as the "White Knight" on horseback who would be the military leader to seize control of the revolution by declaring martial law. Nor is it any clearer what Kerensky wanted or intended when he entered into negotiations with the general in the days leading up to the event. Further complicating understanding of the revolt were the activities of one self-appointed operative, the Ober-Prosecutor of the Holy Synod (the civilian leader of the Orthodox Church), Vladimir Nikolaevich Lvov who claimed he had the support of various conservative groups. What is clear is that Kornilov, after V. N. Lvov convinced him that Kerensky wanted the general to take command of the capital, ordered troops loyal to himself (Kornilov) to march on Petrograd on the night of August 27th. Kerensky, on the other hand, thanks to the intervention of the same V. N. Lvov, came to believe that Kornilov's intent was to oust the provisional government by a coup d'etat to establish martial law. Fearing Kornilov intended to establish a military dictatorship, Kerensky raised the alarm, which served to mobilize the Petrograd Soviet. As a result, the provisional government found itself in the awkward position of rearming the Red Guard, and this act combined with the support of the railway workers who were loyal to the Soviet prevented Kornilov's troops from reaching the capital. Subsequently, the Kornilov Revolt was an abysmal failure. All tsarist era officers became counterrevolutionary suspects and, with its authority and ability to lead now completely compromised, the Imperial Army disintegrated into the ash heap of history. In its aftermath, Kornilov and most every other tsarist general who had indicated any level of support for his efforts and who were in Petrograd and its environs were arrested and incarcerated in the Bykhov Fortress from where they would all escape shortly after the Bolsheviks seized power.[64]

Because of its enormous size, unlike on the Western Front, warfare of the Eastern Front featured mobility. But, the size of the front also proved to be the facet of Eastern Front operations that limited the effectiveness of every major military operation. To put it another way, be it the German breakthrough in 1915 or the Brusilov offensive in 1916, hugely successful mobile operations ultimately failed to achieve their strategic objectives because each respective army ran out of the men and materials needed to continue the offensive until their enemy was completely defeated. Complicating and always contributing to material shortages was the never-ending commitment to operations on different fronts, in some cases not even remotely connected to each other. Each belligerent suffered from this fact—the Austrians by 1916 were waging a war against the Italians in the Alps while fighting the Russians in Galicia. The Germans always had to consider the Western Front before doing anything in the East. And, while always considered a secondary front, the Russians fought the last conflict with the Ottoman Empire during the course of the First World War. Often primary strategic objectives became secondary concerns because of threats to each empire that became immediate dangers that had to be addressed. Hence while saving the Austro-Hungarians from the threat of the Brusilov offensive, the Germans also were engaged in heavy combat both at Verdun and on the Somme. Or, as the Austro-Hungarians withered on the Galician Front, they also had to pay attention to Italian operations in the Alps. All belligerents also struggled with command issues both within their central commands as they sought to determine where to apply resources (Eastern or Western Front or somewhere else) and especially at the operational level where army and unit commanders often did not support each other when engaged in battle, which was the usual case for the Russians. Ultimately, neither side prevailed on the Eastern Front due to its vastness. In the end, material shortages for all belligerents, the German need to concentrate all resources on the Western Front and ultimately the course of the Russian Revolution caused the First World War to end on the Eastern Front.

Epilogue

This book does not have a conclusion! It merits an epilogue instead of a conclusion because imperial Russian military history did not end after the 1917 Revolution. Conflict persisted in the East after Russia's soldiers mutinied in Petrograd at the end of February 1917 when ordered to break up a citywide strike that started as a protest over the price of food. Nicholas II's decision to abdicate came only after he realized that he no longer had the support of his soldiers and his officers. Then, as the spring unfolded, soldiers from across the empire voted with their feet and stopped fighting and started discussing the future of Russia through their newly organized soldiers' committees. The old army was not quite done though as soldiers agreed to fight the Central Powers when they launched their June Offensive and they endured the collapse of the defenses at Riga in August 1917. As a result of these two campaigns, by the fall of 1917 the army had lost its will to fight for the empire. War weariness and the politics of the day had confused soldiers, which combined with the collapse of the authority of officers spelled the end of the old army. Revolutionary events, therefore, undermined the military effectiveness of Russia's armed forces in 1917, which caused a brief hiatus in the Russian's pursuit of empire. But the vision of Empire remained …

In the immediate aftermath of the Bolshevik seizure of power, the imperial army provided the last gasps of tsarism. Its commander in chief General Nikolai Nikolaevich Dukhonin refused to accept Lenin's Decree on Peace. The Bolsheviks were not going to stand for such disobedience. After all, the Bolsheviks had spent 1917 agitating directly at soldiers in what proved a successful effort to undermine command authority and allowed the February mutiny in Petrograd to spread throughout the empire and persisted until the support of soldiers propelled them, the Bolsheviks, into power. According to the decree, Dukhonin was supposed to contact the Central Powers with the offer of an armistice. When he refused to do so and, after a brief period of indecision, V. I. Lenin appointed

Nikolai Vasilovich Krylenko as the People's Commissar of War on November 7, 1917. He was ordered to go to Mogilev to take over command of the army.[1] Upon his appointment as commander in chief, instead of going directly to Stavka to relieve Dukhonin, Krylenko spent two weeks touring the frontline where he agitated among soldiers' committees to build up his base of support. After that he contacted the Germans on November 13th. His point of contact, General Max Hoffman, the de facto commander in chief of the German forces on the Eastern Front, on the next day agreed to an immediate armistice and requested that the Russian government send a peace delegation to his headquarters at Brest-Litovsk. This paved the way for Krylenko to make his way to Stavka where he arrived on November 19th. Upon his arrival he discovered a headquarter's garrison in a state of chaos for which the Bolshevik regime would pay a high price because while the question of who was in command was unanswered Generals Kornilov and Denikin, soon to be the backbone of the civil war opposition to the Bolsheviks, escaped from the Bykhov fortress where they, along with several other officers, had been imprisoned since Kronilov Revolt of late August–early September. Dukhonin was held responsible for their escape and he would be assassinated shortly after Krylenko took command of the army. Nonetheless, the damage was done in that the escape of Kornilov and Denikin provided the forces opposed to the Bolsheviks with the military leaders they needed to fight a civil war.[2]

Even though Dukhonin's assassination marked the death of the tsarist command structure, the Russian military did not disappear from history. What followed has been best described as the continuum of crisis—a crisis whose origins are rooted at least to the early period of Nicholas II's reign and would continue well into the 1920s.[3] The Treaty of Brest-Litovsk of March 1918, the first World War I peace treaty between great power belligerents, exhibited a harbinger of things to come—that peacemaking after the First World War would not be peacemaking at all. Instead, by the autumn of 1918 the Great Powers had exhausted all of their resources—supplies of weapons and munitions were too low to sustain operations and, more importantly, they had run out of men they could recruit into their armies. At the front soldiers in all armies were either suffering from a total collapse of morale or were outright rebelling over inept military leadership that caused endless casualties while civilians found their losses of loved ones combined with wartime material shortages to be unacceptable on all levels. The war of attrition had reached its end. Instead of creating a peacemaking process where everyone met and resolved differences, the assorted First World War treaties all turned out to be punitive. As a result, none of the strategic goals of all of the great powers were met, which set the stage for an uneasy peace that would culminate in a Second World War twenty years later. This "peace" process started at Brest-Litovsk where the Germans were the first to impose draconian terms on their enemies. Because the Bolsheviks had already made it clear that they were not going to honor tsarist wartime debts, the Germans gave up on the idea of assessing reparations to the Russians. Instead they tried to seize control of Russia's western borderlands and create an economic zone that would be entirely controlled by the German Empire. The Brest-Litovsk treaty in fact proved to be the height of folly as the Germans, in desperate need of manpower on the western front, had to keep forces throughout Russia's borderlands to maintain a level of security so that the resources of the region, especially the grain of western Ukraine, could be exploited for the purposes of feeding the people of Central Europe. Once the German forces evacuated the region after signing the armistice with the Entente on November 11, 1918, all sense of peace and security throughout the borderlands between Central Europe and Russia disintegrated.

Conflict in the borderlands between Central Europe and the old Russian Empire did not end when the Germans agreed to an armistice with the French and British in November 1918. Instead, what ensued was a brutal civil war arguably more violent, at least in the way it affected noncombatants, than the World War that occurred in the region between 1914 and 1917. The outbreak of the Civil War in the spring of 1918 consumed the former tsarist empire until 1921 and further defined Peter Holquist's continuum of crisis throughout the early twentieth century. On the heels of their victory over a vast but not well-unified White Army, the Red Army invaded Poland in the summer of 1920 in an effort to spread the idea of their socialist revolution into Central and Western Europe. The failure of that invasion resulted in the March 1921 Treaty of Riga, which ended formal fighting in the borderlands for the first time since 1914. Regardless of the death and destruction of the First World War and the ensuing political chaos replete with unimaginable violence, in the spring 1921 the Russian Empire still existed. What happened next was the new regime, soon to renamed The Union of the Soviet Socialist Republics (USSR), consolidated its authority and control over all of the former lands of the Romanovs ... a formidable task for a group of left-wing revolutionaries who had no practical experience in governing any territory or national groups before 1917. To be sure, one of the tasks they needed to accomplish was to build a military force that represented and served the leadership as well as all of society in post–First World War Russia. Arguably as socialists they were better prepared for such a task than the members of the old tsarist society that had become bitterly divided along class lines especially by the beginning of the twentieth century. The creation of a Red Army in the midst of the Civil War transformed Russia's armed forces from being composed of peasant soldiers serving their tsar to soviet citizens serving their country. This reformulation of the status of soldiers in Russia completed the reforms of D. A. Miliutin, although to be sure not exactly as he envisioned them in the 1860s–1870s. This new Russian army, however, still had the same task as its predecessors … defending Russia from its host of enemies while maintaining control over the Eurasian landmass.

The task was gigantic to be sure! Every Russian military leader who survived the First World War had to make a choice about which side they would serve during the Civil War. Here, patriotism or loyalty to Russia played a far stronger role in the choices people made as opposed to social status during the reign of the Romanovs. After all, General Brusilov who emerged as an early Red Army commander and who remained in the Soviet Union until his death in 1926 was a graduate of the Corps of Pages or the most elite school in tsarist Russia only available to her highest aristocrats. While General Denikin was famously the son of a serf-soldier who graduated from the General Staff Academy and would devote his energies to the White cause until he was forced into exile. Indeed, many members of the Red Army high command until the purges of the late 1930s were graduates of the tsarist military academies. Officers such as Svechin, Zaionchkovski, and Shaposhnikov served the Red Army during the early Soviet period and contributed to restoration of the effectiveness of Russian armed forces at both a doctrinal and operational level. Along with many others, their work provided the Soviet Union with the operational doctrine that the Red Army used as it fought its way to Berlin in the spring of 1945. The Red Army's success in the Second World War subsequently provided the foundation for what became a source of political and military power that resulted in the emergence of a postwar Soviet/Russian Empire that dominated Eurasia and fulfilled the wildest expectations of every vision Peter the Great had of the empire. Although the strength of the empire wavered as Russia tumbled through the collapse of soviet power, at this time (summer 2022) we have every reason to expect that Vladimir Putin will continue his wars in pursuit of his efforts to restore the Russian Empire to its former status.

Notes

Introduction

1. Many works have been written in the recent past on the Russian Empire. Of these some that reward reading are as follows: Kees Boterbloem, *A History of the Russian and Its Empire from Mikhail Romanov to Vladimir Putin* (Boulder: Rowman and Littlefield, 2013); Jane Burbank, Mark von Hagen, and Anatolyi Remnev, eds. *Russian Empire Space, People, Power, 1700–1930* (Bloomington: Indiana University Press, 2007); Janet M. Hartley, *A Social History of the Russian Empire 1650–1825* (London: Longman, 1999); Andreas Kappeler, *The Russian Empire* (Harlow: Pearson Longman, 2001); Valeria A. Kivelson and Ronald Grigor Suny, *Russia's Empire* (New York: Oxford University Press, 2017); Nancy Shields Kollmann, *The Russian Empire, 1450–1801* (Oxford, UK: Oxford University Press, 2017); Dominic Leiven, *Empire. The Russian Empire and its Rivals* (New Haven: Yale University Press, 2000).
2. Carol B. Stevens, *Russia's Wars of Emergence 1460–1730* (Harlow: Pearson Longman, 2007).
3. David R. Stone, *A Military History of Russia From Ivan the Terrible to the War in Chechnya* (Westport, CT: Praeger Security International, 2006).
4. John LeDonne, *The Grand Strategy of the Russian Empire, 1650–1831* (Oxford, UK: Oxford University Press, 2004); John LeDonne, *The Russian Empire and the World 1700–1917. The Geopolitics of Expansion and Containment* (Oxford, UK: Oxford University Press, 1997).
5. The literature of the military revolution in Early Modern European history is vast. The classic place to start reading this material is Geoffrey Parker, *The Military Revolution: Military Innovation and the Rise of the West, 1500–1800* (Cambridge, UK: Cambridge University Press, 1988). For a study that focuses on Russia, see Michael C. Paul, "The Military Revolution in Russia, 1550–1682," *Journal of Military History*, 68:1 (January 2004), 9–45.
6. Brian Davies, *Empire and Military Revolution in Eastern Europe. Russia's Turkish Wars in the Eighteenth Century* (London: Bloomsbury, 2011).

Chapter 1

1. Paul Bushkovitch, *Peter the Great. The Struggle for Power, 1671–1725* (New York: Cambridge University Press, 2001), 12–170 and Lindsey Hughes, *Russian in the Age of Peter the Great* (New Haven: Yale University Press, 1998), 92–131 and 159–202.
2. Paul, 9–45. On the military revolution in general, see Parker.
3. Richard Hellie, *Enserfment and Military Change in Muscovy* (Chicago: University of Chicago Press, 1971).
4. Davies, 57.
5. Alexander Filjushkin, *Ivan the Terrible. A Military History* (London: Frontline Books, 2011), 19–57.
6. Robert I. Frost, *The Northern Wars 1558–1721. War, State and Society in Northeastern Europe, 1558–1721* (Harlow: Longman, 2000), 234.
7. Ibid., 236.
8. Ibid.
9. Ibid., 234.
10. Paul, 24.
11. Richard Hellie, "The Petrine Army: Continuity, Change, and Impact," *Canadian-American Slavic Studies*, VIII:2 (Summer 1974), 248.
12. Vasili Klyuchevsky, *Peter the Great* (New York: Vintage Books, 1958), 45; William C. Fuller, *Strategy and Power in Russia 1600–1914* (New York: The Free Press, 1992), 37–9.
13. For Peter the Great's legacy, see Nicholas Riasanovsky, *The Image of Peter the Great in Russian History and Thought* (New York: Oxford University Press, 1985).
14. Christopher Duffy, *Russia's Military Way to the West: The Origins and Nature of Russian Military Power 1700–1800* (London: Routledge & Kegan Paul, 1981), 10.
15. Duffy, 10; Hughes, 16–17.
16. See Brian L. Davies, *Warfare, State and Society on the Black Sea Steppe, 1500–1700* (London: Routledge, 2007), 185–7.
17. Ibid., 188–207.
18. Frost, *The Northern Wars*.
19. Davies, *Empire*, 54.
20. Frost, 3–4.
21. Ibid., 201.
22. Ibid., 222.
23. Ibid., 212
24. Ibid., 230.
25. Duffy, 17–19; Fuller, *Strategy and Power in Russia*, 67–8.
26. Duffy, 17–19.

27 Ibid., 17.
28 Ibid., 17–19.
29 Davies, *Empire*, 77–8.
30 Fuller, *Strategy and Power in Russia*, 71
31 Lindsey Hughes, "Catherine I of Russia, Consort to Peter the Great," in *Queenship in Europe 1660–1815: The Role of the Consort*, ed. Clarissa Campbell Orr (New York: Cambridge University Press, 2004), 131–54.
32 Davies, *Empire*, 85.
33 Ibid., 79.
34 Ibid., 85.
35 Hughes, 29–31.
36 Hughes, 38–9.
37 Davies, *Empire*, 104.
38 Zenon E. Kohut, "Mazepa's Ukraine: Understanding Cossack Territorial Vistas," in *Poltava 1709. The Battle and the Myth*, ed. Serhii Plokhy (Boston: Harvard University Press, 2012), 22–9.
39 Volodymyr Kovalenko, "The Rape of Baturyn: The Archaeological Evidence," in *Poltava 1709. The Battle and the Myth*, ed. Serhii Plokhy (Boston: Harvard University Press, 2012).
40 Frost, 230; Davies, *Empire*, 87–94.
41 Davies, *Empire*, 88–91.
42 Duffy, 24
43 Frost, 231.
44 Duffy, 26.
45 Davies, *Empire*, 79–80.
46 Duffy, 24.
47 John LeDonne, "Poltava and the Geopolitics of Western Eurasia," in *Poltava 1709. The Battle and the Myth*, ed. Serhii Plokhy (Boston: Harvard University Press, 2012), 177–95.
48 Davies, 102.
49 Duffy, 27.
50 Hughes, 56–7.
51 Stevens, 268.
52 Dmitrii I. Oleinikov, "The Caucasus Factor in Russian Military Reform," in *Reforming the Tsar's Army. Military Innovation in Imperial Russia from Peter the Great to the Revolution*, ed. David Schimmelpenninck van der Oye and Bruce W. Menning (Washington, DC: Woodrow Wilson Center Press, 2004), 205–14.
53 Jacob W. Kipp, "The Imperial Russian Navy, 1696–1900," in *The Military History of Tsarist Russia*, ed. Frederick W. Kagan and Robin Higham (New York: Palgrave, 2002), 155–6.

54 Stevens, 229.
55 The grand embassy was Peter the Great's "fact-finding" 1697–8 tour of Western Europe. See Lindsey Hughes, *Russia in the Age of Peter the Great* (New Haven: Yale University Press, 1998), 12–27.
56 John L. H. Keep, *Soldiers of the Tsar. Army and Society in Russia 1462–1874* (Oxford: Clarendon Press, 1985), 104.
57 Davies, *Empire*, 63.
58 Ibid., 66.
59 Duffy, 17–19.
60 Evgenii V. Anisimov, *The Reforms of Peter the Great: Progress through Coercion in Russia* (Armonk, NY: M.E. Sharpe, 1993), 64.
61 Fuller, *Strategy and Power in Russia*, 69.
62 Evgenii V. Anisimov, "The Imperial Heritage of Peter the Great in the Foreign Policy of his Early Successors," in *Imperial Russian Foreign Policy*, ed. Hugh Ragsdale (New York: Cambridge University Press, 1993), 25; Frost, 294–6.
63 V. O. Kliuchevskii, *Peter the Great* (New York: Vintage Books, 1958), 57–8.
64 Hughes, 445–7.
65 Anisimov, 4.
66 Hartley, *A Social History of the Russian Empire*, 65.
67 Keep, *Soldiers of the Tsar*, 106–7; Frost, 240–1.
68 Hughes, 100–5.
69 Keep, *Soldiers of the Tsar*, 123–9.
70 Hartley, *A Social History of the Russian Empire*, 53–4.
71 Ibid., 126.
72 Frost, 238–9.
73 Paul Bushkovitch, "The Politics of Command in the Army of Peter the Great," in *Reforming the Tsar's Army. Military Innovation in Imperial Russia from Peter the Great to the Revolution*, ed. David Schimmelpenninck van der Oye and Bruce W. Menning (Washington, DC: Woodrow Wilson Center Press, 2004), 253–73.
74 See Chapter 3 of this book for an examination of the Decembrist revolt, pp. 133–5.
75 Davies, *Empire*, 80–1.
76 Davies, *Empire*, 84.
77 Frost, 239; Hellie, 250.
78 Ibid., 244.
79 Arcadius Kahan, *The Plow, the Hammer and the Knout. An Economic History of Eighteenth-Century Russia* (Chicago: University of Chicago Press, 1985), 81–99.
80 M. E. Falkus, *The Industrialization of Russia, 1700–1914* (London: Macmillan Press, 1972), 21.
81 Hartley, *A Social History of the Russian Empire*, 156.
82 Hartley, *A Social History of the Russian Empire*, 61–4.
83 Davies, *Empire*, 82.

Chapter 2

1. Aleksandr B. Kamenskii, *The Russian Empire in the Eighteenth Century. Searching for a Place in the World*. Translated and edited by David Griffiths (Armonk, NY: N.E. Sharpe, 1997), 122.
2. Keep, *Soldiers of the Tsar*, 137.
3. In addition to Keep, other important sources on eighteenth-century Russian military and diplomatic history include Davis; Brian L. Davies, *The Russo-Turkish War, 1768-1774. Catherine II and the Ottoman Empire* (London: Bloomsbury, 2016); Christopher Duffy, *Russia's Military War to the West: Origins and Nature of Russian Military Power 1700-1800* (London: Routledge & Kegan Paul, 1981); Fuller, *Strategy and Power in Russia*; Bruce Menning, "The Imperial Russian Army, 1725-1796," in *The Military History of Tsarist Russia*, ed. Frederick W. Kagan and Robin Higham (New York: Palgrave, 2002), 47-77; and Bruce Menning, "Paul I and Catherine II's Military Legacy, 1762-1801," in *The Military History of Tsarist Russia*, ed. Frederick W. Kagan and Robin Higham (New York: Palgrave, 2002), 78-107.
4. Kamenskii, 132-40.
5. Evgenii Viktorovich Anisimov, "Empress Anna Ivanovna," in *The Emperors and Empresses of Russia. Rediscovering the Romanovs*, ed. Donald J. Raleigh (Armonk, NY: M.E. Sharpe, 1996), 37.
6. Davies, *Empires*, 148-52.
7. Kamanskii, 138-43.
8. Menning, "Imperial Russian Army," 47.
9. John W. Steinberg, "D.A. Miliutin's Impact on the Education of Russian Military Officers," in *The Making of Russian History. Society, Culture & the Politics of Modern Russia*, ed. John W. Steinberg and Rex Wade (Bloomington, IN: Slavica, 2009), 24-9.
10. Duffy, 42-9.
11. Menning, "Imperial Russian Army," 48-9.
12. Fuller, *Strategy and Power in Russia*, 153-5.
13. Menning, "Imperial Russian Army," 50-3.
14. Ibid., 55-6.
15. Davies, *Empire*, 180.
16. Duffy, 53-5.
17. Menning, "Imperial Russian Army," 56-7.
18. Viktor Petrovich Naumov, "Empress Elizabeth I, 1741-1762," in *The Emperors and Empresses of Russia. Rediscovering the Romanovs*, ed. Donald J. Raleigh (Armonk, NY: M.E. Sharpe, 1996), 72-4.
19. Menning, "Imperial Russian Army," 57-8.
20. Davies, *Empire*, 150-2.

21 William H. McNeill, *The Pursuit of Power* (Chicago: University of Chicago Press, 1982), 117–44.
22 Menning, "Imperial Russian Army," 52–3.
23 Christopher Duffy, *Frederick the Great: A Military Life* (London: Routledge & Kegan Paul, 1985), 81–101.
24 Menning, "Imperial Russian Army," 58–9.
25 Ibid., 60.
26 Ibid.
27 Aleksandr Sergeevich Mylnikov, "Peter III, 1762," in *The Emperors and Empresses of Russia. Rediscovering the Romanovs*, ed. Donald J. Raleigh (Armonk, NY: M.E. Sharpe, 1996), 110–13.
28 Duffy, 122–4.
29 Fuller, *Strategy and Power in Russia*, 120–41.
30 Marc Raeff, "The Domestic Policies of Peter III and His Overthrow," *American Historical Review*, 75:5 (1970): 1289–310.
31 Duffy, 166–8.
32 Carol S. Leonard, *Reform and Regicide: The Reign of Peter III of Russia* (Bloomington: Indiana University Press, 1993).
33 Mylnikov, 102–33.
34 On the life and reign of Catherine the Great, see John. T. Alexander, *Catherine the Great Life and Reign* (New York: Oxford University Press, 1989); Simon Dixson, *Catherine the Great* (London: Longman, 2001); Alexander Borisovich Kamenskii, "Empress Catherine II, 1762–1796," in *The Emperors and Empresses of Russia. Rediscovering the Romanovs*, ed. Donald J. Raleigh (Armonk, NY: M.E. Sharpe, 1996), 134–76; Isabel de Madariaga, *Russian in the Age of Catherine the Great* (New Haven, CT: Yale University Press, 1981).
35 Menning, "Imperial Russian Army," 64–74.
36 David Ransel, *The Politics of Catherinian Russia. The Panin Party* (New Haven, CT: Yale University Press, 1975), 62–80.
37 Davies, *Russo-Turkish War*, 4.
38 Norman Davies, *God's Playground: A History of Poland*, Vol. 1 (New York: Columbia University Press, 1982), 511–25.
39 Davies, *Russo-Turkish War*, 7.
40 Davies, *God's Playground*, 345–8.
41 Davies, *Russo-Turkish War*, 8.
42 Ibid., 10–14.
43 Ibid., 48–50.
44 Ibid., 17–21.
45 Ibid., 162–3.
46 Ibid., 28, 41.

47 Menning, "Military Legacy," 89.
48 Ibid., 90–1.
49 David Woodward, *The Russians at Sea. A History of the Russian Navy* (New York: Frederick A. Praeger, 1966), 42–57.
50 Duffy, 173.
51 Menning, "Military Legacy," 91.
52 See Marc Raeff, "Pugachev's Rebellion," *Preconditions of Revolution in Early Modern Europe*, ed. Robert Forster and Jack P. Greene (Baltimore: Johns Hopkins Press, 1970), 161–203.
53 John T. Alexander, *Emperor of the Cossacks: Pugachev and the Frontier Jacquerie of 1773-1775* (Lawrence, KS: Coronado Press, 1974).
54 Duffy, 157–64.
55 Menning, "Military Legacy," 93.
56 See Sebag Montefiore, *Prince of Princes: The Life of Potemkin* (New York: Thomas Dunne Books, 2000).
57 Menning, "Military Legacy," 94.
58 Ibid., 94–5.
59 Duffy, 189.
60 Menning, "Military Legacy," 96–7.
61 Duffy, 195–6; Davies, *Russo-Turkish War*, 241–2.
62 Walter Pintner, "Russian Military Thought: The Western Model and the Shadow of Suvorov," *Makers of Modern Strategy from Machiavelli to the Nuclear Age*, ed. Peter Paret (Princeton: Princeton University Press, 1986), 354–75.
63 Bruce Menning, "Train Hard, Fight Easy: The Legacy of A.V. Suvorov and His Art of Victory," *Air University Review*, 38:1 (November–December 1986), 80.
64 Still the best biography of Suvorov is Phillip Longworth, *The Art of Victory* (New York: Holt, Rinehard, and Winston, 1965).
65 Duffy, 189–95.
66 Menning, "Train Hard, Fight Easy," 83.

Chapter 3

1 Alexander Bitis, *Russia and the Eastern Question. Army, Government and Society 1815-1833* (Oxford: Oxford University Press, 2006), 15–30.
2 Iurii Alekseevich Sorokin, "Emperor Paul I, 1796–1801," in *The Emperors and Empresses of Russia. Rediscovering the Romanovs*, ed. Donald J. Raleigh (Armonk, NY: M.E. Sharpe, 1996), 177–80; Hugh Ragsdale, "The Mental Condition of Paul," *Paul I: A Reassessment of his Life and Reign*, ed. Hugh Ragsdale (Pittsburgh: University Center for International Studies, University of Pittsburgh, 1979), 17–30.

3 David L. Ransel, "An Ambivalent Legacy: The Education of Grand Duke Paul," in *Paul I: A Reassessment of his Life and Reign*, ed. Hugh Ragsdale (Pittsburgh: University Center for International Studies, University of Pittsburgh, 1979), 1–16.
4 Janet Hartley, "The Russian Army," *European Armies of the French Revolution, 1789–1802*, ed. Frederick C. Schneid (Norman: University of Oklahoma Press, 2015), 91.
5 Menning, "Military Legacy," 82; Duffy, 200–8.
6 Hartley, "The Russian Army," 95.
7 See Chapter 4 for more discussion on this.
8 Menning, "Military Legacy," 83.
9 John L. H. Keep, "Paul I and the Militarization of Government," *Paul I: A Reassessment of His Life and Reign*, ed. Hugh Ragsdale (Pittsburgh: University Center for International Studies, University of Pittsburgh, 1979), 91–102.
10 L. G. Beskrovnyi, *Russkaia armiia i flot v XVIII veke (ocherki)* (Moscow: Voennoe izdatel'stvo, 1958), 324. Menning also comes to this conclusion (Menning, "Paul I," 78).
11 Menning, "Military Legacy," 84.
12 Ibid., 84.
13 Hartley, "The Russian Army," 96.
14 John W. Steinberg, "Imperial War Games (1898–1906): Symbolic Displays of Power or Practical Training," *The Military and Society in Russia 1450–1917*, ed. Eric Lohr and Marshall Poe (Leiden: Brill Academic Press, 2002), 253–4.
15 The system of recruitment was irregular at best. Throughout the eighteenth century it changed according to the immediate needs of the moment. Most if not all of what we know ultimately comes from Beskrovnyi, 297. His numbers for the period of the second coalition are 3 men out of 500 in 1797; 1 in 500 in 1798; 1 in 350 in 1799.
16 Hartley, "The Russian Army," 91.
17 Bruce Menning, "Russian Military Innovations in the Second Half of the Eighteenth Century," *War and Society* 2 (1984), 23–41.
18 Norman E. Saul, *Russia and the Mediterranean 1797–1807* (Chicago: University of Chicago Press, 1970), 154.
19 Paul W. Schroeder, *The Transformation of European Politics* (Oxford: Oxford at the Clarendon Press, 1994), 177–210.
20 Fuller, *Strategy and Power in Russia*, 180–1.
21 Menning, "Military Legacy," 99.
22 Saul, 86–114.
23 Menning, "Military Legacy," 100.
24 Ibid., 100–2.
25 Ibid., 103.
26 Hartley, "The Russian Army," 100–1.
27 Ibid., 94.

28 Ibid., 95.
29 In addition to being in the collection edited by Hugh Ragsdale, John Keep's article on Paul I was also published as "Paul I and the Militarization of Government," *Canadian-American Slavic Studies* 7:1 (1973), 1–14.
30 When it appeared that he was assembling a force of 20,000 Cossacks to invade India to counter the British threat, a small group of officers formed a conspiracy and deposed and assassinated Paul I. See Menning, "Military Legacy," 86.
31 Menning, "Military Legacy," 85.
32 Hartley, "The Russian Army," 92–3.
33 James J. Kenney, Jr., "The Politics of Assassination," *Paul I: A Reassessment of His Life and Reign*, ed. Hugh Ragsdale (Pittsburgh: University Center for International Studies, University of Pittsburgh, 1979), 125–46.
34 This section of this study is largely dependent on three studies: David Chandler, *The Campaigns of Napoleon. The Mind and Method of History's Greatest Soldier* (New York: Macmillan, 1966); Dominic Lieven, *Russia Against Napoleon. The True Story of the Campaigns of War and Peace* (New York: Viking, 2009); Alexander Mikaberidze, *The Napoleonic Wars. A Global History* (Oxford: Oxford University Press, 2020).
35 Janet Hartley, *Alexander I* (London: Longman, 1994), 32; Vladimir Aleksandrovich Fedorov, "Alexander I, 1801–1825," *The Emperors and Empresses of Russia. Rediscovering the Romanovs*, ed. Donald J. Raleigh (Armonk, NY: M.E. Sharpe, 1996), 216–55.
36 For a survey of this moment, see Frederick W. Kagan, *The End of the Old Order. Napoleon and Europe 1801–1805* (Boston: De Capo Press, 2006).
37 Frederick W. Kagan, "Russia's Wars with Napoleon, 1801–1815," in *The Military History of Tsarist Russia*, ed. Frederick W.Kagan and Robin Higham (New York: Palgrave, 2002), 109.
38 Ibid., 110.
39 Lieven, 102–38.
40 Lieven, 47–52; Mikaberidze, 228–41; Schroeder, 320–32.
41 Mikaberidze, 368–423.
42 Donald W. Mitchell, *A History of Russian and Soviet Sea Power* (New York: MacMillan Publishing, 1974), 117–25.
43 Kagan, "Russia's Small Wars, 1805–1861," 123–5.
44 Lieven, 102–37.
45 Chandler, 749–67; Mikaberidze, 525–40.
46 Lieven, 138–74.
47 Hartley, *Alexander I*, 2.
48 Alexander Mikaberidze, *Napoleon versus Kutuzov: The Battle of Borodino* (London: Pen and Sword, 2007); Lieven, 192–209.

49 Alexander Martin, "The Response of the Population of Moscow to the Napoleonic Occupation of 1812," in *The Military and Society in Russia 1450-1917*, ed. Eric Lohr and Marshall Poe (Leiden: Brill Academic Press, 2002), 469-90. For the Russian response writ large, see Alexander M. Martin, *Romantics, Reformers, Reactionaries: Russian Conservative Thought and Politics in the Reign of Alexander I* (Dekalb: Northern Illinois University Press, 1997).

50 Lieven, 250-8; Chandler, 814-47.

51 Chandler, 994-9; Lieven, 494-500; Mikaberidze, 552-5.

52 Hartley, *Alexander I*, 128-39.

53 Henry Kissinger, *A World Restored: Metternich, Castlereagh and the Problems of Peace 1812-1822* (New York: Houghton Mifflin, 1957); Schroeder, 517-82.

54 See Janet M. Hartley, *Russia, 1762-1825. Military Power, the State, and the People* (Westport, CT: Praeger, 2008), 1-3.

55 Kagan, "Russia's Small Wars, 1805-1861," 112.

56 Hartley, *Russia, 1762-1815*, 26-7.

57 Professor Hartley has published this number at least twice. See Hartley, *Russia, 1762-1815*, 26; Hartley, "The Russian Army," 89. Dr. Hartley does not make clear if this number includes the peasant/serfs inducted after Tilsit.

58 Frederick W. Kagan, *The Military Reforms of Nicholas I. The Origins of the Modern Russian Army* (New York: St. Martin's Press, 1999).

59 Kagan, "Russia's Small Wars, 1805-1861," 119

60 Hartley, "The Russian Army," 88.

61 It should be noted that this reform was a part of Speranky's drive to reform the entire empire, which ultimately led to the elimination of all of Peter's Colleges and the creation of a State Council to act as a mediator between the tsar and all of his ministries. See Marc Raeff, *Michael Speransky, Statesman of Imperial Russia 1772-1839* (The Hague: Marinus Nijhoff, 1957), 108-9.

62 On Holy alliance, see Schroeder, 586-92.

63 Hartley, "The Russian Army," 89.

64 Although dated, see Richard E. Pipes, "The Russian Military Colonies, 1810-1831," *Journal of Modern History*, XXII:3 (September 1950), 205-19.

65 See Joseph L. Wieczynski, "The Mutiny of the Semenovsky Regiment in 1820," *Russian Review*, 29:2 (April 1970), 167-80. Janet M. Hartley notes that mutiny is too hard of a term to describe what boiled down to a peaceful protest and that dispersing the troops across the empire resulted in fifteen to twenty more such protests by 1825. See Hartley, *Alexander I*, 216.

66 Richard Stites, *The Four Horsemen. Riding to Liberty in Post-Napoleonic Europe* (Oxford: Oxford University Press, 2014) 186-235.

67 Anatole G. Mazour, *The First Russian Revolution 1825. The Decembrist Movement, Its Origin, Development, and Significance* (Stanford, CA: Stanford University Press, 1937); Stites, 240-321.

68 John S. Curtiss, *The Russian Army under Nicholas I 1825–55* (Durham, NC: Duke University Press, 1965); Tatiana Aleksandrovna Kapustina, "Nicholas I, 1825–55," in *The Emperors and Empresses of Russia. Rediscovering the Romanovs*, ed. Donald J. Raleigh (Armonk, NY: M.E. Sharpe, 1996), 256–93; W. Bruce Lincoln, *Nicholas I, Emperor and Autocrat of All the Russians* (DeKalb: Northern Illinois University Press, 1978).

69 In addition to Bitis, 15–36, see Lucien J. Frary and Mara Kozelsky, eds., *The Eastern Question Reconsidered* (Madison: University of Wisconsin Press, 2014).

70 W. E. D. Allen and Paul Muratoff, *Caucasian Battlefields: A History of the Wars on the Russo-Caucasian Border, 1828–1921* (Cambridge, UK: Cambridge University Press, 1953).

71 George Bournoutian, *From the Kur to the Aras: A Military History of Russia's Move into the South Caucasus and the First Russo-Iranian War, 1801–1813* (Leiden: Brill Academic Press, 2020).

72 Robert F. Baumann, *Russian-Soviet Unconventional Wars in the Caucasus, Central Asia, and Afghanistan* (Fort Leavenworth, KS: Combat Studies Institute, 1993), 1–19; Allen and Muratoff, 23–45; Bitis, 274–324.

73 Bitis, 349–77.

74 Kagan, *Military Reforms*, 211–19.

75 Norman Davies, *God's Playground: A History of Poland*, Vol. 2 (New York: Columbia University Press, 1982) 306–33; Curtiss, *The Russian Army under Nicholas I*, 74–96.

76 W. Bruce Lincoln, *In the Vanguard of Reform: Russia's Enlightened Bureaucrats, 1825–1861* (DeKalb: Northern Illinois University Press, 1982).

77 Keep, *Soldiers of the Tsar*, 344.

78 Carl van Dyke, *Russian Imperial Military Doctrine and Education, 1832–1914* (Westport, CT: Greenwood Press, 1990), 1–10.

79 Kagan, *Military Reforms*, 189–209.

80 Baumann, 19–48; Allen and Muratoff, 46–56.

81 Ian W. Roberts, *Nicholas I and the Russian Intervention in Hungary* (New York, St. Martin's Press, 1991).

82 Geoffrey Hosking, *Russia. People and Empire, 1552–1917* (Cambridge, MA: Harvard University Press, 1997), 144–50.

83 David M. Goldfrank, *The Origins of the Crimean War* (London: Longman, 1994); John Shelton Curtiss, *The Crimean War* (Durham, NC: Duke University Press, 1979), 3–267.

84 Curtiss, *Crimean War*, 167–200.

85 Allen and Muratoff, 57–65.

86 Curtiss, *Crimean War*, 267–99.

87 Ibid., 322–41.

88 Ibid., 445–71.

89 Mitchell, 154–82.

90 Curtiss, *Crimean War*, 502–29.
91 Mara Kozelsky, *Crimea in War and Transformation* (Oxford: Oxford University Press, 2019).
92 Pintner, 354–7.

Chapter 4

1 W. Bruce Lincoln, *The Great Reforms. Autocracy, Bureaucracy, and the Politics of Change in Imperial Russia* (Dekalb: Northern Illinois University Press, 1990).
2 To better understand the complex environment of Russian bureaucratic politics at the time of the great reforms, see W. Bruce Lincoln, *In the Vanguard of Reform: Russia's Enlightened Bureaucrats, 1825–1861* (Dekalb: Northern Illinois University Press, 1982).
3 Forrest A. Miller, *Dmitrii Miliutin and the Reform Era in Russia* (Nashville: Vanderbilt University Press, 1968).
4 See Keep, *Soldiers of the Tsar*, 356.
5 Miliutin first systematically expressed his reform plans in a January 1862 report to Alexander II. Keep, *Soldiers of the Tsar*, 356–7.
6 Sadly for reasons of space I have decided not to assess the Polish rebellion of 1863–4.
7 See Lincoln, *The Great Reforms*, 151–2. While Miliutin created fifteen districts, today they have been streamlined into five military districts, yet they do still exist.
8 Lincoln, *The Great Reforms*, 152.
9 John W. Steinberg, "How Military Tradition Prevailed and Reform Failed to Prevent the Collapse of the Russian Empire," in *Victory of Defeat Armies in the Aftermath of Conflict*, ed. Peter Dennis and Jeffrey Gray (Canberra: Big Sky Publishers, 2010), 48–80.
10 John W. Steinberg, "D.A. Miliutin's Impact on the Education of Russian Military Officers," in *The Making of Russian History. Society, Culture & the Politic of Modern Russia. Essays in Honor of Allan K. Wildman*, ed. John W. Steinberg and Rex Wade (Bloomington, IN: Slavica, 2009), 23–46.
11 Miller, *Dmitrii Miliutin*, 182–230.
12 Keep, *Soldiers of the Tsar*, 351–81.
13 A. J. P. Taylor, *The Struggle for Mastery in Europe, 1848–1918* (Oxford, UK: Oxford at the Clarendon Press, 1954), 228–54.
14 On the events leading up to the war, see Dietrich Geyer, *Russian Imperialism. The Interaction of Domestic and Foreign Policy 1860–1914* (New Haven: Yale University Press, 1987), 65–85 and David MacKenzie, "Russia's Balkan Policies under Alexander II, 1855–1881," in *Imperial Russian Foreign Policy*, ed. Hugh Ragsdale

and Valerii Nikolaevich Ponomarev (Cambridge: Cambridge University Press, 1993), 219–46.
15 He was described as such in O. R. Airapetov, *Zabytaia Kar'era "Russkogo Mol'tke" Nikolai Nikolaevich Obruchev 1830–1904* (St. Petersburg: Aleteiia, 1998). This book remains the only complete biography of this significant military leader in any language.
16 Menning, *Bayonets before Bullets. The Imperial Russian Army, 1861–1914* (Bloomington: Indiana University Press 1992), 52–4. For the war plan, see David Rich, *The Tsar's Colonels: Professionalism, Strategy, and Subversion in Late Imperial Russia* (Cambridge, MA: Harvard University Press, 1998), 127–46. For an assessment of this plan, see Fuller, *Strategy and Power in Russia*, 311–17.
17 Ibid., 318–19.
18 Menning, *Bayonets before Bullets*, 71–4.
19 Fuller, *Strategy and Power in Russia*, 320.
20 The best English language survey of the war can be found in Menning, *Bayonets before Bullets*, 51–86. A classic Russian source recently reprinted is A. A. Kersnovskii, *Istoriia Russkoi Armii*, vol. 2 (Moskva: Golos, 1993), 202–80.
21 Taylor, 247–55; Fuller, *Strategy and Power in Russia*, 322.
22 Fuller, *Strategy and Power in Russia*, 324.
23 *Sbornik materialov po russko-turetskoi voine*, 97 vols (St. Petersburg: Voenno-istoricheskoi kommisii glavnyi Shtaba, 1898–1911).
24 Menning, *Bayonets before Bullets*, 83–6.
25 For Dragomirov's biography, see Menning, *Bayonets Before Bullets*, 38–9.
26 For Skobelov's biography, see F. V. Green, *Army Life in Russia* (New York: Charles Schribner's Sons, 1885), 126–42. More contemporary comments about his life can be found in Alexander Morrison, *The Russian Conquest of Central Asia. A Study in Imperial Expansion, 1814–1914* (Cambridge, UK: Cambridge University Press, 2021), 382–3; David Schimmelpenninck van der Oye, *Toward the Rising Sun. Russian Ideologies of Empire and the Path to War with Japan* (DeKalb: Northern Illinois University Press, 2001), 88–9.
27 My understanding of Russian involvement in Central Asia was greatly informed through numerous conversations with Dr. David Schimmelpenninck van der Oye. He also has graciously shared with me three of his unpublished manuscripts that to my knowledge were not published at the time of his untimely death in March 2022. The titles of these articles are "The Seventh Continent. Russian Territorial Expansion from 1450–1850," "Russia Turns to the East 1850–1890," and "Russia's Central Asian Politics and the Great Game."
28 Taylor, 442–5.
29 Baumann, 49–52.
30 Morrison, 349–71.

31 Baumann, 53.
32 Morrison, 220–35.
33 Morrison nicely sums up the role of camels and logistics in "Camels and Colonial Armies: The Logistics of Warfare in Inner Asia in the Early 19th Century," *Journal of the Economic and Social History of the Orient*, 57 (2014), 443–85.
34 The literature on the Great Game is voluminous. A good starting point is Peter Hopkirk, *The Great Game. The Struggle for Empire in Central Asia* (New York: Kodansha International, 1994).
35 Bauman, 57.
36 David MacKenzie, *The Lion of Tashkent. The Career of General M.G. Cherniaev* (Athens: University of Georgia Press, 1974), 207–28; Morrison, 270 and 310.
37 Baumann, 59.
38 Morrison, 240–70.
39 Ibid., 307–49.
40 Ibid., 162–6.
41 On the conquest of Turkestan, see Daniel Brower, *Turkestan and the Fate of the Russian Empire* (London: Routledge, 2009).
42 Bauman, 72.
43 Morrison, 453–7.

Chapter 5

1 Geyer, 86–101.
2 John J. Stephan, *The Russian Far East. A History* (Stanford, CA: Stanford University Press, 1994), 7–110.
3 R. K. I. Quested, *Sino Russian Relations. A Short History* (Sydney: George Allen & Unwin, 1984), 28–50.
4 Steven G. Marks, *Road to Power: The Trans-Siberian Railroad and the Colonization of Asian Russia, 1850–1917* (Ithaca, NY: Cornell University Press, 1991).
5 Geyer, *Russian Imperialism*, 186–247.
6 Robert Warth, *Nicholas II: The Life and Reign of Russia's Last Monarch* (Westport, CT: Greenwood Press, 1997); Dominic Lieven, *Nicholas II Twilight of the Empire* (New York: St. Martin's Press, 1993); and Boris Vasilievich Ananich and Rafail Sholomovich Ganelin, "Emperor Nicholas II, 1894–1917," in *The Emperors and Empresses of Russia. Rediscovering the Romanovs*, ed. Donald J. Raleigh (Armonk, NY, 1996), 369–403.
7 On the Treaty of Shimonoseki, specifically see David Schimmelpenninck van der Oye, *Toward the Rising Sun. Russian Ideologies of Empire and the Path to War with Japan* (DeKalb: Northern Illinois University Press, 2001), 133–47.

8 Francis W. Wcislo, *Tales of Imperial Russian. The Life and Times of Sergei Witte, 1849–1915* (New York: Oxford University Press, 2011).
9 David Wolff, *To the Harbin Station. The Liberal Alternative in Russian Manchuria* (Stanford, CA: Stanford University Press, 1999).
10 Ian Nish, *The Origins of the Russo-Japanese War* (London: Longman, 1985), 1–83.
11 David J. Silbey, *The Boxer Rebellion and the Great Game in China* (New York: Hill & Wang, 2012).
12 Schimmelpenninck, *Toward the Rising Sun*, 196–211.
13 David M. McDonald, *United Government and Foreign Policy in Russia, 1900–1914* (Cambridge, MA: Harvard University Press, 1992).
14 John W. Steinberg, *All the Tsar's Men. Russia's General Staff and the Fate of the Empire, 1898–1914* (Baltimore: Johns Hopkins University Press, 2010), 40–3.
15 Nish, 152–238.
16 John W. Steinberg, "Was the Russo-Japanese War World War Zero?," *Russian Review*, 67:1 (January 2008), 1–7.
17 David C. Evans and Mark R. Peattie, *Kaigun. Strategy, Tactics, and Technology in the Imperial Japanese Navy, 1887–1941* (Annapolis, MD: Naval Institute Press, 1997), 93–9; Julian S. Corbett, *Maritime Operations in the Russo-Japanese War, 1904–1905*, vol. 1 (Annapolis, MD: Naval Institute Press, 1994), 63–109. This is a reprint of this two-volume study that was originally published in 1914. Aizawa Kiyoshi, "Differences Regarding Togo's Surprise Attack on Port Arthur," in *The Russo-Japanese War in Global Perspective. World War Zero*, vol. II, ed. David Wolff, Steven G. Marks, Bruce W. Menning, David Schimmelpenninck van der Oye, John W. Steinberg, and Yokote Shinji (Leiden: Brill, 2007), 81–104.
18 Schimmelpinnick, *Toward the Rising Sun*, 187–95; Igor V. Lukoianov, "The Bezobrazovtsy," *The Russo-Japanese War in Global Perspective. World War Zero*, vol. 1, ed. John W. Steinberg, Bruce W. Menning, David Schimmelpenninck van der Oye, David Wolff, and Shinji Yokote (Leiden: Brill, 2005), 65–86.
19 Hundreds of official reports were published in the period between the end of Russo-Japanese War and the outbreak of the First World War. Good representations of this literature include German General Staff Historical Section, *The Russo-Japanese War*, 9 vols. Trans. Karl von Donat (London: Hugh Rees, 1908–14); Committee of Imperial Defense Historical Section, *Official History, Naval and Military, of the Russo-Japanese War*, 3 vols (London, Her Majesty's Stationary Office by Harrison and Sons, 1910–20); United States, War Department, General Staff, Office of the Chief of Staff, *Reports of Military Observers Attached to the Armies in Manchuria during the Russo-Japanese War* (Washington, DC: Government Printing Office, 1906–7); all of these reports along with much of the work written in the immediate aftermath of the war are cited in A British Officer, "The Literature of the Russo-Japanese War, I and II," *American Historical Review*, 16:3 (April 1911), 508–28;

A British Officer, "The Literature of the Russo-Japanese War, I and II," *American Historical Review*, 16:4 (July 1911), 736–50. For an assessment of this work see: David Jones, "Military Observers, Eurocentrism and World War Zero," in *The Russo-Japanese War*, ed. David Wolff Steven G. Marks, Bruce W. Menning, David Schimmelpenninck van der Oye, John W. Steinberg, and Yokote Shinji (Leiden: Brill, 2007), 135–78.

20 Steinberg, *All the Tsar' Men*, 270–9.
21 David Wolff, "Intelligence Intermediaries: The Competition for Chinese Spies," in *The Russo-Japanese War*, ed. John W. Steinberg, Bruce W. Menning, David Schimmelpenninck van der Oye, David Wolff, and Shinji Yokote (Leiden: Brill, 2005), 305–32.
22 John W. Steinberg, "The Operational Overview," in *The Russo-Japanese War*, ed. John W. Steinberg, Bruce W. Menning, David Schimmelpenninck van der Oye, David Wolff, and Shinji Yokote (Leiden: Brill, 2005), 109–10.
23 Menning, *Bayonets before Bullets*, 157–8.
24 *Kaigun*, 102.
25 Corbett, vol. 1, 178–87; Donald W. Mitchell, *A History of Russian and Soviet Sea Power* (New York: MacMillan Publishing, 1974), 218–37.
26 Menning, *Bayonets*, 172.
27 *Kaigun*, 99–101.
28 Richard Connaughton, *Rising Sun and Tumbling Bear. Russia's War with Japan* (London: Cassell, 2003), 88–105.
29 *Kaigun*, 101–2; Corbett, vol. 1, 228–41.
30 Steinberg, *All the Tsar's Men*, 121–8.
31 Steinberg, *All the Tsar's Men*, 129–33; Menning, *Bayonets*, 172–5; Connaughton, *Rising Sun*, 108–28.
32 Corbett, vol. 1, 284–5; Mitchell, 216–24.
33 Menning, *Bayonets*, 160–71; Connaughton, *Rising Sun*, 227–57.
34 The Baltic fleet would not leave St. Petersburg until October 1904 but discussions were already being held about its transfer to the Far East beginning in the spring, 1904.
35 Corbett, vol. 1, 370–471; *Kaigun*, 102–7.
36 Menning, *Bayonets*, 160–71; Connaughton, *Rising Sun*, 227–57.
37 Steinberg, *All the Tsar's Men*, 134–44; Menning, *Bayonets*, 175–9; Connaughton, *Rising Sun*, 156–216.
38 Menning, *Bayonets*, 179–84.
39 Y. Tak Matsusaka, "Human Bullets, General Nogi, and the Myth of Port Arthur," in *The Russo-Japanese War*, ed. John W. Steinberg, Bruce W. Menning, David Schimmelpenninck van der Oye, David Wolff, and Shinji Yokote (Leiden: Brill, 2005), 179–203.
40 Menning, *Bayonets*, 160–71; Connaughton, *Rising Sun*, 227–57.

41 John S. Bushnell, *Mutiny amid Repression. Russian Soldiers in the Revolution of 1905–06* (Bloomington: Indiana University Press, 1985).
42 Menning, *Bayonets*, 186–95; Connaughton, *Rising Sun*, 279–90.
43 Steinberg, *All the Tsar's Men*, 144–6.
44 Ed Miller, "Japan's Other Victory: Overseas Financing of the War," in *The Russo-Japanese War*, ed. John W. Steinberg, Bruce W. Menning, David Schimmelpenninck van der Oye, David Wolff, and Shinji Yokote (Leiden: Brill, 2005), 465–84.
45 Kaigun, 110–29; Corbett, vol. 2, 1–40, 141–345; Mitchell, 234–67.
46 Tosh Minohara, "The 'Rat Ministry': Komura Jutaro and US-Japan Relations," in *The Russo-Japanese War*, ed. David Wolff, Steven G. Marks, Bruce W. Menning, David Schimmelpenninck van der Oye, John W. Steinberg, and Yokote Shinji (Leiden: Brill, 2007), 551–70.
47 Norman E. Saul. *Concord and Conflict. The United States and Russia, 1867–1914* (Lawrence: University Press of Kansas, 1996), 500–7.
48 Norman E. Saul, "The Kittery Peace," in *The Russo-Japanese War*, ed. John W. Steinberg, Bruce W. Menning, David Schimmelpenninck van der Oye, David Wolff, and Shinji Yokote (Leiden: Brill, 2005), 485–508.
49 Raymond A. Esthus, *Double Eagle and the Rising Sun. The Russians and Japanese at Portsmouth in 1905* (Durham, NC: Duke University Press, 1988), 101–51.
50 Wcislo, 195–241.
51 David M. McDonald, "Tsushima Echoes: Asian Defeat and Tsarist Foreign Policy," in *The Russo-Japanese War*, ed. John W. Steinberg, Bruce W. Menning, David Schimmelpenninck van der Oye, David Wolff, and Shinji Yokote (Leiden: Brill, 2005), 545–64.
52 Ono Keishi, "Japan's Monetary Mobilization for War," in *The Russo-Japanese War*, ed. David Wolff, Steven G. Marks, Bruce W. Menning, David Schimmelpenninck van der Oye, John W. Steinberg, and Yokote Shinji (Leiden: Brill, 2007), 251–70.
53 Akira Iruye, *Pacific Estrangement: Japanese and American Expansion, 1897–1911* (Cambridge, MA: Harvard University Press, 1972).
54 Steven Ericson and Allen Hockley, eds. *The Treaty of Portsmouth and Its Legacies* (Hanover, NH: Dartmouth University Press, 2008), 251–70.

Chapter 6

1 On the Franco-Russian alliance, see A. J. P. Taylor, 325–45. For Russia's strategic concerns, see Fuller, *Strategy and Power in Russia*, 394–451.
2 Walter Goerlitz, *History of the German General Staff 1657–1945* (New York: Praeger, 1953), 69–102.

3 Steinberg, *All the Tsar's Men*, 150–91.
4 Anton I. Denikin, *The Career of a Tsarist Officer. Memoirs, 1872–1916* (Minneapolis: University of Minnesota Press, 1975), 177–83.
5 William C. Fuller, *Civil-Military Conflict in Imperial Russia 1881–1914* (Princeton: NJ: Princeton University Press, 1985), 32–6.
6 Steinberg, *All the Tsar's Men*, 195–208.
7 Menning, *Bayonets before Bullets*, 217–21.
8 Dominic Lieven, *The End of Tsarist Russia. The March to World War I & Revolution* (New York: Viking, 2015), 211–26.
9 Menning, *Bayonets before Bullets*, 221–30.
10 William C. Fuller, Jr., *The Foe Within. Fantasies of Treason and the End of Imperial Russia* (Ithaca: Cornell University Press, 2006), 97–115.
11 Fuller, *War and Strategy*, 423–33; Menning, *Bayonets before Bullets*, 231–7.
12 Peter Gatrell, *Government, Industry and Rearmament in Russia, 1900–1914. The Last Argument of Tsarism* (Cambridge, UK: Cambridge University Press, 1994).
13 Steinberg, "Imperial War Games, (1898–1906)," 253–72.
14 Bruce Menning, "War Planning and Initial Operations in the Russian Context," in *War Planning 1914*, ed. Richard F. Hamilton and Holger H. Herwig (Cambridge, UK: Cambridge University Press, 2010), 80–142.
15 Lieven, *The End of Tsarist Russia*, 313–42.
16 Winston Churchill, *The Unknown War. The Eastern Front* (London: Thornton Butterworth, 1937); John W. Wheeler-Bennett, *Brest-Litovsk: The Forgotten Peace, March 1918* (London: Macmillan, 1938).
17 Most notably, he orchestrated the fifteen-day mobilization agreement.
18 Dennis E. Showalter, *Tannenberg Clash of Empires* (Hamden, CT: Archon Book, 1991), 172–323.
19 Ibid.
20 Melissa Kirschke Stockdale, *Mobilizing the Russian Nation. Patriotism and Citizenship in the First World War* (Cambridge, UK: Cambridge University Press, 2016), 45–74; Joshua A. Sanborn, *Imperial Apocalypse. The Great War & The Destruction of the Russian Empire* (Oxford, UK: Oxford University Press, 2014), 65–108.
21 Holger H. Herwig, *The First World War Germany and Austria-Hungary 1914–1918*, 2nd ed. (London: Bloomsbury, 2014), 81–8.
22 David R. Stone, *The Russian Army in the Great War. The Eastern Front, 1914–1917* (Lawrence: University Press of Kansas, 2015), 81–100; Norman Stone, *The Eastern Front 1914–1917* (New York: Charles Scribner's Sons, 1975), 70–92.
23 Paul Robinson, *Grand Duke Nikolai Nikolaevich Supreme Commander of the Russian Army* (DeKalb: Northern Illinois University Press, 2014), 157–94.

24 Graydon A. Tunstall, *Blood on the Snow. The Carpathian Winter War of 1915* (Lawrence: University Press of Kansas, 2010).
25 Stone, *The Eastern Front*, 144–64.
26 Graydon A. Tunstall, *Written in Blood. The Battle of Fortress Przemyśl in World War I* (Bloomington: Indiana University Press, 2016); Alexander Watson, *The Fortress. The Siege of Przemyśl and the Making of Europe's Bloodlands* (New York: Basic Books, 2020).
27 Tunstall, *Blood on the Snow*, 209–12.
28 David Stevenson, *The First World War and International Politics* (Oxford, UK: Clarendon Press, 2001), 47–64.
29 Peter Gatrell, *Russia's First World War. A Social and Economic History* (Harlow, UK: Pearson Longman, 2005), 21–7 and 108–32.
30 Much work is still needed on the question of supplying Russian during the First World War. Gatrell, *Russis's First World War* offers a good starting point. Still one of the best commentators on the supply situation in Russia during the war is Keith Neilson, *Strategy and Supply: The Anglo-Russian Alliance 1914–1917* (London: George Allen & Unwin, 1984).
31 Herwig, 225–69.
32 Stone, *The Russian Army in the Great War*, 146–77; Stone, *The Eastern Front*, 165–93.
33 Allan K. Wildman, *The End of the Russian Imperial Army. The Old Army and the Soldiers' Revolt (March–April 1917)*, vol. 1 (Princeton: Princeton University Press, 1980), 75–120.
34 Peter Gatrell, *A Whole Empire Walking. Refugees in Russia During World War I* (Bloomington: Indiana University Press, 2005).
35 Gatrell, *Russia's First World War*, 27–38.
36 On the situation for minorities in the borderlands during the First World War, see Alexander V. Prusin, *The Lands between. Conflict in the East European Borderlands, 1870–1992* (Oxford, UK: Oxford University Press, 2010), 41–71.
37 Eric Lohr, *Nationalizing the Russian Empire. The Campaign against Enemy Aliens during World War I* (Cambridge, MA: Harvard University Press, 2003), 17–22; Peter Holquist, "The Role of Personality in the First (1914–1915) Russian Occupation of Galicia and Bukovina," in *Anti-Jewish Violence. Rethinking the Pogrom in East European History*, ed. Jonathan Dekel-Chen, David Gaunt, Natan M. Meir, and Israel Bartal (Bloomington: Indiana University Press, 2011), 74–94.
38 Fuller, *The Foe Within*, 184–256.
39 Richard L. DiNardo, *Breakthrough: The Gorlice-Tarnow Campaign, 1915* (Santa Barbara, CA: Praeger, 2010).
40 Richard C. Hall, *The Balkan Wars, 1912–12: Prelude to the First World War* (New York: Routledge, 2000), 1–80.

41 Allen and Muratoff, 240–8; Michael A. Reynolds, *Shattering Empires: The Clash and Collapse of the Ottoman and Russian Empires, 1908–1918* (Cambridge, UK: Cambridge University Press, 2011), 22–43.
42 Stone, *The Russian Army in the Great War*, 186–90.
43 Reynolds, *Shattering Empires*, 148–55; Ronald Grigor Suny, Fatma Muge Gocek, and Norman Naimark, eds. *A Question of Genocide: Armenians and Turks at the End of the Ottoman Empire* (Oxford, UK: Oxford University Press, 2011).
44 Edward J. Erickson, *Ordered to Die. A History of the Ottoman Army in the First World War* (Westport, CT: Greenwood Press, 2001), 110–19.
45 Robinson, *Grand Duke Nikolai Nikolaevich*, 264.
46 Ibid., 270.
47 Allen and Muratoff, *Caucasian Battlefields*, 320–72; Stone, *The Russian Army in the Great War*, 193–6.
48 Stone, *The Eastern Front*, 232–8.
49 Stone, *The Russian Army in the Great War*, 232–6.
50 Stone, *The Eastern Front*, 221–31.
51 Jamie H. Cockfield, *Russia's Iron General. The Life of Aleksei A. Brusilov, 1853–1924* (Lanham, MD: Lexington Books, 2019), 1–55 and 137–64.
52 Cockfield, 201–9.
53 Timothy C. Dowling, *The Brusilov Offensive* (Bloomington: Indiana University Press, 2008), 160–76.
54 Herwig, 242–68.
55 Glenn E. Torrey, *The Romanian Battlefront in World War I* (Lawrence: University Press of Kansas, 2011).
56 Michael B. Barrett, *Prelude to Blitzkrieg. The 1916 Austro-German Campaign in Romania* (Bloomington: Indian University Press, 2013), 298–314.
57 Wildman, vol. 1, 121–58.
58 Tsuyoshi Hasegawa, *The February Revolution. Petrograd, 1917* (Seattle: University of Washington Press, 1981), 540–8.
59 The literature on the emergence of Dual Power is voluminous—too vast to put in a footnote. A place to start reading about this revolutionary moment is Laura Engelstein, *Russia in Flames* (New York: Oxford University Press, 2018), 101–76; Hasegawa, 313–432.
60 Wildman, vol. 1, 182–98.
61 Boris Kolonitsky, *Comrade Kerensky. The Revolution against the Monarchy and the Formation of the Cult of the Leader of the People (March–June 1917)* (Cambridge, UK: Polity Press, 2021), 231–94.
62 Allan Wildman, *The End of the Imperial Army, The Road to Soviet Power and Peace*, vol. 2 (Princeton, NJ: Princeton University Press, 1987), 3–111; Stone, *The Russian Army in the Great War*, 286–92.

63 Stone, *The Russian Army in the Great War*, 292–7.
64 Wildman, vol. 2, 148–224.

Epilogue

1 Krylenko had served in the army before the First World War, reaching the rank of 2nd lieutenant before being discharged in 1913. In 1914 he was in exile with Lenin in Switzerland and at Lenin's request he went back to Russia in 1915 to engage in underground organizational work. In the revolutionary year of 1917 he first worked as an organizer of soldier's committees at the front and this earned him an appointment to the Bolshevik military organization, which he faithfully served until they came to power in October.
2 Laura Engelstein, *Russia in Flames, War, Revolution, Civil War, 1914–1921* (New York: Oxford University Press, 2017), 240–1.
3 Peter Holquist, *Making War, Forging Revolution: Russia's Continuum of Crisis, 1914–1921* (Cambridge, MA: Harvard University Press, 2002).

Bibliography

Below is a list of essential readings for the Russian Empire and military history. It is far from comprehensive. The readings below should be considered a point of departure for all interested parties. Further, due to space limitations, numerous articles that are available on the subject have not been included. For reference purposes, many of these articles appear in the notes of this book.

Airapetov, O. R. *Generaly, liberally i predprinimateli: rabota na front i na revoliutsiiu*. Moscow: Modest Kolerov i "Tri kvadrata," 2003.

Airapetov, O. R. *Zabytaia Kar'era "Russkogo Mol'tke" Nikolai Nikolaevich Obruchev 1830–1904*. St. Petersburg: Aleteiia, 1998.

Airapetov, O. R. *Uchastie Rossiiskoi imperii v pervoi mirovoi voine*, 1914–1918, 4 vols. Moscow: Kuchkovo, 2014–15.

Allen, W. E. D., and Paul Muratoff. *Caucasian Battlefield*. Cambridge, UK: Cambridge University Press, 1953.

Anisimov, Evgenii V. *The Reforms of Peter the Great*. John T. Alexander, trans. Armonk, NY: M.E. Sharpe, 1993.

Astatov, Aleksandr. *Russkii Front v 1914—nachale 1917 goda: voennyi opyt i sovremennost'*. Moscow: Novyi Khronograf, 2014.

Baumann, Robert F. *Russian-Soviet Unconventional Wars in the Caucasus, Central Asia, and Afghanistan*. Fort Leavenworth, KS: Combat Studies Institute Press, 1993.

Beskrovnyi, L. G. *Armiia i flot rossii v nachale XX veke. Ocherki Voenno-Ekonomicheskogo Potentsiala*. Moscow: Nauka, 1986.

Beskrovnyi, L. G. *Russkaia armiia i flot v XVIII veke*. Moscow: Voennoe izdatel'stvo, 1958.

Beskrovnyi, L. G. *Russkaia armiis i flot v XIX veke. Voenno-Ekonomicheskogo Potentsial Rossii*. Moscow: Nauka, 1973.

Beskrovnyi, L. G. *The Russian Army and Fleet in the Nineteenth Century: Handbook of Armaments, Personnel and Policy*. Gulf Breeze, FL: Academic International Press, 1996.

Bitis, Alexander. *Russia and the Eastern Question. Army, Government, and Society 1815–1833*. London: British Academy published by Oxford University Press, 2006.

Burbank, Jane, Mark van Hagen, and Anatolyi Remnev, eds. *Russian Empire. Space, People, Power, 1700–1930*. Bloomington, IN: Indiana University Press, 2007.

Bushnell, John. *Mutiny amid Repression: Russian Soldiers and the Revolution of 1905–06*. Bloomington, IN: Indiana University Press, 1985.

Chebotarev, A. V., and V. V. Parshin. *Sistema voennogo upravleniia v Rossii (XVIII–nachalo XXv)*. Moscow: Voennyi Universitet, 2003.

Connaughton, R. M. *The War of the Rising Sun and Tumbling Bear: A Military History of the Russo-Japanese War, 1904–05*. London: Cassell, 1988.

Corbett, Julian S. *Maritime Operations in the Russo-Japanese War, 1904–05*, 2 vols. Annapolis, MD: Naval Institute Press, 1994.

Curtiss, John S. *The Russian Army under Nicholas I, 1825–1855*. Durham NC: Duke University Press, 1965.

Curtiss, John S. *Russia's Crimean War* (Durham NC: Duke University Press, 1979.

Davies, Brian L. *Empire and Military Revolution in Eastern Europe. Russia's Turkish Wars in the Eighteenth Century*. London: Bloomsbury, 2011.

Davies, Brian L. *Warfare in Eastern Europe 1500–1800*. Leiden: Brill, 2012.

Davies, Brian L. *Warfare, State and Society on the Black Sea Steppe, 1500–1700*. London: Routledge, 2007.

Davies, Brian L. *The Russo-Turkish War 1768–1774. Catherine II and the Ottoman Empire*. London: Bloomsbury, 2016.

Dixon, Simon. *The Modernisation of Russia 1676–1825*. Cambridge, UK: Cambridge University Press, 1999.

Donnelly, Alton. *The Russian Conquest of Bashkiria, 1552—1740*. New Haven, CT: Yale University Press, 1968.

Duffy, Christopher. *Russia's Military Way to the West: Origins and Nature of Russian Military Power, 1700–1800*. London: Routledge, 1982.

Ericson, Steve, and Allen Hockley, eds. *The Treaty of Portsmouth and Its Legacies*. Hanover, NH: Dartmouth College Press, 2008.

Filjushkin, Alexander. *Ivan the Terrible. A Military History*. London: Frontline Books, 1988.

Frankel, E. R., J. Frankel, and Baruch Knei-Paz. *Revolution in Russian: Reassessments of 1917*. Cambridge, UK: Cambridge University Press, 1992.

Frost, Robert I. *The Northern Wars: War, State and Society in Northeastern Europe 1558–1721*. London: Longman, 2000.

Fuller, William C. *Civil-Military Conflict in Imperial Russia, 1881–1914*. Princeton, NJ: Princeton University Press, 1985.

Fuller, William C. *The Foe within: Fantasies of Treason and the End of Imperial Russia*. Ithaca, NY: Cornell University Press, 2006.

Fuller, William C. *Strategy and Power in Russia, 1600–1914*. New York: Free Press, 1992.

Gatrell, Peter. *Government, Industry, and Rearmament in Russia, 1900–1914*. New York: Cambridge University Press, 1994.

Gatrell, Peter. *Russia's First World War. A Social and Economic History*. London: Longman, 2005.

Gatrell, Peter. *The Tsarist Economy, 1850–1917*. New York: St. Martin's Press 1986.

General Staff, War Office. *Handbook of the Russian Army*. London: General Staff War Office, 1914.

Geyer, Dietrich. *Russian Imperialism: The Interaction of Domestic and Foreign Policy, 1860–1914*. Bruce Little, trans. (New Haven, CT: Yale University Press, 1987).

Hartley, Janet M. *Alexander I*. London: Longman, 1994.

Hellie, Richard. *Enserfment and Military Change in Muscovy*. Chicago: University of Chicago Press, 1971.

Hughes, Lindsey. *Peter the Great: A Biography*. New Haven, CT: Yale University Press, 2004.

Hughes, Lindsey. *Russia in the Age of Peter the Great*. New Haven, CT: Yale University Press, 1998.

Kagan, Frederick. *The Military Reforms of Nicholas I: The Origins of the Modern Russian Army*. New York: St. Martin's Press, 1999.

Kamenskii, Aleksandr B. *The Russian Empire in the Eighteenth Century. Searching for a Place in the World*. David Griffiths, trans. Armonk, NY: M.E. Sharpe, 1997.

Kappeler, Andreas. *The Russian Empire*. London: Longman, 2001.

Keep, John L. *Soldiers of the Tsar—Army and Society in Russia 1462–1874*. New York: Oxford University Press, 1985.

Kersnovskii, A. A. *Istoriia russkoi armii*, 4 vols. Moscow: Golos, 1992–4. Originally published in Belgrade in 1935.

Khodarkovsky, Michael. *Russia's Steppe Frontier. The Making of a Colonial Empire, 1500–1800*. Bloomington: Indiana University Press, 2002.

Kollman, Nancy Shields. *The Russian Empire 1450–1801*. Oxford, UK: Oxford University Press, 2017.

LeDonne, John P. *The Grand Strategy of the Russian Empire, 1650–1831*. New York: Oxford University Press, 2004.

LeDonne, John P. The *Russian Empire and the World 1700–1917. The Geopolitics of Expansion and Containment*. New York: Oxford University Press, 1997.

Lohr, Eric, and Marshall Poe, eds. *The Military and Society in Russia 1450–1917*. Leiden: Brill, 2002.

Lieven, Dominic. *Empire: The Russian Empire and Its Rivals*. New Haven, CT: Yale University Press, 2000.

Lieven, Dominic. *Nicholas II: Twilight of the Empire*. New York: St. Martin's Press, 1993.

Lieven, Dominic. *Russia against Napoleon. The True Story of the Campaigns of War and Peace*. New York: Viking, 2009.

Lieven, Dominic. *Russia and the Origins of the First World War*. New York: St. Martin's Press, 1983.

Luntinen, Pertii. *French Information on the Russian War Plan 1880–1914*. Helsinki: Suomen Historiallinen Seura, 1984.

Luntinen, Pertii. *The Imperial Russian Army and Navy in Finland, 1808–1918*. Helsinki: Suomen Historiallinen Seura, 1997.

Marks, Steven G. *Road to Power: The Trans-Siberian Railroad and the Colonization of Asian Russia, 1850–1917*. Ithaca, NY: Cornell University Press, 1991.

Marshall, Alex. *The Russian General Staff and Asia, 1800–1917.* London: Routledge, 2006.

Mazour, Anatole G. *The First Russian Revolution, 1825.* Stanford, CA: Stanford University Press, 1937.

McDonald, David M. *United Government and Foreign Policy in Russia 1900–1914.* Cambridge, MA: Harvard University Press, 1992.

Menning, Bruce W. *Bayonets before Bullets: The Imperial Russian Army, 1861–1914.* Bloomington: Indiana University Press, 1992.

Meshcheriakov, G. P. *Russkaia Voennaia Mysl' v XIX V* Moscow: Nauka, 1973.

Miller, Forrest A. *Dmitrii Miliutin and the Reform Era in Russia.* Nashville: Vanderbilt University Press, 1968.

Mitchell, Donald W. *A History of Russian and Soviet Sea Power.* New York: Macmillan, 1974.

Morrison, Alexander. *The Russian Conquest of Central Asia. A Study of Imperial Expansion, 1814–1914.* Cambridge, UK: Cambridge University Press, 2021.

Plokhy, Serhii, ed. *Poltava 1709. The Battle and the Myth.* Cambridge, MA Harvard University Press, 2012.

Pankov, D. V., ed. *Razvitie Taktiki Russkoi Armii, XVIII v-nachalo XX b.* Moscow: voennoe izdatel'stvo ministerstva oborony soiuza ssr, 1957.

Quested, R. K. I. *Sino Russian Relations. A Short History.* London: George Allen & Unwin, 1984.

Ragsdale, Hugh, ed. *Imperial Russian Foreign Policy.* Washington, DC: Woodrow Wilson Center Press, 1993.

Raleigh, Donald J., ed. *The Emperors and Empresses of Russia.* Armonk, NY: M.E. Sharpe, 1996.

Rich, David Alan. *The Tsar's Colonels: Professionalism, Strategy, and Subversion in Late Imperial Russia.* Cambridge, MA: Harvard University Press, 1998.

Rieber, Alfred J. *The Struggle for the Eurasian Borderlands. From the Rise of Early Modern Empires to the End of the First World War.* Cambridge UK: Cambridge University Press, 2014.

Rostunov, I. I. *Istoriia pervoi mirovoi voiny, 1914–1918* (Moscow: Nauka, 1975).

Rostunov, I. I. *Istoriia russko-iaponskoi voiny 1904–1905 gg.* Moscow: Nauka, 1977.

Rostunov, I. I. *Istoriia severnoi voiny 1700–1721.* Moscow: Nauka, 1987.

Rostunov, I. I. *Russkii front pervoi mirovoi voiny.* Moscow: Nauka, 1976.

Sanborn, Joshua A. *Imperial Apocalypse: The Great War & the Destruction of the Russian Empire.* New York: Oxford University Press, 2014.

Saul, Norman E. *Russia and the Mediterranean, 1797–1807.* Chicago: University of Chicago Press, 1970.

Schimmelpenninck van der Oye, David. *Toward the Rising Sun: Russian Ideologies of Empire and the Path to War with Japan.* DeKalb: Northern Illinois University Press, 2001.

Schimmelpenninck van der Oye, David, and Bruce Menning, eds. *Reforming the Tsar's Army: Military Innovation in Imperial Russia from Peter the Great to the Revolution*. New York: Cambridge University Press, 2003.

Seton-Watson, Hugh. *The Russian Empire 1801–1917*. Oxford, UK: Clarendon Press, 1967.

Skalon, D. A., series ed. *Stoletie voennago ministerstva, 1802–1902*. 48 parts in 13 vols. St. Petersburg: Voennoe Ministerstvo, 1902–14.

Smele, Jonathan, and Anthony Heywood, eds. *The Russian Revolution of 1905: Centenary Perspectives*. London: Routledge, 2005.

Steinberg, John W. *All the Tsar's Men. Russia's General Staff and the Fate of the Empire, 1898–1914*. Washington, DC: Woodrow Wilson Center Press, 2010.

Steinberg, John W., Bruce W. Menning, David Schimmelpenninck van der Oye, David Wolff, and Shinji Yokote, eds. *The Russo-Japanese War in Global Perspective*, vol. I. Leiden: Brill, 1995.

Stevens, Carol B. *Russia's Wars of Emergence 1460–1730*. London: Pearson, Longman, 2007.

Stone, David R. *A Military History of Russia from Ivan the Terrible to the War in Chechenya*. Westport, CT: Praeger Security International, 2006.

Stone, David R. *The Russian Army in the Great War. The Eastern Front, 1914–1917*. Lawrence: University Press of Kansas, 2015.

Stone, Norman. *The Eastern Front, 1914–1917*. New York: Charles Scribner's Sons, 1975.

Taylor, Brian D. *Politics and the Russian Army: Civil-Military Relations, 1689–2000*. Cambridge: Cambridge University Press, 2003.

Van Dyke, Carl. *Russian Imperial Military Doctrine and Education, 1832–1914*. Westport, CT: Greenwood Press, 1990.

Wahlde, Peter von. *Military Thought in Imperial Russia*. Ph.D Dissertation, Department of History, Indiana University, Bloomington, 1966.

Warth, Robert. *Nicholas II: The Life and Reign of Russia's Last Monarch*. New York: Frederick A. Praeger, 1997.

Warner, Denis, and W. Peggy. *The Tide at Sunrise. A History of the Russo-Japanese War, 1904–05*. New York, Charterhouse, 1974.

Wildman, Allan K. *The End of the Russian Imperial Army: The Old Army and the Soldiers' Revolt (March–April 1917)*, vol. I. Princeton: Princeton University Press, 1980.

Wildman, Allan K. *The End of the Russian Imperial Army: The Road to Soviet Power and Peace*, vol. II. Princeton: Princeton University Press, 1987.

Wolff, David. *To the Harbin Station: The Liberal Alternative in Russian Manchuria, 1898–1914*. Stanford: Stanford University Press, 1999.

Wolff, David, Steven G. Marks, Bruce W. Menning, David Schimmelpenninck van der Oye, John W. Steinberg, and Shinji Yokote, eds. *The Russo-Japanese War in Global Perspective*, vol. II. Leiden: Brill, 2007.

Woodward, David. *The Russians at Sea: A History of the Russian Navy*. New York: Frederick A. Praeger, 1965.

Zaionchkovskii, A. M. *Mirovaia voina 1914–1917*. Moscow: Voenno izd-vo, 1931.

Zaionchkovskii, A. M. *Podgotovka Rossi k imperialisticheskoi voine*. Moscow: Voennoe izd-vo, 1926.

Zaionchkovskii, P. A. *Samoderzhavie i Russkaia armiia na rubezhe XIX–XX stoletiia*. Moscow: Mysl', 1973.

Zaionchkovskii, P. A. *Voennye reformy 1860–1870*. Moscow: Izd-vo Moskovskogo Universiteta, 1952.

Zolotarev, V. A. *Voennaia istoriia otechestva s drevnikh vremen do nashikh dnei*, 3 vols. Moscow: Mosgorarkhiv, 1995.

Index

Abazov, Alexei (Rear Admiral) 202
Abdulmecid I (Sultan) 147
absolutism 10, 42
Administrative College 47
Adolf, Gustav IV (King of Sweden) 10, 22–3, 118–19
Age of Liberty 42
Ahmed III (Sultan) 35–6
Aland Islands 38, 42, 152
Alekseev, M. I. (General) 256
Alekseev, Mikhail Vasil'evich (Major General) 232, 247, 276, 279–80, 284
Alekseevna, Ekaterina. *See* Catherine II/Catherine the Great
Alexander I (Tsar of Russia) 4, 15, 123
   administrative model 145
   conflict in 1804 137
   death of 134
   French Revolution 113–35
   invasion of Europe by the army of 129
   optimism among Poles after 1815 142
   Russian Empire and 113–35
   troops against the French army 129
   war against the Ottomans from 1806 to 1812 137
Alexander II (Tsar of Russia) 5, 6, 168, 177–8, 187, 190, 202
   assassination of 158, 165, 180
   defeat in Crimea 158
   education and mentoring of 155
   Great Reforms 158
   modernization of the empire 241
   overcome disastrous outcome of the Crimean War 208
   restructuring of Russian society to free people 157
   role in Russian state and government 158
   strategic pause on the army's operation 172
   systematic policy of conquest in Caucasus and Central Asia 101, 146
   theater of operations 176
   universal conscription 161, 166–7
   universal conscription act of 1874 161
   war against the Ottomans 169
Alexander III (Tsar of Russia) 5, 100, 180, 197, 198, 242, 269
Alexandrovich, Alexander (Tsarevich) 171
Alexandrovich, Michael (Grand Duke) 175
Alexeiev, Yevgeny Ivanovich (Admiral) 202, 205, 213, 214, 223, 275
Alma, Battle of 151
Anatolia 36, 173, 271, 273
Anglo-Russian Convention of 1907 183, 194
Anisimov, Evgenii Viktorovich 43
Antoine-Henri, Baron Jomini (Marshall) 145
Antoinette, Maria (Austrian princess) 66
Apraksin, Fyodor Mattveievich (Admiral) 38, 46–7
Apraksin, Stepan Fyodorovich (General) 66
Arakcheev, Aleksei Andreivich 132
Aras River 138
Armenia 36, 120, 121, 148, 270–1
Army Corps 148, 173, 182, 226, 232
Artamonov, N. D. (Lt. Colonel) 169
The Art of Victory (Nauka Pobezhda) 94
Astrakhan Khanate 12
Augustus I, Frederick (King of Saxony) 118
Augustus II (King of Poland/Lithuania) 20, 21, 25, 29, 35, 61
Augustus III (King of Saxony) 61, 79
Austerlitz, Battle of (1805) 116
Austria Wars of Succession (1740–8) 66
Austro-Hungarians 169, 251, 255–8, 260–5, 275, 277–8, 284, 286
Azov Campaign (1795–96) 20, 22, 36

Bagration, Pyotr Ivanovich (Prince) 119, 121, 122, 125

Balaclava, Battle of 151
Balkan Mountains 169, 172
Balkan Wars, 1912-13 178, 252, 269-70
Baltic Sea 1, 3, 12, 20, 21, 23, 26, 29, 35, 91, 119, 130, 252, 263
Bar Confederation 80
Bariatinskii, Alexander Ivanovich (General) 160, 183
battles 252-60. *See also* specific entries
Bayonets before Bullets 182
Bennigsen, A. T. (General) 118
Bering, Vitus 43
Berlin Decree 117
Bestuzhev-Riumin, Aleksei Petrovich 64, 66, 74, 76
Bezobrazov, Alexander Mikhailovich 202
Big Program 248
Bilderling, Aleksandr Aleksandrovich (General) 226, 229
Biron, Ernst Johann (Duke of Courland and Semigallia) 59
Black Sea 1, 62, 167, 173, 178
Black Sea fleet 90, 120, 140, 148, 150, 152, 168, 241, 279
Bloody Sunday (January 9, 1905) 232, 236
Bonaparte, Napolean 58, 97, 99
Borodino, Battle of (1812) 123
Bosnian Crisis of 1909 245
Boxer Rebellion 200, 201, 202, 205, 217
Bruces, James David 27, 47
Brusilov, Aleksei Alekseevich (General) 276, 279, 284
Brusilov Offensive 277
Bug River 86
Buturlin, Alexander Borisovich (General) 69
Buturlin, Ivan Ivanovich 46
Byzantine Empire 10, 167

Cadet Corps Academy 58, 59, 145, 163, 164
Campaigns of the French Revolution
    Battle of Austerlitz (1805) 116
    Battle of Borodino (1812) 123
    Battle of Eylau (1807) 118
    Battle of Friedland (1807) 118
    Battle of Jena-Auerstedt (1806) 117
    Battle of Maloyaroslavets (1812) 127-8
Carpathian Winter War 260-1, 263

Caspian Sea 42, 138
Catherine I (Former empress of Russia) 28, 36, 56, 63, 136
Catherine II/Catherine the Great 4, 15, 21, 37, 46, 54, 73-93, 96, 97, 99, 102, 130, 131, 137-8
    death of 71, 73, 96, 101, 107, 108
    reducing term of soldiers 133
    seizure of power in 1762 53
Caucasus 4, 36, 121, 195, 269-73
    after 1828 139
    French Revolution 136-9, 146-7
cavalry army 11, 12, 19, 62
Central Asia 1, 5, 158, 178, 183, 184, 186, 189-92
    conguest of 193
    conquest during the Russian Empire 182-94
Central Europe 1, 3, 55, 64, 66, 75, 107, 108, 115, 117, 129, 147
Charles II (King of Spain) 21
Charles VI (King of France) 62
Charles XI (King of Sweden) 24
Charles XII (King of Sweden) 20-6, 28-31, 35, 38, 41, 58
Charles XIII (King of Sweden) 119
Cherniaev, M. G. (Colonel) 185
Chernyshev, Zakhar (General Major) 65, 72
Chinese Eastern Railway 201
Chlopicki, Jozef (General) 143
Churchill, Winston 251
Chyorny Yar 88
Cixi (Chinese empress) 201
Concert of Europe 242
Conditions (document) 57
Congress of Berlin (1878) 177, 242
Congress of Vienna (1815) 100, 136, 167
Constantine (Grand Duke) 134
Constantinople 5, 10, 81, 172, 176
Continental System 118, 119, 131
Corps of Bombardiers 65
Cossacks 3, 4, 10, 13, 39, 44, 128
Council of State Defense 243, 245, 246
counterreform 165, 180
coup d'état 63
Crimean Khanate 21, 31, 83, 96
Crimean Peninsula 101
Crimean Tatars 30, 42, 86

Crimean War (1853–56) 5, 100, 132, 136, 147, 149, 160, 178
  1856 Settlement Map of 153
  Battle of Alma (1854) 151
  Battle of Balaclava (1854) 151
  Battle of Inkeman (1854) 151
  French Revolution 147–54
  Siege of Sevastopol (1854–55) 150–2
Czartoryski, Adam 114
Czartoryski, Jerzy 143

Dankl, Viktor (General) 256
Danube River 141, 169
Dardanelles, Battle of the 120
Davies, Brian 33, 40
Davout, Louis-Nicolas (Marshal) 116
Decembrist 134, 135, 144
Denikin, Anton I. (General) 244
Description of the Infantry Regiment's Structure 65
de Tolly, Barclay (Prince) 123, 126, 131
Dimitriev, D. R. Radko (General) 261, 265
Diplomatic Revolution 65, 66
Dnieper River 1, 14, 86, 88, 123
Dniester River 85, 90
Dolgorukii, Iakov Fedorovich 48, 57
Dolgorukov, V. M. (Prince) 86
Don Cossacks 87
Don River 1
Dragomirov, Mikhail Ivanovich (Major-General) 170, 181, 182, 219, 228, 245, 246
Dual Power 282
Duchy of Warsaw 122
Duffy, Christopher 27, 33
Dumouriez, Francois Charles 82
dvorianstvo 11, 14, 33

Early Modern/Enlightenment 33, 60
Early Modern Europe 6
Early Modern Military Revolution 10
Early Modern State 50
Early Modern Swedish 36
Eastern Chinese Railway 199
Eastern Europe 147
Eastern Question 100, 136, 147, 153
East Prussia Campaign, August 1914 69, 255
Emir of Bukhara 186, 187

Empire's Staff Academies 165
Eristov, G. Ye. (General) 138
Estonia 12, 24, 25, 35, 48, 64
Eurasia 2
  landmass 3, 4, 51, 101, 129, 159, 196, 290
  poverty in 2
Europe
  gendarme, during the French Revolution 142–5
  Great Powers 114
European Russia 59, 140, 158, 212, 228, 232, 233
Evert, Aleksei Ermolaevich (General) 276, 279
Eylau, Battle of (1807) 118

Far East 1, 178, 195–240
  peacemaking 238–40
  Russo-Japanese War 206–38
  Treaty of Shimonoseki 197–205
Fergana Valley 187
Fermor, William (General) 67, 68, 69
Field Orders 267
Finis Poloniae 92
First Army 84, 85
First Polish Partition (1772) 78
First Siberian Army Crop 219
First Turkestan Rifleman's Battalion 203
First World War 6, 97, 182, 207, 212, 222, 251–2
  end in the East 278–86
  military establishments 245
  Ottoman-Russian Caucasus Campaign 273
Five Siberian Army Corps 226
Fok, Aleksandr Viktorovich (Major General) 218
The Forgotten Peace (Wheeler-Bennett) 251
Fourth Coalition 117–20
Francis I of Austria 132
Franco-Russian alliance 178, 242
Frankfort-on-Oder 68
Frederick I (Holy Roman Emperor) 41
Frederick II (Holy Roman Emperor) 58, 66–9, 72, 73, 79, 82, 94, 102
Frederick IV (King of Denmark and Norway) 20, 21, 25

Frederika, Sophia Augusta (Princess) 74
French, John 274
French Revolution 55, 91, 97, 99–155
  Alexander I 113–35
  Caucasus 136–9, 146–7
  Crimean War 147–54
  gendarme of Europe 142–5
  military reforms of Paul I 101–6
  Nicholas I 135–6
  Paul I Napoleonic challenge 106–13
  Russian Empire 113–35
  Russo-Turkish War, 1828–9 139–42
Friederich, Karl (Duke of Holstein) 71
Friedland, Battle of (1807) 118

Galician Campaign, August 1914 257
Gangut, Battle of 38
General Staff Academy 163, 171, 182, 203, 244, 245, 290
Gentaro, Kodama (General) 230
Geok Tepe 191–2, 203
Glasko, F. F. (General) 220
Golitsyn, Alexander Mikhailovich (Prince) 84–5
Golitsyn, Dmitri Mikhailovich (Prince) 57
Golitsyn, Mikhail Mikhailovich (Prince) 29
Golovin, Nicholas Nikolaievich (General) 248
Golovkin, Gavrila Ivanovich 47
Gorchakov, Alexander Mikhailovich (General Prince) 148, 168, 186
Gordon, Patrick 17–18
Grand Duchy of Finland 119
Grande Armee 128
Great Britain 107
Great Captains 93
Great Embassy of 1697–8 20
Greater Bulgaria 177–8
The Great Game 183, 192, 194
Great Mutiny of February 1917 279
Great Northern War (1700–21) 21, 23, 34, 35, 46, 49, 50, 59, 61, 111
  Battle of Hango/Gungut 38
  Battle of Narva 24, 39, 40
  Battle of Poltava 32, 39, 44
  Pruth Campaign 37
Great Powers 5, 22, 132, 133, 136, 153, 177, 195, 250

Great Reforms 5, 157
  Russian Empire and 159–67
The Great Retreat (Spring-Summer 1915) 262–9, 275
Greek War of Independence 139
Greig, Aleksei (Admiral) 140
Greig, Samuel 86, 91
Grengross, A. A. (General) 220
Grippenberg, Oskar-Ferdinand Kasimirovich (General) 232
Gross-Jagersdorf, Battle of 66
Guard Corps 103
Guchkov, Alexander Ivanovich 246
Gulf of Bothnia 38
Gulf of Finland 28, 37, 42
The Gulistan Treaty (18313) 139
Gumbinnen, Battle of 254
Gurko, Iosif Vladimirovich (Field Marshall Count) 172, 175
Gustav III (King of Sweden) 90

Hamid I, Abdul 88
Hango, Battle of 38
Hanko Peninsula 38
Hartley, Janet M. 131
Hellie, Richard 16, 33
Helsinki/Helsingfors 38
Hermann, Johann 108
Hoffman, Max 253
Hogland, Battle of 91
Holstein Guard 72
Holy League 18
Holy Roman Empire 55, 116
Hompesch zu Bolheim, Ferdinand von 107
Hrazdan River 138
Hungarian Campaign (1849) 146, 147

Ianushkevich, Nikolai Nikolaievich (General) 250
Imperial Army 58, 94, 135, 256, 280
Imperial Germany 252
Imperial Guard 47, 54
imperialism 37, 167, 202
  in British 153
  industrialism and 196
Imperial Military Academy 159
industrialism 158
  imperialism and 196

industrialization 157, 160
  of warfare 245
Industrial Revolution 154
Inkeman, Battle of 151
Ivan III (Ivan the Great) 10, 25, 45
Ivan IV (King, the terrible) 2, 3, 12, 13, 35
Ivanov, Nikolai Iudovich (General) 260
Ivanovna, Anna 57–63, 71, 95, 102
  about her father 57
  Conditions signed by 57
  coup d'état 57
  Russian armed forces 59
  Supreme Privy Council, disbanded by 58
Ivan V (Tsar of Russia) 10, 18, 57
Iwao, Oyama (Marshal) 224–5
Izmailovskii Regiment 59
Iz pechal'nago opyta Ryssko-Iaponskou voiny (From the Sad Experience of the Russo- Japanese War) (Martynov) 244

Jacobinism 91
Japanese Third Army 221
Jena-Auerstedt, Battle of (1806) 117
Jews 80, 267
Joseph, Francis (Austrian emperor) 147, 168, 257, 262, 264
Joseph, Franz 150
Joseph II (Austrian Emperor) 88
Joubert, Barthelemy Catherine 109
July Crisis 249
July Revolution 142
June Offensive and the Defense of Riga, 1917 283
Jutaro, Komura 238

Kamchatka Peninsula 42
Kamensky, Nikolai (General Count) 119
kantseliarii 47
Karelian Isthmus 37, 64
Kaul'bars, Alexander Vasil'evich (General) 232
Kazakh Shamil 184
Kazan 126, 171
  conquest of 2, 12
  defeat of 12
Keep, John L. H. 44, 54
Kerensky, Alexander 281–2
The Kerensky/June Offensive (June 1917) 282–5

Khan, Gassan 138
Khan, Khivan 189
Khan, Khudoiar 189, 190
Khan, Nasr-Eddin 189–90
K'hang Hsi (Chinese Emperor) 196
Khmelnitsky, Bogdan 30
Kiev 10, 14, 45, 84, 181, 246, 247, 283
Kliuchevskii, V. O. 42
Knights of Malta 107
Kochubei, Viktor 114
Kolchak, Alexander Vasilyevich (Admiral) 279
Kornilov, Lavr Georgievich (General) 284, 286
Kornilov, Vladimir Alexeievich (Vice Admiral) 151
Kornilov Revolt 285
Kosciusko, Thaddeus 91
Krasnov, Ivan Ivanovich (General) 152
Krasovsky, Afanasii Ivanovich (General) 138
Krudener, Baron (Lt. General) 173
Krylenko, Nikolai Vasilovich (People's Commissar of War) 288, 311 n.1
Kunersdorf, Battle of (1759) 68
Kuropotkin, Alexsei Nikolaevich (General) 203, 204, 215, 219, 221, 224, 225, 228, 276
Kutuzov, Mikhail Illarionovich (Field Marshal) 115, 126, 127

Lacy, Peter Graf von (General) 61, 63, 64
Lake Naroch, Battle of 275
Lazarev, I. D. (General) 191
Leer, Genrikh Antonovich 245
Lefort, Franz 17–18
Legislative Commission of 1767 75
Leipzig, Battle of 129
Leopold I (Holy Roman Emperor) 18
Leszczynski, Stanislaw (King) 26, 30, 35, 61
Leuthen, Battle of 67
Lewenhaupt, Adam Ludwig 29
Liaoyang, Battle of 232
Liberum veto 79
Life Guard Cuirassier Cavalry Regiment 59
Li Hong Zhang 199
Lincoln, W. Bruce 161–2

Linevich, Nikolai Petrovich (General) 232, 234
Liprandi, Pavel (General) 150
Livonian War (1558–83) 13
Lobanov-Rostovsky, Alexei Borisovich (Foreign Minister) 199
Lodz, Battle of 259–60
Lomakin, N. P. (General) 191
Lord Raglan 150
Loris-Melikov, M. T. (General Adjutant) 176
Louis XIV (King of France) 21, 61
Louis XVI (King of France) 66
Loundon, Ernst von 68–9
Ludendorff, Erich (General) 254, 255, 258, 265
Lvov, Vladimir Nikolaevich 285

Macdonald, Jacques Entienne 108, 109
Madatov, Valerian Grigorievich 138
Mahmud (Sultan) 139
Mahmud II (Sultan) 141
Mahomet-Rakhim, Khan Seid 187
Makarov, Stepan Osipovich (Vice-Admiral) 215, 216, 217
Makram, Battle of 182
Maloyaroslavets, Battle of (1812) 127–8
Manchuria 197
Mark, Frederick M. L. von (Field Marshal-Lieutenant) 115
Martynov, Evgeny Ivanovich (Major-General) 244
massacre 80–1
Massena, Andre 110
Mazepa, Ivan Stepanovich (Hetman) 30–1
Meals, Friedrich von 109
Mediterranean Sea 136
Mejii Restorations 205
Menning, Bruce 58, 105
Menshikov, Alexander Danilovich 28, 29, 30, 46, 56
Menshikov, Alexander Sergeievich (Adjutant General and Admiral Prince) 150
mestnishstvo 45
Miasoyedov, Sergei 268
Michitsura, Nozu (General) 227
Middle Empire 200
Middle Kingdom 198

Mikhail (1613–45) 60
Mikhailovich, Alexander (Grand Duke) 202
Mikhailovich, Alexis (Tsar of all Russia) 12, 13, 15, 16, 30, 49
Mikhek, I. I. 87
military colleges (voennye uchilishcha) 165
Military Commission of 1762 75, 76
military education 5, 14, 95, 145, 160, 163–6, 243
military failure 157, 208, 285
Miliutin, Dmitry Alekseev ich (Field Marshall Count) 5, 146, 159, 160, 161, 183, 203, 208
  Boarding School for the Sons of the Nobility at Moscow University 163
  cautioned aboobut the hazard of bypassing Ottoman fortresses 172
  create military educational system 164
  educational reforms 166, 169, 179, 180
  formation of military historical commission 180
  military districts of 162
  transformation of Cadet Corps Academies 165
Minnikh, B. Kh (Baron) 59–63
Mirsky, Prince (Major General) 175
Mirza, Abbas (Prince) 138
Mobilization Schedule 19 (Variant A) 255
modernization 158, 246
  artillery corps 65
  challenges 144
  curriculum 145
  of education 46
  military 160
  technological 204
Mongol Empire 2, 51, 101
Moreau, Jean-Victor 109
Moskva River 127
Mukden, Battle of 238
Murat, Joachim 128
Muscovites 1, 2, 10, 11, 16–19, 22, 39, 49–51, 59–60, 76
Muscovy 10, 45, 54
  armed forces 13
  battlefields 12
  control of Smolensk 14
  medieval military 16

middle service class 11
Musin-Puskin, Valintin 91
Mustafa II (Sultan) 20
Mustafa III (Sultan) 81, 82
Mustafa IV (Sultan) 120
Myshelaevskii, Aleksandr Zakharevich (General) 270

Nakaz (instruction) of 1767 75
Nakhimov, Pavel Stepanovich (Vice Admiral) 148, 151
Nanshan, Battle of 215, 217, 219, 222, 224
Napoleon II (French prince) 124
Napoleon III (Former President of France) 147, 148
Narshinkina, Natalia 17
Narva, Battle of 24, 39, 40
nationalism 146, 153, 158
Navarino, Battle of 139
Neiman River 123
Nepenin, Adrian Ivanovich (Admiral) 279
Nicholas I (Tsar of Russia) 15, 101, 141, 142, 143–4, 146, 148, 155, 185
 combat experience of 160
 French Revolution 135–6
 pneumonia as cause of death 152
Nicholas II (Tsar of Russia) 6, 197, 203, 239, 276
Nikolaevich, Alexander 179
Nikolaevich, Nikolai (Grand Duke, the elder) 169, 198
Nikolaevich, Nikolai (Grand Duke, the younger) 179, 180
Northern Accord 77, 81
Northern Europe 21, 75, 107
November Uprising (Poland 1830) 142
Novgorod 10, 24
Novosil'tsev, Nikolai 114

Obruchev, Nicholas Nikolaevich (General) 169, 176, 180, 203, 243, 248, 255, 268–9
October Manifesto 241
Office of Tax collection *(Ratusha)* 50
Official Ideology 135
Ogilvy, G. B. 27
Oginski, Grzegorz Antoni 82
Old Believers 87
Old Boyar Duma 50

Olits, P. I. (General) 82, 84
Opalchentsi 175
Orlov, Grigorii 74
Orlov, N. A. (General) 228
Orthodox Christians 80
Orthodoxy 10, 28, 135
Ottoman Empire 18, 20, 21, 36, 81, 100, 136, 147, 169
Ottoman Forts 62

Pacific Ocean 1, 201, 205
Palitsyn, Fedor Fedorovich (General) 243, 246, 248
Panin, Nikita Ivanovich 74, 76, 81, 85
Panin, Peter 65, 85
Partition of Poland 83
Pasha, Baltaci Mehmet (Grand Vizier) 36
Pasha, Enver 270, 272
Pasha, Mukhtiar 176
Pasha, Omar 148
Pasha, Osman 173, 174
Pasha, Talat 271
Paskevich, Ivan Fyodorocvich (Field Marshal) 138, 144, 147
Paul, Michael C. 15
Paul I (1796–1801) 4, 248
 1801 peaceful annexation of Georgia 130
 initial policy toward the French Revolution 106–13
 military reforms, during the French Revolution 101–6
 Napoleonic challenge 106–13
Pavlovich, Constantine (Grand Duke) 142
Pavlovich, Michael (Grand Duke) 143
Pax Mongolia 5
peacemaking 238–40
Peace of Abo 64
Peace of Amiens (1802) 114
Peace of Luneville (1801) 114
Peninsular War 119
Persian Corps 59
Peter I. *See* Peter the Great
Peter II (Tsar) 56, 57
Peter III (Tsar) 69, 72–3, 74, 76
Peter the Great (1689–1725) 3, 5, 9–51, 60, 90, 131, 147, 181
 about eduation 17
 aftermath of 56

assault on Navra 25
Azov Campaign 22
challenges faced by successors 55
childhood 17
conflict faced due to seige of Swedish fortress 25
control over Russia 18
death of 47, 53, 56, 57, 58, 104
efforts to rationalize Russia's government 48
efforts to unify command 46
encouraging Russians to become autonomous entrepreneurs 49
establishment of the woolen industry 48
exiled to Siberia 56
expertise of foreigners in Moscow's military affairs 11–12
failure of military campaigns to south and east 4
Grand Embassy 40, 49
grandson tsarevich 71
Great Northern War 35, 38, 39, 41
inheritance of 12
July assault on Ottoman positions 19
law of succession of 71
military adventures 18, 19
military establishment 6
Military-Field Chancellery, created by 113
military reform 16, 17
military revolution to Russia 10
Military Statute 40, 65
military system 97
poll tax 54
reforms 41, 43, 53, 54, 55, 157
role in Russia's military revolution 4
Rules of Combat 40
setting up the state iron, copper, and silver mines 48
standing army of 47
strategy regarding the Ottoman Empire 37
struggle faced in the Sea of Azov 23
sustaining the army 43–51
Ustav of 1715 104
War College 113, 131
Petrovna, Anna 71
Petrovna, Elizabeth 4, 63–72, 74
Pitt, William 115

Plan and Arrangement for the Army according to Foreign Practices (Ogilvy) 27
Plehve, Pavel (General) 256
Plevna, Battle of 174, 175, 176, 181
Polish-Lithuanian Commonwealth 3, 4, 11, 13, 16, 28, 61, 77, 81, 96, 122
Polish rebellion of 1863–4 158
poll tax 49
Poltava, Battle of 32, 39, 44
Poniatowski, Stanislaw Antoni (King) 79
Port of Taganrog 21
Potemkin, Grigory Aleksandrovich (Russian military leader) 4, 58, 89, 90, 94
Protestants 80
Prozorovski, Alexander Alexandrovich (Field Marshal) 121
Prussianization 103
Pruth Campaign 37
Przemysl, siege of 260–2
Pugachev, Emelian 87, 88
Pugachev, Emil 55
Pugachev Rebellion (1773–74) 87, 88
Pulaski, Casimir 80

Qajar, Fath Ali Shah (Persian king) 137

Radziwill, Michal 143
Razummovskii, Kyrill 74
Red Army 101, 289, 290
Rediger, Aleksandr Fedorovich (General) 243, 246
Rehnskiold, Karl Gustaf 26
Repnin, Anikita Ivanovich 46
Repnin, N. V. 79
Restoration 135, 146–7, 205
Revolution, 1905 208, 244
Revolution, 1917 251
Revolution in St. Petersburg (1905) 233
Rietberg, Wenzel Anton Kaunitz 65
Rimskii-Korsakov, A. M. (General) 109, 110
Romanov, Mikhail 280
Romanov-Ottoman War in 1877–8 158
Romanovskii, D. I. (General) 186
Roosevelt, Franklin D. 238–40
Rostopchin, Fyodor (Count) 126

Rozhestvenski, Zinovi Petrovich (Admiral) 235
Rumiantsev, Piotr Alexandrivuch (Field Marshal) 58, 68–9, 71, 84, 85, 94
Russia-Chinese Bank 199
Russian Army 159–67
Russian Baltic Fleet 152
Russian Empire 9, 50, 88, 157–94
   Alexander I, and 113–35
   ambition against the Turks 4
   cavalry 15–16
   cloth and wool factories 111–12
   conquest of Central Asia 182–94
   dark ages (the Mongol period) 3
   development of 2
   economic growth 48
   foreign policy 79
   French Revolution 113–35
   Great Reforms and 159–67
   international foes 4
   invasion of Moldavia and Wallachia 140
   military educational system 164
   military establishment 10
   military needs 10
   military power 15
   military revolution 4
   need for military establishment identified by Peter the Great 3
   nobles and aristocrats 49–50
   post–Napoleonic period 4
   presence in Poland 82
   Russian Army and 159–67
   Supreme Privy Council 57
   topography and vegetation of 1
   victory at Poltava 35
   war with Turkey 118
Russian Revolution, 1917 251, 278–86
Russian War Council 29
Russian way of war 93–6
Russo-Japanese War (1904–05) 6, 194, 201, 206–38, 239, 245, 252
   attack on Port Arthur (Feb 1904) 207, 209, 210
   Battle of Liaoyang (August 1904) 224, 227, 228
   Battle of Mukden (February–March 1905) 238
   Battle of Nanshan (May 1904) 215, 217, 219, 222, 224
   Battle of Sandepu (January 1905) 233, 234
   Battle of Shaho (October 1904) 229–30
   Battle of the Yellow Sea (August 1904) 223, 235, 236
   Battle of Tsushima (May 1905) 207, 236
   Battle of Vafangou (Telissu) (June 1904) 220–1, 224
   landing at Chemulpo (Inchon) (Feb 1904) 207, 211
   Russia deafeat in the 241
   Russian Far Eastern Fleet 209
   Siege of Port Arthur (July–December 1904) 217, 219, 224, 230
   Theater of Operations 206
   Yalu Actions (April-May 1904) 202, 214–17
Russo-Ottoman War of 1710–11 36
Russo-Persian War (1826–28) 138, 141
Russo-Polish War of 1831 143. *See also* Thirteen Years' War
Russo-Turkish War
   Battle of Plevna (1877) 174, 175, 176, 181
   Battle(s) of Shipka Pass (1877) 169–75, 181–2
Russo-Turkish War (1711–13) 80
Russo-Turkish War (1735–39) 61, 80
Russo-Turkish War (1736–9) 63
Russo-Turkish War (1768–74) 81, 83
Russo-Turkish War (1806–12) 120
Russo-Turkish War (1828–9) 139–42
Ruzskii, Nikolai Vladimirovich (General) 280

Sakharov, Vladimir Viktorovich (General) 279
Saltykov, Ivan Petrovich (General) 80
Saltykov, Pyotr Semyonovich (Count) 68
Saltykova, Praskovia 57
Samsonov, Alexander Vasilovich (General) 228, 254, 255
Sandepu, Battle of (January 1905) 233, 234
Sarikamish, Battle of 270
Saxon-Polish Army 25
Scherer, Louis 108
Schleswig-Holstein 73

Schuldner, Yuri Ivanovich Schilder (Lt. General) 174
Schwartz, R. E. (Colonel) 133
Sea of Azov 36
Sea of Marmara 177
Second Army 84, 85, 86
Second Coalition 114
Second Opium War 200
Second Partition of Poland (1793) 91–2
Second World War 231, 264
Selim III (Sultan) 120
Selivanov, Andrei Nikolaevich (General) 261–2
Senyavin, Dmitri (Vice-Admiral) 120
serfs 5, 16, 44, 49, 56, 105, 130, 135, 145, 147, 154, 155, 157, 158, 166, 208, 241
Seven Years' War (1756–63) 4, 65, 66, 69–71, 73, 77, 81, 93, 94, 102
Battle at Kunersdorf (1759) 68
Shaho, Battle of 229–30
Shamil, Iman 146
Sheremetev, Boris Petrovich 46
Sheremet'ev, Peter 74
Sheremetov, Boris Petrovich 28
Shipka Pass, Battle of 169–75, 181–2
Siberian East 1
siege of Port Arthur (July-December 1904) 217, 219, 224, 230
siege of Przemysl 260–2
siege of Sevastopol (1854–55) 150–2
Sino-Japanese War, 1894–5 198, 213, 218
Sixth Coalition 128, 129
Skobelev, Mikhail Dmitrievich (General) 182, 189–91
Skowronska, Marta Helena 28
Skrzynecki, Ja (General) 143
Sobieski, Jan III (King of Poland) 18
Soimonov, Fedor Ivanovich (Lt. General) 151
Speranskii, Mikhail M. 131
Stackelberg, Berndt Otto 29
Stanislaw I 61
Starck, Oscar Viktorovich (Admiral) 209, 215
State Defense Council 247
Stevens, Carol 39
Stoessel, Anatolii Mikhailovich (General Baron) 217–19, 231
Storkyro/Isokyro, Battle of 38

Strel'tsy 12–14, 16–19, 26, 40, 45
Stroganov, Pavel Aleksandrovich 114
Stuart, J. E. B. 171
Sukhomlinov, Vladimir Aleksandrovich (General) 246–8, 270
Supreme Certification Commission 244, 246
Supreme War Council 219, 228
Suribachi-Yama 226
Suvorov, Alexander Vasil'evich (Russian military commander) 4, 58, 71, 82, 88, 89, 94, 95, 105, 108, 109, 110, 111, 245
Swedish Empire 42
Swedish War 64
Syr River 185

Tannenberg, Battle of 253–4, 258
Tatars 3, 4, 13, 21, 22, 30, 39, 42, 61, 63, 79, 84, 86
Tenth Siberian Army Corps 226
Theresa, Maria (Austrian Empress) 62, 66, 82
Third Coalition 115, 118–20, 130
Third Partition of Poland (1797) 93
Thirteen Years' War 13
Thirty Years' War 23
Three Emperors League 168
Timmermann, Franz 17
Timofeyevich, Yermak 196
Togo (Admiral) 209–11, 216–17, 223, 236–7
Totleben, G. G. 69
Trans-Siberian railway 198, 199, 212
Treaty of Adrianople (1829) 141
Treaty of Andrusovo (1667) 14
Treaty of Campo Formio (1797) 107, 116
Treaty of Constantinople (1700) 20, 21, 36, 81, 84
Treaty of Frederikborg (1720) 41
Treaty of Fredrikshamn (1809) 119
Treaty of Jassy (1792) 90
Treaty of Karlowitz (1700) 81, 84
Treaty of Kuchuk-Kainardji (1774) 86, 87, 88
Treaty of Nerchinsk (1689) 196
Treaty of Nis (1739) 81
Treaty of Nystadt (1721) 33, 35, 39, 42
Treaty of Nystand (1721) 63

Treaty of Paris (1856) 167
Treaty of Pereyaslav (1654) 30
Treaty of Portsmouth (1905) 197, 239, 242
Treaty of Pressburg (1805) 116, 117
Treaty of Prut(h) (1711) 36, 37
Treaty of San Stefano (1878) 177
Treaty of Shimonoseki (1895) 197–205
Treaty of St. Hubertusberg (1763) 77
Treaty of Tilsit (1807) 117, 118, 120, 121, 130
Treaty of Turkmenchay (1828) 138, 141
Treaty of Varala (1790) 91
Treaty of Versailles (1756) 65
Tretyakov, Nikolai Aleksandrovich (Colonel) 218
Troitse-Sergiev monastery 17
Tsar-Peacemaker 180
Tsitsianov, Paul (General) 137
Tsushima, Battle of 207, 236
Turkestan proportion 191–2
Turkish War of 1739 62
Turkish War of 1828–9 87, 90, 144, 182
The Turkmanchai Treaty (1828) 139

Ukraine 3, 4, 14, 61, 62
Ukrainian Uniates 80
Ukraintsev, Yemelyan Ignatievich 20
Ulozhenia of 1649 15
Ulrika (sister of Charles XII) 41
Universal Military Training Act of 1874 166
The Unknown War (Churchill) 251
Unofficial Committee 114
Ura-Tiube 187
Ushakov, Fedor (Admiral) 108
Ustyak Tatars 42
Uvarov, Sergey (Count) 135

Vannovski, P. A. 165
Vannovski, Petr Semenovich (General) 180
Venetian Republic 18
Verevkin, N. A. (Colonel) 185
Vinius, Andrei Andreevich 26–7
Vistula, Battle of the 260
Vistula River 67, 253, 259
Vitgift (Admiral) 223
Voenny sbornik (Military Digest) 163
Volga River 1
Volkonskii, P. M. 132

von Auffenberg, Moritz (General) 256
von Burgneustadten, Hermann Kusmanek (General) 261–2
von Buxhowden, Friedrich Wilhelm (General) 115
von Diebitsch, Hans Karl (Field Marshal) 140, 143
von Eichhorn, Hermann (General) 275
von Falkenhayn, Erich (General) 258
von Hindenburg, Paul (General) 254, 255, 265
von Hotzendorf, Franz Conrad 256
von Kaufman, Konstantin Pavlovich (General) 187, 188, 189, 190, 191
von Makenson, August (General) 265
von Moltke, Helmut (the younger) 253
von Prittwitz und Gaffron, Maximilian (General) 253
von Rennenkampf, Pavel Karlovich (General) 253
von Schubert, Richard (General) 258
von Seeckt, Hans 265
von Shtakel'berg, Georgi (Baron General) 219–20, 229
von Todleben, Franz Eduard Graf (General) 174
Vorontsov, Mikhail Semionovich (Prince) 146
Vorontsov-Dashkov, Illarion (General Viceroy) 270, 272

War Ministry (Voennyi Prikaz) 48
War of Austrian Succession (1740–8) 64
War of Spanish Succession (1701–14) 21
Western Europe 10, 12, 16, 77, 164
Weyde, Adam 40
Wheeler-Bennett, John 251
Wilhelm I (King of Prussia) 168
Wilhelm III, Frederick (King of Prussia) 117, 132
William, Frederick (Duke of Courland) 57
William II, Frederick (King of Prussia) 92
Witgeft, Wilhelm (Admiral) 216
Witte, Sergei Iul'evich (Prime Minister) 197, 198, 199, 202, 238, 242
Wittgenstein, Peter (Prince) 140
World War I
    Battle of Galicia (August–September 1914) 256–60, 265, 276, 277, 282

Battle of Gumbinnen (August 1914) 254
Battle of Lake Naroch (March 1916) 275
Battle of Lodz (November 1914) 259
Battle of Tannenberg (August 1914) 253–4, 258
The Brusilov Offensive (Summer 1916) 277
The Great Retreat (Spring-Summer 1915) 262–9, 275
The Kerensky/June Offensive (June 1917) 282–5
Siege of Przemysl (winter 1914–1915) 260–2
World War Zero 207
Wysocki, Piotr (Lieutenant) 142

Yalu, Battle of the 215

Yalu Concession 202
Yasukata, Oku (General) 215
yellow peril 205, 207, 211
Yellow Sea, Battle of the 223, 235, 236
Yerevan Khanate 138
Yoshimichi, Hasegawa (Lt. General) 226
Young Turks 244, 245, 248
Yudenich, Nikolai Nikolayevich (General) 270–3
Yusupov, Felix (Prince) 202

Zaporopzhian Cossack 83
Zasulich, Mikhail (Lt. General) 213–14
Zemstvos 157
Zerbst, Anhalt 74
Zhilinsky, Iakov Gregorevich (General) 253, 274
Zorndorf, Battle of 68

www.ingramcontent.com/pod-product-compliance
Lightning Source LLC
Chambersburg PA
CBHW071800300426
44116CB00009B/1154